GOOD TIMES

GOOD

Peter Joseph / An Oral History

TIMES

of America in the Nineteen Sixties

William Morrow & Company, Inc.
New York   1974

911.30 392
J71g
119632
oct. 1981

Library of Congress Catalog Card Number 73-17589

ISBN 0-688-05240-1 (pbk.)

2 3 4 5 78 77 76 75 74

TO

The Flemings:
John and Joan
Richard and Katy

A NOTE ON METHOD

The effect I have sought in *Good Times* is of an impressionistic collage, a kaleidoscopic overview of the 1960s similar to the flicker technique used in films, a technique in which a series of images of great variety is quickly flashed to produce a single overall impression. My intention is not to report comprehensively every facet of the decade, but to direct the focus in order best to convey the sense—indeed, the larger shape and gesture—of the times.

The idea owes a large debt to Studs Terkel's *Hard Times: An Oral History of the Great Depression.* Terkel explains his concept at the very beginning: "This is a memory book, rather than one of hard fact and precise statistic. . . . In their rememberings are their truths. The precise fact or the precise date is of small consequence. This is not a lawyer's brief, nor an annotated sociological treatise." *Good Times,* in a similar manner, simply attempts to recapture the tone and the texture of that tumultuous decade just gone by.

Because of the broad scope of this book, it is necessary to focus on, to zoom in for a closeup of, certain events, certain trends and ideas, certain people. At times the people I speak with are well known, people responsible for the events discussed. At other times I speak with the more obscure, those who have only enjoyed—or endured—the decade. With an open mind and an empty tape I set out to hear what America had to say. From the imposing Washington office of Clark Clifford to a welfare apartment in a Chicago ghetto; from a grassy plot in People's Park, Berkeley, to the stifling hot front of E. Moore's Hardware and Implement store in Philadelphia, Mississippi; from a teen-age slumber party in southern Ohio to the dressing room of a nightclub in San Francisco; from Ken Kesey's commune-farm in Eugene, Oregon, to Astronaut Pete Conrad's cramped office at the Manned Spacecraft Center in Houston, Texas; from a living room in Weehawken, New Jersey, to the headquarters of the Strategic Air Command in Omaha, Nebraska—in all of these places and in many more I have spent hours and hours in quest of America thinking. Conversing-debating before-over-after breakfast-lunch-dinner. Acquaintances and strangers, over a drink at the local bar, at home with the family, or at work during the day, the people have told me their story of the Sixties.

The one hundred twenty-five vignettes are ordered in an approximate chronology. Since memories do not always restrict themselves to narrow time slots or limited subjects, the chronology is often broken by reaches into the past and the future. This freewheeling movement reflects the natural intermingling of events and their emotional antecedents and aftermath.

I have chosen the spontaneous spoken thoughts over the washed-and-pressed thoughts of paper and pen precisely because spoken thoughts are not always so organized as the written word. Often they do not come in complete sentences; sometimes they meander in random exploration. Freed of literary convention, people are likely to be more candid and fresh, more expressive. I usually found an initial hesitancy, even fear or nervousness, in my subjects, partly because the impact of the age is still so fresh. Then what followed was often most astounding. I withdrew into the background while the memories flowed. The result is passion, sadness and pride, laughter and bitterness. Here are fear and wonder. Here is puzzlement. Here is history.

FOREWORD

In the fall of 1970, a year when journalists and historians were busying themselves with assessments of the turbulent decade that had just ended, a Princeton junior hit upon the idea of fulfilling requirements for his Senior Thesis by interviewing representative Americans about their impressions of the 1960s. The notion had come to him after reading Studs Terkel's *Hard Times,* a mosaic of recollections of the Great Depression, for History 377, a course taught by Eric Goldman, who had not only written books and articles on contemporary history but had served on Lyndon Johnson's White House staff. Goldman agreed to sponsor the thesis, and the Woodrow Wilson School of Public and International Affairs awarded Joseph the De Witt Clinton Poole Memorial Prize for a thesis with exceptional promise. Both the Woodrow Wilson School and Princeton's history department granted him funds for the project, but most of the money to finance his travels came out of Joseph's own earnings. Founder of the Student Weenie Agency in his freshman year, the ambitious young Ohioan had subsequently taken on the Pizza Agency and the Hoagie Agency, as well as serving as administrative assistant to Provost [now President] William Bowen.

Joseph invested the same exceptional energy and initiative in his Senior Thesis. Tape recorder in hand, he journeyed more than 15,000 miles to take down the words of the movers and shakers of the 1960s as well as those of people who never appeared in the morning headlines. His peregrinations took him from Dean Rusk's study at the University of Georgia to Ken Kesey's farm in Oregon where, despite a case of hay fever, he spent a day baling hay; from Hamburger College, where Mc-

ix

Donald's trainees are awarded "degrees," to the dressing room of Carol Doda, who inaugurated topless dancing in San Francisco's North Beach. "I see myself as a humanitarian," Miss Doda told him. In all he interviewed 250 people and accumulated a 4,000-page manuscript, from which, sifted and edited, has come *Good Times*, a remarkable portrait of an American decade.

Good Times makes a significant contribution to the rapidly growing craft of oral history. Joseph's technique is in many ways similar to that first developed by Allan Nevins at Columbia after World War Two, and afterward taken up by scores of oral history enterprises elsewhere. Joseph acknowledges his debt to *Hard Times*, and some of the interviews of rank-and-file Americans recall the Federal Writers' Project classic, *These Are Our Lives*. But Terkel's people were recalling events experienced more than a quarter of a century before, and *These Are Our Lives* had a regional focus. Joseph's book is unique, for it is the first systematic effort to create a portrait of an entire decade by interrogating people shortly after the era ended.

Joseph's undertaking might easily have failed either because he did not put together a persuasive sample or because his subjects offered only trite or familiar comments. Joseph has escaped both of these snares. Inevitably, some will think of different persons who might have been interviewed, especially those less involved in the momentous actions and passions of the times, but he has taken pains to range widely—to the Pacific Coast as well as the Atlantic, South as well as North, to talk to men and women, black and white, young and old, conservatives and radicals, the lowly and the high and mighty. More than one reader of oral history transcripts has had the experience of coming upon page after page of jejune or self-indulgent remarks. Joseph, however, clearly has a gift for getting people to reveal themselves, sometimes, one thinks, more than they may have wanted to reveal.

Many of the comments are surprisingly guileless. Journalists have emphasized the misery of Resurrection City in the mudflats of Washington, D.C., but a black woman from Mississippi recalls that she did not want to return: "We were livin' comfortable. . . . I lived better than I ever lived in my life." The administrator of the Appalachian program in Alabama admits, "The Appalachian people I have no contacts with," and Paul Ylvisaker reports that when the pioneers of the antipoverty movement reconvened in 1970, "there wasn't a person in the room of twenty who, in individual terms, wasn't two or three social notches ahead of where he was, and four or five income notches above where he was." A New Jersey woman active in the antiwar movement says of her son, who joined an "extremely square" group: "I consider Alan in many ways a Vietnam casualty, just as much as if he had his legs blown off. There are some people who under stress . . . can't take it." Dr. Spock recounts that he voted against the Republicans in 1960 because he thought they were not spending enough on armaments. Later, when his views had changed, he states, "I wrote insulting letters to the President" and got "snotty replies from McGeorge Bundy, which is the personal motive why I want to see him held responsible for war crimes."

Any montage of the 1960s will inescapably allot a good deal of attention to the shortcomings of that decade, especially to the wanton violence. People call to mind painfully the shocking assassinations. George Reedy tells Joseph that after John F. Kennedy's murder, Ted Sorensen said to him, "George, I wish that goddam State of Texas had never been invented." In Oregon a young black woman recollects being awakened by her sister and informed, "They shot Bobby Kennedy." She sat there stunned, stumbled downstairs to where the television was blaring, and "I remember taking a shoe and banging it on our dining room table, totally hysterical. I knew it was all over, that there was no more reason for hope." The following summer found her working in a Black Panther clinic.

Several allude to the racial mayhem. A teen-ager looks back on the games fourth grade children played in Selma, Alabama:

> All these kids would just walk down the street and pretend they were protesting, and some other kids would

pretend to be cops and they'd jump all over them, and knock them down. The first bunch would fall and they'd pretend like they were nonviolent and sit there; and the cops would hit hem over the head and everything.

Loyal Gould, who contributed perhaps the most absorbing interview, reflects on his experience in returning from covering the Auschwitz trial to seeing in his native land Georgia highway patrolmen brutally clubbing black youngsters who offered no resistance and continued to sing anthems of love. "That was the only time that as a working journalist I ever wept," he declares. "I didn't make a sound, but the tears were simply streaming down my cheek." In Los Angeles a police sergeant relates what happened when a white motorist was halted by a black mob in 1965: "They'd take him out. They'd beat him up. They'd beat up his girlfriend, turn the car over and ignite it. When they'd turn the car over, gas would spill— boom!"

Some boldly embrace violence while others reject it. Barbara Walters recalls saying, " 'Mrs. Cleaver, I have a child and you have a child about to be born. You have said that you hoped that in the future this country would burn. What about our children? What about their life together? What do you want for your son?' And she said, 'May he light the first match.' " But an Atlanta police superintendent who had to break the news of Martin Luther King's assassination to his older son testifies: "Not one time did I ever hear one bitter remark by one member of his family, not one. . . . His family's action, through M.L.'s past teachings, saved this city." And when Joseph asks one of King's followers how she responded to news of the slaying, she replies: "I'll be straight honest. My first reaction, when I *first* heard it, it looked like to me violence kind of blurried up in my mind. I got angry, but it wasn't no time before I could think what he had taught us and it soon passed away. I tell you, after that anger flew up and I settled down from there, it was just sobbing and tears and sorry then."

A few are bitter, in particular about racial injustice and the bloodletting in Southeast Asia. A former regional director of CORE sneers at the demonstrators who went from Los Angeles to Alabama in the spring of 1965: "They wanted me to go, and I laughed at them. . . . Here were all these people, piling on planes and trains and buses and cars heading for a great march from Selma to Montgomery when their own city was getting ready to blow right up in their own goddam faces." The father of a Vietnam veteran who won the Congressional Medal of Honor, but might choose jail to being sent again, reflects on one veteran "who lost both legs and his arms and half of his intestines and his insides. If you look at him from his neck up you see a person who is intelligent, a person who went back and got his degree in law; but if you look from the neck down, he's just a mess." Some have learned nothing. Lester Maddox reminisces about pulling a gun on a demonstrator who sought to desegregate his Atlanta restaurant, and the legal adviser to Governor Ross Barnett of Mississippi still believes that President Kennedy's effort to gain admission to the University of Mississippi for James Meredith was a deliberate attempt to provoke violence. Some are scary. The Commander-in-Chief of the Stategic Air Command regrets that America did not "clean out" the Castro government in the Cuban missile crisis, and adds: "I think the time is awfully late and that we're in great danger. I think the silent majority . . . has got to . . . force, somehow, a better understanding of the danger."

Yet Joseph calls his volume *Good Times*, and many of his interviewees agree. Often they highlight the achievements of the civil rights revolution. John Doar, the courageous aide to Robert Kennedy in the Justice Department, dwells on the significance of the Meredith episode: "This was a remarkable thing: one individual, exercising his rights and demanding that his rights be honored, could put in motion the whole apparatus of the federal government to support him. That's the genius of this country." In Atlanta a black woman notes with pleasure: "Now if we do want to go to McDonald's we can go to McDonald's. This is what impresses me now. It's just knowing! It's a good feeling." And in Cincinnati another black woman explains what she owes to Head Start: "The teacher, you know, she invites you into the classroom. So I went and I found out that by being there you learn how to cope with yourself."

Joseph's respondents accentuate too the changes in the quality of life. Tom Wolfe affirms: "The American middle class, including the suburbanites, have really been much more adventurous than most people realize, and certainly more adventurous than any middle class in any European country." The creator of "Peanuts," Charles Schulz, asks: "Do you know how nice it is to have little children and not to have to worry about whether they're going to get polio? Have you ever seen a parent that saw summer come when you lived in the Midwest, where there are lots of lakes and the kids started to go swimming, and all of a sudden the newspapers started to run lists of fifteen polio attacks a day? . . . It's gone now!" Eugene Carson Blake, former head of the World Council of Churches, sums up, "If you take the decade of the Sixties, when historians write it, it will be a tremendous, almost miraculous development of the idea of the unity of the one church of Jesus Christ." So far had the ecumenical spirit gone in a city like Dubuque that by 1965 "the Lutherans and the Presbyterians and the Roman Catholics were thick as thieves."

Finally, they point to the gains in the public realm. The NAACP attorney, Jack Greenberg, harks back to Chief Justice Earl Warren compelling lawyers to come to terms with the question, "But is that *fair*?" and one of Nader's Raiders ticks off the legislative innovations that resulted from his boss's actions, and concludes, "There may be several thousand people alive today who would not otherwise be alive had it not been for the Highway Safety Act. . . . So that's really the ultimate." The former White House aide Joseph Califano mentions that there were some thirty to forty federal grant-in-aid programs when Johnson took office, 450 when he left. Dean Rusk, after cataloguing accomplishments in foreign affairs from the Test Ban Treaty to the Kennedy round of trade negotiations, stresses, "We added eight years to the period since a nuclear weapon has been used in anger." It is left to Wernher von Braun to underscore what future generations may regard as the greatest feat of all. "In some respects," he maintains, "Neil Armstrong's famous 'small step' on July 20, 1969, was probably as significant to the history of life on earth as aquatic life crawling on land."

On occasion Joseph and his subjects claim too much for the 1960s. One of the least attractive characteristics of the Sixties was the conviction that time began with Kennedy's inauguration and that America had no past. In truth, both Kennedy's New Frontier and Johnson's Great Society drew heavily upon the ideas of Franklin D. Roosevelt's New Deal of the 1930s and Harry Truman's Fair Deal of the 1940s. By the chronometry of the 1960s, the Eisenhower era was an utter void. In fact, the 1950s was the decade of the Warren Court's pathbreaking decisions and of the Montgomery bus boycott that made the name of Martin Luther King a household word, of the Salk vaccine that all but ended the plague of polio, and the new rhythms of rock and roll. The counter culture of the 1960s derived in part from the beats of the 1950s, and the novels of the Sixties owe a debt to the literature of the absurd of the preceding decade.

Yet surely Joseph is right in thinking that the Sixties was an exceptional period, an era, as *The Economist* wrote, of "interlocked crises of war and racial conflict and self-laceration." In the 1970s the fault lines from the tremors that shook the decade are apparent everywhere—in political alignments, in the churches, on the campus. It is still difficult to come to even preliminary conclusions about these years. As Robert Lipsyte of *The New York Times* commented, "We won't know what really happened until the films are developed." But our perception of the 1960s will critically affect the course of the final years of the twentieth century. The first expeditions have already set sail to explore the meaning of the Sixties, and many more will follow, but few ventures are likely to advance the inquiry in so lively a manner as *Good Times*.

WILLIAM E. LEUCHTENBURG
*De Witt Clinton Professor of
History, Columbia University*

CONTENTS

We have reached a moment in time when the national condition seems neither lifeless nor deathless. It's like the barren but sensuous serenity of the natural world in late autumn, before Thanksgiving, containing the promise of rebirth and the potential for resurrection. On bare branches whose leaves have fallen, buds bulge visibly in preparation for spring . . . The litter of autumn becomes the mulch, and then the humus, for roots and tender seeds. So it was, so it has been, and so it will be with the growth of the American Civilization.

—MICHAEL KAMMEN,
People of Paradox

INTRODUCTION

Why—in the wake of all the dashed hopes, the torment-
ing malaise, the clinging divisiveness—call this account of the
1960s *Good Times*? Some historians might be more inclined to
call it *Bad Times* or, at best, *Mediocre Times*.

The reasons are several, but most of them concern the
tempo of the period and the collective national metabolism that
made the decade uniquely exciting to live through, and for some
of us, perhaps, too much to bear.

It is rare in any age that a society is offered a vision of
what it can become, as John Kennedy and Lyndon Johnson
offered that vision to Americans in the Sixties. It is rarer still that
such a vision so captivates a people that they are willing to
muster the requisite energy and resources to convert the vision
to fact—or at least to begin the process in earnest. Such a grand
effort was in fact launched in the United States during the first
half of the decade as a whole society rededicated itself to ending
the glaring inequalities within it. It was an extraordinary effort,
whatever the fruits, and reason enough in itself for us to judge
the 1960s good times for America.

Later, the nation's leaders let their vision stray toward
the deathtrap in Southeast Asia—whether from arrogance,
pride, a misguided sense of national security, or steadily deep-
ening conviction is not the point: they let it stray from pressing
domestic matters, and at first the people followed. But then, as
the decade waned, the American people rebelled, in increasing
numbers, at this squandering of lives, resources, and national
purpose. In another day, in another society, the people might
have yielded and let their leaders exercise their sway
unimpeded. But America in the Sixties was not a nation of

sheep, and large segments of the population stiffened in their efforts to resist a disastrous national policy and to redirect wayward energies from the jungle and the ricefields to the home pasture with all its problems. And so one may say, and not merely with poetic license, that a nation with the courage and stamina to weather such a terrible storm—a storm that nearly wrenched it apart—holds the promise to become a very great nation in spirit as well as in riches. To have such a vision as America had, and to hold to it through the accompanying malaise, is a mark of greatness.

For despite all the soaring hopes that had been shattered, throughout all the bitterness and violence, America emerged from the Sixties as a more mature and sobered nation, its people a more knowing and chastened people. Vietnam, among other things, prompted a reappraisal of America's role in the world. This nation finally came to realize that she had no divine mandate to oversee the internal affairs of other nations; she even came to realize that her own house was not in proper order. The nation came to doubt the infallibility of that dogma that said all technological growth is good. She came to understand that natural resources must be preserved and treasured.

How a people conducts itself during such periods of discord and tumult is a severe test of that people. The United States has not failed that test. The final outcome may yet be in doubt, and may remain so for many years, but the Sixties may well prove to have been a most critical testing time for America, for America did not turn her back on the challenge that decade presented.

Finally, one can say that in terms of affluence, America in the Sixties reached a stage that other societies can only dream of. To be sure, large masses of Americans did not share in that affluence, but more of them than ever before benefited from the national bounty. More important, the American people recognized that they cannot go on allowing millions of their fellow citizens to remain at or near the pauper level. A Republican President, elected on a traditional laissez-faire platform, recognized by decade's end that it would no longer suffice to act as if the good Lord helps those who help themselves. The complexities of modern technology and economics could no longer be allowed automatically to dominate our private lives, and programs echoing ideas that had seemed quite radical indeed ten years earlier were on the drawing board in the early Seventies, however inadequately or halfheartedly.

A wealthy nation that has come to recognize that its riches and its successes cannot be measured alone in terms of average annual incomes and the Gross National Product has learned a crucial lesson. The Sixties were such a learning period.

In this larger sense, then, the Sixties were a good, if difficult, time to be alive in the United States of America.

* * *

Although the Sixties officially began on January 1, 1960, and stretched to December 31, 1969, history does not honor these precise dates. The specific time with which I am concerned centers on that period between President John F. Kennedy's inauguration in January 1961 and President Richard M. Nixon's inauguration in January 1969. While some of the themes and some of the thoughts in this book do not respect these artificial boundaries, most do coalesce in that span. Earlier with Eisenhower, and later with Nixon, there was a difference in tone, in flavor. They were simply different times.

* * *

The boom in the private sector during the 1950s left much of America in a state of seemingly secure affluence, but the nation's public spirit simultaneously plummeted to dangerous depths. There was that great race for membership in the middle class, and more than ever a person's accumulation of material goods measured his standing in society. Americans tunneled their vision and worked hard at getting ahead. After the rollicking Twenties, the Depression-dominated Thirties, and the war in the Forties, America had seemed glad to sit back in the easy chair, slippered feet on the ottoman and eyes riveted to the television set, guzzling a sparkling Budweiser. Then, perhaps tired of the fat Roman life, and perhaps fearing a fall, the people listened to the call of John Fitzgerald Kennedy.

When John Kennedy set out in early 1960 to win the Presidency, he exhibited a different brand of leadership. He was young, attractive, daring, and eager for power—traits that most Americans coveted and admired. He surrounded himself with men of intellect and culture, with the New Frontiersmen. He infused in Americans a new sense of pride in their nation and an eagerness to share in the long agenda of unfinished business before them. He so ignited his countrymen that they cheered—they even came to revere—the admonition, "Ask not what your country can do for you. Ask what you can do for your country." One has to go back to Theodore Roosevelt and earlier, to the days of the Revolution, to find the national leadership in the hands of such idealistic and daring young men.

By the late 1950s television had linked the nation in a continental living room, giving the man in the White House an unprecedented power to radiate a mood and a sense of purpose. Dwight D. Eisenhower chose not to exercise this enormous power to rally the nation behind a social program. John Kennedy chose to use all that power. The great cliché of the period was that Kennedy was far more image than substance, that he got by largely on a kind of show-business charisma, that he was at least as much celebrity as political leader. One can accept or reject that evaluation of the man, but it is true that, whatever the substance of his achievement, he *did* affect the national consciousness in a remarkable and stirring fashion. The Kennedy Presidency unleashed enormous energy and passion in vast sectors of the populace, especially in those sectors in which the people had been least powerful and least successful in sharing the fruits of the American Dream.

Kennedy was able to understand and empathize with the young, who were so taken by him that they quickly rallied around his banner. He excited them when he spoke with his nicely cadenced, crisply articulated, unbloated brand of patriotism. Their idealism and his meshed: to the President and to the young alike the hypocrisy evident in the gap between the American credo and the American practice became fair game for reform. The Peace Corps ideally embodied this new sense of mission. The Office of Economic Opportunity, incorporating VISTA as the domestic Peace Corps, would later work in the same manner. Once unleashed, the young were not to be halted by the blows and harassment that came raining down on them as the decade wore on, though the dreams of many would soon lose their glow.

In President Kennedy the blacks found a man in charge of the national government who was committed to ending their degraded state. Though the Supreme Court had outlawed segregation in 1954, President Eisenhower had declined to speak out with any moral fervor on the matter. The Kennedys spoke out. Attorney General Robert F. Kennedy ordered the Interstate Commerce Commission to force the desegregation of interstate transportation facilities in November of 1962. The President personally stood up to the effrontery of Governors Ross Barnett and George Wallace, thus forcing the integration of the Universities of Mississippi and Alabama. During his showdown with Governor Wallace in June 1963, Kennedy asked a nationwide television audience:

> Are we to say to the world—and much more importantly to each other—that this is the land of the free except for the Negroes; that we have no second-class citizens except Negroes; that we have no class or caste system, no ghettos, no master race, except with respect to Negroes?

Reaching out for the understanding and conscience of America, Kennedy sought to soften the hardened hearts of a nation that might have rendered meaningless the laws to come. With such a powerful ally rallying the nation to their cause, black Americans began themselves to lead the fight for long-delayed equality. And in that fight they made remarkable progress.

Under Kennedy the age-old conception of the poor as society's sinners and misfits gave way to a recognition that they were, for the most part, victims of an oppressive environment. By publicizing their plight, the government spurred national concern for the poor and heralded what would eventually become the War on Poverty by initiating the thinking that would lead to such programs as Head Start for preschool children, VISTA, the Job Corps and Upward Bound programs for the jobless and college students, the Appalachian program, and the Community Action Program to channel local energy and needs. It all amounted to an assault dedicated to help the poor break the stranglehold of the culture of poverty. That it was an insufficient effort for the ends sought mattered far less than that the battle was at last joined.

And it was Kennedy who called attention to the accelerating crisis in the cities. The fiscal, racial, and psychological problems of the urban areas affected people from all walks of life; they affected the health of the country as a whole. The entire range of problems—from transit to pollution to safety in the streets—was intensively studied. The task force on the cities broke new ground in its analysis of the urban doldrums. City strategists discovered that urban renewal often meant urban destruction and enormous psychological dislocation; they came to realize that the bulldozer could not make deep-seated problems of race and poverty disappear. Spurred by the seriousness of the problems and the Kennedy eagerness to tackle them, universities and colleges made urban affairs a fully recognized field of study. Not only did Kennedy shed light on the festering problems of the cities, but he also began to muster the resources necessary to develop the remedies. Yet it was a sobering lesson to learn that the problem was deep-seated and that overnight cures were without potency.

In the lively (some said permissive) climate John Kennedy had brought and left behind him, the women's liberation movement flourished. It grew out of the atmosphere that freshened one's perspectives and attitudes on basic values. Women in the Sixties stood up to demand their rightful place in society and to seek recognition as equals with men.

Across the land this sense of new beginnings and freshness prevailed. In almost every art form new things were happening: in the theater, from the theater of the absurd to nudism to a new sense of social content; in the novel dark comedy and surreal renderings took on a powerful role, and an old-fashioned romanticism won a new lease on life; in painting and sculpture, "happenings" and Pop Art turned one's vision back toward society itself, often in bitingly critical assessments; in religion and philosophy a new and simple set of creeds washed away encrusted dogma and cut through all the hairsplitting of the theorists as ecumenism became the cause of the crusaders; in fashion and popular dancing a relaxed openness emerged— a new naturalness that seemed suddenly very radical and shocking to many of the older generation, still inhibited by taboos and totems whose forms had long since exhausted their substantive values. The movement was marked by a return to nature, to natural feelings, and the earth itself came to be cherished in a way it had not been in generations: ecology would become a national passion, and groups who disagreed on many other matters would join hands to support the preservation of the American land and the rescue of the air and waters.

John Kennedy thus heralded a decade that would foster new beginnings in almost every sphere of human activity and every sector of the population. Springing from the challenge of the New Frontiersmen was a zeal that seemed to reach throughout America, and the actions that followed were the actions of an intensely committed people. Not since the Progressivism of the first decades of this century had there been a period of such broad social reordering. Not since the Civil War had there been such rampant internal strife. Not since the Industrial Revolution had there been such a staggering jump in the material well-being of the American public. The passion to begin anew, coupled with a remarkable intensity of purpose and dedication, made the Sixties a decade of extremes, a decade that was a kaleidoscope of love and hate, progress and breakdown, ambition and despair. They made the Sixties a decade that seems likely to count in the lengthy span of history.

Such was John F. Kennedy's contribution—a vast churning of energy, hope, action, an era of experimentation and new beginnings. America was on the move. Nor did her advances end with the shots in Dallas, although Kennedy's traumatizing death did signal the beginning of a countermovement of sadness, of frustration born of unfulfilled hopes. Kennedy had promised to lead the country to a New Frontier. In his thousand days in office he did just that. For indolence does not go down well on the frontier, and he left America far less indolent than he had found it.

President Lyndon B. Johnson could not himself have blazed that trail to the New Frontier; but once there, he could do the building. An old-line politician whom Kennedy had defeated for the Democratic nomination in 1960, Johnson had served for years as the Senate Majority Leader. With his wealth of experience Johnson proved himself a master craftsman in building on the foundations the previous administration had laid. Under his guidance Congress passed some of the most sweeping social legislation in America's history. Tom Wicker, writing in *The New York Times,* noted with a certain sense of awe:

> They are rolling the bills out of Congress these days the way Detroit turns super-sleek souped-up autos off the assembly line . . . and some of the bills—on medical care, education, voting rights, and Presidential disability, to pick a handful— are of such weight as to cause one to go all the way back to Woodrow Wilson's first year to find a congressional session of equal importance.

After the Congressional debates and the White House signing ceremonies, mention of the legislation dropped from the newspapers, but slowly the laws did begin to take effect. The quality of American life did start to improve. More people could —and did—vote. More people could—and did—attend better schools and colleges. Steps were initiated to save the ravaged environment. The poor were not quite so poor. The elderly finally were offered more nearly adequate medical care. The consumer found his position not quite so vulnerable. The white- and blue-collar workers saw their paychecks bolstered, even after inflation was figured in. President Johnson, reflecting on his five years in office, noted with justifiable pride in January 1969:

The statistics of progress were all recorded. Almost to the day we had entered the ninety-fifth month of sustained economic growth and prosperity, the longest and strongest period in American history. The previous five years had produced an unparalleled standard of living for most Americans: an estimated 8.5 million additional jobs had been created by the growing economy; only 3.3 per cent of the work force was unemployed, down from 5.7 per cent in 1963; approximately $460 billion had been added to family net assets. A total of about $535 had been added to the average yearly income of Americans, after accounting for taxes and price rises; and federal revenues had increased by $70 billion, helping to send children to Head Start classrooms and men around the moon.

Lyndon Johnson was mindful of history: he was an able, highly intelligent man with a powerful dream—he wanted to earn for himself a chapter in history as the founder of the Great Society of all time. In pursuit of his radiant dream President Johnson harnessed the passion and the energy of the New Frontier and molded them into the beginnings of his own vision of the just and bountiful society.

At the grassroots level the Kennedy verve and the Johnson ability to get things done inspired private citizens to take up the crusade against injustice. Two relative unknowns, for example, committed their lives to fighting for a more equitable distribution of the fruits of an affluent society and, in the process, they came to be national heroes. More important, they achieved triumphs unthinkable just a decade earlier.

Cesar Chavez organized the grape-pickers of California into the United Farm Workers Organizing Committee. After long and bitter strikes and boycotts that involved tens of thousands of Americans from coast to coast, Chavez and his union eventually gained recognition from the growers. The support of these Americans from all walks of life and all parts of the country —most of whom knew the movement simply as "La Causa"— finally broke the growers' cruel grip on the impoverished migrant workers.

Ralph Nader was a missionary of a different stamp. A

quiet young bachelor, he almost singlehandedly took on all of big business in his fight for consumer rights. *Fortune* magazine, itself a barometer of big business, could not help but note the accomplishments of this intense public-spirited lawyer:

> He is chiefly responsible for the passage of at least six major laws, imposing new federal safety standards on automobiles, meat and poultry products, gas pipelines, coal mining, and radiation emissions from electronic devices. His investigations have led to a strenuous renovation at both the Federal Trade Commission and the Food and Drug Administration. . . . Nader can point to at least one quite tangible result. Last year [1970], for the first time in nine years, traffic fatalities in the United States declined to 55,300 from 56,400 in 1969. Unless the decline was a fluke (and officials at the Highway Traffic Safety Administration do not think it was), then for those 1,100 living Americans, whoever they may be, Nader can be said to have performed the ultimate public service.

Nader's muckraking continued to bear fruit and to inspire countless other young lawyers to practice as servants of the public interest. Now he is demanding "full-time citizenship" of all Americans.

That two such men as Ralph Nader and Cesar Chavez undertook the battles they did, their eagerness to upset the old order in pursuit of justice, their ability to rally the masses around their causes, and their eventual success—all may ultimately be credited to the fertility of the Kennedy legacy and the Johnson vision.

But John Kennedy had planted another seed, a deadly seed that cannot be ignored: he had sent advisors to help the South Vietnamese in their struggle with the Communist North. The war in Vietnam quietly escalated through the early years of the decade—at least halfway around the world the escalation seemed quiet enough—and more advisors were sent. Slowly, deceptively slowly, the advisors began to take up positions beside the inept and dispirited South Vietnamese troops; later they began to fight in place of them. When Lyndon Johnson succeeded to the Presidency, part of his inheritance was twenty thousand advisors involved in that distant war.

In 1964 Congress passed the Gulf of Tonkin Resolution, giving the President almost unlimited warmaking powers in Southeast Asia. The vote in the Senate was 88–2; in the House, 416–0. Of the American public, 85 per cent approved. By 1966 President Johnson would bolster the troop level twentyfold. To him, and apparently to most Americans, Vietnam was seen as critical to our national security. Although it takes a tortuous stretch of the imagination to see how such a small remote country has much to do with the security of the United States of America—the mightiest nation on the earth—both the leadership and the people still held to the domino theory. A paranoid fear that America could not survive if challenged by other nations and by other systems of government obsessed them.

Bit by bit America was swept down the vortex, and by 1968 over half a million Americans were fighting a war that could not be won. Not only could that war not be won, but its existence spelled defeat for the more important and historic effort at home, the drive to build a Great Society. In time the American citizenry came to see the error, but not before the war drained money and men from the shining and crucial domestic programs—from the War on Poverty, from education, from urban programs, from antipollution efforts. More seriously, the war drained the spirit of the nation. It drained away the enthusiasm, the excitement, and the idealism of the Kennedy years. By decade's end nearly forty thousand Americans had died in Vietnam; another three hundred thousand had been injured, maimed, or declared missing; $125 billion had been diverted to that quagmire in Southeast Asia.

As the war in Vietnam escalated, pessimism, divisiveness, despair, and anger took command where optimism had previously prevailed. In the minds of many America simply had no business in Vietnam—and too much unfinished business at home.

The vast involvement in Vietnam angered American blacks as concern for the Vietnamese superseded concern about the plight of the Negro. About the time when the war began to make a shambles of the country's priorities, the blacks in the ghettos of Northern cities began to tire of the role of the invisible man. For years the poor ghetto dwellers of the North had watched white Northerners head south in their crusade for justice, while they themselves were ignored. When it became obvious that progress would not come as fast, if at all, in the North as it had in the South, and when they saw the idealism and the crusading spirit of those early years dim, urban blacks threw one of the most violent tantrums in the history of the United States. It began with the Watts riot in August 1964, taking a five-day toll of 34 dead, 853 wounded, and 4000 arrested. In the next three years 57 more cities exploded in holocausts that would leave another 107 dead and another 3693 injured. Watts, Detroit, Newark, Plainfield, Chicago, Cleveland . . . the story was nearly always the same: exceptionally high unemployment rates, corrupt city administrations, deteriorated services and decrepit housing in the core city, and continued overt discrimination. In one word—frustration.

Kennedy had directed the national attention to all of these problems. Johnson followed up with plans and programs to alleviate them. Vietnam wiped the slate nearly clean—of funds and of hope.

Urban decay continued apace. The war-stimulated inflation soaked up a good part of whatever real gains in productivity were realized, and the workingman, caught in the price-cost squeeze, fought back with an unending series of costly strikes. For the young the dreams all but faded to nothingness as the war intensified month after month. An overall curtailment of domestic monies eroded the effects of the social legislation of the Great Society.

The compounding frustration spilled over. The year 1968 witnessed an overwhelming sense of malaise and a basic fear that the political system simply was not working. In January the Têt Offensive shattered what little confidence there was in the American position in Vietnam. Senator Eugene McCarthy nearly upset the President in the New Hampshire primary, and then Senator Robert F. Kennedy announced his candidacy for the nomination. Facing an almost sure defeat in the Wisconsin primary, President Johnson stunned the world by announcing on March 31, "I shall not seek, and I will not accept, the nomination of my party for another term as your President."

> As your President, I have put the unity of the people first. . . . In these times, as in times before, it is true that a house divided against itself . . . is a house that cannot stand.
> There is division in the American house now. There is divisiveness among us all tonight. And holding the trust that is mine, as President of all the people, I cannot disregard the peril . . . [this brings to] the progress of the American people.

While the Johnson withdrawal ignited hopes that the political system might, after all, begin to function properly again, the respite from despair was all too temporary. After Martin Luther King and Robert Kennedy died at the hands of assassins and after the travesty at the Democratic National Convention in Chicago, most Americans saw their country on the verge of a national breakdown.

At the Chicago Convention most people thought the election had already been decided—Nixon would win. Not that it mattered, for the electorate saw little difference between the two major party candidates. There seemed to be no choice at all until George Wallace—a Southern governor whose reactionary repertoire included racism—offered himself as an alternative to the tumult and the distress of the decade. In November Richard Nixon defeated Hubert Humphrey by the slimmest of margins —0.7 per cent of the popular vote—while 13.5 per cent of the electorate had cast their votes for Wallace. An era had ended.

President Nixon promised to "bring us together," a herculean task in the face of the division then in the country. It is questionable whether any leader could have snatched America from her despair at that time. Richard Nixon won the right to try, but he did not succeed. The tumult continued as Vietnam continued. Young people rose up in anger, only to be beaten— and, on occasion, shot—back down. Dissenters cried that their civil liberties were being denied them.

Many liberals and moderates feared President Nixon's basic philosophical perspectives. According to his record and his public statements, he seemed opposed to the general direction of the country during the 1960s. He seemed opposed to the basic foundations of the Great Society.

Because the social programs of the mid-Sixties broke new ground, they did not always work as planned. The Kennedy-Johnson years were a time of experimentation, of failures as well as successes. The problems of a complex society had proved to be enormous. Many people tired of the expense and the effort devoted to this experimentation, and Richard Nixon, it was thought, would be in a position to erase much of what had been accomplished.

But, surprisingly, he did not do so. Ideas and attitudes had been planted. They flowered for a time, later they withered and wilted, but they did not die. Laws were on the books. The Supreme Court had ruled. A powerful current had been slowed, but it was not possible to rechannel the flow of American life. Swept up by the current, President Nixon espoused positions that he had denounced most of his political life. The Nixon record is, moreover, testimony to the progress made in the first three quarters of the decade, testimony to the growth in spirit and idealism of the American nation. For President Nixon it was an evolution. For America, it was hardly less.

PETER JOSEPH
Princeton
September 1972

PART 1

Don Ferguson

 All at once you had something exciting. You had a young guy who had kids, and who liked to play football on his front lawn. He was a real human being.

A 1962 graduate of the University of Nebraska, Don Ferguson works for the Lincoln Public School System as Administrative Assistant for Publications and Information. As a student he campaigned for John F. Kennedy in 1960. In the summer of 1971 he decided to run in the Democratic primary for Congress, but had to withdraw six months later because of insufficient funds.

What was it about John Kennedy that so excited you?

Eisenhower had done absolutely nothing for a marvelous term of too long. So I was kind of interested in seeing something happen. Kennedy came along with a new, fresh, young image; with his slogan the "New Frontier," which was a pretty good one. For once there was kind of some excitement about the whole country. There was a whole different attitude. Right now, you know, we're going to kill ourselves in negativism; and we were about to at that point, I think, before Kennedy.

3

Everything was down. I think it's just the emotional attitude, the psychology of people.

It was kind of nice after he was elected to be able to sit back and think that the country must be in pretty good shape or that guy wouldn't be getting in his golf cart and taking the kids down to the ice cream shop. That kind of thing breeds confidence.

All at once you had something exciting. You had a young guy who had kids, and who liked to play football on his front lawn. He was a real human being. He was talking about pumping some new life into the country, into its economy, into its agriculture, into its industrial life, into its foreign relations—just giving the whole country a real shakedown and new image. I kind of think people need to have some heroes, and there aren't many heroes for people to identify with in this country today. They shoot them all. . . .

I think just the fact that the Kennedys were young and they were doing things that everybody else wished they did. Having fun together. Everything they did showed that America was alive and active. Family ski trips. Football games at Hyannis Port, riding around in the golf cart, going out in the ocean on a boat, going to nightclubs. Jackie with her new hair styles—everybody started getting the Jackie hairdos. People were getting their hair fixed with those big puffy jobs and straight down the back. I think it was kind of a fad, and I don't think that's bad. It's good. To run a country it takes more than just mechanics. It takes a psychology. It takes a confidence, and you don't build that confidence by a bunch of old men or women who plod around and don't do anything very stimulating and exciting, or who don't take much advantage of the things that are good about this country. They were enjoying entertainment, having music in the parlors, and giving out awards. The Space Age was hatched. There was a whole batch of things to bring a whole new feeling of enthusiasm. In a way, it's cultism, or hero-worship, or royal family, or whatever you want to call it. But I think a country has to have that. Even a democracy.

James Sackellson

 What's the difference whether you're Greek, whether you're Catholic ... ? What should that stop anybody from becoming a President if he's an American born ... ?

A Greek immigrant, Mr. Sackellson has waited tables for forty-nine years at the recently defunct Occidental Restaurant in Washington, D. C. The motto of the restaurant was "Where Statesmen Dine," and for Sackellson it was an honor to work there.

I waited on President Kennedy. Not as President, but when he was a Senator. He used to come in here. Well, not too often, but I waited on him many times. He used to come in here and sign personal checks, and we were good enough to let him have the money he needed. We knew he was going to run for President. Everybody liked him. Especially me. I always thought the world of him.

Well, that time we were there, we had a snowstorm before, you know. The night before we had a terrific snowstorm. And the government, they ordered the army in and cleared the Pennsylvania Avenue overnight. During the parade, Pennsylvania Avenue was almost just as dry as. . . . And yet snow all around it, but not on Pennsylvania Avenue. The army trucks, they cleared and the soldiers cleared the snow for the parade and the inauguration of President Kennedy.

And that day, when he went from the White House, when he went to the Capitol and he was inaugurated, I was up on the roof of the restaurant. This is eight, nine stories high, but the restaurant is only two stories high, and about a half a dozen waiters, we got up there. And we were watching the parade, you know. Going down and coming back. During the day like that, we're not busy during the parade. After the parades break up, then we get *really* busy.

How do you remember the assassination?

I got off work about quarter after two, twenty after two, and I went right off. That was Friday. Because Saturday and Sunday and Monday I was off, you see. And I stood by that TV from Friday from about 2:30, 2:45, til Monday when he was buried. And I never left the set. I had many fears in myself during that time, because I thought the world of that person. I had memories of him, and of course everybody could remember him. They felt awful about that assassination. Because, as I say, he was a well-liked person. I remember when he was making that inaugural speech and he says, "Don't ask what the country can do for you, ask what yourself you can do for your country." I don't remember exactly.

What was it about Kennedy . . . ?

Well, I tell you. A lot of people are just like me. They're broadminded people you know. And I'm one of them. Everybody was thinking at that time, how is somebody going to break that tradition, you know, for a Catholic to become President of this country. You understand? Because before him there was never a Catholic President of the United States. He was the first one to break that tradition. I remember when I was just here a few years. Of course I didn't know much. I couldn't speak a word of English. And even now . . . because I never had no schooling in this country. And I had always heard that there's never going to be a Catholic President of this country. Well, to me, I couldn't see that. I could never see that. What's the difference whether you're Greek, whether you're Catholic, or whether you're any religion whatsoever? What should that stop anybody from becoming a President if he's an American born and is of age to become a President? That's why I was one hundred per cent for him before he was elected.

When the time came for Kennedy, I said I think he's the person. He's well liked by the people. He's well liked by the women of this country. They're going to vote for him, and they did, too. And he had a big fight with Nixon, you know. Because at that time Nixon was running against him. And I listened to every debate. And to me, he made Nixon look like two cents. But he really did.

Frederic Fox

 . . . the Eisenhower Administration was dull, unpoetic, unimaginative . . . while the Kennedy Administration looked so artsy, so cultural. . . . But it was so phony.

During John Kennedy's brief stay at Princeton University, Frederic Fox was a classmate. Later, Fox worked in the White House as Eisenhower's liaison with voluntary organizations. Now a minister, he works in the administration of his alma mater.

After reciting his favorite stanza from Gray's "Elegy"—all about pomp and glory disappearing—Eisenhower left us at the breakfast table. The reason he left was because he had to go upstairs and get dressed, you know, in a top hat which he didn't want to do—the Kennedy uniform of the day was much more formal than his in 1953. He wore a Homburg, but Kennedy wanted to go all out, all the trappings, the black silk hat. Eisenhower said he didn't want to wear the silly hat, but if Kennedy had chosen it, he certainly would wear it. He'd do what he was supposed to do. He was such an obedient guy. So, he went upstairs and then I went over to my office, which was in the East Wing of the White House.

I had a little tiny office. So I went over to clear the pictures off the walls and last-minute things. And then I didn't really want to leave. My wife kept feeling that I should have resigned while I still had a Presidential title. It was easier to get employment when you did. But I thought it would be more fun to see the whole thing just sort of fade away. I just wanted to be there.

So, I went to the front door and at about a quarter of twelve or so Kennedy drove up with Mrs. Kennedy, and then they left with the President, and I waved good-bye to them as they left. Then I went back to my office and got some boxes, and I called the White House garage to see whether I could get a ride home. Every once in a while they'd give me a car or take me someplace. They said if I got over there before twelve o'clock they would, but after twelve they couldn't. I said, "Oh, gee whiz," and I lugged all this stuff over to the garage and they gave me an old beat-up car and took me home and that was the end. But that did sort of introduce the new decade for me. 'Cause I was out of a job, and I'd gone through this really glamorous period—you know, to work in the White House, it's really a gorgeous place to work.

I don't in any way have the respect for that Administration that present history seems to have for it. You'll find that I'm very prejudiced—my feeling is so colored by the prejudice of the 1960 election, the fact that our party lost. I don't think I have in any way Eisenhower's generous feeling toward Kennedy. I didn't share his respect.

His Administration seemed so disorderly, filled with public relations. No one seemed to know who was responsible to whom. The Eisenhower Administration maybe was too orderly. Some people claimed he ran it like a chief of staff would run an army, but I don't think it was. You can't run a government that way. But Kennedy was so slapdash and informal and spontaneous, which had a certain appeal to it. It seemed so creative, but I think in the long run it just wasn't effective. The Cuban business was so enormously disastrous and was a sign of this lack of orderliness, lack of responsibility in reporting to Kennedy.

If the Kennedy Administration hadn't been cut short in such a ghastly way, it would have been wrecked anyway. It was headed for disaster in one way or another. Dean Rusk suggests that Eisenhower and Johnson and Nixon were sort of alike, part of the same tradition, and that Kennedy was different. But I don't think the difference is necessarily good or desirable. There was a spontaneity to it—but I don't know really whether that's a virtue when you're talking about a nation of two hundred million people.

He was so young. Eisenhower had fame before he became President, so he had a kind of personal security. He didn't care what people would say about him, but Kennedy was always trying to prove himself, and I really don't think he had the inner security, although obviously he had a certain—not arrogance—but a certain conceit, a certain self-assurance. I think Eisenhower had it to a magnificent degree. He was a leader and he knew it. He had been tested and proved it. While Kennedy was just growing up, so he didn't have the security. You had the feeling he was always trying to make points, even while he was in the White House.

And the way he used Robert Frost was an example of this. I was one of the links between the Eisenhower Administration and Frost. Frost complained that nobody used him in Washington. So I immediately ran up to the Library of Congress and started talking to him. And from then on we'd take things to him and ask him for his help, and let him read the stuff and add words. I became reasonably close to him. He kept calling me his chaplain. He invited my children down for tea, and we had a very glorious time with him.

We were trying to get him a gold medal. It was a special medal, struck just for Frost. It had been given to other outstanding Americans. Like Lindbergh and Jonas Salk. Admiral Byrd got one. It was for great heroic Americans of one kind or another. But we thought it would be nice if we had one for Frost. You have to have legislation, you have to get it introduced, and then Congress puts up the money. And we had it, by 1960, almost done. All the necessary authorization, but not the appropriation. It was being held up. We had the thing designed. Then it looked like there wasn't going to be enough time to get the medal struck unless we could raise some money in a hurry. The Treasury said if we could get an outside source, like Dartmouth, for example, or somebody to put up some money, and we could get the medal struck and then Congress would give the money back to whomever had put it up in the first place. This had been done in other cases. When the institution wanted something done, for some public-relations purpose or some other legitimate purpose, it could be done and then Congress would pass a bill for the relief of Dartmouth College.

So I called Frost and asked whether he wanted this done, whether he was in a hurry to have this done, whether he'd like to have this medal in 1960. He was very funny. Frost was tremendously an ego, and filled with tremendous conceit. As he should have been. Frost told me, "Gee, I need every honor I can get. This is a wonderful thing, but maybe we ought to wait for the incoming administration and let them have the honor of presenting this to me."

So we turned over all of our paper work, all the medallions and everything, and about a year later, Kennedy made the first hoopla about honoring Frost, the great American poet, using all our material. So that in the eyes of the American public the Eisenhower Administration was dull, unpoetic, unimaginative, the military establishment type; while the Kennedy Administration looked so artsy, so cultural. They liked good music, good poetry. But it was so phony.

McGeorge Bundy

 We all felt that the Cuban regime had hardened into a very tight dictatorship, that there really had been an extinction of free choice in Cuba . . . and that the national thinking was genuinely unenthusiastic about Castro.

At fifty-three McGeorge Bundy is now President of the Ford Foundation. From 1961 to 1966 he served as Special Assistant for National Security Affairs under Presidents Kennedy and Johnson. His brother, William, held a key position in the State Department. Since then, the Bundy brothers have weathered heavy criticism for their roles in formulating the United States' foreign policy, particularly in regard to Vietnam.

The Bay of Pigs was certainly the first major foreign policy trouble, but I'd have to say that a sense of the troubles of foreign policy was a part of the administration from the beginning until after the Missile Crisis. The most important real issue of foreign policy was Berlin—the tension of the Soviet threat to make a separate peace and let the future of Berlin be decided by that. There was more danger in that in the view of most people; in President Kennedy's view it was the most important.

Were the people of America as concerned as the administration was with Berlin?

That's a very good question. The country as a whole probably felt more confident about the position in Berlin than the President and the administration did, because there was no dramatic moment of crisis to correspond with the Berlin Blockade of the Forties. Then, in the summer of 1961, the reserves were called up. The Wall of Berlin created a considerable public outcry, but before that the level of concern of the government was much higher than public concern.

What provoked this high level of concern within the government?

The kind of situation you had was one in which if Khrushchev does conclude a separate peace, he then lets the Republic of the East announce that the Western powers no longer have rights in Berlin and various forms of blockade are imposed. Then the next move is up to the West, and it's a very difficult thing, what moves to make. The acceptance of the extinction of the Western presence in West Berlin and its absorption into the surrounding German Communist Republic would have been an enormous international shock in the 1960s. It still would be in 1972. And there was a finite chance that Khrushchev might force this issue. The danger that he would was the greatest international danger of those years.

What was your first knowledge of the Bay of Pigs? What role did you play?

As I recollect my reactions, my own thoughts were that we probably did not want to do it, but it was important to get all the evidence and arguments on both sides before the President. I was quite surprised when he came back from a weekend in Florida, probably in March, and said that in principle he had decided to go ahead with it. I didn't disagree with that decision because I underestimated the costs of failure by a very great deal, and I could see a good many of the arguments in favor of letting a battalion of Cubans go. So long as there was no major American military engagement, this was a contest between Cubans. In the President's own mind it was very clear that beyond the very marginal and supposedly covert air support which was initially scheduled, we were going to keep the organized American armed forces out, which we did.

You mentioned that you seriously underestimated the cost of failure?

Well, it seemed to me . . . I guess I'm trying to say that I don't think I supposed that the American role in training and launching the battalion could be a secret, but it did seem to me that when the President had shaped the operation, it was genuinely an operation by Cuban exiles, to which Americans had given a lot of support and encouragement, but not primarily an American operation. That's the reshaping *I* thought he gave it, but not many others perceived it that way.

President Kennedy felt strongly that he had been given very bad information as to how strong and lively the two opposing groups of Cubans were: the Castro people and their armed forces were very much stronger than he had been led to think, and the Cuban battalion was less effective than its enthusiasts had argued. His own process of decision-making seemed to him to have been very unsatisfactory. Gradually there was a pronounced development in the way in which President Kennedy went about making hard decisions in foreign affairs.

Why did you think it advantageous to train and to encourage a group to invade Cuba?

The group was there already when we came in. We all felt that the Cuban regime had hardened into a very tight dictatorship, that there really had been an extinction of free choice in Cuba, that it was not wrong to let a group of Cubans have a test, and that the national thinking in Cuba as a whole was genuinely unenthusiastic about Castro. Looking back on it, I would be inclined to agree that we reached that decision on less than perfect evidence. There was a fairly general view, which may sound funny to you now, not only in the administration but in the country as a whole, that any time you had a Communist takeover in a country, most people in that country really wouldn't like it and would be in favor of liberation.

What about the Cuban Missile Crisis of 1962?

The hard intelligence was a shock. Most of us believed that they would not do that. The subsequent discussions were very serious and very intense and very prolonged. They lasted from the Tuesday morning until the President reached a clear-cut decision to adopt the quarantine and blockade policy on Sunday. That's about five days of some of the most intense committee meetings, deliberation, memo-writing, and examination of alternatives that I suppose ever happened in the United States government. The following period was equally intense but quite different after the crisis became public with the President's speech of Monday evening. This period lasted until Sunday morning when we got the message from Khrushchev that he would take the missiles out.

How did you think the President's speech that Monday night went?

The world took it extremely seriously. It became a tense time in the minds of most people, except perhaps in the Soviet Union, where there was not so much publicity given to it. But elsewhere in the world. . . .

It was somewhat easier at this time to be a part of the immediate governmental process than it was being an ordinary citizen, because the danger, clearly, was the danger that there might get to be a full-scale war which would be a nuclear war. I do not think that the danger ever seemed instantly imminent in the minds of the United States government. I don't recall any night where it seemed to be too dangerous to go to sleep or anything of that sort, while I'm sure a lot of other people did have very wakeful nights during that period. We never did lose diplomatic contact with the Soviet government. So for us, while it was very tense, it was not unendurable.

The danger that was in the air in that week of open crisis had a maturing effect on world foreign policy. The readiness of governments to get that close to danger is lower than it proved to be in the case of Khrushchev's gamble. I don't know whether you've read any accounts of the Cuban crisis from the Soviet point of view, but no matter how you estimate the Soviet motives, they clearly involved a willingness to accept a very high risk of American reaction. There's been much less of that in the ten years since 1962. In that very serious sense the Seventies are less dangerous than the Sixties. The other area in which this was demonstrated is Vietnam. A lot of terrible things happened, many excesses occurred, but what did *not* happen is more important. What did not happen was a second war between us and the Chinese. We had a very large war with the Chinese in 1950–1953 and this time we didn't.

Joseph Barbera

 Nothing seemed to work. Until the idea came up, 'Why not make them cave families?' . . . everybody could identify with them.

A partner of Hanna-Barbera Productions, Joe Barbera has won several Academy Awards for animated cartoons. *The Flintstones* and *The Jetsons* are two of his more notable creations.

The first series was *The Flintstones*. The basic conception of it was, "Why not try to do a family situation show for nighttime? Let's put together a typical family in animation and make neighbors for them."

We made thousands of drawings: we made tall fathers and short mothers, and sons and dogs and dressed them in regular clothes; we dressed them in sports clothes; we dressed them in shorts; we dressed them in hunting outfits; we tried different homes. But nothing seemed to work. Until the idea came up, "Why not make them cave families?" Although they spoke . . . and everything else was contemporary . . . everybody could identify with them. They were neither capitalists nor in the ghetto. They were not black; they were not Oriental. They were just caricatures of the average family.

No one could criticize them for their status or their living standard or where they lived because they were cave people. We were universally accepted because there was nothing they could really criticize. We weren't putting anybody down. It was a great uniform they had on, cave people clothes, a skin, bare feet. The whole concept took off. We began doing caricatures or satire on their ways of living: their dishwasher and their garbage disposals and lawn mowers, which were usually prehistoric animals who were chewing the grass with their teeth.

Almost any average American was able to identify with these people as being average people. Everybody identified with them and their problems. It gave adults a reason to watch it because these were not animals or little pigs or bears. These were people, and they had children, and they had babies. They had a baby born that was a sensation! All the middle of the United States—and the ends, too—all identified and all were able to laugh at them, or with them.

Their problems were just normal. Fred was going to lose his job, or he went in to ask for a raise, or he wanted to go out bowling and Wilma said they had tickets to the opera. Or Barney invented something and Fred decided they should go into another business. Or they decided to go camping without the women, and the women go camping and show them that they can do it as well as men. We had all the Women's Lib touches in it. All the situations were events that are actually taking place. They're contemporary. If you ran one ten years ago, their problems were different. They didn't have hair problems on the men. They didn't have miniskirts on the women or see-through blouses. Actually the problems are the same; they just vary a little with the times.

The Jetsons?

We decided to come up with another family and another situation. This time we went centuries into the future. We had them living in an apartment of tomorrow. We designed what we thought were the kinds of apartments they would live in. We had them on long pedestals, up above the smog. You'd get there by high-speed elevators and you had garages up there. You had space vehicles that were like the Mustangs or the Pintos. They had drive-ins to drop in for food that were space stations that kept circling. We just gave the same identifiable problems a whole new look. In fact, when they built the World's Fair in New York City, the style of architecture they used there was exactly what we had already done in our show. It was amazing. As you drive to Kennedy Airport you see those space needles . . . it's incredible.

We wanted to show the future. We wanted to show that there would be "people-movers"—instead of walking, you'd step on these moving things, which they have now. They lived in space apartments: but the dishwasher broke, the water wasn't hot enough, the maintenance man had to come up all the time.

The Jetsons, like The Flintstones, will hopefully run forever. We were just portraying life as it is and as it will be forever. I don't care where we live, or what happens, or how we clean up pollution or whatever we do. Human beings will never change. The situations will still be there; I think the school problems, the generation gap . . . nothing will ever change. Your style may change, your cars may change, your clothing may change, but people, I don't think, will ever change.

Stuart Cohen

 I felt there were a whole lot of specialized ideas that I was supposed to fulfill. . . . I didn't like that so much, but I didn't have any idea of anything else to do.

The son of Wilbur Cohen—Secretary of Health, Education and Welfare under President Johnson—Stuart Cohen is a Harvard dropout. In his mid-twenties he heads an anti-war group in southeast Washington. He and some of his young neighbors have joined in a loosely knit group called the Alley Crowd, often sharing meals and other times normally devoted to the family.

The decade of the Sixties encompassed most of my growing up—all the high school and all the college and what I've done since then. I didn't like school! I felt that there were a whole lot of specialized ideas that I was supposed to fulfill: supposed to go to high school, get a diploma, go to college, graduate school and go into a variety of professional arts. I didn't like that so much, but I didn't have any idea of anything else to do. I had mentioned to a number of people that I didn't want to go to high school. It was always a great tension. I didn't like going to study halls. I never used them. I never needed to use them. And yet I couldn't find some way out of the social structure so that I could go do something else.

It came to a head in one scene when I wanted to go fly a kite. This is a metaphor for a much larger thing. The study hall teacher said, "No, I can't let you go fly kites unless I let everybody." We got into an amazing larger argument about how you let some people do some things and restrict other people. It seemed quite reasonable that if I never used the study hall and was able to do well, that I could go out and fly kites. But it didn't happen, and it was very frustrating. This got to be a larger and larger kind of thing, and less and less did the academic subjects concern me. More and more did I feel physically trapped. The same way as being stuck in the study hall.

Well, when it got time to go to college, I went to school and felt the same thing, except on many, many, many more levels. An example, not very detailed, much more frustrating than I can describe:

Widener Library has access to eleven million books and yet it closed at nine-thirty. Due to the fact that there was a rigid time to eat dinner—five or six or something like that—it would be seven-thirty or eight o'clock before I was ready to study; and then normally studying till two or three in the morning or something like that. Yet if I got at the library at eight-thirty and it closed at nine-thirty, there was only an hour to use all these amazing materials.

I wrote letters back and forth, trying to find out if I could have the library open later. One letter was saying, "I'm dissatisfied, can't it be opened later?" and a letter comes back and says, "No." It was funny that it was conducted by letters but I couldn't find out who it was I was supposed to talk to. I said, "Why not?" and a letter came back and said, "Because we don't have the staff for it." So I said, "How many do you need to keep it open at night?" and they said you could keep it open all night with seven people. And I said, "Well, good, do it." They said, "We don't have the money and furthermore, we couldn't find seven people who would work at night and want to do it." I thought to myself of all the people in Cambridge who are always out in the middle of the night. . . . I went to the Bursar's office. Being a student of economics, I said I was writing a paper on economics and I got a financial report of theirs and found that they had returned eleven million dollars to the endowment fund, so it was clear that they had more money than they were spending that year. They certainly could hire seven students at minimum wage to keep this library open all night. I felt surrounded by absurdities. I didn't know what to do. Here I get a letter that says they can't find seven people. The only thing I can do is laugh in the guy's face but I can't even find him! . . .

Once I got out of the academic business, I began to really enjoy life. I worked in a variety of jobs. Worked at the post office, which was a fairly rigid job; but I enjoyed memorizing the *Postal Manual* and being able to quote it for humor effects. I worked for a friend who owned a book shop. Did bookkeeping, which I could do asleep, which I frequently was.

Working in this bookstore was also good because I was working for a friend and it began to be a whole different feeling toward the job. The manipulation of the numbers was so easy that I didn't ever think about it, so what was much more important was to develop some way to work with all these people. I brought in my record player and the Jefferson Airplane. A woman asked the other bookkeeper if he wanted to dance and we'd carry on and bring in soda pop. My boss was also my friend and he was satisfied with the work, so he didn't care if we danced. If we were happy, all right. So more and more of my friends began to be hired there, mutual friends especially. We frequently had parties, birthday parties. Close the store early. None of this affected the profits at all, but it made the place incredibly wonderful to work in. Quite an antidote to the absurdity of everything else. Why *not* work *and* have fun? Everybody else makes it such a Protestant ethic. Working for money has to hurt. We just abandoned that and had a good time. It continues even now, four years later.

At what point did you drop out of the academic structure?

I dropped out in the middle of my third semester. There was just a tremendous amount of pressure at that point. I hadn't been going to all of my classes. I spent more and more time going to sporting events. The fencing team practiced just a few yards away from my room and I'd go and watch them and think about that a lot. The Knights of King Arthur or something like that. I'd just walk back to my room and all of these other things would be going on. The feeling that I had walking back from the fencing matches and seeing all these other things going on. It was the architecture. It was the bonds going up. The English-style architecture and the way the streets were laid out and so on. There was just amazing organization. All this kind of stuff was going on and I couldn't quite understand it. Why did they put the streets this way? Why is that gymnasium located there?

What does the future hold for you now?

I know exactly what's ahead for me. I will do for the rest of my life exactly what I'm doing now. I'm quite comfortable, actually. The issues in life that interest me are: How do other people deal with their life issues? And some of those are: As a bachelor, how do you eat, clothe yourself, keep clean, be happy? As you begin to involve yourself with other people, what are those relationships between a male and a female? Then as that gets more and more involved, what are the relationships between adults and children? As that gets more and more involved, what are the relationships between families and other families? Now all these things are just tremendous, and I really enjoy thinking about them and acting on them.

What is the Alley Crowd?

The Alley Crowd is a set of people who are all families who have interesting needs that suggest various things to get them together. Why not convert one person's apartment into a kitchen—the whole floor into one gigantic kitchen and have all these twenty families eat together. You could have one person cook on a large enough scale. It would be infinitely cheaper. I'm not so interested in doing exactly that, although I would like to. I've lived that way myself. But what's more interesting is to see why the people either do it or don't do it. Why does this person here hesitate? Why does this person here say, "Terrific!" Is it the monetary savings; is it the emotional savings; is it the time savings? Is it the fear of losing oneself or control of the family that makes another person not like it? I find these incredibly exciting ideas. I'll just continue doing this. Working on these kinds of ideas. It doesn't matter to me whether I have a job in the post office or in a bookstore or if I work for the government or whatever. I just have to solve my life issues.

Loyal Gould

 . . . these poor souls, these . . . Klan types, couldn't get it through their bloody heads that they're in the same boat with the black fieldhands. . . . It's crazy.

Loyal Gould was a European correspondent for the Associated Press before returning to this country to cover the civil rights struggle for NBC. He now chairs the fledgling Journalism Department at Wichita State University.

They had to build that bloody [Berlin] wall for economic reasons. They were losing hundreds and hundreds of thousands of people who were fleeing to the West. They couldn't have cared a tinker's damn about the old people. They were glad to get rid of them because they wouldn't have to support them, but what they were terribly concerned about were the young people with skills. The East German regime invested an awful lot of money training them, and then literally hundreds of thousands of them skedaddled over to the West for better-paying jobs. Then this wall all of a sudden goes up.

It goes up, the beginnings of it, in one night. It started shortly after midnight on August 13, 1961. There must have been a tremendous amount of advance planning for this. They strung out barbed wire on the sector frontier along the border separating East Berlin from West Berlin. Then the second stage consisted of concrete posts and barbed wire strung around the concrete posts. Then a third stage consisted of cinder blocks with barbed wire on the top. The fourth stage consisted of these huge slabs of concrete, several inches thick, very wide, piled on top of each other. The next stage—which is the way you see the wall now, though they are continuously working on it; they say they're "beautifying" it—but the stage that it's in now is concrete blocks reinforced by steel and, on the top, long, long cylinders. The wind that blows through the Brandenburg Gate keeps those things spinning so that if by some chance you get through all the minefields and the preliminary barricades on the East side leading up to the wall—past the dogs, the guards, the watchtowers, the trip wires that set off sirens and at night turn on floodlights—it you get beyond that point, if you do get to the wall, you can't jump up and get a grip on anything. That fool cylinder just spins!

From that point on, those in East Berlin did not go into West Berlin. Until that time they could walk across, they could take an elevator, an elevated train. They could take a subway or they could take a bus. Then they were sealed in. At that time there were thousands of East Berliners who worked in West Berlin, worked in West Berlin plants, in the Zieman's Electric Plant. Now those people who had been on the midnight till eight in the morning shift—and they were by and large women—when they were on their way home to East Berlin, they had the choice: either go over into East Berlin and know full well that they weren't going to get back to West Berlin, or stay in West Berlin. Thousands of them opted to stay in West Berlin. This meant the split-up of families, all manner of hardship. I still do believe, though, that President Kennedy was correct. We did not go to war over the Berlin Wall because it would have been World War Three.

Exactly how did President Kennedy react?

The diplomatic protests were lodged with the Soviets. He sent Vice President Lyndon Baines Johnson over. Johnson was actually the first politician from outside Berlin to visit Berlin after the wall went up. This was when Willy Brandt was Mayor. Johnson actually got there before Konrad Adenauer, the Chancellor of West Germany. The word we got in Bonn and Berlin was that Adenauer was madder than a hatter that the American Vice President went to Berlin before he did.

Were there many escapes in the period after the wall went up?

There were quite a few escape attempts after the wall first went up. Quite a few successful ones, some not so successful. But as the wall got bigger and stronger, these escapes went down, down, down. They tried all manner of things to flee, all sorts of tricks. Some of them were pretty good, pretty shrewdly thought out. Then you got into the tunnel-digging episodes. The East Germans eventually gave the order for their wall guards to shoot on sight. Kill them! And they did! They killed an awful lot of them.

Two years later President Kennedy himself journeyed to West Berlin. You've got to realize the situation of the Berliners. There's a pretty gutsy bunch of people living there. Here they are, eleven miles inside East German territory, surrounded by the East Germans on this little tiny island. It tends to give some people a certain degree of claustrophobia. Kennedy came in and he made this speech. He had an official translator, an American, a fellow by the name of Lochner. Kennedy was speaking and Lochner was doing the interpreting to the crowd in German, and Kennedy noticed that they weren't getting anything. It was a good speech and they weren't getting anything at all. He then disposed of his prepared text and he went into this phrase, *"Ich bin ein Berliner."* With that he had that crowd in the palm of his hand. They went wild for him. They loved him. The next day had he run for Chancellor of West Germany, he could have won hands down. He was able to convey his sympathy for these people. They loved him for it. Hell, they loved him all over.

What kind of country did you find when you returned from your European assignment?

The last major story I did for the Associated Press before I joined NBC was Germany's biggest war crimes trial, the biggest ever held by the Germans—the Auschwitz trial. It lasted twenty-two months. The defendants were a collection of over twenty former Auschwitz SS guys. For twenty-two months I'd gone through this unbroken series of horrors. This was a trial where they had absolutely first-class classical witnesses. Former Auschwitz inmates, prosecution witnesses who came from all over the world. And for twenty-two months we had just one bit of horror after another from these classical witnesses who were describing exactly what had transpired in only one of the Nazi extermination camps.

Then I went from that down to Crawfordville, Georgia. Well, when you're covering a trial like that in a foreign country, you're hit by all this horror and you fall into thinking, "Well, it can't happen in my country." I was the only reporter from the English-speaking world to cover that trial from beginning to end, and after that I flew to Atlanta and became acquainted with Martin Luther King and some of his colleagues in the Southern Christian Leadership Conference in Atlanta . . . trying to get an idea of what they were doing, how they were doing it, and why. Then, ninety miles south from Atlanta, straight down to Crawfordville, Georgia. It was one of the most dramatic experiences I'd ever had up until that point . . . to go down to this small Southern town and witness the reaction. All these people from King's group—King was down there himself—all they were doing was simply trying to implement the law of the land. They wouldn't even raise a finger in defense of themselves. They'd get down there and they'd start off this ritual every morning. They'd have usually about one hundred fifty to two hundred area schoolchildren, black, ranging in age from about six to eighteen; and they'd line up every morning in front of the County Court House, and they'd sing these Southern spirituals *cum* civil rights songs. These were youngsters who were being barred from the white schools. The first time I was down there we were watching this: recording it, filming it, taping it. About one hundred fifty of these youngsters lined up and they began singing this song, "I Love Everybody. I Love Everybody in My Heart." Members of the Georgia State Highway Patrol came up from behind—and with these youngsters just singing spirituals in supposedly good southern Christian territory—these patrolmen would go up behind them, each one with a club, and just go down the line from behind, hitting one after another of those youngsters over the head. These youngsters were terrified. They didn't run. They didn't offer any resistance. They didn't offer any defense of themselves. Just one after another would crumble under those billy clubs. All the while they were singing, "I Love Everybody. I Love Everybody in My Heart." That was the only time that as a working journalist I ever wept. I didn't make a sound, but the tears were simply streaming down my cheeks. I had never seen anything until that time that I considered quite so brutal. I went through World War Two. As a journalist I've covered a lot of wars, a lot of fighting, but I'd never seen anything that I thought was quite so brutal as this. This went on, this ritual, almost every day for almost two weeks. Finally, that particular action of King's just fizzled out.

We'd have to run our film into Atlanta every single evening to be fed out from a TV station into the NBC network; and one of the things that I learned down there was how to protect myself as an American reporter in the United States. I had been locked up before. I had been arrested in various places outside the United States, arrested as a journalist. Been roughed up a number of times previous to this. Here I was, coming back to the United States after a five-year absence, back in my home territory, and in covering these civil rights stories down South, one of the first things I learned was that as far as the rednecks, wool-hat boys, crackers—whatever you want to call them—poor white trash, were concerned, was that, along with the blacks, the other category of humanity that they hated most were the newsmen covering this. They especially hated newsmen with cameras. I was taught pretty quickly what you had to do when you came in to cover a story like this. One of the things that we did was to rent about the biggest car we could find. It was a Chrysler Imperial. I was told that we had to find a big heavy one that went awfully fast, stuck to the highway, and one, such as the Chrysler Imperial at that time, that was controllable—the windows, the doors—from the inside, from the dash. Also that it had to have air-conditioning.

On the first run back to Atlanta with film I learned why. At that time the Klan was led by Bobby Shelton. These Klansmen all through the South had their little pickup trucks—Fords and Chevys—and you'd always notice on the back window of the cab they always had these gun racks. They'd have their weaponry on that. They all had these civilian band radios. They'd be in evidence at these civil rights demonstrations, take as much pertinent information as they could about the journalists: what they looked like, the car they were driving, the license plates, this and that. Then they'd follow up, and in some ways they were pretty effective. In that town of Crawfordville, at the time, we couldn't go into any restaurant. They'd chase us right out. They wouldn't even let us buy bread in the local grocery store. We couldn't buy any gasoline. Even in the County Court House they wouldn't let us use their johns. We found that we were safest, had the greatest sense of security, when we were out in those piney woods of South Georgia in all-Negro territory. King's followers in that area maintained a so-called Freedom House out in the back woods of Crawfordville. It was an old abandoned schoolhouse. If you wanted a bit of respite from this harassment, you'd head straight out for that Freedom House in the Black Belt of Georgia. Then, in going to Atlanta, we found that the Klansmen with their civilian band radios passed the word down the highways giving our descriptions. They'd give chase in their beat-up pickup trucks. Some of them were pretty well souped up. They'd put up roadblocks and try to stop you, confiscate your film, beat you up if they could. They hated newsmen with a passion. One of their favorite tricks was in that heat down there if you had an open window and you were stopped at a red light, all of a sudden you found somebody in the back seat of the car.

That was the reason we always wanted automobiles that had doors and windows that could be controlled from the dash, and with air-conditioning. Usually these men had pistols or revolvers. The idea was to get you to drive outside of the community and then they'd take the film, destroy it, burn it, try to wreck your equipment, beat you up if they could. This was one helluva surprise coming back to the good old USA!

Did you ever protest this harassment to the local authorities?

I tried it down in Crawfordville, to the local policeman. His only answer was, "Go tell your troubles to the niggers." That was it.

You said you once covered a Klan meeting?

That was before he [Bobby Shelton, Imperial Wizard of the United Klans of America] went to jail. He's out of jail now. It's kind of funny in a way. He showed up down there and then eventually again in Hainesville, Alabama. He had a public-relations advisor, of all things, and he formed something like the KBI, the Klan Bureau of Investigation. We made an arrangement to shoot a Klan meeting, to film it. It was an awful affair; they had the members of the Klan Auxiliary—women. These were women that you could only have compassion for. The poor, bedraggled, overworked, southern white women; the poorest of the poor. Hanging bellies, sagging bellies from too many children, not enough good food; many of them missing either all their teeth or many of their teeth; those with teeth stained from chewing tobacco; overly rouged, overly lipsticked. Skinny, scrawny imitations of women in their Klan regalia, their white robes, comical sort of headgear. Listening to them trying to convince each other that somehow, by some hook or crook, they were the superior ones of the world. Intellectually, physically [*he leans backs and laughs*], you name it. We shot this whole Klan meeting.

One of the men making a speech was that self-pro-claimed minister from Birmingham who did the bombing of the Birmingham church where the three little black girls were killed. He was justifying his activities, saying things like, "Them's weren't children, them's were animals."

It was all so frightening, frightening as hell, to see this going on in your own country. To also see this vast amount of white poverty, along with this black poverty, and to realize that these poor souls, these white Klan types, couldn't get it through their bloody heads that they're in the same boat with the black fieldhands down South. It's crazy.

Paul Ylvisaker

 We . . . said, 'Look, these problems are here. You can't forever turn your back on them. Which one of you has got the guts to come on out and start working at them?'

Paul Ylvisaker, of rugged Norwegian stock, has been active in urban affairs for the past two decades—from Executive Secretary to the Mayor of Philadelphia to Director of Public Affairs at the Ford Foundation to Commissioner of Community Affairs for the State of New Jersey. Now he is Dean of the Harvard Graduate School of Education: "I've retreated to academia—to step back and see what I've done and to decide where to jump back in."

I've been working at what you would call community problems ever since I was in graduate school. Way before the current interest in the cities, I had a feeling that American government and foreign governments would have to come to terms on everything from sewage to school problems. The outlook was kind of bleak until the late Fifties. Not many people were interested. At the Ford Foundation there were just the beginnings of interest, and several of us began making grants to the cities, to bring the country to terms with the problems. Those grants evolved into what became the poverty program under, first, Kennedy, really, who started some of these programs, and then Johnson in 1963 and 1964.

The black revolution broke at that time, and that produced a huge tidal wave of action. The poverty program, later the Model Cities program, and that continued until the Vietnam War began chewing up not only our resources, but our souls.

When 1970 came, the last year of the decade, there was this spirit of deep despondency on the part of a number of us that promising beginnings had ended up in some vast disillusionment. There were some ironies during that time. When we reconvened the early poverty warriors, people who during the late Fifties and early Sixties had been working out in no-man's-land, we reconvened them in North Carolina last fall. I looked up and down the table, and there wasn't a person in the room of twenty who, in individual terms, wasn't two or three social notches ahead of where he was, and four or five income notches above where he was.

After we agreed that most of the programs we had been involved with were shattered, that the central city was still in some hell of a position, we raised the glass to another generation of individual success and social failure. I say that with a kind of wry irony, because so many more people in America have "made it" individually during that time. There is that juxtaposition of individuals, many individuals, probably most individuals, doing better; and some individuals doing no better and, therefore, given a decade of relativity, doing worse.

In the middle of the 1950s, we started working away from the normal research organizations that foundations do business with; partly because Ford had so much money that we would have simply produced inflation if we put more money in the same constituency, but mostly because we thought that the country during the Eisenhower period was not doing much venturing on social problems.

Social problems were accumulating. The migration from the South, rural areas, was at its peak during that period. The cities were bursting, and the infrastructure was failing. Knowing that the problems were beginning to grow and fester, we knew that the Foundation was a prime place to start America thinking and moving. We took the money, therefore, to individual cities and states—North Carolina, Philadelphia, Washington, Boston—began talking to the mayors and school boards and said, "Look, these problems are here. You can't forever turn your back on them. Which one of you has got the guts to come on out and start working at them?" And that's when we got about a dozen, two dozen communities in a couple of states venturing out prior to Kennedy.

We had about a four-year work time before Kennedy. During the Eisenhower regime, when things were slow, we stockpiled ideas and experiments. We worked with leading figures who, during the Sixties, achieved great national renown but at that time were completely inconspicuous.

Then, during the Sixties we moved into a transitional period where what we were doing at the Ford Foundation, where many of our experiments there became law during the 1960s. I spent a lot of time in Washington under the Kennedy and Johnson Administrations tying into the governmental operations.

Then, having successfully tied them in, I went back at Ford and began working on the next wave of things, knowing that these ideas were too fragile to survive by themselves. They'd have to be reinforced. That's when we began talking about income maintenance, talking about dealing with the ethnic communities, working with state governments which were at that time completely unequipped, talking about changing the ground rules, not just getting bureaucratic programs going.

I continued that, but when the Vietnam War came that forced on the Democratic regime the same kind of almost do-nothingness, the para-paralysis that you had during the Eisenhower regime. The Ford Foundation had pretty well cleaned out its equities. Part of the reaction against philanthropy was a reaction against what we had done. I moved out for some personal reasons at the time and took the job in the State of New Jersey —against Bobby Kennedy's advice, who said that it would be a disaster—because I sensed that the states were having to emerge, that you could start from a place that was almost like a clean slate. That turned out to be exciting. Probably the most exciting three years of my life were over there. I hit the state government just when the riots broke, and the states began coming alive to urban problems. So again we could work in advance of the period on some pretty creative things.

Then, just like the reaction came against the Foundation intervention, the reaction also came after three, four years to the kind of interventions we were making through state government, and the conservatives' regimes did take over in 1968 and 1969. It's interesting to watch that the same people who took over as conservatives are now moving just as radically on the problems as we did two years ago. Life forces you to do that. So I closed the decade by having a chance to go back and look at life from the sidelines again, decide where it was going, and where to jump in once more.

What was this first wave you speak of?

It was our shop in the Ford Foundation that found the man working at the New York Medical College on early childhood education. We financed his experiments, brought them to the attention of Washington, and that became the Head Start program. We also early identified a program dealing with bail and poverty, the Vera Institute of New York. An early experiment which we helped finance has now become a national law signed by Johnson which institutionalized the procedures about bail, completely revolutionized the court and police systems in New York City, and is now traveling around the country in state courts as well. We are the ones who began identifying through the educational plant different innovations and experiments in teaching minority students—there must have been fifty different experiments we tried, many of which have survived. There are scores of these things which began small and turned out to be *the* things in national legislation. The poverty program. Community Action was invented in our shop also.

In the Kennedy and Johnson period a number of Ford people became consultants in Washington. I was a member of Kennedy's Task Force on the Cities, and then under Johnson I headed his Task Force on the Cities. The Kerner Commission report was really a rewrite of the Task Force on the Cities report of the year before. The same people writing the same document, but it emerges as the Kerner Commission. The VISTA program, by the way, is another of ours.

One thing I've learned through this period is one has to be terribly careful—so much that we call optimism or despair is perceptual, and therefore extremely subjective. If my agenda isn't adopted, I'm inclined to despair. But if my agenda was wrong, and if there was a different way of doing it, and I've seen enough now—twenty years of my own cleverness—to know that it isn't always right, there's also a survival path. A society usually does what it has to do to survive. That means it addresses the same problems that you've noticed earlier than society. When they accumulate to attract society's attention, society may not have followed the same rational way out of it that you projected, but they do things that are interesting. Take an example: I would not have liked to have gotten into the balance of terror that now is the savior of our communities. Just like the Russians and the Americans have held each other off by atomic stalemate, often the army of Italian and black communities against each other stabilize the situation. Now this is not what a rational man projects, but mutual fear has kept the peace in many of our communities. Now the question is, "How do you get your way out of that one?" While I might invent a number of T-groups or similar programs, it may turn out to be a couple of fistfights. So, I'm constantly trying to correct for that in my own perceptions.

I find something especially exciting happening in the country. As we become more pluralistic, and sometimes nearly more anarchic, I find a growing rugged individualism that is affecting the black communities. This is making it difficult to get social programs going, but means a much sturdier base. The same thing with students. The students are, on the one hand, a cause of anarchy in the country. On the other hand, they're pretty rugged individuals more and more. They have different perceptions of how to proceed. You can count on this kind of society doing things a lot more spontaneously than they ever could before; and the spontaneous is maybe better than the organized, because every time you try to organize a society, you get into the failure of bureaucracies, and bureaucracies are sometimes worse than the problems they attempt to solve.

So there is a great strain of optimism, despite my pessimism that my agenda isn't doing well. There are some cases where I see the survival logic not moving fast enough. There are some cases where we get into an engineered disaster, like the Vietnam War, which is the greatest disaster this country's ever gotten into as far as I'm concerned. I see no way out of it since our institutions are paralyzed. Congress never declared the war, can't stop the war. The President keeps playing with the war, two Presidents, three Presidents. The society is now completely against it and can't stop it. *That* scares me.

How effective have your programs been?

There are certain times when you have to throw a rope across the chasm to make a bridge. All these were ropes across the chasm. Not strong enough to sustain the whole society marching over. Therefore you had to weave, and there was the need for more ropes to get some strength, and later to produce a bridge.

But somebody had to throw the first rope across, and that's what a lot of these programs were. The poverty program. In fact, the poverty program has outlived its time. It was a grea thing in the era of the Sixties, and now it's kind of an embarrassment to the country. I don't like to kill it for the wrong reasons, which is now being done, but there are many things we can do now that go far beyond these programs, like income maintenance.

Many people have criticized the failure of these social programs, haven't they?

This is where hindsight is so damned often wrong, and most of this stuff is hindsight. At that time, when we came up to the chasm, there were probably, figuratively speaking, two or three people who arrived there first. And they had one rope which they could carry with them because they had to run fast up to that chasm, and they threw that rope, and it's a miracle they got that damn rope across. Now later when everybody arrives, they say, "Hey, why didn't you throw a steel arc across?" That's utter nonsense. Which of those runners is going to carry a big steel girder up ahead of the crowd? When you get there, then you can stop and say, "Okay, now let's put a steel girder across."

The other thing is that to talk about income maintenance in 1958 would have been regarded as absolute folly. Some people do get out there first, but they don't ever arrive with enough to do the whole thing. What bothers me now, we don't have so many frontrunners very far out in front of us.

* * *

The Chinese have a proverb, or not a proverb, but a greeting that says, "May you live in interesting times." The Sixties were interesting times, extraordinarily interesting. I suppose they had a fatal fascination in the last years because of the Vietnam episode.

We've discovered one thing: that you have to be assertive, but violence is another thing. I predict an increasing amount of violence during the Seventies, but sporadic, sometimes of a disciplined sort. It's a fact of life; you're going to have to get used to it. The question is going to be whether the violence will so sour American society that it won't allow the more constructive efforts to go forward. If that happens, then violence will become the order of the day, and we will see, I think, an explosive end to this society.

But I have some odd feeling that ninety-nine per cent of the people don't want to die, and they'll do what's necessary to stay alive. The Seventies are going to be damned exciting. One difference is we won't use bureaucratic methods. You'll find more and more a need and, I hope, a willingness to fight for men's minds in the streets, in the vernacular, in the ethnic wards, where you don't train the elite to inherit a job somebody else appoints him to. He goes out and struggles for power, by running for political office or by running Ralph Nader kind of things. But you can't escape the responsibility of pluralistic society. Now you have to persuade the guy on the bottom, on the outside. You can't assume loyalty or automatic consent. We have to negotiate that consent.

Tom Wolfe

 People started learning how to use freedom. . . . Try something weird. This would even hold true for the poorest people in the country. . . . They could start cutting up a bit.

Best known as the propagator of the New Journalism, a kind of free-form intuitive rendering of moods and basic social conditions behind the headlines, Tom Wolfe sprang to fame in the pages of the now-defunct New York *Herald Tribune* and its unique magazine, *New York*, a thriving offspring on its own for the past four years. A graduate of Yale University's doctoral program in American Civilization, he is the author of *The Kandy-Kolored Tangerine-Flake Streamline Baby*, *The Electric Kool-Aid Acid Test*, and *Radical Chic*, all withering insights into national mores.

The American middle class, including the suburbanites, have really been much more adventurous than most people realize, and certainly more adventurous than any middle class in any European country. They've just done weirder and weirder things. They really have more of an instinctive feeling of the advantage of being in such a class, whereas the Europeans are still hung up really on the vapid model of being middle class.

There are older people, like the trailer caravans, who are a fairly recent phenomenon. These are mostly retired people. I've run into them in Washington State and in California. They find that their income isn't enough for them to live in the style to which they were accustomed in their working days, especially in this inflationary period. So they have the choice in many cases of either going to live with their children—at which point you get that deathray look from your son, who says, "Oh, sure, Dad and Mom, that would be wonderful," and you know you're just going to be waiting to die in an upstairs room—or you buy a trailer. It's the only form of low-cost housing that's really available. At first the tendency is to build a trellis around the bottom round of wheels so it doesn't look like a trailer and you put a canvas out over the entryway and call it a breezeway. A little brick extension onto the trailer—anything to make it look like a home. But a lot of them have discovered that you don't have to do that. You can actually start moving. So they've begun to travel in these caravans. There's one group of them called the "Blue Berets" in California, made up of Air Stream trailers. Do you know what an Air Stream trailer looks like? It looks like a silver bullet—kind of pretty. And if you've ever seen a caravan of thirty-five, forty, forty-five Air Stream trailers going down the superhighway at dusk, with the last rays of the sun shining off their roofs, it's a sight you won't soon forget. There are other groups that are not so exclusive. Any trailer can join in. Some go out of Laredo, Texas. These trailer caravans often go into, not just the safe tourists' paths, but they'll go down into Mexico and then into the rather beautiful tourist Mexico, and then into western Mexico, down along those terrible roads on the west coast with all the dead armadillos lying on their backs with their bloated stomachs. It's all dust and dung and all this stuff. Skulls. Or they'll go into Death Valley, or the Glacier Parks in the wilds of Canada. Because suddenly they find out that they have a life that they are more a master of than the younger people are.

It's a whole new esoteric sense of expertise. They even

develop their own initiation rights and so forth. There's one called "Plugging In." After you've been on these caravans, on the road for a long time, eventually you've got to come to a campsite. There has to be a utility pole. They have been especially made for trailer camping, in which you can plug in your trailer so you can run all the equipment. In some of the older ones of these camps the poles are made in such a way that if you didn't plug the thing in right, with the right prong on top and the right one on the bottom, you'll get this terrific shock. There's a lot of juice in these things. So you see people sitting around at dusk talking, or making out like they're talking . . . rhubarb, rhubarb, rhubarb, nudging each other, kind of looking at each other . . . there's a new man, a new couple coming in to plug in for the first time. You'll see this guy, he takes his utility line and plugs in. He does it wrong. Pow!!! There's this tremendous jolt in his face! The poor guy, he does a back flip. It can really knock you down. Then everyone starts laughing. They all break up. It seems pretty funny until you realize that this guy who just did this involuntary one-and-a-half backwards is seventy-two years old. Or seventy-three. It doesn't matter any more, because they're into this whole esoteric sphere of just trailering.

People started learning how to use freedom. To use a little Kesey term, they learned to move off dead center. Try something weird. This would even hold true for the poorest people in the country. They found that they could move off dead center too. They could start cutting up a bit.

The young started cutting up a bit, too, didn't they?

In the late Fifties, in the early Sixties, the real decor was litter. There was a sock over here, a Band-Aid here, one of those old doorstoppers sitting out in the middle of the floor, just odd things sort of spread around. Everything was bare, messy, and legless. There was such a glorification of living in a very funky way, sleeping on the floor, everybody drinking out of the same pop bottle, not cleaning up. People who came from the middle class got a tremendous kick out of this, out of getting rid of all the inhibitions about comfort and cleanliness. This was a departure because it was an abandonment of the idea of the Bohemian life being a variation of the genteel life. Of course, marijuana was the key. Drugs, but even before we get to the psychedelic or hippie period, I can remember kids showing their parents even then, back around 1959, 1960, copies of Huxley's *Doors of Perception* as if to say, "If you don't read this, you won't understand what it's all about."

You often see people explain what they're doing by explaining that this is a way of breaking ties with the bourgeoisie, aside from perhaps feeling good. And in dress, a lot of seeming military dress in the New Left. So there'll be a military shirt, maybe combat boots . . . you see a lot of green Vietnam combat boots. But then always something to take the curse off: Levi's or turtleneck sweaters, this kind of thing. Sort of to say, "I'm not really a uniform freak, you know. This is just a thing I do." Actually, in the psychedelic world, the same thing was done. A lot of people would wear something like a doorman's coat or a West Point tunic. They're great, as a matter of fact, a terrific coat. Or part of a clown suit. But never the whole thing. Again you'd have something like sandals or Levi's to take the curse off, as if to say, "I'm not really a costume freak." In San Francisco in the wintertime I've seen heads wearing really nice maxicoats, which meant that you really couldn't tell their status by this coat. It would come down to their ankles, but then they'd be barefooted. They kept on this coat but then they'd go barefooted, which kept their credentials.

There were runaways then, but they weren't called that. People would just disappear. And then the mother would get a letter which said, "Dear Mom: I know you've been worried about me and I'm sorry about that. It just didn't work out with . . ." and then you fill in the blank. Me and school. Me and the job. Me and Danny. Whatever. "I'm now in . . ." and then you fill in another blank with one of the groovy places like San Francisco, several places in Mexico. Even in places in the Southwest. "But don't worry about me. I've met some beautiful people. And everything is all right." There was something about the way this word "beautiful people" came in there that just struck terror into the hearts of parents all over the country. It was somehow . . . it either meant spades or dope. And that was another thing.

Did these "beautiful people" quickly drop back into society after their romantic fling?

I assumed, as most people did when this began, that as long as somebody was young they'd stay in this, but that eventually the time would come when you have to settle down. That they couldn't be going on like this. They'd have to get back into the network. But in fact it doesn't happen. I got to know quite a few people in this particular world when I was working on *Electric Kool-Aid Acid Test,* and I don't know of one who's ever come back.

There are two reasons, and one is that they don't want to. It becomes such an important part of their whole way of looking at the world that to go to work for Monsanto Chemical is just totally unthinkable. But quite aside from that, once you've been in this kind of life for about five years, you run into a terrible thing if you want to come back. You run into personnel officers. There's nothing worse than a résumé with a gap. It's much better to be able to say that you were on welfare for five years, because at least you had a regular income; they know what you were doing. But to have a gap! To people in personnel, that means one of two things: either that you were in jail or that you were in a mental institution. So what do you tell those guys when they say, "What did you do between 1966 and 1971?" And you say, "I was with some beautiful people, man! I was just getting by, grooving it a little bit."

One of the best things about this life is that you can drop through the net. If you can stick it out for two or three years, you can drop off the lists of the credit bureaus, the draft boards, and everything else. You can really drop through the net. But you can't get back in again. At least it's very hard.

Eugene F. O'Neill

 It was a huge antenna, a tremendous radio ear trumpet, a big horn . . . we put it
under an inflated structure . . . the largest
inflated structure ever built to that point.
It was two hundred and ten feet in diameter!

Eugene F. O'Neill directed the American Telephone &
Telegraph Company's Telstar project.

This was very special. I'd been with Bell Telephone
Laboratories for twenty years and it caught everybody's imagination in a way that nothing else had. There was a great esprit
de corps and a lot of midnight and six A.M. Sunday work. It did
look like a new era and a whole new way of doing things. It came
right at the peak of excitement of the space race. We'd all been
bothered by Sputnik and we'd said, "We've got to get in there
and show them that the United States can match their technology."

In 1961 President Kennedy said—and nobody noticed
this but us—that communications satellites would be a private
venture. There was a great debate in the Senate as to whether
communication by satellite should be a government operation
like the Post Office, or whether it should be done by the private
sector. There was a great deal of stimulation to get this thing
done. There were aspects of a race, too. Other firms and other
corporations were interested in doing this as well.

We had to build a ground station, an earth station
. . . we did that up in Maine. That's an enormous installation;

we put a lot of money into it. This was as novel in its way as the satellite—a station to receive signals. It was a huge antenna, a tremendous radio ear trumpet, a big horn. Since it was in Maine, we put it under an inflated structure, a radom, which was the largest inflated structure ever built up to that point. It was two hundred and ten feet in diameter! We built that station all through the winter of 1961, early 1962, getting ready for the satellite launch.

We launched Telstar at about four-thirty in the morning of July 10, 1962, and the first transmission took place at about seven o'clock that evening. I was up in Maine at the ground station. All that we had hoped to do on that first transmission was to transmit from the ground station, up to the satellite, and back down again to the same station. We succeeded actually in transmitting from the ground station in Maine to the satellite and getting a television picture received in France. This was a wholly unexpected bonus. We didn't give ourselves a prayer of having that station finished in France.

The first transmission was a very simple picture. A white square on a black background. Most people didn't even recognize that as a television picture, but we did. As soon as we saw that, we knew that the thing was working. Then we had prepared a videotape of a motherhood-patriotism scene. We had a picture of an American flag rising over the radom of the ground station in Maine with the band playing "The Star-Spangled Banner."

As soon as we got transmission through it, we placed several telephone calls. The first call was between the man who was Chairman of the AT&T at that time, and then Vice President Lyndon Johnson. We have photographs in our file of that call being placed.

There wasn't too much of this "What has God wrought" or something of that sort. Heck, people talk on the telephone all the time. I remember for example, that Fred Kappel [the Chairman of AT&T] said, "Good evening, Mr. Vice President, this is Fred Kappel." "Yes, Mr. Kappel, I can hear you fine." And then Kappel went on to say, "You know this is the first telephone call ever placed via communication satellite." And Johnson said, "Yes, that's very nice." It was a low-key kind of thing.

Satellite communications now is a well-established everyday sort of thing. If you place a call to Europe, there's no way of knowing whether you get a circuit over a submarine cable or a satellite. Both are in use, hundreds of both kinds, and you're connected without any discussion as to which it should be. Millions of calls are being placed by communications satellites every year now.

Before the satellite the best that you could do was to take a film and put it in a jet. Jets weren't around very long before Telstar either. But put it on a plane and six or twelve or fifteen hours . . . or however long it took to fly it back, develop it, and transmit it. Before Telstar, there was no live transoceanic television. It was a first.

James Seff

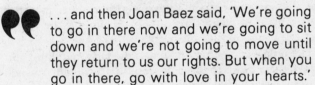 . . . and then Joan Baez said, 'We're going to go in there now and we're going to sit down and we're not going to move until they return to us our rights. But when you go in there, go with love in your hearts.'

Jim Seff is in his late twenties. A graduate of Bolt Hall, the law school at the University of California's Berkeley campus, he now specializes in the legal problems of wine producers. He and his wife, who works in public relations, live in San Francisco.

I remember some of my classmates putting themselves on the line with the Free Speech Movement people. At that point they were putting themselves on the line because nobody knew what the State Bar Examiners were going to do with people who were arrested for these kinds of political expression. Ultimately, they did nothing, which was probably the right thing, but at that time there was a strong feeling that those people who participated in this and who did get arrested might very well not be admitted to the practice of law in California. And if, after all, you're going to be an attorney or a lawyer, it's very important that you be able to practice.

I remember the day of the Sproul Hall sit-in when all those kids were arrested and carted off to jail. Joan Baez was there, along with a number of other luminaries. There were a number of speeches on the steps of Sproul Hall and then Joan Baez said, "We're going to go in there now and we're going to sit down and we're not going to move until they return to us our rights. But when you go in there, go with love in your hearts." Or words to that effect. Then she started singing, "Blowing in the Wind," the Dylan song. It was like the Pied Piper of Hamelin. Everybody wanted to go. It was really an inspiring moment. Unfortunately, as I recall, Joan Baez left before the police said that the doors would be locked and that anyone who remained in the building would be subject to arrest. But I don't know how important that is. She certainly has taken her stand in other areas, the payment of taxes, for example, to support the war in Vietnam.

The police came that night, and the kids went limp and they dragged them down the marble steps, bouncing their heads on the steps, which was uncomfortable at the very least. Throughout the Free Speech Movement I can't remember a time when there was violence on the Berkeley campus. It was really passive resistance, kind of a noble thing.

One of the bad things that happened, one of the offshoots of the Free Speech Movement was what came to be called the "foul speech movement," where some students were carrying around signs with the word "fuck" on them and walking up and down the streets. Other students were reading passages from *Lady Chatterley's Lover* to the Berkeley campus police. All under the guise of First Amendment rights. But the First Amendment rights are not absolute: for example, I believe Justice Holmes said, "You can't shout 'Fire' in a crowded theater under the First Amendment." Whether they were legitimately trying to test the First Amendment and to press it to its ultimate extreme, or whether in fact they were just having a lark, is something about which I know nothing. My guess is that they were probably just having a good time.

Clark Kerr

 It was a free speech area, free activity area. . . . It was the most precious right the students had.

An economist by profession, Clark Kerr served six years as Chancellor of the Berkeley Campus of the University of California before being named President of the entire system in 1958. He was ousted by Governor Ronald Reagan in 1967, and now heads the Carnegie Commission on Higher Education.

I won't soon forget that ill-fated September 14 [1964] order, doing away with the "Sather Gate" tradition—there was this area in which the students could do anything they wanted to. It was the famous twenty-six feet. It was a free speech area, free activity area on campus. It was the most precious right the students had. When I came back from Tokyo two days later and heard about it, I was absolutely aghast. It was unthinkable to take away that "Sather Gate" tradition. That day when I got back from Tokyo was the only time in eight and a half years as President I ran on to campus the day I heard of something to tell a Chancellor he'd made a terrible mistake, he'd better take it back. Then I made a very bad mistake. I advised the Chancellor that he ought to withdraw the order, but he refused to do it, and instead of ordering him to do it, I stood with my advice.

The first big episode was when a guy refused an order of the Berkeley campus police. The campus police did a stupid thing. Rather than just arresting him or having some policeman carry him off—just at about the noon hour, when all the students are going to flow through this Sproul Plaza—they sent a police car to pick him up with its siren going. Now I have never, in all the years I've known the Berkeley campus—graduate student, research assistant, faculty member, Chancellor, President—I have never seen a police car inside the campus itself. I just never have. This crowd gathered around the police car. In those days any time you didn't like anything, you just sat down. The police car was imprisoned. Students looked upon this as an expression of their power. To everybody around the state it was a flouting of authority, that you could capture and hold a police car. Public opinion was inflamed. Then things were off!

It went through October, November, to the middle of December. And it was solved by some new policies by the university, and by Christmas vacation. . . . When we got through with the episode, we were back to where we had been before September fourteenth, with a larger area for the activity. What could take place previously on the twenty-six feet could now take place on the whole Sproul Plaza.

There was not a single windowpane broken. There was only one claim of violence. A policeman claimed that Mario Savio [a student and the acknowledged leader of the Free Speech Movement] had bit him on the thigh. And apparently he claimed that he had teethmarks to prove it, but he didn't go to the hospital. I guess that's a little bit of violence but it was never proved.

During the time I was President, despite all the furor around the state, there wasn't any violence on any campus of the University of California. All the violence came under Reagan. And when he said he was going to clean up "the mess at Berkeley," the first move was to get rid of me. For what he considered to be a mess of peaceful resistance . . . what he got in return was violence.

Michael Harrington

  Kennedy said to Heller . . . , 'Is there anything to this, that there is a peculiarly intractable kind of poverty in America?' Heller said, 'Yes, there is.' Kennedy borrowed Heller's copy of *The Other America*, which Heller said he never returned.

Forty-eight-year-old Michael Harrington is one of the group that Paul Ylvisaker labels "the early poverty warriors." He also worked closely with Bayard Rustin and Martin Luther King in organizing many of the first civil rights demonstrations. In 1968 he campaigned for Eugene McCarthy, then switched to Robert Kennedy. Harrington has been active in the democratic socialist movement since 1952, and in 1968 the Socialist Party USA elected him Chairman; he was reelected in 1970. He has written a number of books, including *The Other America, The Accidental Century,* and *Toward a Democratic Left.*

I finished *The Other America* in 1961. In one sense it took me two years to write the book. In another sense it took me ten years to write the book: all during the 1950s, when I was at the *Catholic Worker,* and two years down on the Bowery, and when I was traveling around the country talking to socialist students' groups . . . in that period I did a lot of hitchhiking and so forth. I got into just about every area of the country. Wherever I would go I would talk with people actually involved in this. I would talk with union organizers, civil rights people. *The Other America* was a book which utilized academics, but in major part it utilized my experiences. It was published in March of 1962. Made a modest splash. No great resounding success, but a modest success, getting nice reviews here, there, and the other place. Then in January of 1963, Dwight Macdonald published a review in *The New Yorker*. It was about forty pages long. Not just a review but a long analytical discussion of the problems of poverty. It relaunched the book and made it a topic of cocktail- and dinner-party chatter in New York City and Washington.

At the same time—we're now in the winter of 1963—the unemployment figures did not behave like the Council of Economic Advisors told Kennedy they were supposed to behave. Unemployment was perplexingly high from Kennedy's point of view. So these things converged: there was Kennedy, worried about unemployment, having seen West Virginia in the 1960 primaries; and here's this book being talked about. At that point—Walter Heller [head of the Council of Economic Advisors] told me this; I never met Kennedy—Kennedy said to Heller he'd heard about *The Other America* and he said, "Is there anything to this, that there is a peculiarly intractable kind of poverty in America?" Heller said, "Yes, there is." Kennedy borrowed Heller's copy of *The Other America*, which Heller said he never returned.

The President asked that a study be prepared on poverty in the United States and was apparently considering making it a major theme for the 1964 race. Then, when he was killed in 1963 and Johnson had his first meeting with Heller on domestic issues, Heller told him that poverty was in the pipeline, that work was being done on it. I get the feeling that Johnson—finding a program somewhat in progress which had not been publicly identified with Kennedy—that Johnson lapped at the opportunity to himself identify with this. He gave the full-speed-ahead to the project, and it was in his State of the Union Message in January 1964 that he made this unconditional declaration of the War on Poverty. Then I went down to work with Shriver on his task force for about two weeks, by which I mean fourteen days, eighteen, twenty hours a day.

There had been a tremendous amount of bureaucratic fighting within the government. Specifically, as far as I can tell, there was a big fight between the Department of Labor, which wanted the poverty program to emphasize manpower programs, and the Department of Health, Education and Welfare in alliance with the Council of Economic Advisors, which wanted an emphasis on Community Action Programs. It had become impossible to get agreement between these people by the normal process of Cabinet juggling and discussion, so Johnson appointed Shriver as an arbiter with Presidential authority to break this impasse. Shriver didn't know anything in particular about the subject. He was appointed on a Saturday, called up Frank Mankiewicz [the director of the Peace Corps in Lima, Peru, at the time] and said, "I'm working on poverty, so can you come over and sort of describe to me what the problem is." Frank called up a good friend of his by the name of Paul Jacobs, a writer out on the West Coast, and then they called me up. Jacobs and I flew to Washington on Monday, ostensibly to have lunch with Shriver. We stayed for two weeks. During those two weeks, we did a number of things. We conducted a seminar for Shriver on poverty in the United States. We talked about the various aspects of it: unemployment, migrant labor, children, aging. It was Pat Moynihan, Jacobs, a guy now in The Brookings Institution by the name of James Sundquist, Adam Yarmolinsky, and myself. We would go over various topics, then Shriver would raise the questions, "Well, what can be done about the children of migrant laborers? What can be done about Appalachian unemployment? What can be done about this, that, or the other thing?" So after each one of these discussions, we would then write out a memo to Shriver, describing what the existing legislation was and what the broad options were. Out of this brainstorming consideration of the various programs came the underlying theory behind economic opportunity.

How much of an effect did the Poverty War have on poverty in America?

It made a dent. Those people who say that it didn't are foolish. The most important single dent, I suspect, was made by the decrease in unemployment. In that winter of 1963, when

Kennedy was worried about it, unemployment was 6.7 percent. It was reduced by 1968 to less than 4 percent. It meant that all of the poverty which was the result of unemployment and underemployment was improved. Secondly, I think that in the same way that the Wagner Act [formally, the National Labor Relations Act; it was passed in 1935 and prohibited certain unfair labor practices while strengthening the privilege of collective bargaining; it also established the National Labor Relations Board] of the Thirties did not really give workers rights— they had to go out and win them after the Act was passed—it did give them an aura of legitimacy in society, it did give them a national mood where they could seize their rights. In the same way, the poverty legislation legitimized Cesar Chavez, helped Martin Luther King, helped George Wiley in the Welfare Rights Organization. I think all of the insurgencies of the poor which came out of this have been extremely important. Thirdly, it was not part of the War on Poverty, it was a struggle that had been going on for a long, long time; but Medicare and Medicaid represented basic new innovations. Now National Health Insurance is finally going to get around to doing the job that Harry Truman wanted to do in 1949.

I think there were some smaller aspects of the Poverty War which were successful: things like legal services, focusing on the need for lawyers for the poor, changing very much the spirit of the law schools of this country. They are now much more action-oriented, policy-oriented. Those are pluses. The big minus in my mind is that there are still ten million jobs under the minimum wage; that a third of the poor still live in families headed by full-time male workers; and, above all, the problem in which there have been no dents to speak of for a generation now—housing.

Chubby Checker

 It was a really good time for America, the whole country . . . the Twist was a very happy scene.

A thirty-one-year-old black recording artist from South Philadelphia, Chubby Checker is best known for the Twist.

How did the Twist start?

It just happened. It's just something that just happened. Why it happened I don't know. My two brothers, Tracy and Spencer, got together with me and made a dance from a record that was five years old called "The Twist." I recorded it and everything else happened after that. In 1960 the record was a big record, but the Twist never made world acclaim until 1962. That's when it became big. Before that it was a successful thing, but in 1962 it really took ahold.

The Twist is every dance that anyone's doing right now. The dances they're doing are still basically the Twist because they're still dancing apart. So basically the dance is a thing that you do your own thing—self-expression. Only you're doing it apart. You're looking at each other.

When it first made it big, everything was going along really great. People were having fun for the first time. Before that they just danced close together and wore long skirts. When the Twist first came along, the dresses got shorter and things got much cooler. It was real nice. It was a very nice time. People were very happy. It was Reconstruction the second time around, I think, for our country. John F. Kennedy at that time, Martin

Luther King, Robert Kennedy. So many things were happening. So many things went on. It was a really good time for America, the whole country. The Sixties were a very good period for adjustment. It's brought us up to this time where we're able to cope a little better with the society that we don't really understand. But the Twist was a very happy scene. Everybody was very happy.

Margaret Mead

 Women . . . began to realize that staying at home in the suburbs with small children and being scullerymaids, bottlewashers, chauffeurs was not a very rewarding life.

One of the world's most distinguished anthropologists, the grandmotherly Dr. Margaret Mead is Curator of Ethnology at the American Museum of Natural History in New York.

The Sixties gave rise to all sorts of things. With Kennedy's election, people felt that somehow a new life had been given to the country. Eisenhower had been so old. He represented a grandfather, somebody who came in when everybody was tired and carried them through a period of transition. I often called it the "period of low-level goodness." Everybody got married and moved to the suburbs and was very domestic. It was a dull, dull period. With Kennedy's election things started to happen. Life began to stir.

One of the first things that happened in relation to the women's movement was a drive to get married women with partly grown children back to work. This was the period when we had the electronic revolution and we were looking for cheap, intelligent labor, and women were the last source of cheap intelligent labor. We were tapping high-school science teachers, robbing the schools to get people. So there was a tremendous push to tell women that they were unfulfilled, that just living at home and looking after their children wasn't making them as happy as they thought. Women began doing something, under pressure from the society, for purely economic reasons. Then they began to realize that staying at home in the suburbs with small children and being scullerymaids, bottlewashers, chauffeurs was not a very rewarding life.

Hasn't this trend been limited by the need for more day-care centers?

I think it would be just fine if we had enough day-care centers for the children who have no homes. This screaming about day-care centers for the middle class is ridiculous. We have over two million broken homes where the mothers need day-care centers. Do they get them? No. After all, the legislators belong to the middle class. They don't belong to the broken-home group that need the day-care centers.

If this present women's movement is going to amount to anything except a few frills, a few changes in composition of offices and things, it will be because of the population explosion. With that, society realizes it doesn't need as many children, and the pressure on women to have children will be released. If that's released, then it's possible for women to take their place as individuals in society.

In the press the men laugh about it, but it's become quite fashionable now. They've succeeded in associating rules about sex to other civil rights and fair employment practices. There are very definite changes being made in the employment of women. The only trouble is finding women to put in high-status jobs. Lyndon Johnson announced that he was going to appoint fifty women to high-status jobs. Well, the only way he could do it was to take them away from other high-status jobs.

There weren't that many women. Because women just gave up in the early 1950s and settled for a life in the suburbs. So come 1965 when we should have had a group of women—about forty, competent and educated—they just weren't there.

Dean Rusk

 We added eight years to the period since a nuclear weapon has been used in anger, and that's no small accomplishment, given the seriousness of the crises to which we've been subjected.

A former Rhodes scholar, Dean Rusk was President of the Rockefeller Foundation when President Kennedy asked him to serve as Secretary of State. In that position he was a primary architect—and defender—of America's policies in Southeast Asia. Rusk continued as Secretary of State under President Lyndon Johnson, proving to be one of his more hawkish advisors. Now out of government, he is a Professor of Law at the University of Georgia.

John F. Kennedy was a most extraordinary man, an incandescent man. He was on fire, and he tended to set people around him on fire. Those were very interesting and stimulating days because almost every question was up for review and reexamination. He wanted to chart his own course. He campaigned on the general theme that "we should get this country going again." During the Fifties there had been a kind of lethargy in American politics. President Eisenhower was looking for stability and serenity and cohesion. President Kennedy thought the country ought to come alive again.

Although Kennedy was a man of peace and wanted to

get on with such things as the Kennedy Round of Trade Negotiations and the Peace Corps and the Alliance for Progress and the Nuclear Test Ban Treaty and things of that sort, he was faced with crises that were imposed upon him from the outside by other people. The mood was one of adventuresome new initiatives, but modified by the harsh necessity of having to face up to some terrible crises.

* * *

The worldwide reaction to President Kennedy's assassination was very hard indeed to describe. We were told that Chairman Khrushchev burst into tears when he got the news. We had black men walking forty and fifty miles out of the bush in Africa to get to our nearest consulate or embassy to say, "I didn't know President Kennedy, but he was my friend. I just want to tell you that I'm sorry." This reaction was felt very deeply by the visiting heads of state and chiefs of government who came to Washington. When I met President de Gaulle at the airport and thanked him for coming, he said, "Don't thank me. The little people of France required that I come." We had similar expressions from all the other dignitaries that were there. The Soviet Union sent Mr. Mikoyan. Emperor Haile Selassie of Ethiopia came. We had a most extraordinary gathering of the peoples of the world for that funeral. It was an outpouring of affection and esteem for President Kennedy and his wife that we may never see the like of again.

* * *

For President Kennedy, the story started officially on the day before Inauguration, in a conference with President Eisenhower in connection with the turnover of responsibility. Almost all of the discussion in that meeting was about Southeast Asia. The only specific recommendation which President Eisenhower made to President Kennedy was to put American forces into Laos, because at that time it was in Laos where the North Vietnamese troops seemed to be most active.

We had the problem on our plate as soon as we took office. The more we looked at it, the more we thought that a major effort ought to be made to bring about peace in Laos itself. The Laotians were obviously a gentle, civilized people who were not interested in killing each other. When the forces on the battlefield were made up solely of Laotians, there was very little fighting. Very few casualties. A few big bangs made quite a battle. I remember one incident where it was reported that the two sides left the battlefield and went to a water festival together and then went back to the battlefield. So we came to the conclusion that if everybody would get out of Laos—let these people manage or mismanage their own affairs—then this would be an island of stability in an otherwise turbulent part of the world.

President Kennedy suggested this to Chairman Khrushchev in Vienna in June 1961 and Mr. Khrushchev seemed to agree. So in the Laos Conference, which had been meeting in Geneva, we made what at that time appeared to be some significant compromises to get an agreement on Laos. We accepted the Soviet nominee to be Prime Minister of Laos, Prince Souvanna Phouma. We accepted a coalition government in Laos made up of the right-wingers, the Communists, and the neutralists. We accepted the international neutralization of Laos. We felt that this could have been a major step toward peace in Southeast Asia. The difficulty is that we got no performance from the North Vietnamese. They did not pull their troops out as the agreement required. They did not stop using Laos as an infiltration route into South Vietnam as was required by the agreement. They didn't permit the coalition government to operate in those areas of Laos held by the Communists. They didn't allow the International Control Commission to visit those areas held by the Communists. This was a major and bitter disappointment to President Kennedy and had a lot to do with his attitude toward Vietnam. It was President Kennedy who made the basic decision to use American armed forces to assist South Vietnam to defend itself against these people coming in from North Vietnam.

The first major turning point was the failure of the Laotian Agreement in 1962. That put everybody on notice that the North Vietnamese were not going to take this major step toward peace and were going to continue their effort to get what they wanted. Projecting ahead a bit, the next major turning point occurred at the end of 1964 and the beginning of 1965, when the North Vietnamese started moving the regiments and divisions of their regular army from North Vietnam into South Vietnam. That shaped the scale and force of the struggle until by 1968 a military position had been achieved in South Vietnam that could not have been overrun by North Vietnam. By that time, however, there was so much internal dissension in this country that Hanoi clearly decided to stick with it and wait it out and see how far this dissension would go. It must have been obvious to them in 1968 that they did not have the military capability of achieving in South Vietnam what they had set out to accomplish.

You served as Secretary of State for eight years. How do you evaluate that term in office?

There were many rewarding aspects to that period of service. One thing the public does not understand is the enormous amount of constructive and positive international cooperation that goes on day after day, week after week, right through the years, which they don't hear about. Not because it's secret, but because it's not news. I've said to some of the young people down here that the simple truth is that the overwhelming majority of international frontiers are peaceful. The overwhelming majority of treaties are complied with. The overwhelming majority of disputes are settled by peaceful means. Now, if this is not their impression, it's because agreement, normality, serenity are not news. It takes controversy, violence, even blood, to capture the attention of the news media for the most part. So that when I looked at the enormous amount of habitual and routine cooperation which is rapidly expanding among the nations of the world, this provided a very satisfying and encouraging backdrop to the highly controversial and highly publicized crises.

What do you consider the accomplishments in the realm of foreign affairs during the decade?

We had the Partial Test Ban Treaty. We had the Non-proliferation Treaty, the Civil Air Agreement with the Soviet Union, the Kennedy Round of Trade Negotiations, the Consular Treaty with the Soviet Union, the Outer Space treaties. We launched the SALT talks on strategic missiles. We encouraged the Latin Americans to move toward a Latin American Common Market. We continued to encourage the Europeans to move toward a broader base of European unity. The nations of Asia came together to form organizations like ASPAC [Asian and Pacific Council, a regional cooperative organization of Asian nations for mutual assistance and defense], the Association of Southeast Asian Nations, and the Asian Development Bank with its headquarters in Manila and with a Japanese president. Yes, there were many constructive things that were going on in that period.

I think we came out of the Sixties with a little better prospect for peace than we had at the end of the Fifties. For example, those who experienced the Cuban Missile Crisis came out of it a little different people than they were before they went into it. I think that's true both in Moscow and Washington. There was a certain amount of additional prudence in world affairs as a result of that crisis; I think the jagged edges of ideology tended to smooth over a bit. President Kennedy and President Johnson looked for points where we could reach agreement with the Soviet Union, despite the fact that there were unresolved problems that were difficult and dangerous. I think we got away from the notion that you could pursue a policy of total hostility across the board toward any country.

We added eight years to the period since a nuclear weapon has been used in anger, and that's no small accomplishment, given the seriousness of the crises to which we've been subjected. We're turning over to your generation now twenty-five years since a nuclear weapon has been fired at anybody. If

you can add another twenty-five years to that, you'll be doing
very well.

Graham Jackson

 You know the change of the season is
near at hand. Unconsciously, here come
the buds. Maybe a hailstorm will come
and kill out everything. But it's still time
for that change.

Graham Jackson is an eclectic and versatile black musi-
cian who has played at the White House for every President dating back to Franklin Roosevelt. His favorite in-
strument is the accordion.

I find that in the Fifties—the Forties, the Thirties, the
Twenties—there was a period of contentment, a period of re-
served contentment, of tradition. The change came about . . .
not only in buildings, in dress, in style, in planning, in city life
. . . the change came about like a season. I don't care what you
say, you know spring is here when you see those leaves budding
out there on that tree across there. You know spring is approaching. You know the change of the season is near at hand.
Unconsciously, here come the buds. Maybe a hailstorm will
come and kill out everything. But it's still time for that change.
I'm trying to find a way of answering your question as humble
as I am and as best I can. Now it is just time for a change!

When I was a youngster, if it was mentioned that a man
was a sissy, if I can be this blunt, he was ostracized from society.
It was never known. He didn't let the person next to him know
what was happening. Now it seems to be if you don't share your

thoughts of sexual relations, get together, do this, or be identified, you're not living in the times. I've heard that in my playing. I noticed that at one time you were ostracized from society for having long hair.

Rudi Gernreich

 People began to play a game and . . . to wear clothes . . . like a kind of spoof. They were not really representing themselves. . . . I think it was very healthy what went on.

Although Rudi Gernreich's topless bathing suit catapulted him to fame, within the fashion world he has commanded respect for many years as a leading innovative designer. Gernreich's collection includes the no-bra bra, Swiss-cheese swimsuits, and disposable underwear monokinis. Commercially, he limits himself to two general categories of design—knitwear garments and his own couture sportswear—using fabrics that range from chiffon to cellophane.

Fashion became more reflective of what people are really all about. Dress codes prior to the Sixties were not to be related to things that were sociological or interesting. It was a thing in itself, dictated down from the top. Then all of a sudden codes became symbolic of what people really were all about; and it became much more important and interesting, much more involved with serious issues rather than just the frivolous, stupid things that codes used to be.

What fashion stood for is dead now because it was objectionable to today's society, because it stood for snobbishness, it stood for capitalism, it stood for a few select people and then the rest of the world had to sort of catch up with it. To be in style, you had to ape that, and it really got to be a resented thing. Today this is clearer. During the Sixties these attitudes began to reshape themselves and form themselves. It really started, I would say, in the late Fifties in London. The young London people began to instinctively change their attitude in the way they dressed, to symbolize what they stood for. Then all the young people from all the world started to identify with what the British started. It started to really influence fashion as such because fashion as *haute couture* just wasn't sensible anymore. Even people who were very wealthy began to think about it, began to reevaluate their attitude on clothes, began to think that one really shouldn't put that much money on their back. Serious people, intelligent people, began to resent the attitude that clothes really involved prior to that. Then certain opposite values that these clothes represented became the status symbols. It became rather confusing.

The major thing that happened was a much more realistic attitude toward clothes—the attitude that made clothes much more alive, much more of a living thing, which related to people much more directly. Prices began to drop and people began to understand that to be looking right and to be representing what they stood for did not involve having to spend a great deal of money. All of the value judgments began to disappear. You could almost say the old adage "Clothes make the man" just didn't apply anymore.

Today we are in a period of something that I'm not really very much in agreement with. It has taken on an attitude that I don't like. It's understandable too; but, as a designer, I can't go along with it. I don't like this reverting back to history and representing all kind of . . . really going to grandmother's trunk and taking out all kinds of old stuff. But it is in a way understandable because when there's too much progress and too many technological jumps that are so fast, then people get scared and insecure, and they revert back to something that is familiar and secure to them. That is the reason why we see that the Twenties and the Thirties and even now the turn-of-the-century clothes are being worn, but I think the tendency toward that will be short-lived. Then we will be able to continue and live in our time.

What about the miniskirt?

It started in the early Sixties and it took about five years, six years, before it really cracked above the knee. Then very quickly it became the mini- and the microskirt. From about 1965 skirts shortened very quickly and this began to infiltrate into every area of society.

It was an abrupt change. All the influences and indications were there in the early Sixties; but when you look at the 1960 clothes now, they really look like from a different century. They are really conservative and uninteresting-looking. Also the attitude of the male began to change at that time towards his looks and the way he wore clothes. That all began in 1960. By 1965 there were enough indications in other areas, of breaking down and reevaluations of everything, that clothes really began to change. People were aware of it. It was fashionable to accept this. There were people who didn't really want it but they thought they had to do it in order to be fashionable. Clothes became very spoofy, and by the end of the Sixties fashion was quite absurd, almost surrealistic. People began to play a game and began to wear clothes that were playing a role, like a kind of spoof. They were not really representing themselves but they were representing characters of different plays, which was fine at that time. Today this is still around, but I don't think it applies nearly so much now. Today clothes must be more real, more realistic, and less a game-playing.

The skirt above the knee was fought against because revealing the knee was considered ugly and immoral. Then, of course, all the changes of attitude towards morality and more skin showing and nudity and all of that began to change very radically. Always the thread underneath all of these changes was freedom. It was related to all types of freedom. Not just freedom of the body but freedom of the mind, freedom of thinking. I think it was very healthy what went on, extremely so. Amazingly quickly new values, sound values that apply to today were found more and more comfortable by greater segments of the society.

How was this freer look reflected in your work?

Very, very much in my own work. Really the freedom of the body actually started in the mid-Sixties. No, it started earlier, but by mid-Sixties it was there. The topless swimsuit which I did in 1964 was a symbol of the freedom of that period, related to women's emancipation and to freedom in general.

I'm so tired of talking about that. It's been quite some time ago. Of course, a lot of sensationalism happened during that time. People were up in arms against it. It was very interesting how different nations reacted to it. That was the most fascinating part of it. Naturally Scandinavian countries, Holland, more so than the democracies, reacted in a very favorable manner. It coincided with their own ideas of freedom and freedom of women. They praised it. Then countries such as Catholic countries, or puritanical countries like America, were very much offended by it. I would get lots of letters from below the Bible Belt saying, "The Devil's going to get you." In the first months there were about three thousand pieces sold. How many were actually worn I don't know. A lot of them were bought, I think, for gags and publicity. There were women who wore them around their private pools; and some women put them on to attract attention to themselves; some of them got arrested.

It really hit the freedom of the body. Immediately the type of underwear the women were wearing prior to that period disappeared and changed very quickly, and today there's hardly any underwear worn. For instance, it was impossible for a girl or a woman to walk around without a bra prior to 1965. Today you see most young women wearing absolutely no bra. You feel that it is absolutely correct and perfectly all right and completely logical to see a breast move under a dress. Prior to that, that was unacceptable, totally immoral, wrong to do that. Women really became free in their walks, in their postures. The body began to relax. It wasn't trussed up and corseted and stiff and rigid. The body has been freed, in relationship to a free spirit. It was inevitable. The topless swimsuit was a kind of symbol of that freedom. It speeded it up, maybe, or clarified it.

I think that in the Sixties, when we talk about clothes, the old concepts have to be put down, be done away with. That's why people have to be very lighthearted about clothes, make fun of it, be very humorous about it. All right, we've done that. In the Seventies, I think, a much greater tendency towards serious-ness has evolved, because people are really involved in serious matters and serious issues. If you relate the clothes to what you think, you cannot be spoofing something that isn't to be spoofed. We've said this, we've done this, now let's be done with it. Today I think the clothes that people wear must relate much more to the reality of their lives.

Malcolm Forbes

 The young people . . . [have] introduced a whole new set of values, but that doesn't mean they want to do away with capital-ism. What do you substitute? There has to be some way of making things.

Fifty-three-year-old Malcolm Forbes is publisher of *Forbes Magazine*, a semimonthly business magazine begun by his father fifty-four years ago. A staunch Republican, he was for a time State Senator in New Jersey, and in 1957 ran for Governor of that state. He holds memberships in at least a half dozen exclusive clubs. He is the father of five children.

It's simply that it's no longer essential to grub for material things. The success of capitalism has created such a degree of prosperity, not just in things, to where now young people don't have to think, "How am I going to earn a living?" They can think, "How am I going to live?" The economic pressure is off them. This is the success of capitalism.

The whole purpose used to be . . . the thesis I was taught in college was that the measure of a civilization was when people could afford to be interested in the arts and finer things of life. They didn't have to sweat for their daily bread. Now the average Indian in India today, his total concentration is getting enough food to stay alive. In this country the concern of more young people—and not just those in college—is doing something they enjoy doing. They don't want to be rich per se, because what the hell do you do with riches when you have them?

I don't feel the feeling against capitalism is stronger than before. Remember, there have been revolutions since the Industrial Revolution against the conditions that result from capitalism. Free enterprise, which basically is private ownership. In other words, you can own your own home; it doesn't belong to the government. That is, in essence, what you mean by free enterprise. They've got to realize that capitalism is an essential ingredient of what we think of as personal freedom. What they are against are abuses of an economic system that is far from perfect.

But when weighed against the so far available alternatives, I think they have to come down and decide that the more truly liberal, the more truly liberated a person is, the more he will come to realize that what he wants is to reform the evil, not do away with the system. Because the alternative systems so far require the Big Brother dictatorial approach. Everybody owns the automobile factory, so there are none in Russia. Or there might be three. And nobody has a car.

Part of the freedom that youth values is to get in and go, to take their own camper and live in it if they want, instead of living in New York in their family's apartment. But their freedom also relates to a thing that we happen to have much of —campers. The whole emphasis today is great—that kids just don't care about cars. That isn't the big status symbol it was in my generation. The kids have educated us. We've graduated from the big car syndrome to where we are more concerned with preserving a forest.

They don't have the same set of end values. They want their own lives to be useful. And where it can be very useful now is in these voluntary efforts to halt abuses. Ralph Nader has got them turned on. They feel, gee, this is an avenue of achieving a better life for more people. Putting an end to exploitation, putting an end to the phoniness of business. And others just want to do their own things: commune, or write, or think, or just enjoy. But you can get a surfeit of any one of those. You just can't make a life of total pure thought. You've just got to make the lean-to, you've got to make the campfire. The young people today, they don't measure success by money. As a matter of fact, the rich are sort of looked down on as people who are imprisoned by their things. They're not free to rove and to roam and to live and to do what they want to do. They've introduced a whole new set of values, but that doesn't mean they want to do away with capitalism. What do you substitute? What do you put in its place? There has to be some way of making things. You know, you can't go back to caveman days. There are too many people and not enough caves.

*   *   *

From where I sit, it seems to me youth are accomplishing. They are doing much to rectify the wrongs they are concerned with. And tomorrow there will be other things that need rectification. Like ecology. It has not succeeded poverty, but it's a new concern. Immensely important. Nobody gave it a thought before. We were all concerned with getting out our magazines, not concerned with who threw them where, and how you got rid of them, how they got recycled. Everything was inexhaustible. It was who made the quickest buck. Well, there's a new awareness.

This generation has achieved far more than they think they have. They think nothing has changed. Changes have been enormous, but the impact of it isn't immediately visible. You know, if you want to get something done today, and God, it hasn't been done in six months, it's the end of the world! But it isn't. It's the beginning of a new world.

Julian Bond

 What is at issue for such a person is power, the ability to control a part of his life, the ability to control some of the economic forces that now only act on him, the ability to make them act in his own behalf.

Julian Bond was born in Nashville, Tennessee, in 1940. Twenty years later he was one of the founders of the Student Non-Violent Coordinating Committee [SNCC]. In 1965 he was elected to the Georgia House of Representatives from Fulton County, but subsequently was barred from membership, ostensibly because of his statements against the Vietnam War. The Supreme Court ruled, however, that his constitutional rights had been violated and ordered that he be readmitted to the House. At the 1968 Democratic Convention, Julian Bond was considered for the Vice Presidential nomination. Bond continues to serve in the Georgia House of Representatives.

I was the Communications Director, which meant that I was in charge of publicity and printing and photography. SNCC at one time had five photographers, they had a beautifully equipped double darkroom, one for negatives, one for prints. A printing press, paper cutter, stapler, stitcher, addressograph machine. We had a newsletter of which, in the summer of 1964, we published fifty thousand copies a week, distributed all over the South.

*   *   *

When the movement began it was simply interested in integrating lunch counters, integrating buses, and integration was thought to be the solution to the problems Southern black people have. As it moved from integration of places, it began to rethink its integrationist ideology, particularly as it began to move deeply into the rural South, and where it saw that for a sharecropper in rural Mississippi, integration was not really an issue. What is at issue for such a person is power, the ability to control a part of his life, the ability to control some of the economic forces that now only act on him, the ability to make them act in his own behalf.

The shift was away from the integrationist ethic and toward—not exactly a nationalist ethic—but toward sort of an anti-ideology. An ideology which suggested that what is good for a black man in Mount Bayeau, Mississippi, may not be good for a black man in Birmingham, Alabama, but each of these black men individually must develop his own ethic, his own ideology, and that we on the SNCC staff are simply technicians who help him do that.

The first project we began was in rural southwestern Mississippi. The notion was that these young college students, who had been registering voters in big cities like Nashville and Baltimore, could do the same thing in rural Mississippi. Of course, the two things are directly opposed. What you could do in Baltimore, you can't do in Mississippi. But in our naïveté we didn't know that, so we sent a team to Mississippi. When some of them were run out of the State of Mississippi, they went into Albany, Georgia, and eventually spread out from Albany into Dougherty County and the rural area around Albany. That's how we saw ourselves, as voter registration technicians. Increasingly, we began to see that the ability to vote was tied to a great many other problems—one of them being the ability just to live, to earn a living. But in the first two or three years I think most of us saw ourselves as community organizers whose main thrust was to be technicians, to show local people how to do the things they wanted to do; and what most local people wanted to do was to become registered voters, to become a part of the system of government that prevailed in their city or their county or their Congressional District or whatever.

When John Lewis was defeated for the chairmanship and Stokely Carmichael elected, there were two things at issue. One was simply a matter of personality: John being rural, Southern, soft-spoken, and a firm believer in nonviolence; Stokely being urban, Northern, and not a firm believer in nonviolence. A great many people who analyze and philosophize about SNCC disagree with me on this point, but I think the issue was not so much philosophy as it is cultural. By cultural I mean that John Lewis, as a black rural Southerner, represents one section of black culture; Stokely Carmichael as an urban black Northerner, represents another section of black culture. What you had was a clash of cultures, with Stokely's style being forceful, hard-hitting, aggressive; John's style being more Southern Baptist. That's what the issue was: Which of these two styles would prevail?

What happened after Stokely Carmichael became Chairman?

Well, I left about six months after that. The effect was a couple of things. First thing, when I became involved in the antiwar controversy, that began to cut off contributions to SNCC. SNCC began to suffer financially. Many people who supported the concept of civil rights generally, didn't want to see it linked with antiwar sentiment. Then, when Carmichael began to articulate black power, money began to be cut off again. About two years after that SNCC took a position on the struggles between the Arabs and the Israelis—supported the Arab side—and that just about finished SNCC financially. Those three things, coming about a year and a half apart, just decimated the coffers, the treasury of the organization. Another thing that happened is that under Carmichael's direction, SNCC wanted to stop being a rurally-oriented Southern organization and become an urban-oriented Northern organization. This transition was just unworkable.

SNCC should have continued doing what it was doing, which was political organizing, the development of an alternative political structure, an alternative economy, in the rural South. That's where it worked the best. That's where it did the most. And that's where the need was the greatest. If you go to New York City there are hundreds of organizations trying to do this, that, and the other thing in Harlem, Bedford-Stuyvesant, someplace else. But in Chickapee, Mississippi, there is no one. Thankfully, SNCC worked long and hard enough in towns like Chickapee so that local people have begun to take a great deal of this burden on themselves. But there's a tremendous void left by the absence of college-age young people who could be working now all over the rural South, and who could have made some radical changes, particularly in Mississippi and Alabama, had they chosen to stick it out. It's a tragic mistake that they abandoned the South.

Among the SNCC people, we didn't think in terms of the passage of national legislation. SCLC [Southern Christian Leadership Conference] did. The SCLC modus operandi was to come into a town like Selma, to create enough national excitement to focus attention, not on Selma per se, but on the problem of black people in the South not being able to register and to vote, and to hope that that reverberated back to Washington —to the White House, to the House and the Senate. The SNCC process was to go into a town like Selma, begin organizing, working, over a period of a year, two years, working to build up a movement which could in and of and by itself force local authorities to register black people to vote. It's obvious neither of these two things works by itself. The SCLC approach resulted in the 1965 Voting Rights Act. If it had not been for their ability to really capitalize on what happened in Selma—the Selma-to-Montgomery march—you wouldn't have had that Act. But we didn't think about it in terms of legislation. We thought about building a movement. They . . . very correctly, I see now, but I didn't see then . . . thought about legislation, and were able to put together what we had worked on so long and so hard in

Selma and to turn it into a national movement involving church people, labor people, and liberals all over the country.

What's happened to white Southerners and black Southerners is that now that white and black people sit down together in Woolworth's, they never remember a time when they couldn't, and therefore don't remember the struggle and sacrifice that went into making it possible. When black Southerners, rural Southerners vote, they remember the struggle around the vote. They remember the day when the vote was out of their grasp. And they, I might say, put a great deal of hope and faith in politics. They really believe that if they ever do something about themselves and improve their condition, one of the ways it's going to be is going to be through elective politics.

You talk of what you hope for the future. Has the civil rights movement pretty well petered out?

That's very interesting. The other day we were talking about helps for syphilis. And someone said, "They'll probably just saltpeter out." I think it's petered out in the sense that SCLC, the NAACP, SNCC, and CORE are no longer the big four. Instead, in a city like Atlanta, or a small town in rural Louisiana, you will find a local coalition organization that may have the NAACP in it, but no longer do these four organizations set Southwide policy for what's going to happen in the South. And in a way I think that's very good. So you don't see any Selma-to-Montgomery marches any more, but you will see people marching around the block in a small town that most of us never heard about.

Can the progress in the North be compared to the progress in the South?

It's more obvious in the South. Things were so bad and are so bad in the South that any progress immediately becomes apparent. Thirteen people get elected to the Georgia Legislature, that's news. Ten in the New York Assembly, and no one thinks anything of it. Black people can now eat at Rich's in Atlanta; they've been able to eat at Woolworth's in New York for many, many years. But I think what is happening is the South is becoming like the North. We're going to progress to the level of black people in the North, which is not a very high level at all.

How do you sense the mood of the Southern black today?

I think they're optimistic, and not naïvely so. They're optimistic in the sense that they say to themselves, "It used to be we couldn't do this; now we can. It used to be this was prohibited for us, and now we can do it. It used to be that things were uniformly bad, now there's one or two bright spots. We think we can do it. We know we're going to have to do it pretty largely by ourselves. The federal government is not going to help us. College students who used to help us don't come down any more. Liberals who used to hold big fund-raisers in New York don't do it any more." But I think they have a feeling of optimism. Northern black people, on the other hand, I think have the very honest and open feeling of pessimism.

Wernher von Braun

 It was really a rather inadequate response to this very sophisticated Sputnik I. It was kind of an improvised solution. Sputnik weighed a hundred eighty pounds and ours weighed thirty.

Briefly but broadly stated, Dr. Wernher von Braun is the father of modern rocketry. After contributing to the development of the German V-2 rocket during World War

II, von Braun came to the United States as the war neared an end. He became a naturalized citizen in 1955. Since the earliest days of the United States space program, von Braun has played a central role. He directed the project that developed the Redstone rocket, and progressed through a series of assignments to become Deputy Associate Administrator of NASA in Washington. He remarks of his job: "My personal responsibility ends really with the launch rocket. In other words, inject the people to the moon and wish them good luck." Now, he is vice-president of Fairchild Industries.

Through the period of 1957–58, the scientific academies of the world had agreed on a project called the Geophysical Year, which meant that the academies of all these countries would collect certain data about the earth that could be put together and would provide mankind with a better overall understanding of the physics of the earth: the atmosphere, the shape of the earth, the seasonal pattern, all that. It was in the framework of the planning for this International Geophysical Year that the Russians rather casually announced that they would also try to launch a scientific satellite to measure the shape of the earth. Nobody really took that Russian statement very seriously because a majority of people felt, "With the Russian technology, this is probably too much for them." Very few people believed that they would be able to pull it off. Then, to everybody's surprise, all of a sudden there was a Russian unmanned satellite in orbit. Sputnik I. Soon to be followed by Sputnik II.

[When Sputnik first appeared over American skies, Dr. von Braun was with the newly appointed Secretary of Defense, Neil McElroy.] About two weeks later we had a call from him; he gave us the go-ahead to put our own Army rocket up. The first experiment with a Navy Vanguard had resulted in failure, which made it even more urgent to put some money on a second horse. That is how our own Explorer I went into orbit. The Redstone rocket was the booster, with which I was associated.

It was really a rather inadequate response to this very

sophisticated Sputnik I. It was kind of an improvised solution. Sputnik weighed one hundred eighty pounds, and ours weighed thirty. It did one thing though. It discovered the Van Allen Belt, if you know what that is. It had a little Geiger counter and we were very fortunate in that we made that major space discovery right there on the very first flight. This was something that had escaped the Russians' attention.

Between Explorer I, which was in early 1958, and Kennedy's announcement to go to the moon in 1961, there were three years. In these three years we built some smaller satellites, all unmanned. One of them even left the gravitational field of the earth's orbit, and became a planet of the sun. But all this was relatively small-scale stuff. The Russians had beaten us to the first satellite around the earth. They had beaten us to the first manned flight in orbit, and the first animal flight in outer space. They had beaten us to the first photographs of the far side of the moon. Whatever first there was, the Russians had always chalked it up for themselves. We either didn't come in at all, or a poor second. The announcement to fly a man to the moon and back really made us hit the big time. It required a quantum jump.

*   *   *

I believe that man's activity in space, both with manned and with unmanned equipment, is something very fundamental. I think it is as fundamental a step in man's development as his conquest of the air was. Or like man's ability in crossing the ocean. All widened man's arena of activity. Man will never ever pull his nose out of space again. I believe that by the end of this century, people will even wonder how man could ever hope to manage the limited resources of the planet Earth without being able to look down on Earth with space sensors and space laboratories in orbit. Even now we use space satellites as the most important communication links for worldwide telephone and television. Satellites have become a new mode of our life. There will be tremendous direct benefits accruing from these observation laboratories orbiting the earth, or even from laboratories on the surface of the moon.

The geology of the moon makes it perfectly obvious that the moon and the Earth were born at the same time. Clouds of dust and particles going around the sun in roughly the earth's orbit led to the gravitational collapse of some of that matter into what is now the planet Earth. Some of the matter that had higher speed with respect to the earth accreted in a gravitational center orbiting the earth, and that center became the moon. The earth, being bigger, cooled down slower; the moon being smaller, cooled faster. On the moon things assumed final form after about one-tenth of the duration of Earth's geological history. So when you visit the moon today, you find a circumstance corresponding to page one in the Book of Genesis. That's why the moon is so important to science. Since the moon never had an ocean or an atmosphere, or winds, or vegetation—all these things that have worked the earth's surface over and over again—the moon is a unique museum of the conditions existing in the earth's early history.

In some respects Neil Armstrong's famous "small step" on July 20, 1969, was probably as significant to the history of life on earth as aquatic life crawling on land. There was one notable difference though: when marine life tried to establish itself on land, millions of attempts probably failed, while occasionally one succeeded. Man doesn't use this hit-and-miss procedure any more. Man simply decides: as I consider seventy-two degrees Fahrenheit a pleasant temperature for me, I'll take life-supporting equipment along with a thermostat to give me that seventy-two degrees. He just takes his environment along to his new spheres of activity and no longer gambles with actual adaptation and survival of the fittest.

Space exploration is a worldwide thing. Our astronauts tell us that one of the most impressive experiences is that you go around the world in ninety minutes; you see seven different oceans, and when you turn your radio on, you hear something like two hundred fifty different languages and dialects. I don't know if you heard that statement . . . who made it? Alan Bean, I believe, who was with Pete Conrad on the moon. . . . He said, "You stand there on the moon, and over there's the earth, and you can cover up the entire earth with your thumb of the space-suit glove." If there is anything that can forcefully bring home the feeling "Aren't we all brothers on this spaceship Earth?" it is really looking at the earth from that distance. That is the one measure that comes through loud and clear.

Art Buchwald

 The pain threshold of today's youth is so much lower than it is for our generation. We dealt with [problems] because we had no choice. This generation seems to think it's got a choice.

As a comic observer of society, Art Buchwald has been favorably compared with Mark Twain. He writes a humor column that is published in more than 450 newspapers around the world. Nearing fifty, Buchwald lives with his wife and three children in Washington, D.C.

Everything is short-term in this country now. I think the big effect of the Sixties is how middle America and the straight people have been affected by the hippie people. In their dress. In their mannerisms. The effect that music has had on this generation! It's all the youth culture that has affected our styles. I think that the things that we rejected in the youth culture we've all adopted. Advertising agencies are using all the youth culture words. The dress is getting wilder and wilder. You go down the street now and everybody is dressed like they're on a Broadway stage. I mean, it's all costumes. The flower children! They had a tremendous effect.

What's happened now, though, is that from flower children and people doing their own thing we've gone into the drug culture—which I think we're going to live with through the Seventies and the Eighties. And it's probably the worst inheritance we can have. Everything else pales in comparison to the drug culture that was introduced during the Sixties.

What provoked this culture?

The kids had to be turned on by things. First they were turned on by music. Then that didn't seem to be enough. All of a sudden drugs started popping up. First it was pot. Then the reaction of middle-class America to pot was so strong that the youth decided, "Hey, they don't like it. Let's do it." There's a lot of putting the Establishment down by smoking, by doing drugs. Plus it was their own thing. Alcohol was our thing and drugs were their thing. This was something that they had of their own.

The drug thing has infected the world with something that I really believe is the biggest threat to civilization, in a strange way even more than the atom bomb. They start off with pot and all of a sudden they're into hash, then they're into what they call kef, and then they're talking about LSD. The end of the road is heroin.

The pain threshold of today's youth is so much lower than it is for our generation. We can deal with problems—we did —that were very serious. We dealt with them because we had no choice. This generation seems to think it's got a choice. If it doesn't work out the way they want, they turn to drugs. They turn off. They're in their own world and it's a world of music and a world of . . . I don't know . . . they think it's beauty and they always say, "We've got our heads together." But they are seriously getting into a psychological situation where instead of dealing with what life is, they just can't take it. They cop out. There are more dropping out of schools. There are more kids who refuse to work at any job because they say the system doesn't work, that they're being co-opted. Everybody, at least the bright ones, want to go back to the farms. We're losing a generation of very valuable people.

Julie Shepard

 After living with Daddy for so long, it was like a dream come true.

Julie Shepard, the twenty-year-old daughter of astronaut
Alan B. Shepard, attends the University of Arkansas.

When we were real little, back in 1959, the original
seven families were very close. It was just because there were
seven of us and it was a good number for all the kids to know
each other and all the families to know each other. At parties and
everything they were always together. Then after we moved to
Houston and they started to enlarge the program . . . I couldn't
even begin right now to name all the astronauts that they have.
It's kind of sad, but then it comes to a time when there has to
be more people. The last time I heard there were sixty astronauts. It's probably even larger now.

The night they landed on the moon, Mrs. Slayton, Mrs.
Schirra, and mother—who were the only three that were left of
the original seven in the NASA program at that time . . . no, Mrs.
Cooper, too, but she wasn't there—it was something I don't
think anyone else could have shared. If anyone else had been
there except a person from the original seven, they probably
would have felt out of place. There was just complete contentment and satisfaction. Just happiness.

When they landed on the moon, I was thinking, "We
made it!" but then after seeing them walk on the moon, I started
thinking about the people who give NASA a bad time when
things are going bad. I was wondering what they were thinking
about then. Then I started thinking about the people who have

put so much into the program. The four that died, wishing that they could be there to see it too.

When did the impact of the space program really come home to you?

First with Daddy. Just getting a man into space. I don't think anyone really thought about space until after that flight. People thought about it in cartoons and movies and things like that. It was just something impossible. For a rocket to go up. He just went into space and then came back down. It was about a fifteen-minute thirty-second flight.

It was 1961 when he first went up. I can't remember the feelings I had. Everyone else was excited, and being a little child, I was excited too. That's about how it was. After living with Daddy for so long, it was like a dream come true. It was just happiness.

John Creighton Satterfield

 . . . the Attorney General decided that he would ignore all pending legal process, abandon the courts, and use military force to obtain the admission of Mr. Meredith. . . .

John Creighton Satterfield was admitted to the Mississippi Bar in 1929. A former member of the Mississippi House of Representatives, he was President of the American Bar Association from 1961 to 1962. During the crisis over the admission of James Meredith to the University of Mississippi in 1962, Satterfield was legal advisor to Governor Ross Barnett. Now he is legal counsel for the Mississippi Chemical Corporation.

The status on September 30 [1962] which is the date involved, was there was pending in the Supreme Court of the United States a petition for writ of certiorari in the Meredith case, a petition filed by the proper officials of the University of Mississippi. There was pending a temporary restraining order against Governor Barnett and Lieutenant Governor Johnson, as to which final action had not been taken, and there was pending a citation against the Governor, claiming a violation of the restraining order which had already been set to be heard on October second—which, of course, was after these incidents occurred. Now, on September thirtieth, the Attorney General decided that he would ignore all pending legal process, abandon the courts, and use military force to obtain the admission of Mr. Meredith to the University of Mississippi.

The first representative of the Department of Justice to arrive on the campus was Mr. Ed Guthman, who was the head of their public-relations department. He did an excellent job, as this was one of the most spectacularly successful public-relations stunts that has been pulled in the United States in the last sixty years, since I'm now sixty-seven years of age! When the public-relations man for the Department of Justice arrived at the university campus, he found most students were at a football game in Jackson between the University of Mississippi and Houston University. At that time, during the afternoon, Mr. Meredith was brought to the campus. He was put in a dormitory, approximately a half mile from the Lyceum Building, which is the center of the campus, and around which these incidents occurred. He [Ed Guthman] was advised by the proper top official of the University of Mississippi that Mr. Meredith's application would be considered, as all student applications pending would be, on Monday morning, this being a Sunday.

Mr. Guthman decided that the admission could be obtained by promoting violence. Therefore, he used the marshals —there were a few marshals that had been sent, some border guards and penitentiary guards who had been sworn in as deputy marshals, there being a total, I believe, of approximately

556 of these persons. In order to attract attention, they were lined up shoulder to shoulder around the Lyceum Building in the center of the campus, by which the students would pass coming from the football game to their dormitories. They had put on very loud-colored jackets—orange-colored jackets used to protect them from tear gas—helmets, and were armed with three types of tear-gas projectiles. One shooting a can of gas for close use, another shooting a light type of projectile which contained tear gas, and the third having a stronger and a heavier projectile containing tear gas. These so-called marshals remained around the building which Attorney General Kennedy and President Kennedy knew would not be utilized in any way in connection with Mr. Meredith until Monday morning, in my opinion solely to attract the students and to provoke violence.

John Doar

 We had lots of energy. We worked like hell, and we believed in what we were doing. There weren't very many of us, and the South is an awfully big place.

After ten years in private practice John Doar joined the Civil Rights Division of the Justice Department in the Kennedy Administration. He was named Assistant Attorney General, and in late 1964 took command of the Civil Rights Division, where he remained until 1967. Robert Kennedy, by then Senator from New York, again called on Mr. Doar, this time to head the Bedford-Stuyvesant D & S Corporation, a group of businessmen organized to revitalize and rebuild that vast impoverished community in Brooklyn. He also served briefly as President of the New York City Board of Education.

At the University of Mississippi, I went up with James Meredith. I took James Meredith into the university and had a number of meetings with Ross Barnett.

My relationships with Meredith were always pleasant. He was a good guy. He and the Chief U.S. Marshal, Jim McShane, and I spent a good deal of time together that fall. We walked up to the University of Mississippi several times and were turned back before we were finally able to bring Meredith in, each time with a higher level of force supporting us. It was a period of considerable excitement and emotion in Mississippi. Jim Meredith always took it calmly and coolly. He was never perturbed. He was determined, persistent. He never panicked at any time.

It took five times before he got registered into the University of Mississippi. The first time I was not with him. I was trying a case down in Hattiesburg, Mississippi. John Barrett, the second assistant, and two marshals accompanied him to the university. They had the Governor there and rejected him. The second time we went to the State Office Building in Jackson and the Governor rebuffed us there at the Office of the Board of Trustees. The third time we got up to an entrance of the university and were blocked by the Lieutenant Governor, Paul Johnson, with a line of sheriffs behind him across the road. We didn't have the force to force our way through and we didn't want to be reckless and try to do that anyway. We were accompanied by two or three marshals, that's all. McShane, Meredith, and me. The fourth time we were going down with about thirty marshals, but it was reported that the situation was so emotional and out of control that it wouldn't be wise for us to push our way onto the campus with thirty or forty marshals. So we turned around, halfway down the road between Memphis and Oxford. The fifth time we came in a light plane and entered the university at about six or seven o'clock P.M. on Sunday, after some three hundred marshals had gone onto the campus at about four o'clock to secure the entrance. Disorder was just breaking out at the main building of the University of Mississippi campus when we got there. We came into one of the lesser-used routes and went immediately to a dorm which had been assigned by University officials to Meredith. I spent that evening with some marshals at the dormitory while Meredith slept, then later I went down to the university headquarters, the Lyceum Building—the main administration building—where there was a riot going on, lots of violence. Two people were killed.

He had some security for some time, maybe all the time he was on the campus. The practice was that I would go with him to class—not go in the class, just walk along and talk to each other until he got to the classroom door. Sometimes I would fall off and follow from a distance. There were always one or two or three marshals around the area. In front or behind him. We kind of played it loose or tight, depending upon what kinds of crowds there were, what kinds of attitudes there were among the students, what time of day it was. I usually ate with him in the cafeteria.

I stayed there for about three weeks, and then I gradually broke in younger lawyers to stay with him. We rotated a lawyer down there with him for months. There was a lot of social pressure against anyone who tried to be friendly with him. Keep in mind that he was the very first guy to break the caste system in Mississippi. The caste system was enforced by every public, social, and private institution in the state—from the cradle to the grave. Here was a guy who was saying, "I'm not going to have you do that. I'll put up with all the anxiety, trouble and harassment, discrimination and threats, violence; but I'm going to have my rights." It was his decision that triggered the response by the federal government. This was a remarkable thing: one individual, exercising his rights and demanding that his rights be honored, could put in motion the whole apparatus of the federal government to support him. That's the genius of this country.

It was a great moment in history. It was a situation where the country had not lived up to what it said it stood for; its deed was in no way consistent with its word. Here was a situation in which my colleagues and I found ourselves where we had an opportunity to narrow the gap between the country's word and the country's deed. We [lawyers in the civil rights division] were very high about that. The juices in all of us were running very fast. We had lots of energy. We worked like hell, and we believed in what we were doing. There weren't very many of us, and the South is an awfully big place.

The political leaders had lived with this hypocrisy for one hundred years. Political leaders and all our leaders. So when you find yourself in that kind of situation, the emotion you have —at least the emotion I had—was just to work. Stay in there. Keep at it and keep at it.

How did you keep at it after Senator Robert Kennedy left the administration?

Senator Kennedy didn't think the city programs, the poverty programs, were working at all. This country was beset with a great number of racial disorders, rioting, and violence in the city. The standard government programs didn't seem to be making any impact. He thought the Bedford-Stuyvesants of the country were awfully frustrated and bitter and disillusioned because they'd heard the political leaders who had constantly talked about goals and objectives where everybody was going to be equal and there was going to be freedom for one and all. Yet, admitting the progress that had taken place in the South, a citizen in Bedford-Stuyvesant couldn't see a hell of a lot of difference in his situation then and what it had been three, four, five years before. He was still the sufferer of all sorts of discrimination. Somebody still had their foot on his neck. So Robert Kennedy, after being challenged by some people about the deplorable conditions in Bedford-Stuyvesant, took a tour out here and decided to see if he could develop a new kind of program to try to rehabilitate and revive Bedford-Stuyvesant. That's how this program began.

Precisely what is the program?

Well, you see, we're two corporations. There is a community corporation—the Bedford-Stuyvesant Restoration Corporation; and there is a corporation made up of businessmen, of which I'm the President—the D & S Corporation. There's nothing permanent about the business corporation. We're here to help. We're here to help create and develop a viable community institution. Once that's done, we'll no longer be needed. We're not here to build an empire for ourselves, not to build an empire for John Doar.

I sometimes feel that this is just a different aspect of making the law work to correct this gap between word and deed. Here I'm not working as a lawyer. I'm really not trying to ensure legal rights, to ensure political rights. Rather, I'm trying to help a community, help a city, the city of Bedford-Stuyvesant, to acquire some economic power.

You speak of the Bedford-Stuyvesants of America. What kind of place is this particular one?

It's 450,000 people in 600 square blocks. All minority people, mostly blacks, eighty-five per cent black. Poor. More unemployment than the average. Lots of people on welfare. Lousy schools. There hasn't been a new public school built in Bedford-Stuyvesant in fifty-five years. Inferior health facilities. No communication system. No radio station, no television station, no newspaper. No credit. No internal flow of money. Few goods exported from the city of Bedford-Stuyvesant. Terrible sanitation service. Pretty bad to bad police service. Bedford-Stuyvesant is ringed by a number of high-rise public-housing buildings, reflecting what I call the "national clean room" policy, the policy the national government had for thirty years to solve the problems of the citizens who lived in Bedford-Stuyvesant. If "they" just had a clean room, everything would be fine. It didn't matter who built the room. It didn't matter if all white carpenters built the room. It didn't make any difference whether a white architect designed the room. It didn't make any difference whether a white developer developed the room and made money on the room. Or it didn't make any difference whether whites managed the room, collected the rent from the room. But if "they," the people in Bedford-Stuyvesant, just had a clean room to live in, everything would be all right with them and with us. That policy was a miserable failure. That's what the situation was in 1967.

We act as a commercial bank in that we make loans to businesses that are forming and trying to grow in Bedford-Stuyvesant. We make loans through a consortium of banks to homeowners so that they can get reasonable mortgages, government-insured mortgages on their homes; buy them, repair them, and maintain them. We are building new housing projects. We've just got one under way now; it's a six-floor, fifty-two unit project. We rehabilitate housing. We are trying to develop, and are developing as you can see from the area where we are now, a commercial center to stimulate retail trade—commerce—within Bedford-Stuyvesant. We plan to restore the confidence of businessmen in Bedford-Stuyvesant as a place to do business. If we could just get the people and the market to have confidence in Bedford-Stuyvesant, then conditions will improve.

The state of mind has a hell of a lot to do with how well we can do. If the market forces are running against you, then no one has confidence in the area. If nobody has confidence in the area, then the market forces run faster the other way. We're trying to turn those market forces. I'm very optimistic about that. I think both Bedford-Stuyvesant and Brooklyn have a great future. I see Brooklyn at the turn of the century, around the year 2000, as being one of the great cities in the country. Really we're going to have a renaissance in Brooklyn. And what is happening in Bedford-Stuyvesant is a very important part of that renaissance. Brooklyn is going to be a great place to live. It's going to be closely tied to Lower Manhattan. Manhattan is really two cities: Lower Manhattan and Midtown Manhattan. I envision Lower Manhattan and Brooklyn having a marriage where they will both work to improve the other. Lower Manhattan needs Brooklyn to survive, and if Lower Manhattan would focus on Brooklyn, then we would have the economic power to put some muscle behind this renaissance. This is really the great frontier of the country. The West and the Southwest are now settled. This is the place to be, in Brooklyn.

Elmer Valentine

 Here, all you have to do is keep time to the music. You do whatever you want. You ad lib. You're the creator of your own dance.

It was Elmer Valentine who, with his Whiskey à Go-Go, first brought the discothèque to America.

I had owned a nightclub, PJ's, in Santa Monica. I sold out my interest in PJ's and decided to go to Europe. This was in 1961, and I was touring all over around the countries. Over there is where I got the idea of the discothèque. There was Whiskey à Go-Go all over Europe. In Cannes and Nice and all these small clubs. All the big nightclubs that cater to the tourists weren't doing as well as the little discothèques, where they were dancing just to music. I saw the young people: they were just dancing and having fun. This was it. After about a year I came back to Los Angeles and decided to open a club for the young people.

I opened the Whiskey. It just was an immediate success. We signed Johnny Rivers for one year. Johnny Rivers was like the Pied Piper. The girls in the dancing cage . . . that was a fluke. The go-go dancer is almost a household word now, but it originated at this Whiskey à Go-Go. I like to take credit, saying I invented the go-go dancer, but I didn't. It was just an accident. I didn't think Los Angeles was ready for a pure discothèque only with records, but I would bring Johnny Rivers in and then play records in between. We were going to have a female disc jockey play the records and talk to the people. Well, the night we opened up here, she called up crying—her mother wouldn't allow her to work in a nightclub. So we were stuck without a girl!

We grabbed one of our waitresses. Her name was Patty Brock-hurst. It was a French motif and our waitresses had short skirts and leotards. "Tonight, you're going to have to play records." So she got up there and she started playing records. Well, if you just play records, you have nothing to do, so she started dancing with the music. Everyone thought it was part of the show and it became an immediate hit. We were doing such business that Saturday night didn't vary from Monday night.

We were the originator of the Go-Go girls; I also think we were the first ones to stop it. The kids are too hip today. They were better dancers than the girls I had in the cage. They only want their music. They're not lookin' to look at dancers.

The Whiskey opened in 1963. The dances were called the Watusi and the Frug. The Watusi was a dance where they moved but they kept their feet in the same position and never moved around. That's when they started not holding one another, when you were on your own. Years ago to be a good dancer you had to get ballroom dancing. If a person was a little shy, he went to the dance studios and got taken for a lot of money. Here, all you have to do is keep time to the music. You do whatever you want. You ad lib. You're the creator of your own dance.

When I first opened, it was strictly adults—twenty-one and over. It was the Jet Set type and the Hollywood crowd. Very influential, upper middle class, management, Madison Avenue. With a buck. But today my business is successful because it's really not for the Jet Set. The kids live for today. I charge anywhere from two dollars a night on up. They can get the best music going. In my generation I would go to a nightclub to see Frank Sinatra or whoever and it would cost twenty to thirty dollars for an evening with tip and headwaiters. Today they can come into the Whiskey, pay two dollars to get in, spend fifty cents for a Coke . . . or if they're twenty-one, a dollar for a beer . . . eat a hamburger and have a great evening for five or six dollars. If they bring a date it's ten or twelve dollars. They can come out four or five times a week. The average nightclub-goer years ago would go out once a week on the weekend, or once or twice a month.

That's why I'm successful, because the young people live for today, not for tomorrow. They want to hear their music. They love their music. They won't sit home and have their intelligence insulted by the trash they put out on television. They want to be out every night.

Bruce K. Holloway

 It doesn't take a deep study of history to realize that the confrontation is real. . . . They intend to take us over and eliminate all the things that America has stood for. . . .

A West Point graduate and fighter pilot during World War II, General Bruce K. Holloway has held numerous high-level commands and has earned a warehouse of military decorations and awards in the course of his thirty-four years of military service. In July 1965 he was awarded a fourth star and the dual command of the United States Air Force in Europe and of the 4th Allied Tactical Air Force of NATO. A year later his superiors recalled Holloway to Washington and appointed him Vice Chief of Staff of the United States Air Force. Then, in 1968, he assumed command of the Joint Strategic Target Planning Staff and became Commander-in-Chief of the Strategic Air Command, which carries a broad mandate: "In peacetime to maintain a force capable of deterring Communist aggression, while in wartime the mission is to destroy the enemy's warmaking capability. It is responsible for the delivery over enemy targets of over seventy per cent of the Free World's nuclear firepower."

The series of events proceeded quite rapidly from the discovery and validation that there actually were offensive-type missiles based in Cuba by the Russians. Reconnaissance flights determined it.

I'll skip the preliminaries and the diplomatic discussions because I'm not too privy to exactly what they were, but it fairly soon resulted in a marshaling of forces and a buildup of forces—particularly Air Forces, but also ground forces—in Florida. Bases in Florida were poised for action. This was, of course, very visible to anybody that wanted to see it. The feeling began to run pretty high in Florida as this happened. A lot of people left and went north because they were afraid for their own safety. This particularly applied to some of the older residents there around St. Petersburg, and all manner of tourists. The tourist business dropped off to about zilch for a while. We obviously meant business when we said, "Get the missiles out of Cuba" with this buildup—showing resolve. We had the underlying strength. We had what most people estimate to be a five-to-one superiority of strategic forces over the USSR. We showed this resolve by posturing all these general purpose forces in Florida. This included tanks and a great number of aircraft.

Then in the insistence of getting them out—in the give-and-take of messages—we established a blockade but never enforced it, as far as I know, against any ships of Russian nationality or that operated for the USSR.

Anyhow, the net result was that with that show of force and resolve, and the unwavering insistence on the part of the President of the United States to get those things out of there, they got them out. We did not attack. We did not invade. We did not fire a shot to the best of my knowledge. Whether or not we should have gone down there and cleaned out the Communist government of Cuba is another subject. I think if we had cleaned out that rats' nest, it would have cut back a lot of the Communist growth in South America for a long, long time. But they did get their missiles out and I think it was a tremendous loss of prestige for the USSR amongst all the Communist world to do so. Very shortly after that was when they started this priority drive to improve and build up their strategic force structure. They learned a big lesson.

What was the atmosphere in your office during this tremendous buildup?

Well, it was one of working pretty hard around the clock. Examining and refining plans on a daily basis as the situation developed. We drew up a number of plans for going in there to eliminate those missiles if we had to go. Just ordinary strike plans. Contingency war plans, without any consideration for using nuclear weapons, of course. Just conventional forces. The decisive part, the immediate quick-reaction part was air force, followed up by ground forces, if necessary. My feeling was that it wouldn't have been necessary.

Were you at all caught off guard by such a fast progression of such major events?

I was surprised in only one respect, and really not terribly surprised. I was surprised that we didn't actually go in there. I thought we were going.

How in overall terms do you view the course and peril of the Cold War?

I would characterize the Cold War as a confrontation without bullets that results from the vast difference in ideology between that of the Soviet Union and that of the United States. This is the underlying genesis, and the catalyst for a Cold War that's gone on since 1948 or thereabouts.

The fact that there is a Cold War, and the fact that it hasn't basically changed, is very directly resultant from the fact that we have this diametric ideological view of how people ought to live and be governed. The USSR is a dictatorship. It's not the will of the proletariat. It's not the will of anybody else except that minority dictatorship. The facts of the case—how Communism is run and controlled—are so different from the theory as espoused by Karl Marx and Engels that there's no resemblance at all. They explain it by saying that "We're going to get there, but we've got to get there by eliminating all the other evils of the world, such as capitalism/imperialism before we can establish this great utopian structure of the rules of the proletariat and common property." There is a lot of similarity, to me, when you study the theory of it, between the idealistic preachings of Communism and Christianity, but in practice it's something else. In practice, it's very purely a ruthless, totalitarian dictatorship whereby the individual is precisely controlled.

Up to the Korean War things came out generally in our favor; but only because we were dealing from relative strength, very decidedly superior strength. That condition doesn't apply any more. So the changes with respect to the Cold War from here on out are going to be pretty frightening. The changes are in degree. There's not going to be any change in the fact that there is a Cold War and why there is one. But it's going to be very different, because we don't have any more of that margin of superiority in basic strategic military power. It's gone.

The Cuban thing, this is when the big change began. This was another test of will and resolve. It was established without any question that there were offensive missiles based in Cuba that could reach the United States—which, incidentally, was contrary to assurance that we'd been given from the highest level, by Khrushchev. So we said, "Get them out." We had the superiority and we showed resolve. Those are the necessary ingredients. We showed resolve by posturing tremendous weight of conventional forces in Florida, particularly Air Force. I was down there. Every big base, like Homestead and McCoy and MacDill, was loaded with fighter aircraft. So we showed resolve; we told them to get them out and they got them out.

Now it's changed. Shortly after that the Russians started their drive, their unrelenting effort—without any constraints except natural constraints—to establish a strategic force structure at least as good as and hopefully superior to that of the United States. They've at least reached parity now, perhaps passed it—depending on how you want to evaluate it—and I think we're going to see some very discouraging things happening in the not too distant future with respect to further prosecution of international confrontations. We're not going to be able to control them like we have in the past, and then the Cold War will shift definitely in their favor. Their motivation being entirely different: to move in, aggrandize, and swallow up bit by bit other nations, other peoples, other sources of economy; ours being just the opposite: to live and let live—it's going to be kind of bad.

The United States has always been dedicated to the dignity and the rights of the individual, to allow freedom of expression to nationalities, freedom of choice in all things. We recognized right after World War Two that to be able to take a stand, forcefully, to keep those countries free that want to remain free, it required strength from which to deal. We understood it real well apparently, and this is why an awful lot of money went into building up the strategic forces all during the 1950s. Then, about 1960, a new administration came in and immediately announced one of their dedications was to improve, in a most significant way, the strength of the non-nuclear forces, the general purpose forces. President Kennedy adopted such a platform almost immediately and said, "To underline and exemplify what I'm talking about, which is to give us some choice between show of force and all-out nuclear war, I'm going to spend during the next year a minimum of five hundred million dollars on improving general purpose armaments." And we did.

So the shifting of emphasis took place about that time. The buildup in general purpose forces was valuable. It was a good move. But that has gone on now to a point that the strategic forces which, after all, give underlying strength and meaning, particularly against the Communist movement, were relatively neglected and are badly in need of modernizing today. The emphasis has shifted back somewhat. Along with the emphasis shifting back, the pressures to decrease all things marked "Defense" have been so persistent and effective lately that nothing is getting as much attention as it ought to now. This was the general emphasis on priority for military modernizing during the 1960s. It was carried on particularly to the beginnings of the war in Vietnam, and then, of course, after Vietnam started, most of the priority money and attention went to that.

I call the period 1962 to now as the period of . . . well, I don't know if I have a name for it . . . but the period of shifting emphasis in strategic power passing to the USSR from the United States. All through the Fifties, the United States had had an overwhelming position of superiority, a monopoly feeding into a position of overwhelming superiority. That superiority existed, a definitive superiority, until about 1966. Then it started dangerously changing, on a daily basis, in favor of the Russians, until now we're past parity. I think it's shifted in their favor.

*   *   *

There are a lot of people who will say we've had twenty-five years of nuclear peace. There have been no nuclear weapons used, and that proves that this strategy is sound. Well, it doesn't prove any such thing to me. There are reasons we haven't had a nuclear war. The first one is that we've had a preponderance of strength, so that if anything started, there isn't much doubt in the minds of those who would do it who'd come out on top. This is the real reason. When you've got that kind of strength, the kind we had in 1962 versus theirs, most any old strategy will do. It doesn't make much difference what it is. The second thing is that I would question severely whether the forces of communism want to destroy us in the first place. If they can, they'll do it through power negotiations, which they understand so well—coercive negotiation. If they can do that and thus gain, gradually or otherwise, the great wealth of the United States, certainly they want to do that rather than destroy us in the process of driving toward an end goal of world communism.

How do you react to those who question the necessity of this antagonistic relationship?

I kind of like that slogan you see sometimes on car bumpers these days that says, "God Bless America. Love It or

Leave It." I think there are a number of people in the United States today who have been variously motivated against the government and most everything it stands for, and are in a destructively critical mood. I think they are more or less oblivious to the priceless advantages of being an American citizen. The silent majority that represents the will of the United States has got to do better in communicating with these people. I think the time is awfully late and that we're in great danger. I think the silent majority that has been described variously in late years has got to get more active and less silent, and force, somehow, a better understanding of the danger that we face. They should study a little bit of the history of the last fifty years where it's mighty clear. It doesn't take a deep study of history to realize that the confrontation is real. It's not a matter of adjustment to the ideology of the two: they're absolutely diametric. They intend to take us over and eliminate all the things that America has stood for and that we have, at least up to now, fought for.

You were somewhat involved in the planning concerning Vietnam from '66 to '68.

That's right. That's when it built up to its peak in the air action over North Vietnam. It was a very interesting period. Combat was very closely and precisely controlled from the highest governmental level to a degree way beyond anything that ever occurred, as far as I am aware, throughout history in military operations. The commanders in the field had very little flexibility: of targeting or tactics or strategy. In a broader sense, they had a certain amount of control in their tactics such as in attacking a certain target—how would you do it, how much cover, how much going in? But not with respect to targeting and rules of engagement. The show was run precisely like a puppet show, from the very topmost levels of authority.

This, of course, made it difficult and frustrating to the military commanders, especially in targeting. I don't think there's ever been a contingency in modern times where the Achilles' heel was more prominent than it is and has been in

Vietnam, and that's the logistics complex at Haiphong: the harbor structure controlled all movement of the goods and support of war through that port. There are those, of course, who argue that "So, suppose we close it. That would just force them over the beaches and they could still go over the beaches." Well, sure they could, but they'd be reduced to fight it like Murphy fought the war in *Murphy's War* [A movie starring Peter O'Toole as Murphy, who is the sole survivor of a torpedo attack by a Nazi submarine and is forced to use all sorts of makeshift methods in his quest for revenge].

Precisely what types of targets were you allowed to hit?

We were allowed to hit certain types of logistics targets, like rail tracks and transportation points, but only on an individual, case-by-case basis with respect to location and timing. We had to get authority on a case-by-case basis.

Where did these directives come from?

They came from above my level, and I was Vice Chief of Staff of the Air Force.

I am not saying by this that I am openly critical of the administration that was in power for doing it the way they did. Well, I am critical, really, regardless of how I'm saying it. But I want to make it clear that within a framework of going in in the first place . . . if we went in there, we should have gone in to accomplish the end desired result, which was to force the North Vietnamese to talk turkey and come to terms at the conference table. We haven't done that yet. We should have either not gone in or we should have gone in there with the resolve and the latitude of targeting and the use of the tremendous amount of air power we had in there to hopefully force them to do it. We didn't do either one, and this is my criticism.

Have you had to deal with any opposition to the war at home?

No, not from my daughters. I have with a couple of their friends. I've argued with them in my house two or three times. I think with some effect, some good effect. Their general stand was this whole hackneyed business that if each side has enough nuclear weapons to kill each other X times over, what's wrong with laying down some of our arms and saving some money and putting it on more useful things like welfare? Then, if we just do this—they say—we will show our good intent to the USSR or to the communists, or whoever they desire to pick out, and they will do the same thing.

I try first to contain myself and explain patiently that they ought to take a little broader view of the communists, and review the record a little bit, how they operate. That not many people look at things this way and that this is just exactly the kind of attitude and conditioning that the communists would like to generate in this country. I say that if they really believe these things, they are becoming part of the problem, and they'd better quit thinking so much down here [*gesturing to his heart*] and a little bit more up here [*gesturing to his temple*].

Bayard Rustin

 If one is to struggle for justice, one must avoid concepts of optimism and negativism. The joy must be in the struggle and not in the achievements.

Bayard Rustin has been active in civil rights since he finished working his way through college in the early 1930s. A partial list of his activities includes: the Free India Committee (1945), the first Freedom Ride (1947), work with Kwame Nkrumah and Benjamin Nnamde Azikewe in Africa (1951), the Montgomery Bus Boycott (1955), original planning for the Southern Christian Leadership Conference (1956), the thirty-five-thousand-strong Prayer Pilgrimage to Washington (1956), the March on Washington for Jobs and Freedom (1963), the New York School Boycott (1964), and many more. This

master international organizer and social critic has been
arrested no fewer than twenty-four times for his efforts.
Currently he is executive director of the A. Philip Ran-
dolph Institute, an organization devoted to developing
and promoting programs to cure the basic economic and
social ills of the United States.

I'm not optimistic, I'm not pessimistic. I say that the
only way for a social engineer—which I consider myself—to
behave is not to be fundamentally concerned with whether or
not you are getting there. I've been in this thing for almost
thirty-five years now and I expect to be in it for another twenty.
I'm here for the long pull. I'm not like the kids you hear of—
Stokely Carmichael one day, Rap Brown the next, Huey Newton
the next—those people are never here for the long pull. I am
here for as long as it takes.

Instead of being optimistic or pessimistic, I am realistic.
It will be good sometimes. It will be bad sometimes. We'll be
disgusted sometimes. We'll be elated at other times. But the
struggle goes on. I am here because I am opposed to injustice
wherever it is. I am working because I am for justice, and therefore I go on. I know something very fundamental: man's struggle for justice and equality is eternal. It never will be solved.

If one is to struggle for justice, one must avoid concepts
of optimism and negativism. The joy must be in the struggle and
not in the achievements.

*   *   *

We took about three months to organize the March on
Washington in 1963. We had about two hundred people working in the national office and we had people working in almost
every city in the country. The way in which a person really
organizes anything is to assume that everybody involved has a
third-grade mentality. I'm not joking. You say to yourself, "Now
suppose these are just children coming. What would you do?
What would they need to learn? What do they need to know?
What do you need to tell them?"—because the most intelligent
of men will be very unintelligent when they are moving in num-

bers. There is just something about people moving in numbers which reduces their ability to function carefully. So we had to spend hours and hours. We even told people what to bring in their lunches and what not to bring. We wanted to get everybody—from the whole country—into Washington by nine o'clock in the morning and out of Washington by sundown. This required all kinds of things that you had to think through. You had to think how many toilets you needed. Where they should be? Where is your line of march? We had to consult doctors on exactly what people should bring to eat so that people didn't get sick. We had to arrange for drinking water. We had to arrange what we would do if there was a terrible thunderstorm that day. We had to think of the sound system. There were just a million things. We had to set up a bank. We had to notify everybody where the bank was in the event that anybody got lost or lost their pocketbook and didn't have money to get home. The interesting thing is that there were over a quarter of a million people and we only had to spend something like four hundred dollars for welfare. Absolutely fantastic!

If you ever want to organize anything, assume that everybody is absolutely stupid.

And assume yourself that you're stupid. What would I do under the circumstance? Or if this happened? Then, of course, we had to notify people along the main routes coming into Washington. We had to have places for them to stop along the route. Every place there was a public toilet, we stuck a red flag along the road so that people knew where to stop; because there were so many people and the closer you got into Washington, the more congested it was to become. We had to notify the Police Department and sit down with every other department of government to work out the details.

People started coming in the night before. There must have been fifty thousand people who got in before dawn. What we had to do was to have blankets for them to lie down on the lawn and sleep. We had to have food for them. We had to have water for them. I had to be up all night in the event that something went wrong. We were expecting the reactionaries who would try to create trouble; and, of course, Rockwell [George Lincoln Rockwell, head of the American Nazi Party] and his crowd came. The police blocked them, but we didn't know when they were coming, so somebody had to man the post.

The march really went according to schedule and that was because I've learned one thing. The best organizer in the world is the guy who sits down and does what appears to be nothing. That is to say, the good organizer is the man who delegates authority to responsible people, and merely keeps an eye open as to whether they are doing their job; and if not, he immediately replaces them with someone else. So on the day of the march I had absolutely nothing to do except watch my lieutenants.

We had twenty-five men who looked after the sound equipment. We had a meeting of some twenty people a week before the march, and we said, now we're going to role-play. I want everybody here to assume that he is a racist, he is against this march. I want you to tell me everything you think you could do by way of disrupting it. I had a secretary who took down every suggestion. The most serious one that emerged was that if someone were to slice the cable at the source, we could be in serious trouble. Therefore, what we had to do all night long after the cables had been put into place was to erect lights which played all along the cables so that if anyone came near them we could see them. I had some fifty people who spent their whole night looking after that sabotage possibility. We had brought in fifteen hundred police officers, black, from cities all the way from Boston to Richmond; and I had to get them in two days ahead of time to give them a kind of on-the-spot training which we wanted. None of them were using guns or had any weapons, of course.

The other problem was that we had to get the leadership over to the White House for an appointment with President Kennedy and then back in time to start the march. Another thing that one always has to think of is to protect your platform. That meant that I had to find eight thousand people who would go over early and fill in the front seats so that nobody would be in a position to shoot at anybody, or to throw anything.

We had a program beginning when the sun came up at the Washington Monument . . . we had people like Harry Belafonte speak, Ossie Davis read poetry, Josephine Baker was flown in from Paris to appear, Jimmy Baldwin to read something; singers, dancers. That's where Ossie Davis introduced all the celebrities who were there. Then, of course, the second most important thing was the most fantastic movement down the avenues to the monument. The third thing that was important was the program at the Washington Monument in which King's "I Have a Dream" speech turned out to be the highlight of the day. The people felt it was a tremendous speech. He was continuously interrupted with applause. I think that it is one of the most poetic . . . it's not actually the content of the speech, its intellectual content, it was its emotional fervor and the sheer poetry of it. The repetition of the language. It was tremendously poetic. Another important item was the pledge that the people took to go back home and try to do something to press for the legislation and for a Voter Rights Bill.

By sunset almost everybody was out of the city. There was not a single arrest in Washington that day. The only day that Washington has ever recorded when there was not a single arrest. The most orderly dispersement of people.

Has much progress been made since then?

You must always measure progress not so much by what has been achieved, but in terms of the gap between achievement, no matter how great, and aspiration. Once you begin to achieve, people want achievement geometrically as against arithmetically. The demand for progress is born of hope, not despair; so the more hope there is, the more difficulty you can have—even in the face of vast achievement. So that the question never is, "How much progress have we made?" We have made tremendous progress. The problem is that aspiration has outstripped progress. That's one side of the coin.

The other side of the coin is that you must not only think of aspiration in regard to progress. That's external. There's also an internal problem, particularly where people have been deprived. You get a gap between their need to progress and their inability to do so. That makes another type of problem. That leads to intense frustration on the part of the most ambitious of people, and this can go into a very bad syndrome where they turn inward to avoid the external problem which they don't feel capable of dealing with. That's one of the problems of black studies today, that it's not an effort to solve any problems but an effort to turn inward because people do not believe problems can be solved.

*   *   *

The blacks have only one way to solve their problem and that is in an integrated America. Now I understand this tendency because it's a result of . . . it's like young whites in America saying the political process doesn't work. How stupid can they be? The political process works perfectly. The problem is who controls it. Our problem is not that the political process is not any good; it is that we have never controlled it. It's in the hands of others. It works perfectly for those people. For Wall Street, it works magnificently. For General Motors—the poorer people get, the more money they make—because they manipulate the political process. So the question is, who has the process?

It always happens at the same point. It happens when people are in despair and do not believe they can get justice. It happened in the Twenties with the Marcus Garvey "Back to Africa" movement. If you'll look at the Twenties, you'll see that this was a very difficult economic and social period for blacks. The Palmer Raids were on [mass arrests of political and labor agitators by the Justice Department; all aliens arrested were immediately deported]. It was a very despairing period. The ghettos were being formed. They were being run off the land in the South. Lynching was at its height. So out of the despair they attempted to turn someplace else, and it is always to Africa or into your own bosom. You get concerned with how you wear your hair, what you eat, black poetry, the cultural revolution. All of this. It won't work. It never has worked.

Is this inward movement larger than before?

No. It's diminishing now. I would say in two years from now it will be practically all over. There will be remnants of stupidity. Like the Ford Foundation giving one hundred thousand dollars to study black English, as if there is any such thing. There is just bad Southern English, which blacks and whites speak. You can't make anything of it except that it's just bad. Now why people want to have Negro children speaking that language when one of our problems for Negroes is that we do not have the language, reading, and mathematic tools for existing in this society . . . ? This is radical chic bullshit.

Jesse Curry

 As we went into the triple underpass I checked with the dispatcher to see how near we were on schedule. We were only a couple of minutes late.

After a long history of police work Jesse Curry was promoted to Dallas Chief of Police in 1960. He was Chief at the time of President John Kennedy's assassination in 1963, and was widely criticized for his overall handling of the Presidential visit and its aftermath. He is now Director of Security for the Texas Bank and Trust.

At the time of Kennedy's visit to Dallas, I wasn't very happy with the thought of him coming here. Dallas was known as a right-wing extremist town, and since his philosophy was not in harmony with some of the groups here, we didn't particularly look forward to a visit from him. He had been here with Johnson when they were campaigning and we had no trouble at that time, but the feelings were not quite as strong at that time as they were when he visited here as President.

We tried to foresee any group that might try . . . we didn't think *kill* the President, because we didn't believe that anyone would try to physically harm the President. We did think that we had some groups that would perhaps try to embarrass the President.

*   *   *

Everything progressed well. People gave him a tremendous ovation. He stopped a couple of times because the people had just crowded out around him on the parade route. He stopped and shook hands with groups. He really got a tremendous reception here. More, I believe, than nearly any President that I've ever seen visit the city of Dallas. Everything was exceptionally nice. Everyone seemed cordial to him. They seemed to be wanting to show him that Dallas did like him. I think he was very pleased. I know I was pleased that we had brought him all the way through town and nothing had occurred to embarrass him. There was just no indication that people had anything but admiration for him. We brought him right down Main Street.

As we went into the triple underpass I checked with the dispatcher to see how near we were on schedule. We were only a couple of minutes late. I think I made the comment to the people in the car with me: "Well, five more minutes and we'll have it made!" I felt once we got him inside the Trade Mart . . . where they had invited guests, and we had over two hundred men in that building . . . once we got him there, why, security-wise we were in good shape! We were going down the ramp on this triple underpass when the first shot was fired. I didn't know what it was. There was a railroad yard there and I really thought that it was a railroad torpedo. I said to the people in the car, "What was that? A firecracker?" About that time there was the second shot fired and then the third shot fired. The first one and then there was a pause of a few seconds there . . . well, it couldn't have been many seconds, because the entire fusillade of shots only took up close to six seconds.

By that time I knew it wasn't a firecracker, that shots were being fired. I looked into the rearview mirror of my car and I could see a lot of activity in the President's car about fifty feet behind me. I waved for a motorcycle officer who was a few feet behind me and who had been right beside the President's car and I asked him what happened. He said, "Those were shots." And I said, "Was anybody hurt?" He replied, "Yes, they were." I said, "Get us to Parkland Hospital," the nearest hospital to where this occurred. I took them to Parkland Hospital and got them inside. I stayed there until he was pronounced dead.

*   *   *

After the announcement was made that the President was dead, shortly after that it was decided that we would take the new President, Johnson, back to the airport. In discussing this with various members of the Secret Service, Congressmen, Senators, and people that were there at the hospital, there was some question in our minds as to how widespread this was: if it was a conspiracy to overthrow the government, if attempts would be made to eliminate other high government officials. So the Secret Service decided we should get Johnson out of the hospital and get him on board the Presidential plane. They felt we could protect him better there than we could anywhere else. One of the Secret Service men came out and asked me to get my car. He [Johnson] came out with a couple of Congressmen and Secret Service men. They got in my car and I drove them to Love Field and put him back on the plane. We waited there until Mrs. Kennedy arrived. Mrs. Johnson wanted her there for the swearing-in ceremony. When she arrived, she still had blood on her clothes and was distraught, but not hysterical or anything like that. She went into the plane into what had been Kennedy's room and her room . . . she went in there for a few moments until we got ready for the Oath of Office to be administered to the President. We had found Judge Sarah Hughes and she was en route. When she arrived, we had this swearing-in ceremony for President Johnson on board his plane.

I stayed there until President Johnson departed. Then I went back to the City Hall. When I arrived there, I was told by one of the supervising officers that they thought that Oswald might be the man. There was utter bedlam there. The news media had just swamped City Hall. This was the first time that anything like this had ever occurred in this century. There was a large press here and there was a large press traveling with the President. They literally were covering up the City Hall. They had TV cables strung down through the halls, through the windows, for live TV. There were big trucks parked outside for all the local stations around here: these are big trucks that they can put on location for direct pickup of programs. You had to work your way through to get into the offices on the third floor. We were highly criticized for permitting the news media to be in the City Hall, but you see this was the first time that anything like this had ever occurred. It was only after this that we began to realize that nobody controlled the press, that they had "Open Sesame" anywhere in the United States. They hindered us in our preparation and finally had been instrumental in making it possible for Ruby to go down to where he could shoot Oswald.

*   *   *

Captain Fritz [head of Dallas Homicide Bureau; responsible for Oswald's interrogation] told me that he was through with Oswald and ready to transfer him. We had seventy men in the basement of that City Hall and had searched out every nook and cranny and cut off the elevators. We had men on the entrances to prevent anyone from going in there except the news media. I started down from the third floor to the sub-basement where we had taken him to put him in the car, but before I left someone came and told me that I had a call in my office from the Mayor. So naturally I went to talk to the Mayor, and I was talking to him when someone rushed in and said, "My God, they've shot Oswald." So I was sitting in my office talking to the Mayor when this happened. He just said, "Oh, my God!" and then, "What else is going to happen?"

For several days in Dallas, it looked like . . . well, when you've lost a member of the family, you know how the family is. They seemed stunned and in deep grief. That's the way the whole city seemed for several days. That's all you could hear, how terrible it was, this thing that had happened here. I got phonecalls, telegrams from all over the *world!* Immediately they held us solely responsible for the assassination of the President. It was a pretty gloomy city around here for several days. I felt badly about it.

Frank Castora

 Here comes Mrs. Kennedy with the two little kids, in the middle of the night . . . you could hear everybody crying. It was the saddest thing you ever saw in your life.

During his service in the Marine Corps, Frank Castora was detailed to the Marine Drill Team for the White House. A few weeks before President Kennedy's assassination, he injured his leg in a football game and was assigned to light duty—bartending at the club on base. Now working as a Xerox repairman, he lives in Denville, New Jersey, with his wife and two sons.

I was playing football. It was Friday afternoon. We were playing a game against the color guard. We were driving back from the football game and we heard it on the radio. It was a bulletin on the radio. So I ran right into the captain's office and told him about it. That was the first he heard about it. He didn't even get it from the upper brass.

Everybody went down to the club and turned on the television and we were watching it. The captain got on the phone. He got to all his officers, called in all the troops, because he knew we'd be involved. When Kennedy died, the captain just canceled all leaves. Every man was committed.

When Kennedy died, he got on a plane and we knew it was going to the White House. We met the plane. There were two groups that went out in the middle of the night. One met the plane at Andrews Air Force Base and carried the casket to the hearse, and then we had a unit at the White House gate. We escorted it up to the White House. Nobody knew we were going to be there. The Secret Service didn't know we were coming; nobody knew we were coming. The captain said we should be there, 'cause that was our job. Every time the President officially made an entrance into the White House for any affair, we were always there on the driveway.

We had a double squad. Fourteen men in each squad. Twenty-eight men. Two ranks. We just walked along with the hearse as it drove up. The captain just called us and woke us up and said, "They're going to be there at such and such a time." We were standing there at attention when he got there and marched in with him. I was on that one.

We really didn't know what was going on. Well, I did, because I was in the bar all day long and the television was on and I kept switching stations and listening to all the big news-casters. So if anybody asked, I had the rundown of who was next, and next. After Johnson was the Speaker of the House. Why? And etc., etc. Then the Majority Leader of the Senate, some-thing like that. As a matter of fact, Adam Clayton Powell was very high on the list, and people didn't realize it. Maybe four or five down. Something like that. He was a very big man in the House at that time and the House was the thing, because the House was elected by the people.

The funeral procession I had to stand. They took out the cooks and everyone. We just didn't have enough people. I stood on the side. The Marines don't have that many dress Marines available. If they were prepared, if they knew about it, they could have had them there. There's a unit on every base and they would have had them all flown into Washington.

I'll tell you. We had this guy. I'll remember it forever. I was watching it on television. There was this one fellow. He was a very mousy guy, skinny kid. A fairy. Not a fairy, really. He was a corporal. No strength, no fire at all for a Marine. Terrible! He was always sick. A sickly kid. Really no authority, nothing to him at all. He happened to be standing at the casket. He looked good in his uniform, which was what they were looking for, and it was in the middle of the night, so they said, "Okay, give him a chance." I was in the club at this time and the captain and the major were there. The two of them were sitting in the bar watching television and they almost died. We were just joking who was on now and I said, "It's ———!" The captain looked at the major and said, "I don't know! I didn't assign him."

Here comes Mrs. Kennedy with the two little kids, in the middle of the night. She's standing there and you could hear everybody crying. It was the saddest thing you ever saw in your life. The guy never moved, never budged, like a rock. The other guys all broke up. We were breaking up at the bar. Really a sad-looking thing: those little kids, they didn't even know what was going on. He never broke. They said he was pretty wobbly in the car coming back and when he came back he really broke down. You've got to give a guy like that a lot of credit.

PART 2

Floyd Mann

 This same group of people had followed the bus and they set the bus on fire. That's when we realized how important it was to have had that state investigator on the bus.

A redheaded Southern Baptist, Floyd Mann was Director of Public Safety in Alabama from 1959 to 1963, and again from 1968 to 1970. In between was the George Wallace Governorship, when Mann worked in the private sector. He is currently Special Assistant to the President of the University of Alabama.

I think the change began when this group of people decided to ride the Freedom Rider bus. I don't know where that bus started but it wound up in Montgomery, Alabama and Birmingham, Alabama.

By the information we had, we felt we probably would have police problems in the State of Alabama, so we dispatched a state investigator to Atlanta to ride this bus into Alabama. The first stop was at Anniston. While the bus was stopped there, a group of people surrounded it and wouldn't let the people off.

Our investigators advised us about the situation and we called in additional troops from the Anniston area. While the bus had been parked there in Anniston, a group of people had cut the tires. The tires leaked down after the bus left the Anniston area. Several miles outside Anniston, in the rural area, the tires went down to the point where the bus had to stop. This same group of people had followed the bus and they set the bus on fire. That's when we realized how important it was to have had that state investigator on the bus. Everyone would have burned if he had not gotten to the door and pulled his pistol and identified himself as a state trooper. By this time the help that we had called while the bus was in Anniston had arrived on the scene and dispersed the crowd. We got these people back to Anniston —some of them to the hospital and to various places.

From that point arrangements were made through various groups to get these people on to Birmingham; and after they got there a real problem developed. They had another riot around the bus station. Bull Connor was Police Commissioner in Birmingham, and those people stayed there for I don't know how many days. The information we had in Montgomery was that they could not secure a bus driver to drive that bus on into Montgomery. Attorney General Kennedy got extremely involved, personally and otherwise; got to talking with the bus managers and different people in the Birmingham area, and finally they did secure a bus driver. Kennedy dispatched a deputy attorney general to discuss the whole thing with Governor Patterson. He had had a personal discussion with the Governor about it, in the Governor's office. So one night late he called me and told me that arrangements had been made to bring the bus on in to Montgomery.

The bus would arrive in there about noon. It was leaving Birmingham about eight o'clock. We dispatched about thirty-five highway patrol cars to escort this bus. There were sixteen cars in front of the bus, maybe sixteen behind it. We made arrangements for a small aircraft to fly reconnaissance overhead because we had information they were going to blow up some bridges, stop the bus along the route someplace. The bus did get safely into Montgomery, but there was a problem when it got there. I had asked for one hundred state troopers to be brought into Montgomery and had them quartered at the Alabama Police Academy, secured there just in case something happened that we were not aware of. Sure enough, when the bus stopped, there was a riot that broke out. Several people were hurt.

What provoked the specific incident?

One person walked up to one of the Freedom Riders and started to fight with him. This broke out into other fights, and then it just began to draw a crowd. Huge crowds were drawn downtown. Streets were blocked. That was on Saturday. Finally, we got those people to one of the churches and got the church secured after bringing in those hundred state troopers and blocking off the streets. On Sunday the United States Marshals were dispatched to Montgomery. Sunday night the Freedom Riders met all night in the church and the Governor declared martial law in the city of Montgomery. The people were kept in the church until daylight the next morning for fear of what would happen. There were approximately twenty-five hundred people in that church.

Then we made arrangements to take those people on into Mississippi. We had the same type escort, with the state investigators guarding the bridges, and airplane reconnaissance and helicopters and state trooper cars, both in front and behind.

The Boulware Family

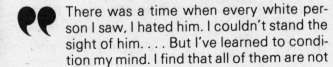

There was a time when every white person I saw, I hated him. I couldn't stand the sight of him. . . . But I've learned to condition my mind. I find that all of them are not alike.

Carol and Frank Boulware grew up in Charlotte, North Carolina, and were married there in 1960. They are both devout Southern Baptists. After a five-year stay in Phoenix they returned to the South and now live in Atlanta. Their two young daughters, Jade and Jarmal, are attending classes at a newly integrated elementary school. Mr. Boulware is an accountant.

Do you know who Martin Luther King is?

JADE   He was a great man. A man shot him and he died. He was a preacher, I think. He thought that the blacks and whites should be equal. He walked the streets and he preached. He preached that it wasn't right for the whites to be against the blacks.

Have things changed much? Are blacks and whites more equal now?

Yes. Well, in some ways they're not because like in the Pepsi-Cola Company they won't hire any Negroes.

In what way are they more equal?

They don't fuss and fight. They don't curse at each other and have those kind of like fights that everybody in town goes and beats up each other.

Do you remember that?

I've heard of it. It wasn't long ago.

Do you believe that America is the greatest country in the world?

JARMAL   Some of the problems. Some of them they can't stop. Problems like the war. It's kind of hard to stop that. The race against blacks and whites.

You don't think they can solve that?

They maybe could. But it's kind of hard to all the way. [*She pauses.*] I don't think they'll ever be able to do it.

What makes you think that?

Well, it was worse before when there was slaves. Now if somebody who was a slave was still living, he would think it would be great. He'd probably think that nowadays was a great day because then it was slavery but now it's gotten better. But a man today our color would still think it was bad because he wasn't living in the old slavery days. When they used to go sell them on a block. Chain their arms together and then go sell them. That's what I think. But it might, it just might get over with.

In school do the whites treat you well?

They always used to call me mean names and they said I was sad-looking because I wasn't white.

Did this bother you?

I don't care.

Have racial attitudes in the South really changed over the past ten years?

MRS. BOULWARE   The first week we were married we went to McDonald's restaurant. My husband went to the window for a hamburger and the lady said, "We don't serve colored here."

I used the example of McDonald's. We wanted to go there! It was a part of America. White people were going. Poor white trash, they were going. Those that had to steal a dime. Here we were, making a living, why couldn't we go? McDonald's . . . well, who wants to go to McDonald's now? But now if we do want to go to McDonald's, we can go to McDonald's. This is what impresses me now. It's just knowing! It's a good feeling, knowing that these things are available to us now. In the Sixties they would look at you and shake their heads.

MR. BOULWARE   There's still lots and lots of room for improvement. We like to think of it like a robber would approach it. That is, a lot of white people are saying, "Well, what do blacks want?" It's just like a robber, "We want what you got." We want everything. We want the same type of education. We want the same type of jobs if we're qualified for it. America is a strong country, the greatest country, and it was built primarily because of the black man's strength. All the hard labor. You look around at the various firms and large companies—we still see token prejudice today. We see one or two persons with white-collar jobs, the jobs that are making a little money. I have about a twelve-to-fourteen-thousand-dollar-a-year job, but taking a survey of the black people as a whole, you can still see that they're far underpaid. If only we could catch up, if we could get some of the jobs where you can actually make some money . . . until we do there's going to continue to be this big problem.

Will attitudes ever change?

MR. BOULWARE   The young whites and blacks today will solve the problem. A good example, my daughter Jarmal. Last year in school she was the only black in her class, and there's no way in the world you can tell the other twenty-some students that Jarmal is not as good as they are. They're just not going to believe it, because she was the A student and they had Cs, Bs, Ds. There's no way you're going to tell them that Jarmal is dirty. They see her every day.

MRS. BOULWARE   It has to do with the mind. You're going to have to get your mind straightened out first. It's just like washing a glass. Before you're able to drink clean water, you've got to get that glass clean. You can't put clean water in a dirty glass and expect the water still to be clean. You've got to clean it out completely.

There was a time when every white person I saw, I hated him. I couldn't stand the sight of him. Because it was still like. . . . When you were growing up in the South and you go downtown, you get thirsty and you want a drink of water. You go to a fountain that says "Colored" and it doesn't work, and you better not drink out of the one that's "White." Then there comes this white man that looks at you and laughs. I can remember saying that the first one I ever saw I'd want to spit in his face.

I just hated them! But I've learned to condition my mind. I find that all of them are not alike. I've learned to accept people. Frank has helped me quite a bit. He's helped me condition my mind that people are people.

MR. BOULWARE It's easy to be a quitter, but it's great if you pursue the challenge and move ahead. I spent three years in the service. Upon getting discharged I applied for a job as a telephone installer. During my three years in the service, I had worked installing telephones. I went down and applied for this job, and they told me they weren't hiring. I asked them why because I had just looked there in the paper. He said, "No, we're not hiring." So I went back out to my car and showed the ad to him, and he said, "We're not hiring colored boys." I had just spent three years in the service for my country and about thirty of those months were spent over in Germany. This really kind of irks you and it could make you bitter. You could get real bitter at the war. But again you have to think back: hate destroys you.

Adrian Fisher

 . . . the thing to do was to get the test-ban discussions going back on the track again . . . word had come back through the Pugwash channels that once you guys get in, maybe we can make a deal.

Approaching sixty, "Butch" Fisher has spent much of his life in the employ of the United States government, starting with the State Department in the 1940s. In 1961 he was appointed Deputy Director of the United States Arms Control and Disarmament Agency and held that position until 1967. He also represented the United States at the Geneva Disarmament Conference in 1964, and again

from 1966 to 1969. Fisher is now Dean of the George-
town Law School.

During the course of the 1960 elections, there came to
be an awful lot of "missile gap" in terms of U. S. psychology. We
thought we were behind. I wasn't so sure at this stage about our
survival as a nation because of the growing nuclear arms threat,
and the missile gap made people even a little bit more nervous.
The Soviets were ahead. It turned out that Mr. McNamara dissolved the missile gap fairly soon after that. It didn't exist except
in the minds of some excitable columnists and some irritated
CIA types. But the country went through sort of a missile-gap
psychosis, a fairly tough Cold War psychosis. There's Khrushchev the bully pounding his shoe at the United Nations. The
Cold War was pretty heavy on people's minds at that point. The
Bay of Pigs didn't make it any better, although the vibrant personality of President Kennedy and his immediate apologies to
the country increased his popularity.

President Kennedy recommended setting up the Arms
Control and Disarmament Agency, lobbying like mad to get the
thing passed through Congress, which it was at the very, very
last minute of the session in 1961. It suffered a little bit in that
Jack Kennedy didn't want us to get ahead of the Peace Corps on
the priority list.

We felt that the thing to do was to get the test-ban
discussions going back on the track again—in terms of tone and
attitude, at least an ongoing discussion with the Russians. An
awful lot of word had come back through the Pugwash [a private
Soviet-American consulting group conceived by American capitalist Cyrus Eaton] channels that once you guys [the Kennedy
Administration] get in, maybe we can make a deal. Now it turned
out that the whispers and murmurs that the Soviets had said
weren't true, but nevertheless it was worth trying.

A couple of things had happened. You'd had the
Vienna Conference, which was rugged. This was Khrushchev
hazing the new boys, and it was tough. He talked in two terms.

Two things were really dealt with in Vienna in the summer of 1961. One was Germany and Berlin . . . and hell, Khrushchev was talking about stopping the Autobahn, another blockade, this, that, and the other. Secondly, there was the discussion of the test ban. Khrushchev was rugged to the point of being insulting. We then had a moratorium on testing in effect, and Khrushchev said, "Well, you're cheating through the French." This was a bilateral, private equivalent of banging the shoe. With all his good points, Mr. Khrushchev was a bully, and he was trying to see if he could bully the new boys.

You had the [Berlin] wall thrown in, which followed Vienna. That was sort of saying, "I'll show you that I'm not bluffing, buster." Then the other thing that followed Vienna was that the Soviets called off the moratorium on testing and started testing, bang, bang, bang . . . one of them fifty-seven megatons. While we had gotten some structure organized by the end of the summer of 1961, the substance wasn't doing too good.

The big Geneva Conference started again in March of 1962, and it turned out to be purely forensic. Just posture positions. Nothing really happened until the aftermath of the Cuban crisis. Then, at the end, one of the last observations made by President Kennedy in his letter to Khrushchev—the "now we step back from danger" statement—suggested that "Isn't it a good idea. . . ." The unofficial letter made some references to the test ban, and President Kennedy said, "Perhaps now, as we step back from danger, we can make real progress in this vital field. I think we should give priority to questions of proliferation of nuclear weapons on earth and in outer space, and to lend a great effort to a nuclear test ban." Strangely enough, every one of those has been done.

You've seen the secret correspondence that was later released between President Kennedy and Khrushchev on the test ban. There were three letters, in which they suggested negotiations. The hangup on the underground tests were on-site inspection, and Khrushchev suggested, "Why don't we just have one or two. They don't matter a hell of a lot."

The Joint Committee and all our friends on the Hill—

they were then somewhat more hawkish than they are now—they were almost saying, "You need a thousand on-site inspections and an army of a million each to have a test ban." The whole tone was, "You can't possibly do it," primarily because of those horrid Soviets who'd cheat on underground tests and we couldn't tell. How could we know—a test or an earthquake?

Then, two things happened. Hubert Humphrey sweet-talked [Senator] Tom Dodd into sponsoring a resolution on atmospheric tests, and the Soviets began to take an interest in it. One thing led to another . . . and there was Averell Harriman and his delegation in Moscow initialing a test ban. Limited to atmosphere, outer space, and underwater, but nevertheless the first step.

Why'd they want to do it? I think part of it was the reaction from the Cuban crisis, both of us shook up a little bit . . . let's do something to calm this thing down.

How effective was the treaty, in your estimation?

Well, I wish it had included underground testing, but it didn't. We've both gone ahead and banged away like mad underground, but it has put some inhibitions on the superweapons, and to that extent it's worthwhile.

*　　*　　*

The progress that President Johnson started was of nuclear containment policy. You'll find it in his 1964 message to the Geneva Conference. What this really ended up with was the Non-Proliferation Treaty, which in many ways is as important as the Limited Test Ban Treaty.

President Johnson was interested in this in 1964 . . . but not really. Not really, to the extent that he had outstanding the other issues of how to handle the nuclear problems within the North Atlantic Treaty Alliance. The MLF [Multilateral Nuclear Force] was held out to our NATO allies. It was the idea that the bomb could be a form of candy for increased NATO cookies. As long as the MLF was an active part of the negotiating structure, the Non-Proliferation Treaty wasn't going to get off the ground.

Even though some of the MLF suggestions were unreal, you couldn't advance anything at Geneva that was inconsistent with any option held open in the MLF negotiations. So there was really no prospect of any success.

From 1966 on, after it was clear that MLF was not going anyplace, President Johnson and Dean Rusk, who was not the world's most enthusiastic supporter of arms-control matters up to that point, really went all out for the Non-Proliferation Treaty. There was no problem about their support.

One of the other reasons you wanted the Non-Proliferation Treaty was it was a precondition to any real dealings with limitations of strategic arms generally, what is by now the SALT [Strategic Arms Limitations Talks] talks. It's perfectly clear that the Soviets were not going to do much in the way of negotiations on SALT until we had a fairly firm deal with them on the Non-Proliferation Treaty.

Now, why is a Non-proliferation Treaty important? Well, we look at it differently. For the Soviets the Non-Proliferation Treaty is important for one purpose: to enlist U. S. support to prevent the Federal Republic of Germany from getting nuclear weapons. What is our interest in a non-proliferation treaty? Our interest is in signing up various countries—who might be the sixth, seventh, eighth, or ninth nuclear power—that we couldn't sign up by ourselves, but who might be receptive to a joint approach with the U.S. and the U.S.S.R.

Do you recall how many countries ratified the Treaty?

Oh, fifty or sixty. A couple of critical ones have not. Neither India nor Israel signed up, at least to the extent of having ratified the Treaty.

In many ways the Non-Proliferation Treaty was quite a significant treaty. You're going from something that's fairly small to something that's in a sense seminal. The limited test was fairly small, but something that prevents the fifty-seven-megaton superblasts of the Soviets. The Non-Proliferation Treaty, which is in some ways more controversial internationally, less controversial domestically, laid the foundation for the Strategic Arms Limitations Talks. You had something fairly good there. Unfortunately, Czechoslovakia intervened and LBJ felt that under the circumstances SALT talks couldn't begin. They didn't begin for another year, not until sometime in November 1969.

>*Has the Cold War pretty well subsided by now? Are the Soviets still a major threat to the United States?*

Sure they are, in that they have the ability to kill us all tomorrow. There's a Soviet missile someplace in Transsiberia that's aimed in an area that would clearly strike this building. When we do still have these loaded forty-fives aimed at each other's bellies, I don't think they're going to do anything silly. On the other hand, while they don't want to start an aggressive war, they will never return any loose change. That's the basis on which you deal with them. While I'm not a super Cold Warrior, I don't believe you should leave too much loose change lying around. They think, "Hell, if he leaves all this lying around, he expects me to pick it up." That's their general approach to life.

Lester Maddox

 For every civil right there is a civil wrong. ... This civil rights legislation has the idea that everybody is equal. And they're not. Only in the sight of God.

Lester Maddox and his wife opened the Pickrick restaurant in Atlanta, Georgia, in 1947. Prospering on their specialty of "skillet-fried chicken," he expanded the restaurant nine times in the next fifteen years. The national eye began to focus on Lester Maddox in the 1960s, when he barred Negroes from his restaurant by threatening them with axe handles. He finally closed the restaurant to avoid serving blacks. Maddox then turned to politics and in 1966 won the Governorship of Georgia in an election that had to be decided by the State Legislature. The state constitution prevented Maddox from running for another term as Governor in 1970, so he ran for the office of Lieutenant Governor and won in a landslide.

I guess I've been in trouble all my life. I grew up as a kid that had trouble in school. In second grade they pulled me out and were going to put me in a special school because I couldn't read the regular printing. I finally talked the educators and my mother into letting me stay on in the regular school. I had difficulty because of this. I had injuries. This poverty that I talked to you about. I had trouble with the other kids in my neighborhood because of my eyesight. I couldn't play ball with them oftentimes. I was so thin that I wasn't physically able to compete with the better-fed boys in the neighborhood. So the problem I had at the restaurant was no more than the others.

The environment was a homelike atmosphere. The food was not like you eat in a normal restaurant. It was home cooking that people liked so well. We had the pick handles that you've heard so much about. They called them axe handles but there had never been axe handles. The pick handles were there because it was named Pickrick. There never were axe handles. I don't know why it was in the news media that they were axe handles. I guess it's because they just don't know the difference.

For seven months the FBI stayed there. They counted the customers and counted the cars. When we finally went to court I was denied a trial by jury . . . if I had had a trial by jury I would still be in business and not in public life. And I would rather be free than be President of the United States or governor of all the states. Knowing that the Supreme Court had ruled that my actions were constitutional previously, and knowing that the Presidents, all of them up until that time, had decided that my actions were constitutional, I proceeded to protect these property rights, basic human rights.

The first time they sought to invade my place I had gone home for a few moments in the later afternoon. That was about my seventeenth year there in the business. I was to come back at five-thirty. These people who called themselves "Reverend" but who were not reverend, one of them had been charged with theft in the Atlanta public school system. They put the name "Reverend" in front of them in their scheme to get a whole lot of respect and assistance and were excused for their criminal actions and their attacks upon other people and upon our society. I was called at my home about four-thirty and told that these four ministers had been by the place and asked for me. The manager told them that I was not in. They stated to Mr. Duncan [the manager] that the reason I was not there was because I was afraid of them and I was running. "You get word to him that we're going to be back at five-thirty."

Mr. Duncan called me at home and told me that they had been out there and said that I was afraid and running from them. I got my wife and we went to my restaurant. They attempted to come into the place. They were going to destroy my business and my home and all. I carried a gun with me, the first one I ever owned and I still have it. I have never fired a gun in my life, but I had one then for personal security for me and my family. When they proceeded to get out of their car I told them not to do that, to get back in, that they were not going to be served, and one of these great big ones got out of the car and started toward me. When he started toward me from around the car, this is when I pulled out my gun. I have no regrets about doing it. If I had it to do over again, I think I would have stayed there and forced the United States government, my government, to violate the Constitution by moving toward a socialistic and communistic form of government by destroying the right to private enterprise. I would have stayed there until it brought my death or my imprisonment.

Had your policy always been not to serve blacks?
The law in the city was that.

The whole city?

Yes, sir. Most of your licenses stated that.

The real issue was the authority of the federal government. I was fighting, and still am, for every white *and* black man in this country and his right to the private enterprise system. When a man loses his right to private property, the propertyowners and the non-propertyowners lose some of their rights. This is a basic human right. This is what I was fighting for.

What is it about the black man that makes you refuse to serve him?

It was a tradition in our part of the country. It was law in our part of the country. Had been for a long time. President Johnson had stated, before becoming President, that this legislation [1964 Public Accommodations Act] was wrong and unconstitutional, that it would make a police state out of this country.

Why was it the law? Why was it tradition?

Every man has a right to his private property.

Sure. You can kick whites out and you can kick blacks out. Why was it the blacks that you kicked out?

Because the federal government had said that you've got to do this, regardless.

So it hangs on the fact that the United States Supreme Court and the federal government told you that you had to serve blacks. If they hadn't, you would have served them?

I had served a number of them in my business. I had sixty-five employees and about forty-seven of them were blacks.

*   *   *

I think any time you pass civil rights legislation for any group of people, you create civil wrongs. For every civil right there is a civil wrong. When you pass special legislation to give to some person, whether it be the rich or the poor, the weak or the strong, the black or the white, then you've got to take it from someone else. This civil rights legislation has the idea that everybody is equal. And they're not. Only in the sight of God. Other than that you are not equal to me in some instances and I am not equal to you probably in many, many more. This is true in my family and in your family and between our families. Civil rights legislation desires to treat everybody as equal and they're doing a lot of harm.

Ulli Steltzer

 You talk about poverty . . . you don't have to remember names. But the people have names.

A photographer at various times for the Department of Labor, the Office of Economic Development, and the Southern Christian Leadership Conference, Ulli Steltzer has spent recent summers photographing Indians on reservations in the Southwest.

There were several reasons I went south. My first contact with black people were the migrants, and I photographed those around southern Jersey for the Labor Department. It was a miserable state of affairs. At that time there were hardly any rules or standards set for farmers. The shacks migrants lived in —just repulsive! And I kept wondering why the migrants come to the North and live in these miserable conditions. Was it really better than what they had at home? I kept going back to South Jersey, and I photographed for the OEO [Office of Economic Opportunity] later, and I found that it wasn't only migrants. The blacks in the southern part of Jersey, they lived in housing that literally were just cardboard boxes. Filthy, poor, just terrible. There were babies all over. The women had sometimes work, but not always. The men had sometimes work, but not enough. There was no baby care in the way of doctors. People didn't know about birth control. There was a lot of stealing going on.

All the white hatred, because the white egg farmers in southern Jersey were out of business. I think the eggs came from Virginia or someplace, so all of a sudden all of southern Jersey had no more egg farming. The whites were poor, and that made them even more bitter toward the blacks.

Then the OEO came in and they hired the Quakers to help them, because the Quakers had worked in that area before, and had done a pretty good job because they were really concerned people. So the OEO was smart enough to hire the Quakers who were already down there to continue working in the particular villages or towns that they were at, but work under the OEO. That's when I got to meet one woman in particular, Harriet Adams, who is black. And we worked together. She was to take me around and show me the areas where I was to photograph. I went back again and again and saw a lot of her and her friends. She had a way to really appreciate the individuals she was working with, and she opened my eyes very much toward what it means to be a black individual in this kind of setup.

After I was finished with the assignment in Jersey, I had a few other assignments, in Chicago, in Columbus, Ohio. By that time I'd learned to make my own contacts, and I just walked the streets. In Chicago I photographed the urban training center. In Columbus I was involved in photographing a poor neighborhood that was basically white, but there were also blacks there. It didn't matter. They were all poor. After a while, you get the feel for it. You can tell from the outside of a house what's going on inside.

Then I went down to Atlanta. Harriet had moved down to Atlanta, and I kept asking her about the rural areas. When I went down the third time to Atlanta, she was working for Martin Luther King. They took me on an assignment, and I photographed Liberty County, which is probably the poorest county in Georgia. That was for Martin Luther King, and it was in the spring before he was assassinated. We went from house to house, or from shack to shack rather. There were not even outhouses. That was really the worst I had ever seen. There was one woman . . . we tried to explain to her why we were taking pictures. We told her we were doing it for Dr. King. So she says, "As long as you're doing it for a doctor, it's okay." These people were so far from everything. The kids didn't go to school. Nobody cared. The people owned the land that they were living on, ironically enough, but they didn't have the tools to work it. So the land was just sitting there, and—oh, it was terrible, it was terrible. No food, people just sitting around the floor, people having no beds.

You said you learned what it was to be a black individual from Harriet Adams?

You never really learn what it is to be black, as you never really learn what it is to be poor, unless you are that. But you do get a feel from the repetitious impressions of what it maybe is like. There are certain things that you know. You know after a while how it is to cook when you have no pots and pans, and you know how it is when you have to go and find yourself a tree when you have to go to the bathroom. You know how it is when father and mother and the children all sleep in the same bed. I have seen it again and again. Sometimes it wears me out, and sometimes I almost get numb towards it.

There is a lot of laughter. There are a lot of tears. It seems the emotions are much more alert, and maybe more so than the emotions of white suburbia. I don't know what it is. I suppose that when there is nothing else to communicate with, no television, no telephone, no letter-writing, not much visiting —then you have a human need to communicate with those who are close to you. I had the feeling people were much more lively. Seemingly happy, though miserably poor. I've often wondered about this strange phenomenon of emotions, where their emotions are so strong, and their happiness is so much stronger than our happiness, and their misery is so much more visible than our misery. What really does this? Maybe it's the temperament. Maybe it's the South. I don't know.

I decided that there were too many states I hadn't seen down there, so I took a long trip. I think it was October of 1968. I wanted to know what the different organizations were really doing. I wanted to photograph wherever there are black people in communal efforts trying to make it on their own. I left Atlanta and went to Birmingham, and then further down into Alabama.

I had trouble there because I was harassed for doing what I was doing. I was rather open about it, which was rather stupid, but I didn't know at the time. I had a little red Volkswagen and that was a mistake because people down there don't drive red Volkswagens. So they were suspicious from the word "Go."

I remember it was the night before my birthday and I decided I was worth celebrating, so I went to the bar and had a drink all alone. All of a sudden there were all of these crummy businessmen around who wanted to know what I was doing there and tried to get friendly. I was friendly, you know. But then they wanted to know what I was doing, but I had courage because I'd had one drink. It doesn't take more for me to have courage. So I took out my photographs from Jersey—not only blacks. Whites, poor people from Columbus, Ohio. And I spread them out on that bar in Tuscaloosa. They got furious. They went wild. They wanted my identification. Oh, you know, this wasn't the thing to do. I was identifying with the wrong people. Shouldn't waste my time on blacks. They are no good. It was before the elections [1968] and some of them were for Wallace and some of them were for Nixon. The better ones were for Nixon. Can you imagine? It was sick.

At one point, I remember, the conversation came to killing. One guy said, "Why don't you kill all the niggers?" So I just quietly said that I thought there had been enough killing done. They had killed Gandhi and they had killed Malcolm X and they had killed Martin Luther King and two Kennedys, and they had killed Jesus. When I said Jesus, they got really angry because I was using the word "Jesus" in vain, and the name Jesus was holy to them and how could I name him in connection with gangsters.

Three times they tried to get in my room that night. They didn't get in. I locked it. [*She laughs*] Banging on the door, yelling, "Open up! Open up!" So I waited in the morning until it was nine. Since they were all typical businessmen, I figured they had to be somewhere for work. When I came down none of them were there. And I went right ahead and went where I wanted to go.

*   *   *

If things are going to be overcome, they are going to be overcome because individuals make the break and pop the bag. You talk about poverty, and as you talk about poverty you don't have to remember names. But the people have names. And once you meet a person, you just don't treat them as a bag, particularly if you become friends, and if they take you in and if they treat you so nicely.

All the civil rights acts have helped. Some people have more food than they had before. Some people get jobs easier. Some kids get into schools. Some schools are integrated. But what it does to the heart of the human being I don't know yet. I can't judge it. You find very rarely whites in the ghetto visiting. Now that does not mean that they are not welcome, but they are not very freely invited because they have never done it. It seems very dumb and sick.

The blacks, they say they feel very insecure. They never know where they are, because nobody lets them know. How this is to be solved I could not tell you. For sure, not by white paternalism. Dishing out the goodies, sending off the clothes may be helpful to a family at the moment. But it also throws them back, and it throws you back. As long as you give out these things it makes you feel superior and as long as they have to accept them it makes them feel inferior. It's not a good thing.

Peter Lloyd[*]

By the time Haight was over in late August, everybody knew that the scene had gotten so big that they'd destroyed it. Too many people. Too many runaways. . . . You bring in one hundred thousand kids, you got trouble.

A college senior, Peter Lloyd took a leave of absence before his senior year to live on communes in the West. He is from a well-to-do New York family.

A friend of mine and I started hearing about Haight-Ashbury. It was in *Newsweek* and stuff. That was the place to go. We knew through the general news that there were hippies out there and these cute little broads, and people were having a great time. After going to prep school for six years, we just hated it. It was a petty place. It was the first set of instances in which I really ran into adult evil, let's call it, people who lied to your face and could. My parents knew I was pretty disgusted and they said, "Oh, surprise of surprises."

As we were traveling across, Scott McKenzie was singing on the radio, "If you're going to San Francisco, put flowers in your hair." Sure enough if we didn't arrive with flowers in our hair. We went into that town and I couldn't believe it. It was a carnival. That one big street, Haight Street, running from about Masonic to Clayton, was just packed with every kind of freak you could imagine. Guys with Mohawk haircuts, people walking around in commodore uniforms, you know, the hat with the fuzz all over it. Everything! You couldn't believe it. It was an incredible street scene.

*A pseudonym. All pseudonymous interviewees are similarly indicated by this mark.

We went to work for about six weeks, until about the middle of July. Then we quit work. That's really when Haight-Ashbury and my experience got started. I wasn't working any more, so I had twenty-four hours a day to just dig that big scene.

There was a freshness about it. I'd been down to communes in Arizona, communes in Colorado, communes in the Northwest. I had been to a couple of folk and rock festivals. I had been to peace marches. You know, gatherings of five hundred thousand people and things like that. Gatherings of freaks. But there never was the innocence that there was there. It was so fresh, so fresh that you could leave the door unlocked and you didn't have to worry about it.

We lived at 1668 Page Street. We had one room, a small kitchenette off to the side, and we shared a bath down the hall. In this room were living about ten of us. Somebody would say they were looking for someplace to live and I'd say, "Come on up and live with me." Originally we had a lot of young kids with us. But anybody younger than eighteen was trouble because runaways were always being looked for by the police. That kind of shit I didn't need. They'd look for runaways, find the drugs, then they've got you. So after a while we all decided it wasn't cool to check anybody who was under eighteen.

The good things I remember were like the mutual freedom that everybody gave each other. I mean there were ten people living in a room, and just having lost my virginity about six months before, I really wasn't up for balling in front of nine hundred people. But before you knew it, you finally realized that that was the only way to do it. You couldn't very well lock out nine people. So before you knew it, it became a natural thing. There wasn't any superficial unselfconsciousness about it.

I started selling newspapers for the *Oracle*, just to do something. I met people playing flutes on the street. You met people passing a joint. You meet people giving you flowers. That sort of bullshit. It was very nice. You met people giving you clothes. You met people giving you weird raps on the death of Vivien Leigh. I remember one guy coming up to me and saying, "My God, Vivien Leigh's dying." [Vivien Leigh was Scarlett

O'Hara in *Gone With the Wind.*] I remember one time we met this blind kid who was walking on the street with his dog. And I said, "Are you looking for someplace to stay?" He said, "Yeah." So he moved in with me. It turned out he was from Rochester, heard about Haight-Ashbury, got on a plane, hitchhiked from the airport to Haight-Ashbury and just arrived . . . fucking blind! And he didn't have to worry about it, because things worked out very well.

After I stopped working, days were like . . . oh, I'd get up about twelve or one, smoke a joint or two, go out there and hawk some newspapers, mess around, go into the park, hear people talk, play Frisbee, mess around, go to various parts of the city, sell newspapers up on Telegraph Hill, go out to the woods to see people, go to a rock concert at night, or just sit around on the street and watch thousands of people go by.

The drugs didn't seem to be that important in that nobody was in a particularly straight mood to begin with. Nobody was dashing for buses or trying to go to work or anything like that. What difference did it make if you were tripping out on acid, or speeding, or stoned? It literally didn't make any difference. A logical, straight consciousness is necessary for certain things. If you aren't doing those things, if you're not trying to form logical sentences, then why do you have to be straight? There's no necessity for it.

On a Saturday afternoon the traffic would just be slower than you could walk, with all these tourists sitting in these cars. They'd be going by and they'd be looking at us, and they'd have their windows rolled up and the buttons pushed down, scared shitless of the freaks. We weren't doing anything to them. It was funny. Everybody had police whistles. Imagine the scene when five thousand people have police whistles, and a police car drives down the street and everybody starts blowing their police whistles. It makes a parody of police and the whole bit. It becomes a whole charade. It's a joke.

I once went down to Market Street and handed out Carvel ice cream cones. I mean these are commuters and Market

Street is the business district. They almost went out of their minds. Half of them thought I was trying to poison them and half of them just about fell over in gratitude.

Why did it happen there, and then?

It was a complete generation . . . the baby boom grew up under parents who were not like the grandparents. I talk to my parents and ask how they were raised. It's the usual thing, "Children are to be seen and not heard." But our parents didn't operate that way. They could remember their childhoods, the coldness of their parents, the selfish dullness of love. Both of them resolved that when they had children they wouldn't do that to them, that they would give their children time and love and patience. When you give that much love and that much attention to a whole generation of people . . . [he shrugs.] It was almost a resentment. Get off my back. I don't want it. I want to be myself. I don't want to be loved into a certain individual. Everybody all of a sudden decided we'll zoom out and be ourselves.

*   *   *

There was a riot once, a pretty bad riot. It was Saturday and it was incredibly crowded. Full of tourists, full of hippies, and I heard a noise and commotion. They'd just busted another kid for selling newspapers. People started yelling and screaming and before I knew it the tactical squadron arrived, which was about fifty guys with these long pine sticks, about four feet long, and dogs. German shepherds. By that time there were just thousands of people on either sidewalk yelling at the police in the middle. The police cleared the traffic at both ends and just stood in a line in the middle of D'Arcy Street, saying through bullhorns, "Everyone off the street." Well, the sidewalks were so crowded that no one could stay on the sidewalk. The tension began to really rise, and there were taunts, and then somebody would push a policeman and they'd arrest him. One of his friends would go out and try to help him and they'd arrest him. A girl got arrested and her friend ran out to help her. Somebody from a second-story window threw a bottle full of orange juice down at the policemen. The bottle bounced on the roof of a car, hit the girl, shattered, cut her up bad. She was bleeding. Lots of blood. The noise and the screaming and the chanting got higher and higher and higher. You could just kind of smell it—boom, it was going to happen, and sure enough, boom, it happened!

The police all of a sudden shouted an order and they broke into two groups: one group ran into the middle of the sidewalk on one side of the street, and one group ran into the middle of the sidewalk on the other side of the street. Then they split and started pushing people down the sidewalk towards the end of the block on either side. It was like cutting cheese. You just saw these big pine sticks going up and down. People were trampling each other. You don't realize it at the time, but the worst sound you could ever hear is hysterical women. Men yelling doesn't bother you that much. It's a lower pitch. But when women start screaming, it's like eerie. It pierces your ears. It was frazzling, you couldn't stand it. We ducked into this laundromat which is right on the street. It had this big plate-glass window. It was like watching through a TV set. I watched people getting clubbed and getting the shit beat out of them as they were being pushed down the sidewalk. Then afterwards, all the people on the street got together and surrounded the police station and started chanting, "Love, love, love."

How did the police react to that?

They couldn't believe it. For a week later people were washing police cars, trying to get the police to realize that they really meant it.

*   *   *

By the time Haight was over in late August, everybody knew that the scene had gotten so big that they'd destroyed it. Too many people. Too many runaways. Drugs were getting pretty bad. Heroin was showing up. The street carnivals were crazy. When I was there, there weren't that many blacks. When I returned on a trip two years later, Haight was mostly full of blacks. In terms of Haight, blacks meant trouble. Because it was like "flower child yields to drug culture." It sounds brazen, but I'm not kidding, that's the way it worked. Harlem is not a cool place. The Harlem drug culture is murder and self-destruction. Haight was never that. There was a black district. This was a culmination of the Bowery, sort of a hip Bowery. Grimy, filthy, violent, a lot of dirty broads, a lot of dirty people. A lot of hateful people. I once went to a rock festival in Haight. I was stoned out of my gourd. I didn't know where I was. I just got in a car after the thing was over, and before I knew it I was home. Now sure as hell, I'm not going to do that at a New York rock festival. I'm not going to get in a car, no matter how stoned to the eyeballs I am. I just fried my brain that night and I didn't worry.

Drugs are followed with money. They're followed by criminals. They're followed by ripoffs. They're followed by murders. A hell of a lot of people living on the street is followed by disease, poverty. It drives out stable people in the neighborhood who sweep their walks and keep their houses nice. Before you know it you've got a slum. In a slum you have people walking around knifing each other in the middle of the night. Haight-Ashbury was a nice stable Italian neighborhood before we took it over. It's a no-man's-land now. You should see it. All the windows are boarded up. Nobody goes there now.

Drugs aren't that cool. If you can handle them, they're okay. A lot of people don't handle them. What happens to them? They get victimized. They're helpless. With speed, you're eating up protein. That's what it does. You're eating up your body cells. It emaciates you, destroys your mind. It makes you incredibly paranoid to the point of being a self-destructive whore. Acid's a bad drug too, for some people. I've taken acid a half dozen times and it never bothered me. I don't do it any more because it's a bore.

*   *   *

Haight really got fucked over . . . and Haight got fucked over by people like me. You bring in one hundred thousand kids, you got trouble. They can't all coexist together.

I was on holiday. I couldn't care what I did. I did a lot of good things. The easy, calm, very calm, sexual relationships

I had at Haight-Ashbury don't happen around here. One of the impacts of this explosion was that people are nicer to each other. I don't think there's any doubt that this is a kinder, more tolerant generation.

Abigail van Buren

 The young people refuse to buy the good phrases—they want to *live* what they have been taught. . . .

Best known as "Dear Abby," Abigail van Buren has been writing her syndicated column since 1956. The column—the basic staple being advice to the lovelorn—appears in papers throughout the United States and seven other countries. Her twin sister is Ann Landers—"That's the column in the other paper in town," says Abby, who is fifty-four years old and the mother of three children.

The sexual revolution . . . young people have begun to ask questions and demand answers. Due to the exposure to television, more frankness in literature, they have begun to cut the apron strings at an earlier age. The media in general have become much more, well, shall we say, uncensored.

A number of people have questioned the theory of a sexual revolution. They maintain that there is just greater openness in discussing sex.

That's ridiculous! Oh, they'll say, "We did the same things in parked cars. We didn't talk about it but the same things were going on." Yes, we did do the same thing in parked cars, but we certainly could not have lived openly without marriage, and with having our parents knowing about it. Every once in a while some kid would go away to school and live with a girl or live with a guy, but people are now telling their parents, "Look, I'm of age and I want to live with this girl, and no, we're not married. We'd love to have you accept it, but if you don't, that's rough." We could not do that, but they're doing it now. It's getting more prevalent. Girls are becoming pregnant and keeping their babies; they didn't do that years ago. They were stigmatized and disgraced and thrown out of the house and told not to come home! Today, the adoption agencies are having a heck of a time getting babies because girls are keeping their illegitimate babies. This is probably related to the feminist movement and Women's Lib. I don't say that that's good. In fact, I think that children belong in a family with married parents. But there are many children born out of wedlock among intellectual, intelligent couples because women feel that marriage is not necessary.

*　　*　　*

Of course the sexual revolution happened! It caused young people to change their values rather than to accept the values of their elders, as my generation did. We didn't question whether Mom and Dad were right or wrong. We listened to them talk about brotherhood and equality and justice, and it didn't occur to us that something was askew when we saw them behaving in a contrary manner. The young people refuse to buy the good phrases—they want to *live* what they have been taught, what previously had not been lived in their families, in their lives, in their communities. They're going to give the next generation a lesson in how to *live* instead of *talk* a better brotherhood, a better community, justice and equality for all. They have more responsibility toward their fellow man than their elders did.

Happiness is a . . . I don't know how you would even define a "happier" people. From appearances it's become apparent that we're in an awful lot of trouble, but still the people have become better able to handle problems, and therefore probably better adjusted or happier people in that sense. They're more conscious of who they are, and what they are, and where they're going. It does create some disturbing thoughts, but they aren't just Pollyannas tripping along and chasing sunbeams.

Alice Williams[*]

 But like I get five dollars and sixty cents a month for utilities, and my electricity is never under twenty-five dollars bimonthly. . . . That money has to come from some place.

The mother of seven children—three to fourteen years old—Alice Williams is divorced and on public assistance. "My husband and I had married very young. I was sixteen and he was eighteen. We ended up getting a divorce while he was still in the service." Mrs. Williams worked at skip-tracing ("That's finding people that have not paid their bills") for a time. She lost that job, held several more, lost her apartment, moved into one room with her children, then suffered a nervous breakdown. She is now in her mid-thirties and lives in a ghetto in Chicago.

Mayor Daley has lots of signs up and down Chicago that talk about the fact that "This site has been cleared to enhance the neighborhood." Well, you know, the site has been cleared and the land has been standing there for years and all he did was make more people double up into smaller apartments and create more slums, because it makes those apartments just get torn up when you have so many people living in them. I'm very upset that Mayor Daley is talking about building an athletic stadium and we don't have houses to live in. I think it's nice that we've got good transportation back and forth through the city. Then I seriously question whether or not we have such good transportation because Mayor Daley was really concerned about all of the people of the city, or if he was concerned about people that wanted to come from suburbia through downtown without having to look at the blacks of the slums.

I get kind of upset because I don't think it's a good idea to have all of the people on public assistance shacked together, because there is nobody to provide incentive to these people. When you live in a community where everything is downhill and you don't have the Joneses to look up to, it's not a very good thing.

I live in this rehabilitated apartment, this five-room apartment. When I moved in here, it was a lovely apartment. There were a lot of faults, like the wiring isn't very good and the plumbing isn't very good, even though it's rehabilitated. The windowsills are dry-rotting. Some of the floors are very bad. They didn't put up new doors.

We had all hardwood floors, and in order to keep hardwood floors, you have to buy wax. With seven children you have to scrub and wax at least twice a week. Yet on a public-aid budget you can't wax once a month. So therefore your floors got looking horrible and there's no money to buy linoleum or anything else. The whole apartment starts to fall apart.

We talk a lot about the rent ceilings, there not being enough money for clothing, not being enough money for food and other things. I firmly believe that if people on public assistance were able to spend the entire amount allotted to them for food, they would be able to eat pretty well. But like I get five dollars and sixty cents a month for utilities, and my electricity is never under twenty-five dollars bimonthly, every two months. That money has to come from some place. When you think of the fact that the clothing allowance for one of my children in school is something like five dollars-something a month, and that means that I have to save up for five months to buy him a decent winter coat and hat, just for the winter. That means that there are only seven other months that you can buy him shoes, gym shoes, clothing, underwear, sweaters, and all the other essential clothing that he must have. It doesn't leave any room for a child tearing his pants or his shoes wearing out before a year's time. So this money must come out of the food money too.

Lilly McCullough

 They teach them everything, including how to tie their shoes and how to use zippers and buttons. . . . Just a little bit of everything.

The mother of six children, Lilly McCullough has worked as a teacher's assistant with the Cincinnati Head Start program. Her four youngest children have been enrolled in Head Start.

How satisfied were you with the Head Start program?

The teacher, you know, she invites you into the classroom. So I went and I found out that by being there you learn how to really cope with yourself. I found that a lot of times with six kids—I got six kids—that with me screaming and yelling and pulling my hair out . . . you really sit down and learn how to organize yourself. Like, out here in the hallway I got all the toys and things organized on the shelves that my husband built. This is the way the classroom is. This is what they showed us to do. Like, we take Clorox bottles and made Easter baskets for our kids because we couldn't buy them. We took milk cartons and things and made wagons and toys and different things. They showed you how to take paper and make dolls and things to paste on paper and to teach a child how to use scissors. I've given them a magazine and let them sit and cut, and you don't get aggravated. They teach them everything, including how to tie their shoes and how to use zippers and buttons. . . . Just a little bit of everything.

We had such a good teacher, Mrs. Magee, she was perfect as far as having patience with children.

The kids, when they first started, they really didn't know the colors that well. They taught them how to count from one up to twenty, this is for a four-year-old. Then they taught them the colors, and they teach them how to talk. Not to say "cookie" and "candy" and stuff; but, "I want a piece of candy," or "Can I have some cookies?"

Now these two here, like we're sitting down having a conversation, and all six of them are sitting here, now these two youngest ones catch on much quicker than the two oldest ones. They catch on very quick. I think that it's more that they teach them how to listen. A lot of people hear things, but they do not listen to what's said. You can give them an order, tell them, "Go upstairs and bring my purse down here." My second one is likely to get up to the top of the stairs and come back down and say, "What did you say?" Then I tell the other one to go upstairs and do what I told you to do, and she goes up there and does it. They listen better.

George E. Reedy

 Johnson has a fantastic faculty, and it's genuine . . . I used to think he was lying, but over a period of years I came to the conclusion that he was not . . . for convincing himself that what he was saying as of the moment was the truth. The man could just blot out every contrary fact.

A child prodigy from Chicago, George Reedy reported for the UPI before becoming Press Secretary to Senator

Lyndon B. Johnson in the early 1950s. He served as President Johnson's Press Secretary after John Kennedy's assassination until he was replaced in 1965. After a return to private life, he was called back as Special Counsel to the President in 1968. Since then he has been a Fellow of the Woodrow Wilson International Center for Scholars at the Smithsonian Institution.

I was in Washington. And shortly after the [assassination] announcement came over the wire—I had the news ticker in my office—I got a call to come to the White House. Walter Jenkins was already there. And the two of us were in a rather embarrassing position. Because with Johnson down in Dallas, they more or less regarded me and Walter as the two who were in control, and neither one of us wanted to be in control.

The major thing was still the grief of all the Kennedy people. And I can remember Arthur Schlesinger walking up to me and just saying, "George, this is terrible." And then bursting into tears. They were bringing every decision to us. Very minor ones, very petty ones that really they should have made themselves. And we were trying to tell them that. Such things as having a forklift out at the airport to bring the coffin out of the plane. We got the whole feeling that the Kennedy people here were trying to transfer power. And of course neither Walter nor I wanted to be in that position. In the first place, the President wasn't here. And we didn't want to be the people laughing at the funeral feast. I can recall that when the plane finally arrived and we got into a helicopter, I sat next to Ted Sorensen, and he said, "George, I wish that goddamn State of Texas had never been invented." I knew the man was overwrought. It was a foolish reaction. It could have happened in Arizona or Boston or anyplace else. I just didn't comment.

How well did Johnson make the transition to the White House?

I knew Johnson well enough to know that his press relations were going to be one of his most vulnerable points, and that there was nothing that anybody could do about it. This was an insuperable problem, because of his attitude and because of his psychology.

I was hoping that I wouldn't wind up as press secretary, although knowing that it was almost inevitable. I knew I was going to lose no matter what happened. If I did a good job for him, I was going to become so unpopular in the White House that life wouldn't be worth living, and if I didn't do a good job for him, I wouldn't be much of a man.

The major thing is that Johnson had certain aspects of the pure politician. I don't mean that in any derogative sense. It's basic in the psychology of the successful politician that he look at the world from the standpoint of friend or enemy. Politicians are always committed to causes, even the worst of them; and in their minds those causes have a certain sanctity. Anybody that is opposed to them, or anybody that casts doubts is either corrupt or venal or misinformed. The real world isn't like that. Political leaders have to be that way. Otherwise, nothing would ever get done. Politicians have no sense of perspective, because you can't be a political leader if you have a sense of perspective. You have to be a monomaniac to a certain extent. Johnson carried that to an incredible extreme, insofar as he regarded the press in terms of friend or enemy. The press is not that. Individual reporters are as partisan as any politician. In fact, most of them are partisan, but they still have a basic responsibility for putting down what's happening. It's a responsibility they can't avoid. They may not do it well, but they still have the responsibility. If a man commits a foolish act, they don't have to say it's a foolish act, but they have to describe the act. This was the sort of thing that would send Johnson into a towering rage, and convince him that he was dealing with some form of conspiracy. He was deeply wedded to this absolutely childish idea that the way to handle the press was to reward those who write nice stories about you and to punish those who don't. Most politicians do have that concept, by the way; but most of them are not sufficiently powerful personalities to persist in those tactics after they've proven to be failures. Johnson was a much more powerful personality than most of the men who have occupied the

White House. By powerful, I mean a man who would run everything into the ground, who would follow out a tactic to the point of absolute destruction.

Now, of course, when he first came into office, he was quite a hero of the press, and I think this misled him a bit too. He came in under circumstances where I think he was almost everybody's hero for a while. The tremendous traumatic shock of the assassination of Kennedy. There was Johnson, a man not too well known to the public, and he took over the office superbly. I don't think there was a single misstep. All of a sudden the American people had the picture of this calm, determined hand at the wheel. A man who knew what he was doing. A man of sense and yet a man of strength. There was a period of four or five months where there was almost adulation. During that period, the press, being human, shared the adulation.

Then he started doing things that to the press were totally irrational. They didn't understand it at all. They were perfectly rational in his mind, but that was because he had a different picture. Little things.

For instance, Helen Thomas of the United Press wrote a story about his visit to Cousin Oriole. He has an aunt, Cousin Oriole she's known as, who has a small piece of property adjoining his ranch. She's Pentecostal something or other and I think the whole Pentecostal church has its national assemblies in her house, which is very small. She's deaf. She's an elderly lady, rather determined. She's still living back in the early part of this century, when that part of Texas was really the frontier, and it still has many aspects of the frontier. If you get off the main roads around Johnson City, you'll think that you're in the West of the 1880s or 1890s.

President Johnson liked to walk up to her house. It was a habit he'd gotten into after the heart attack when the doctors told him to walk a mile every day. He walked over there one night; he had some reporters with him and he banged on the door and went through all the horseplay. Cousin Oriole came out and she was in her bare feet. So Helen Thomas wrote what I thought was a very warm, very sympathetic story that did him a world of good. But he flew into an absolute rage over it because of the line that Cousin Oriole showed up in her bare feet. To him that indicated that Helen Thomas was saying that these people are nothing but ignorant Texas hillbillies, and therefore Helen Thomas was his enemy. His whole concept had been shaped by his mother, who was one of these genteel turn-of-the-century Victorians. One of those persons who regarded no picture as any good unless your hair was combed and your face was composed and your suit was pressed . . . something like a Chambers' Funeral Parlor ad. He made a very deadly enemy with that one, when Helen had actually written a very warm story.

When he became President, these incidents began to accumulate. He started to apply the carrot-and-the-stick technique in which he tried to reward those reporters who would write friendly stories about him, and try to punish those who wouldn't. Well, of course those who wouldn't had a very simple technique—they'd dig up nasty stories. Now, if it had just been press relations, I don't think that would matter, because strangely enough, a man's press relations have very little to do with his success in politics, but it's hard to convince politicians of this. They're all obsessed with the idea that if they get the right public-relations man they'll become not only President, but maybe even Pope. And Johnson had this overdeveloped.

Again, however, that was not the serious point. The trouble was that this attitude carried over into all of the things that he was doing politically. He started regarding the whole world as friend or enemy. This meant that he began making powerful enemies in the Senate. If a Senator would get up and say something critical about Johnson, something that he would interpret as critical, well he would immediately do something. Call the man or make some snide remark in public. In no time at all he had men like Bill Fulbright and Vance Hartke—both of whom had been his closest friends while he was in the Senate —he had them on edge so much that he couldn't get the time of day out of them.

The "credibility gap" didn't arise when I was Press Secretary. We had an information gap when I was Press Secretary. I just found it impossible to act. Because he was so thoroughly convinced that successful public relations meant feeding the press stories that they liked, that he liked, I wasn't going to go in for that nonsense. And yet, at the same time, the Press Secretary is the spokesman for the President. Therefore, we got into kind of a stalemate. What really happened was that the press got virtually no information while I was Press Secretary. When he got rid of me . . . until I left and he got in someone who was willing to play his game . . . then the press started to get a lot of stories. They were malarkey stories but they didn't notice that particularly. For a while. They finally caught on.

If you check the history, you will find that every President and every press gets into it, but usually when trouble arose out of these things, Presidents pull in their horns. Johnson wouldn't. He insisted on pushing this thing. The other aspect was that Johnson has a fantastic faculty, and it's genuine . . . I used to think he was lying, but over a period of years I came to the conclusion that he was not . . . he had a fantastic faculty for convincing himself that what he was saying as of the moment was the truth. The man could just blot out every contrary fact. He was a master debater and therefore he was constantly capable of smothering people with arguments. Now in the Senate, of course, that didn't go over too well because you'd have somebody like Bob Kerr there who'd just very bluntly tell him to go soak his head in a bucket of water. But nobody really argues with the President, and therefore he'd come out with some of these things which were really quite outrageous but which he himself believed. I don't think he lied any more than any other President. But he was more persistent in unworkable techniques.

How do you explain the feud between Lyndon Johnson and Robert Kennedy?

Here you had two men who were remarkably similar in certain aspects of their personalities. This was obscured by the fact that Johnson was a big mid-Texas rancher and Kennedy was sort of an Irish Boston bronco. Therefore, when you heard the two talk, it looked like they were worlds apart, but both were deeply committed to this friend-enemy concept of the universe. Bobby had it just as bad as Lyndon Johnson. Bobby was one of those persons who if you weren't for him you were against him. Johnson wasn't quite that bad. When you put two personalities like that together, they really clashed. Jack Kennedy was a somewhat more reasonable man, which was why Johnson was nominated Vice President in 1960. Jack was absolutely right: I do not think Jack could have won that election without Lyndon Johnson. I think that's one of the few elections in American history where the Vice Presidential candidate made a real difference. Without him Kennedy could not have made it.

Now Bobby resented that right from the beginning. There's no doubt in my mind that after the election, Bobby became the central focal point for the various rumors and inspired stories that Kennedy was going to dump Johnson in 1964, which I didn't believe for a second. This irritated Johnson. Any politician in this town soon learns where those things are coming from. So really there was this undercover seething argument all during the Kennedy years. I think this was largely Bobby's feeling that Johnson was a very unworthy man. Bobby was quite sincere about that. He really thought that Johnson was something less than ideal. After the takeover I can't avoid the very strong impression that Bobby sort of thought that Johnson wasn't entitled to the job. This led to this increasing scratchiness, which finally culminated with Johnson, in effect, ruling Bobby out as a Vice Presidential candidate.

Did Johnson give any consideration whatsoever to Kennedy as the Vice Presidential candidate?

I imagine that Johnson would tell you . . . he'd probably have lots of documentation to prove it . . . that he did; but when you work in the government for a while you learn about documentation. Even though I never heard him say this directly, there's no doubt in my mind whatsoever that he wouldn't have let Bobby Kennedy on that ticket if he had to drown him.

When Johnson refused his party's nomination in 1968,
did that surprise you?

Early in the spring of 1968 I started getting calls from
the White House. Never one directly from Johnson, but from
people who were very obviously representing him. Marvin Watson, for instance, and Johnson's brother, Sam Houston, the idea
being that Johnson wanted me back. Well, it didn't make much
sense to me and the only thing I could figure out was that in the
years since I had left he had developed a staff whose knowledge
of politics was absolutely nil. The only interpretation I could
give was that he was getting set to run again and wanted somebody around who had had some actual experience, that could do
something about it.

I was in the White House about two weeks when I heard
that he had this big address scheduled. When it actually happened, I was at a Chinese restaurant with some Chinese friends
enjoying an excellent dinner. The management set up a television set for us and I realized about a quarter of the way through
the speech that he was going to resign. I knew him well. I could
see the direction in which that speech was moving. That was the
first real knowledge I had of it, right while he was doing it. Since
then I've run into an awful lot of people who allegedly knew
about it in advance . . . I don't think so.

Really, even if I had been told he was going to do it, I
wouldn't have believed it. This was an old Lyndon Johnson
stunt. He was constantly announcing to people immediately
around him that he was going to resign. He was going to resign
as Majority Leader of the Senate. He was going to resign as
President. The night before the nomination in Atlantic City in
1964 I spent two hours walking up and down the White House
lawn with him. He really had me a little scared that night. He
kept insisting that he was going to quit . . . the hell with it! I could
just see the Convention being thrown into absolute chaos, a
situation so bad that even Barry Goldwater might get elected.
Well, the next day he just went up and accepted the nomination.
I came to the conclusion after that that this was really sort of an

appeal for sympathy. That he'd say things like this so that people around him would start importuning him not to quit, begging and pleading with him not to quit, that they loved him. So therefore if I had been told two hours before that broadcast that he was going to resign, I wouldn't have believed it.

As a Johnson intimate, how would you have advised him?

About resigning? At that point I would probably have given him some bum advice. I would have told him that he shouldn't resign, but that was because I would have been influenced by my own personal position. I had just cut all my bridges; I had given up some rather fine stock options; I had closed down all of the projects I had launched. In effect, I had just resigned myself to live in the White House. Now I'm not sure that my judgment would have been a good one.

I recognized as soon as I got into the White House and started to look around that the situation was an impossible one, but I was still suffering under an illusion that he could correct it, that he could bring some people into the Democratic National Committee who at least knew the names of the state leaders, that he could get some reasonable people managing things, that he could make some moves. Now, in retrospect, I realize that while I was right about that—that the situation was not lost, provided he did the right things—that he would not have done the right things. He had reached the point where the people would always be wrong, where the moves would always be wrong. In retrospect, I'm rather glad he resigned. I think the Chicago Convention and all that happened there was inevitable. Given his temperament and given his mood at the moment if he had actually been the nominee, I think you might have had a major bloodbath in Chicago rather than just . . . I'm trying to think of a word between "disaster" and "unpleasantness."

Benjamin Spock

 So I said, 'Oh, President Johnson, I know you'll be worthy of my trust.' And it was only three months later that he did what he promised not to do.

In many ways, Dr. Benjamin Spock epitomizes the Establishment: descendant of a pre-Revolutionary Hudson Valley Dutch family, Yale, tailored three-piece suits, $80,000 in annual earnings. "I was born and brought up a Republican—voted on my father's recommendation for Calvin Coolidge in 1924." He wrote *Baby and Child Care*, the bible of child-rearing that has sold twenty-two million copies in twenty-five languages in the last twenty-three years. In the Sixties, however, Dr. Spock distinguished himself in a different manner. As an opponent of the Vietnam War, he marched, spoke, wrote, and demonstrated with a frenzied avidity. In late 1968 Dr. Spock was tried in Boston on a charge of "conspiring to counsel, aid and abet the violation of the Selective Service Act." He was found guilty in May 1969, fined $5000 and sentenced to two years in the penitentiary. Later the conviction was overturned. He continues his opposition to the war as standard-bearer of the People's Party, a coalition of radical groups that grew out of the frustrations of the 1968 Democratic National Convention.

Some people think that I jumped right out of the pediatric office one day when I was measuring a fat baby and jumped on the barricades. It was actually a series of steps, none of which seemed very significant in themselves. I joined SANE [National Committee for a Sane Nuclear Policy] in 1962 because I was reluctantly convinced we had to have a test-ban treaty. Otherwise more and more children would be born with mental and physical defects. So, I thought it was a pediatric issue.

Actually I was not a dove at that time. I had voted for John Kennedy in 1960 on his say-so that there was a missile gap; and that Eisenhower and especially George Humphrey [Secretary of the Treasury from 1953 to 1957] were skimping on our defense in order to save money. In other words, I felt that the way to cope with the Soviet Union was to be armed. I was made co-chairman of SANE within two years, not because I knew so much about radiation or tension areas or disarmament, but because I would have an influence on the mother vote.

I knew very little about these things, but by the time I became co-chairman then I had to find out. Including the fact that we have no business being in Vietnam. And furthermore that it was very dangerous to be there. So that's how I got concerned with Vietnam. Then came the Lyndon Johnson and Barry Goldwater campaign. As a spokesman for the peace movement, I felt absolutely compelled, when I was asked to participate, to participate; because Barry Goldwater said the way to solve Vietnam is to escalate, to bomb them into submission. Lyndon Johnson said, "No, no escalation, no sending American boys to fight." So I participated. I did a number of radio and TV things. There was a half-hour commercial put on by Scientists and Engineers for Johnson. They got a very impressive group of people to do a round-table discussion of how outrageously irresponsible Barry Goldwater was, and what a statesman and a pacifist, practically, Lyndon Johnson was. We sat around the table for half an hour, sneering at Goldwater and admiring Johnson. They say that it made such an impression on Johnson that he showed it three times.

Lyndon Johnson called me up two days after the election to thank me and he said in this humble-sounding voice, though I know now that there was no scrap of humility in him, "Dr. Spock," he said, "I hope I will be worthy of your trust." I was so embarrassed. The President of the United States hoping to be worthy of my trust! And it was only three months later that he did what he promised not to do.

Now, with the kind of upbringing that I had, the kind of personality, I was a very careful person always. I had to listen to my conscience. Before I could take any public position I had to be terribly careful. I was a very hesitant sort of person. This betrayal by Johnson relieved me of all restrictions of conscience because my conscience was now in total agreement with me, my ego. It energized me, and it also released me from carefulness. I mean, here was a case where it was absolutely crystal-clear that I was not wrong. I was right and Lyndon Johnson was wrong. Everything that I read confirmed this. So I developed a tremendous increase in activity and have been increasing it ever since. I wrote insulting letters to the President and I got no answer from him.

I used to get replies, snotty replies from McGeorge Bundy, which is the personal motive why I want to see him held responsible for war crimes. He has always been, I gather, one of the most arrogant and condescending people. I remember when we had the first Professors' Teach-In, the spring of 1965. He couldn't be there. I think he had to go to the Dominican Republic to find out just what was going on there. But he sent a message—there were something like eight thousand professors in Washington at this hotel—and he said it was clear that we had not done our homework. Typical of McGeorge Bundy.

So I said in this letter that I sent—somebody told me to send it care of Valenti—and I said, "Dear Mr. Valenti: Please put this on the President's desk in case he wants to read it. I am not interested in a reply from an assistant." I got a reply from the President. Of course, I had belabored him on ten points about the illegality and the immorality of the war, and he only answered me on one of the ten points where he technically had me. I slightly overreached myself in the accusation. I implied that he never told the country that he held North Vietnam the aggressor. I thought that he had invented this in the throes of the escalation. Well, it turned out that I was wrong. So I wrote back saying that I apologized on that one point but that I still knew the war was wrong.

In July, he was still debating how far to go. "The President is having a review of the whole situation to know whether we need to escalate further." The escalation went by stages at first. So I took that occasion to write another letter and tell him, "For God's sake, don't you know how hard it will be to get out?" Well, he wrote me, he signed it anyway, and it said he wished he could count on my support. Well, with the kind of boiling feeling that I had, I of course took the occasion to tell him exactly why he couldn't have my support.

Then he kept on escalating for two more years, and in the late spring of 1967 I signed the "Call to Resist Legitimate Authority," and was one of the promulgators. This was the cornerstone of my life of crime, according to the federal government. Then we had a press conference and later a demonstration before the Department of Justice, during which we harangued an Assistant Deputy Attorney General. There was also a discreet draft-card burning, which I was not involved in. The fifth episode was at the Whitehall Street Induction Center here in New York, where I was one of the leaders of the demonstration. Those are the steps of my involvement. It seems to me every one was a relatively small step following another. It started with what I thought was a pediatric concern.

Sol Myron Linowitz

 . . . people forgot that technology is amoral and it's a tool. It's what you do with technology that makes the difference.

Sol Linowitz culminated a career of government service by representing the United States in the Organization of American States from 1966 to 1969. He is a senior partner of Coudert Brothers law firm and serves as a director of a number of corporations, including Time Inc. In 1947 Linowitz represented and advised the Haloid Corporation in the acquisition of the process called xerography.

Eventually he became Chairman of the Board, and the Haloid Corporation changed its name to Xerox and became a household brand name.

There was understandable concern as to whether the new technology was going to cause massive unemployment, whether the machine was going to be in the saddle riding man, and whether we were at a new era when all of a sudden the machine that we created was going to become a Frankenstein monster and take over the world. We got carried away by the wrong concerns.

A friend of mine once said that it's dangerous to extrapolate a curve, even on a woman. The fact is that this extrapolation of curves as to where we're heading with the new technology frightened a lot of people. Those people forgot that technology is amoral and it's a tool. It's what you do with technology that makes the difference. Technology can bring you on television everything from the Boston Symphony to the Beatles to heaven knows what else. A car can transport you or kill you. It's what you do wth a piece of equipment that makes the difference. The answer to the hand-wringers is "not yet."

When we became involved in Xerox in trying to take this new process and harness it to serve human needs, what we had in mind was not how many copying machines could be turned out, but what could be done to have people in a position where they could communicate better, more effectively, from one part of the world to another.

Suddenly we found that we could do so much. Technology was making massive new changes—suddenly we could telescope time and distance, and the world suddenly shrunk. Somehow we had found that we had technological capacity almost beyond our abilities to absorb. There is the process called xerography, which makes possible copying in a way that has never before been possible: librarians, scholars, physicians, artists are now able to get the benefit of what has hitherto been simply unavailable to them. You go into the old archives and see copies of documents, yellowed and crumbling, which could never before be examined and now, through the xerographic process, reproduced and made available for study. Scholars all over the world have expressed their gratitude that this has happened. The same process has developed a new way of taking X-rays, called xeroradiography, which makes it possible now to see things that no X-ray system has ever been able to see before. Again, technology serving the human condition.

There are so many things we now can do. We can cure illnesses. We can help doctors operating in one part of the world to know what's going on, what has happened in similar cases in other parts of the world. We can speed up learning in the developing countries where, heaven knows, unless we can overcome this massive illiteracy, we're never going to move into the twenty-first century. Everything from ways of using nuclear energy to the Salk vaccine. When you talk about the Salk vaccine today, the name itself means that this dread disease has been virtually eliminated. In short, we *have* been able to use these tools to advance the human condition.

*   *   *

I don't think of the Sixties so much as a time when cataclysmic new inventions in technology were suddenly propelled forward. It was rather a time of gaining, advancing, improving, moving forward in connection with technological achievements.

I'm very concerned about where we are in this country, less with technology than I am with our social problems. Our failure to reorder our priorities in this country. If there is anything that troubles me more deeply than anything else, it's that we haven't put first things first. We still are wracked by racial problems in this country. We still have our cities as areas of potential disaster, tragically abandoned. Socially we haven't made progress. In our concern with the military and the defense, we have relegated to subordinate positions those things which ought to be on the top of our agenda. I'm troubled, deeply troubled, by all these things.

When I use the phrase "reordering priorities," I mean

using our resources as a nation in a way that will best advance the lot of the average American. In the Sixties there was pressure to put our hopes in defense in order to protect ourselves and remain strong. When you make that decision, then obviously you're taking your resources from purposes that make a difference in the life of the average person in housing and education and health care and those things that are integral to a good life. When I talk about reordering our priorities, I'm talking about taking the federal budget and reshuffling our allocations and insisting that we not place in second or third or fifth place what makes a better life for people just a few blocks from here, within the shadow of the Capitol and the shadow of the White House.

Do you think the average American is ready to make the commitment, to make the sacrifice necessary to a reordering of our priorities?

I think so . . . if their leaders will tell them to do what has to be done. I'm very high on Americans simply because I think as a nation, as a people, we've always been willing to respond—properly challenged, properly called upon—to do what has to be done. No one has said to the American people in the way it has to be said, "Look, it costs greatly to be great. If you want to be a great nation, that's going to cost. You can't look for tax breaks. You can't look for gimmickry that will get you out of paying the pricetag. The pricetag is going to be a heavy one. You've got to understand that if you want your kids to live in a nation that isn't torn apart, that if you want your kids to live in a nation where they can breathe the air, somebody is going to have to pay the bill. All of us together are going to have to pitch in and insist that what has to be done is done." This people is capable of rising to that kind of a challenge. Unhappily nobody is issuing the challenge today.

The American people are a warmhearted, generous, optimistic people, susceptible of major commitments and major sacrifices if they think it's worthwhile. Somebody has got to let them know why it's worthwhile.

H. Edward Smith

 It was the doggondest Christmas Eve that I'll have to remember. . . . The impact of what we had had a chance to see was very firm evidence of God's creation out-side of our own earth planet.

Ed Smith works for the National Aeronautics and Space Administration as a journeyman engineer.

I think everybody should want to make his mark in the sands. Some people do it one way: they build tall buildings, and they amass great fortunes. Then there are some that group together and do something unusual in life, cause some great event to occur. They will be well remembered if the event was good. I think in this case there was a large group of people that massed together to cause an event. The print in the sand was big. My portion of the print may have been just one toenail. I wouldn't trade it.

* * *

I saw the ad in *Aviation Week* that they were looking for engineers in the Manned Spacecraft Center down here. At that time MSC was not centrally located near Clear Lake as it is now. It was spread all over the city of Houston. The Thought Group Operations Division, which I was being interviewed by, was in an old dinky apartment. I went over there and it was crummy. It was unlike anything I had ever seen in the aircraft business. They showed me around, and there was nothing to see! No computers, no calculators, no airplanes, no hardware. People were just sitting around scratching their heads and slipping slide rules and talking about the next mission, which at that time was Cooper's Mercury mission, the last of the Mercury missions, which was going in May of 1963.

My position was as a journeyman engineer. We did much of our work wtih flight simulators. We'd take large computer complexes and attach a cockpit to them with a TV screen driven by the computer. We'd actually simulate the lunar landings with these computer complexes. We'd put Apollo in there and we'd fly the LEM and actually size the engine and design the control system by doing these little tasks where we actually landed on the moon. We might land on the moon as many as one hundred times a day in simulation, and break a few doing it.

I still had to earn my keep on something besides flying simulations, and I broke into the Gemini program. I was on Gemini IV as Debriefing Officer. That was when Jim McDivitt and Ed White flew the first three-day flight. Ed walked in space. I was waiting for him on the *Wasp* and debriefed him. We spent two days talking that one over and putting it on tape. The highlight of that mission, of course, was Ed White's extravehicular activity, what they called the "walk in space." You've got to remember that all of these astronauts are in beautiful physical condition. Ed was a fine athlete anyway, a tremendous track man. To get Ed off of about a fifty-seven pulse rate, you almost had to hit him over the head. Well, after he'd done his walk and got back in, they couldn't close the hatch. They worked for over two hours. They made a complete revolution around the earth trying to close that bloomin' hatch. The rubber seal didn't close enough, and his pulse rate went up to the order of one-sixty or one-seventy trying to get that bloomin' hatch closed.

But they got down and all the medical fraternity had predicted dire trauma for their being three days up in space—they'd be all disoriented. The first thing Ed did when he got out on that red carpet was do a little hop, showing how good he felt about it. It was a tremendous breakthrough, the thought that man could live up there in the weightlessness for three days, and come down feeling like a million.

*   *   *

Gemini was just built to test some of the techniques that were going to be used in Apollo. The critical techniques, like the possibility of having to walk in space, getting out, and recovering the instrumentation. The rendezvous—which they have to use every time when the LEM goes back to the Command Module in lunar orbit—was demonstrated by Schirra and Stafford on Gemini VI. It was all a buildup to where the first Apollo flight went. Then we had a terrible disaster where we lost Ed White and Grissom and Chaffee, but we finally got Apollo off the ground with Schirra and Cunningham and Eisley. That was the first Apollo rendezvous and it marked a real interesting point in life because we rendezvoused without any sort of radar. Just looked out through a sextant and measured the angles and let the computer work on it. This was the difference between Apollo and Gemini. Gemini was more a state of the art of the aircraft world and Apollo took a big giant step forward and used the computers to estimate the navigational state of the vehicle.

In Apollo VIII for the first time man voyaged beyond Earth's gravity and circled the moon. It was a flight that was designed on the spur of the moment. The original design of Borman's flight was to go out into deep space about thirty thousand miles and then reenter at a high rate of speed to test the entry system. Then we had navigation problems around the moon, so send Apollo VIII to the moon, test out our ground-based radars and see what the problem was. Of course, the beauty of the thing was that the best time to fly was at Christmas. Gosh, they insert into orbit Christmas Eve and that evening—it's been our habit to have Christmas Eve dinners instead of Christmas dinners—and we had it and we sat down for that TV session. They came on and you just sat spellbound listening to their description of the moon, and they were taking TV pictures of it that were being sent back simultaneously. It was almost weird to think that on Christmas Eve these people were up there showing you pictures, very close pictures of the moon. Then the closing prayer that they made. I don't remember just what the words were, but each one of them said a few words, and I guess the Lord's Prayer was said. That's when Madeleine Murray got all upset. It was the doggondest Christmas Eve that I'll have to remember. You couldn't top it. The impact of what we had had a chance to see was very firm evidence of God's creation outside of our own earth planet.

What were you doing during the Apollo XI flight when our men first landed on the moon?

I was in Systems Evaluation Center, which is in Building Forty-five. All the systems specialists were gathered there. I guess there must have been a hundred of us: various subsystems like Propulsion, Environmental Control, Guidance and Control, the Telecommunications Groups. We were all over there. The Mission Control Group are the people who look at the data and have a good working knowledge of each of the individual systems, but if something very unusual happened, they felt they should have the people who designed the stuff sitting in another room, the boiler room. If something silly happened we could figure out fairly quickly what a fix would be, and that's what we did! In many cases, there would be some unusual happening and they'd call over there and give us the symptoms and the fellow that designed the crazy thing could sit down there and figure out what happened pretty quickly. There must have been between three hundred and five hundred people that were on the line, on call almost instantaneously, during the mission. We had two monitors in front of us that we could call up special data straight off of the telemetry.

What was it like in the "boiler room" as the LEM descended closer and closer to the moon?

It was embarrassment for me. In the latter stages I was responsible for all the integration testing of all the guidance control system's hardware and software for the LEM. We actually had a LEM guidance control system strewn all over the

Grumman Aircraft Corporation floor, hooked into a simulator with a computer, faking it out, making you think you were flying. Except that there were a few pieces that we didn't have. Wouldn't you know, one of them acted up. Neil was coming down, he had gotten through high gate, which was the point at about eight thousand feet where it pitches over and he can see out the window. The computer got overloaded due to a faulty insertion of a signal from the rendezvous radar, which was supposed to be off, and it made the computer stand up and try to throw up. Fortunately, we had thought about it and we had protected the computer from quitting. We had protected high-priority things like keeping the engine going and steering and told it to drop some of the lower priority routines that the computer was doing, but one of the routines that was dropped was Neil's instruments. His display went blank on him, and all I could think of was, "Gee, I'll bet Neil will want to kick me when he gets back."

They were still seeing blanks, I think, down around five thousand feet. They were coming down in the order of one hundred feet per second or six thousand feet per minute. It meant in a minute they would bounce. We had some long probes hanging off of the landing pads and the probes were about four feet long so if they were coming down about three feet per second, they would get the light from the probes touching the ground and then they'd shut off the engine and drop. Lunar gravity being what it was, you don't drop very fast. All I can remember was I heard Aldrin yell "Contact" or "Lunar contact," which usually meant the light came on, the blue light. I waited about two seconds and I whacked the table and said, "They're down!" Everybody looked around at me and said, "Hush," 'cause everybody was in dead silence. And then it came across. . . .

"Tranquillity Base here. The Eagle has landed," is the way he did it, I believe. It was stone silence for a second and then everybody made a muffled cheer. This group, you know, they're not a real demonstrative group. They're a bunch of engineers. It was kind of like "We knew it would work all the time." The twentieth of July 1969. It's a day I won't forget.

What so intrigued you about going to the moon? Was it really worth the cost?

In the early stages there was to me no scientific value to going to the moon. The ability to demonstrate a flight system, the vehicle that could do it, to me was a matter of technological pride. Well, we were going! Ever since I was a kid the moon, or anything relating to going to the moon or jumping over the moon was something I heard in Mother Goose. Since then, I think, my thoughts have matured somewhat about what it means. At that time the moon was a klinker pile to me. Nothing else. It set out a quarter of a million miles away. It moved and so it was hard to hit and yet you wanted to hit it softly. After that first landing, I went home and I sat down to just casually watch the moonwalk. It was a very casual thing. My job was done. When they got down there and got out and started walking around, you suddenly realized that you were looking at a foreign body that had a very close relationship to our history. From there on, going to the moon meant something else to me. Dave Scott may have found something that really is a key to how the earth was born. [While on the second moon rover expedition of Apollo XV, Dave Scott found a rock that scientists conjectured was part of the original moon crust, dating back nearly 4.6 billion years.]

That in itself makes me think of Columbus. The first time they funded Columbus and sent him off on his merry way and he got back and they all met him and clapped him on the back, there was a kind of dismay that there was no gold or silver and jewels. He had some feathers and some Indians with him. But they funded him up again and fired him off again to the Indies and he câme back again. He found some more land but he had some more feathers and more Indians. They didn't appreciate it too much. They were beginning to grumble, but they sent him off again. The next time he came back he didn't have anything else, and they clamped him in chains and put him in prison. Well, I've heard the chains rattling out at NASA, because we're not coming back with gold and silver and jewels.

History, or my impression of history, is such that the

more you learn about where we came from, the more you understand about how to handle yourself, your life.

Robert Lopez *

 They were shooting not only at policemen
but at firemen. . . . A fireman doesn't have
any protection. . . . But if you have three
hundred people . . . and these people who
start the fire actually want it to burn.
. . .

Sgt. Robert Lopez has worked for the Los Angeles Police
Department since 1961. He has seen duty on almost every detail but traffic in that time. "Ninety percent of my
job I enjoy," he says. "I'm eligible for retirement after
twenty years. I may do twenty-five, maybe thirty, depending on the family situation."

A highway patrolman stopped a drunk driver in Watts,
which is the southeast area of Los Angeles. It was a very hot,
stifling night. I worked four and a half years in that area, got to
know some of the people, the type of people, some of the attitudes they have. During the summertime, people as a rule get
out and they drink. They get out in the open air because it's hot
in their homes.

How did events unfold that first night?

It's difficult to say, mainly because there were so many
people. I'm not really sure that they knew this was going to
happen. Some bricks started flying. Bottles started flying. So
naturally, more police were called. People begin to get arrested.
Well, when this happens, then other people who were generally

not hostile at that time become more hostile. When a person becomes combative, the police have to use force to restrain him. The people aren't happy with what they see. They don't see the person striking the officer or throwing the bottle or hitting him on the head. All they can see is the officer taking whatever necessary force he has to take to restrain the person.

From that day on until two weeks later, we averaged anywhere from fourteen, sixteen, eighteen hours a day. The whole city was in turmoil. They were in fear. The families of the policemen—my wife wasn't happy, my kids didn't see me. I'd come home to sleep four or five hours. I'd get up and go back. We'd recon in an area and then we'd get specific areas to patrol.

Back to that first night, what was your assignment?

On that particular evening I didn't get involved in anything as far as physical arrests. I was standing at one of the intersections there—at Avalon and Imperial. There were a number of police cars parked in blocks. I saw approximately two or three hundred people standing on the corner at a gas station, and kids and young adults and teen-agers were running back to the Coke machine where you'd have the empty soft-drink bottles. There were retaining walls of brick which had been broken . . . pretty soon you'd start seeing these bricks flying. Hitting policemen, windows being broken. Windows were being smashed out of one of the new media station wagons. When that started, well naturally, troops moved in. They more or less broke up the groups.

Later we were more or less assigned to work in teams of three cars. Six men working in three cars, patrolling, more or less telling the people, "Go home! The whole thing's over. Start a new day tomorrow."

I think the biggest problem was on Imperial, east of Avalon. If you're familiar with the area, it's a wide highway. Normal commuters were using three or four lanes each way. It's a transition road off the freeway. It runs just south of what they call the Watts area and just north of Willowbrook. Cars were being stoned. Cars began to be overturned. People were being assaulted. Now when I say "people," I'm referring to the white race. And generally speaking, these assaults were being committed by the black race. Guys were driving down the street with their girlfriends, and they'd just start rocking. When I say "rocking," I mean rocks and bottles. The guy would sometimes stop because he was panicky. They'd take him out. They'd beat him up. They'd beat up his girlfriend, turn the car over and ignite it. When they'd turn the car over, gas would spill—boom! Many cars all up and down Imperial were just set ablaze.

How many people were killed during the Watts riot?

There was something like thirty-three, thirty-four total killed, and that was over a period of a week or ten days. I don't really know what ethnic group they were. I think the majority of them were Negro. Some of those were killed by the rioters. There may have been some killed by the police.

Here I'm working in an area. I might have been with four or five other policemen. All of a sudden a call comes out: "Rioters looting a building at 104th and Avalon." Then you hear that the place is on fire. So you shoot on over there and there's three or four hundred people. They break up and you can see them grabbing things and carrying them and running in every direction. The fires started in the whole area down around Imperial and Avalon and Main and Broadway: these are all streets that parallel each other. They just started moving north. Eventually, when they got up to around 103rd Street, there are a number of pawnshops. They had guns and they had property, cameras. This is one of the big targets that these people started hitting later, so they could arm themselves.

I got hit on the back of the shoulder the second or the third day. A call had come out at Avalon, just south of Imperial, and something like ten or fifteen cars responded to it. There were like three hundred people there. They just took off running. The majority of the guys in uniform took off running after them. I stayed with maybe two or three other guys. It looked like a Christmas tree. All the red lights. Thirty, forty lights going. I'm surrounded by three or four hundred people, everybody throwing rocks and bricks and bottles. So I'm flashing my light on them, more or less to keep them from throwing the bottle. Well, it turned out my partner got involved in an arrest and he took the prisoner in another car and took off. I'm here waiting, "Where's my partner?" I'm concerned maybe he's killed or injured, but yet I can't leave these cars unattended. I might leave and they'd all be burned to the ground. So I got back into my car—and it wouldn't start. Finally I had to hail another car to push me out of the area. Later I located my partner at the station.

It was a situation where no one really had a set plan. Things would happen. And, naturally, when a call comes out where a policeman is being shot at or being jumped or mauled, the policeman's first instinct is to help himself, help the guy that you work with. So people were just riding all over, trying to help one another. It was terrifying. I was just twenty-four, twenty-five years of age and I can remember not knowing what was going to happen here. I worked with a guy and we were able to work together pretty well. We tried to set plans for each other in the event that something happened, like, you would say a given word and by that we would just take some immediate action as need be.

They were shooting not only at policemen but at firemen. This was what was really bad, because a place would get looted and then they would set it ablaze. Naturally you had fire engine units responding from all over the city and other jurisdictions. A fireman doesn't have any protection, and he can't fight back if he's being shot at. He's got the hose and maybe an axe. But if you have three hundred people . . . and these people who start the fire actually want it to burn, and here's the opposition because he's the good guy and wants to turn it off, what are they going to do? They don't want him to turn it off so they start rocking him. They start shooting at him. They start harassing him. The firemen, if it got bad, they'd load up and take off.

Eventually it got to the point where policemen had to ride like the old stagecoach: you had the shotgun rider.

There was a lot of sniping, especially the third and fourth day. A lot of that. Fortunately not many policemen were killed that I know of. I can't recall offhand if any were killed. Many were injured, but I think the majority of the injuries came from beatings or bricks or rocks. I got hit a couple of times with some pretty good-sized rocks. Nothing that was lasting, but it was painful for a few days. Yet, the following day you had to come back to work, and it was an anticipation where "Hey, what's going to happen?" You don't really know, except that there's a lump in your throat when you think that maybe you might be killed, or maybe your partner will be.

It was something that will remain in my mind forever. At that time a lot of guys had been studying for promotional exams. The guys had been studying eight hundred hours or one thousand hours prior to this thing. Then when this thing happened, it left such an imprint of what had happened, it was such a shock that I had trouble getting back and studying. You'd start studying and all of a sudden your mind would wander to an incident that happened here, or you'd remember running into an area and you'd hear the bullets zinging by your head, or the cry of a policeman when he's been shot or when he's been hurt. You couldn't really concentrate.

How valid were the charges of police brutality?

Very frankly speaking, I think there was probably more verbal abuse than there was physical. Maybe there's a policeman driving down the street and they're calling him obscene names. So he might give them the finger. These similar-type brutality complaints have come out in the past, after the riot, before the riot. It always amounted to verbal abuse by the police. Sure, I heard some. Sometimes possibly there was a little bit of force beyond the necessary force. But here's the situation. Everybody is emotional. How do you handle the situation? A guy throws a rock at you. Boom! He smashes your window. You see him and you jump out of the car and grab him. But there are fifty other people standing around. This guy is fighting, he's kicking, so what are you going to be doing? You're either going to stay there and try to handle the guy with kid gloves and let these other ones jump you, or you use as much force as you can then to restrain him, get him in your car, and get the hell out of there. Sure, there was some extra force taken. I probably used it myself, but I felt that it was my life.

I can only say what I did and what I saw, but there were another couple thousand policemen, and there was a lot of National Guard there, too. I'm sure a lot of the shooting was by them. In the National Guard, you had younger, less mature men. There you've got seventeen-, eighteen-, nineteen-year-old kids. Oftentimes they'd hear a shot that might have been three blocks away, but they think they're being fired on. So all of a sudden, a National Guardsman will pull his M1 and he shoots one off. It travels a hundred yards, or two hundred yards, or even a mile, and it goes by another National Guard, and he turns and he fires somewhere else, thinking they're shooting at him. A lot of this went on.

Every day seemed like the same. It seemed like you never left because you would be gone a few hours and then you'd come back. You were like in a daze continually. You didn't get enough sleep. And when you were sleeping, you weren't really sleeping because here's this thing on your mind. It's in the sun and it's hot and you're trying to get some sleep. You might sleep three out of five, and those three aren't really restful. You come back to work and you might have a cup of coffee and something to eat, and you meet with the guys that you're going to go out with.

The radio was just a continuous rumble. It never stopped. An officer being shot here. Major 415 which is a major disturbance. You were just jumping all over. Especially later, when it was really intense, and fires were going, and shootings, and people looting. You really didn't know where to go, what to do. . . .

Frank and Musette Rose

 About twenty of them . . . broke in and carried out the cash register. . . . If that many men worked . . . at something constructive and productive . . . , just think of the wonderful things they could do.

The Roses live in a small white frame house on the edge of Watts. Their tiny yard is surrounded by a weatherworn white picket fence, and several dogs stand watch from within. They are the only whites in the area. "We moved here Halloween of 1938, and we're not about to move out now," Mrs. Rose says. Mr. Rose, at seventy-one, still works full time as a plumber. His wife works at the school library.

MR. ROSE   Well, I know what started it was a drunk. They said they wasn't drunk, but it was a damn drunk and they arrested him and that was it.

MRS. ROSE   Thursday night it started. Where the drug store is now, the pharmacy, was a sandwich stand. I heard a couple of motorcycles roar in. I heard glass break, and one of the girls screamed. They started going right down Avalon Boulevard, destroying. That was Thursday night. And, of course the Bee Drug Store, right across the alley . . . we could see right through here to its back doors. Next to the drug store was the laundromat, and then a liquor store with apartments back of it and an ice house.

Later on they broke in the back end of the pharmacy. About twenty of them we counted broke in and carried out the cash register. They carried it across 107th Street to a little corner place there. About twenty men. If that many men worked as hard at something constructive and productive as they were working to destroy, just think of the wonderful things they could do.

MR. ROSE   I bought a truck in Englewood, and my son-in-law and I went out to get it. Well, I made a mistake. I knew they were raising hell. But instead of coming up San Pedro or one of the other streets, I, like a damn fool, came up Avalon. Well, as I got down south of Imperial, about 119th Street, about five hundred of them started throwing rocks and bottles at us. There wasn't enough glass left in my camper . . . I'd like to show you holes in the camper yet. There was a five-gallon can of bricks and bottles that I took out of the front end.

     I tried to run over them if I could, but they're fast. Luckily I had a good truck that I could do it with. Good tires. I jumped the curb, tried to run over them. I had to go way over on Main Street and then circle over and come back to come in the alley. I didn't have any glass or nothin' left in the truck. Not a damn thing left of it. It cost one hundred and seventy dollars to put glass in it, so you can just imagine. Then I went up to the country and come back. By then, hell, all this stuff here, that would make you hair stand on end, all this stuff afire. Imagine how close it is here. Big buildings with flames shooting up, and this tarpaper here was so hot it was melting.

MRS. ROSE   Thursday night we watched from our bedroom window back here. I would have shot them in the back with a shotgun had I not been able to keep my wits with me. It went on until about midnight or so. Then the good old County Sheriff's Department sent in . . . oh, I don't know what you'd call it. They were walking four abreast, weren't they? There must have been a dozen of them with guns across their shoulders. You could have heard a pin drop or a whisper. Before that, there were great big women dressed in white up there. Some would be pointing this way and that way and looking up and down. I couldn't figure it out. But they were running pretty wild. That was Thursday night, before the fires.

MR. ROSE   There's a sense of humor to it, too. You've seen cartoons of monkeys with a wheelbarrow. Well, somebody went down the alley here and got a wheelbarrow. And here he comes up here running—a little short guy, it was funny. Now the liquor store warehouse, they were hauling beer and whiskey and stuff out. One guy was hauling it over to the corner and putting it on the sidewalk, and the guy with the wheelbarrow he was just agoin' down here. He'd go down here somewhere and dump it and then he'd run back with the wheelbarrow and load it up again and take off again. That was comical.

MRS. ROSE   They're misled people, Frank.

MR. ROSE   Well, that's all it is. They're misled.

MRS. ROSE   They chose the wrong leaders that led them into the trouble.

MR. ROSE   They just do not have the thoughts and the brains, to be honest with you. Anything skulduggery, they're smart, but when it comes to mechanical or progressive, they haven't got it. I don't care where they come from it's the same thing. They're giving them loans here to start businesses. When they start the business, fine, they do good; but inside of six months they're broke. When I was a kid about four or five years old, I heard the saying "nigger-rich," and that's just what it is. I had a friend who had a service station and he rented it out to them. Well, they took in $400, $500 that day. That night they went out and celebrated. Fine. Well, the second day they took in $300, $400. On the third day they didn't have any money to buy gas or oil with. It was all gone. That's the big deal with the people. Like I say, I understand them in a way. I get scared of them.

MRS. ROSE   There's a lack of respect for law and order, and where there's a lack of respect you'll find that there's a lack of self-respect.

MR. ROSE   It's just one of those things. As I said before, they're jungle people. They called in the Army. What did the poor Army do? They only walked with their guns and got rocks knocked in their head. Now what? Now, if somebody is throwing rocks at you and you've got a gun, what are you going to do? Stand there and take the rocks? I've seen police thrown end over end. Police don't dare shoot them. Well, cut them down. They'll quit. Awful quick. Damn right. If you were throwing rocks at somebody and you knew they were going to shoot you, you'd quit. They're not that dumb. I have a friend who was down at the Olympic Games in Mexico. Some colored people went down there and started a riot. Well they cut down about twenty-five of them—no more trouble. They haven't had any more trouble down there since.

Theodore Jacobs

 No question was ever asked about representation of unrepresented people, about new rights, . . . new involvements. . . . Nader's great contribution was really that he began to ask these questions.

A former New York lawyer, more recently counsel to a Presidential Commission on Product Safety, thirty-nine-year-old Ted Jacobs directs Ralph Nader's Center for the Study of Responsive Law. In this position he is essentially Nader's chief-of-staff.

Ralph Nader was always a person who had great interest in social injustice, political and economic injustice. He espoused the cause of a great many underdogs in a very quiet way throughout the years that I've known him. He was interested in the American Indians and their plight, and a great many other underdog causes. As he tells it, he's always been interested in the problems of technology and their applicability to social and economic issues. The question of auto design was not new.

People were talking about crashproof vehicles and methods of saving lives on the highways many years ago. The materials were all there. It wasn't a matter of Nader inventing auto safety. He certainly didn't. How he became interested in it? It was during law school . . . it was not one traumatic experience, but he does tell the story of seeing a child decapitated by the glove compartment door springing open at the time of an accident that he witnessed. The child was slammed against it and it cut her head off. Rather a gruesome experience, I suppose. I don't know that that was the sole determinant in his becoming interested in auto safety, but it probably helped.

At law school . . . well, it was like a factory for turning out high-priced, highly trained specialists to work in corporations and high-priced law firms. Harvard Law School was a trade school in the Fifties and for many, many years before. There was a great emphasis on excellence and honing of skills, but there was no question at all paid to the value systems to which these excellent skills would be applied. That was simply taken as given. No question was ever asked about representation of unrepresented people, about new rights, new representation, new involvements. I think Nader's great contribution was really that he began to ask these questions. There have always been lawyers involved in public-interest law. [Louis D.] Brandeis, for one. And many, many partners of the prestigious and Establishment law firms have traditionally sat on the boards of charities and given part of their time to the Salvation Army and the Red Cross and the church—that kind of public interest involvement. But Nader, I think, for the first time began to question the role of lawyers in terms of the interests that they represented and the people they represented.

Nader was cast into the public spotlight by his book **Unsafe at Any Speed.** *Why did this particular book have such a powerful impact at the time?*

You've got to talk about the book in terms of the GM trailing, the investigation of Nader by General Motors. I think without that investigation the book might not have had the impact that it did. It would have taken many, many years for auto safety to become the political issue that it did as quickly as it did. The book was published in 1965, I believe, and the auto safety law was passed a year later.

What happened was that in March of 1966 Nader began to believe that he was being trailed by detectives, that his phone was being tapped, that sex lures had been used, that credit checks were being run, that his friends were being interrogated. It quickly appeared that General Motors had conducted this investigation. It probably would have ended there, except for the fact that the detectives made the mistake of trailing him into the Senate Office Building. At that time he was under arraignment to testify before Senator [Abraham] Ribicoff's committee. Ribicoff interpreted General Motors' investigation as interference with a Senate witness. He consequently called the Chairman of General Motors to Washington to appear before the Committee. This was the famous confrontation in March of 1966 between James Roche and the committee, consisting of Bobby Kennedy, Ribicoff, and a few other known Senators. Roche apologized for General Motors' behavior. Nader testified primarily in the area of Corvair safety, and secondarily in the area of "Why can't someone criticize a big corporation without being investigated for it?" It was carried by all the networks. It was on the front pages of all the papers. It probably created Nader as a national institution in one fell swoop. The sympathies were quite apparent here, with the little guy—no resources, no money, no power—bucking the world's primary corporation. I think the natural reaction almost everyone had was sympathy and rooting for the David in the David and Goliath scene.

Why was GM so concerned about Nader?

He did a very, very thorough job of analysis of the engineering defects of the Corvair. The Corvair was a car which I think probably for the first time in the American auto industry was an innovative job. It was a rear-engine automobile that had a tendency to swing out of control in certain kinds of turns. Nader analyzed in the first chapter, which is called "The Sporty Corvair," exactly what happens to the Corvair. It was a rather devastating critique. Subsequently, the Corvair was phased out. General Motors ceased producing Corvairs.

Shortly after this incident he sued General Motors for invasion of privacy. The case dragged on for years and years, again David and Goliath against one another. Goliath had all the cards. They could go on and on and on and on. It's estimated that they spent six hundred thousand dollars in legal fees. They made every conceivable kind of motion to prolong the case. Finally, the second or third appeal that went up to the highest court of the State of New York found in Nader's favor in terms of the liability. The problem in settlement was again that Nader was in a hurry to settle and they weren't. The long and the short of it is that it was settled for four hundred and twenty-five thousand dollars.

With a broad perspective, what has Nader accomplished?

Let's see. . . . Consider what he's accomplished on a number of levels. First, there have been a number of specific pieces of legislation that are normally attributed to Nader's influence. The four or five laws dealing with auto safety, gas pipeline safety, meat and poultry inspection, X-ray radiation equipment, occupational health and safety. He's presently working on a consumer protection agency. You also can attribute to his work a reform of several of the regulatory agencies. The Federal Trade Commission and the Food and Drug Administration are really very different places today than they were before Nader came along. One of his first studies—done with students who had become known as Nader's Raiders—was of the Federal Trade Commission. It found lethargy, sloth—an agency with an enormous potential not using that potential at all. A potential, that is, for protection of the consumer. Nader's report had an astounding impact: Nixon appointing an American Bar Association group to review the Federal Trade Commission. As a result, different people have been appointed to head the agency. These people have been far more energetic, far more determined in their enforcement of consumer rights than the previous people who had headed the agency.

Beyond that I think he's had an impact in the way a great many decision-makers—in government and out of government—view their role. He's made them think more seriously about their responsibilities to a wider public. You'll often hear stories, for example, about a decision being made by some chemical company that we never heard of. Someone will say, "Well, we'd better do it such and such a way. What if Nader got hold of this? What if he found out about it?"

On an even broader scale—not decision-makers, but just the man in the street—people have a renewed sense that it is possible to fight city hall. That one man, given determination, given the will, can make a dent on the most mammoth institutions facing him: unions, big government, big corporations. It's had a significant effect in encouraging a whole host of movements. The ecology movement is the product of this kind of thinking. It's the idea that the individual who's affected by enormous institutions, enormous forces, is going to make an effort to regain some control over these institutions. Nader's successes have encouraged this kind of activity.

What's really been accomplished so far is a change in consciousness rather than in behavior. I think that Nader is asking the hard questions of, "Are citizens going to change their life styles? Change their value systems? Devote themselves to full-time citizenship?" He thinks that is the only solution for the problems that beset any society. And with respect to that, the results are not yet in. It remains to be seen whether there'll be an enormous growth of a citizenship movement. Right now there are no more than a handful of people really working full time in areas allied to what Nader is doing, that is, full-time citizenship.

It might fade away after the phenomenon of an individual like Nader fades away, because he's asking difficult . . . he's asking for sacrifice, and we're not a people who really enjoy sacrifice. Sacrifice is always a short-range thing. We're willing to sacrifice for the war. During the Second World War there was a great spirit of patriotism and the feeling that we were doing something for mankind. The civil rights movement had that feeling. And Chavez's movement had that feeling. They don't always last. It really remains to be seen. We're doing a good deal of work in attempting to get student organizations under way, student-financed public interest groups. If these things can get under way and become self-fulfilling, the United States will be a very different place in ten more years. There are hundreds of thousands of private-interest lawyers and special-interest lawyers. If there were ten thousand *public*-interest lawyers in this country, you'd just begin to see what can be done. It's just too early to tell.

Things are very much the same today as they were before Nader ever came on the scene. There's just as much pollution, just as much bureaucratic ineptness, just as much corporate secrecy, just as much unresponsiveness of institutions as there was before he started. In terms of what really has changed in the world, very little has changed as a result of Nader's work. People think somewhat differently. There are, as I said before, certain laws on the books. Maybe . . . maybe the most significant work that he has accomplished are these laws. Because one of them . . . no, they're all designed to save lives. There may be several thousand people alive today who would not otherwise be alive had it not been for the Highway Safety Act, and *he* was responsible for the passage of that. So that's really the ultimate . . . if you've been successful in saving any lives . . . those people who are alive today might have reason to think that he's been extraordinarily successful.

Nancy Tate Wood

 I became more and more involved simply as a mother. I'd be damned if I was going to have my boys sacrificed for this ridiculous cause.

Nancy Wood is the wife of a well-to-do New Jersey psychiatrist.

In 1965 my husband and I both felt that the war was a lousy affair. However, we were caught up in the thing about our sons, who were obviously going to be drafted. We had the conventional attitude, "Well, if you're drafted, it's just unfortunate. You must go and try to arrange your education around it." But by 1966 we both had changed very much. News of the war began coming through. Because of these two boys of ours we became more interested in reading the news closely and examining the situation. We became more and more disenchanted. I became more and more involved simply as a mother. I'd be damned if I was going to have my boys sacrificed for this ridiculous cause.

I believe it was in 1966 that we really began the bombing heavily. I'm sure that did it. This brought it closer. And, of course, I had always disliked Lyndon Johnson. I thought he would be a terrible President, disastrous. Then the racial troubles beginning. All of these things sort of focused my attention on what was going on in the country more and more. I'd been a completely apolitical person until then. Completely. I never voted for a President but once in my life, no twice. I voted for Jack Kennedy and for [Adlai] Stevenson. That's it. A political idiot. Politically irresponsible.

As things began steaming up in 1966, my younger son graduated from school. His brother was two years into college by that time. First, we began hoping to advise them about how to perhaps join the Reserves or the Coast Guard, and then I began to talk to them about conscientious objection. The whole thing began. We began gathering steam in the family. Then, by the summer of 1967, by that time we were absolutely opposed to the war, and both boys were too.

I think that one of the major elements was reading about this whole business of the draft, and coming to understand that. This was another thing that got me started, because after all what did we found this country for? You know, one of the basic things was not to fight in any wars that any king should dream up for us. I suppose it was the spring of 1967, or that winter, I was reading de Tocqueville. This really got me fired up. I became absolutely impassioned about what seemed to me to be happening in America. And one thing just led to another, very rapidly.

It's curious that somebody who has been so absolutely uninvolved should become so involved. But I think that's partly being a war generation. Because my husband . . . we were married when we were terribly young and he went off to the war. I had one baby. Then when he came back, he went to medical school and then we became very much involved in forgetting about the war and his becoming a doctor and having babies and living. Trying to manage the whole thing. I think this often happens with a war generation.

Then by 1967 I got involved with a group called Negotiation Now. These were people very, very correct and sort of mild in their demands. With some other women here in town I helped raise money for it. Got speakers to come down, and petitions and that whole business. That was my first experience in any sort of political pressure group. I was one of their delegates to Washington, and there I became aware of how this group was put together, and all the political infighting. There were some old-line socialists, sort of muddy-headed in their thinking, and there were all sorts of undercover political Dump

Johnson things going on. It was a very uneasy alliance. Some church people. Well, since I'd never done anything like that before I was amazed at the success I had raising money for it. It seems it gave me the encouragement to get further involved. That was the summer of 1967, and that fall I made them ten thousand dollars.

Then Eugene McCarthy comes in the picture, and I jumped onto that bandwagon with all four feet. I'd worked all that summer and all that winter for antiwar things, but by Christmas 1967 I felt that the Negotiation Now people were far too muddle-headed. This simply wasn't strong enough, because the war was getting worse and worse. I knew that Eugene McCarthy had announced his candidacy. He's a friend of my father and my mother. Archibald Alexander came and asked me if I'd be the moneyraiser for the Fourth Congressional District for McCarthy, and I said, "Sure!" I got his sister to join me and we became co-finance women. Then we further became involved with the State Committee for McCarthy, and then we ended up being the state finance people, and raised one incredible amount of money through these United States.

But I was still extremely naïve about politics until, I suppose, July of 1968. Then I began to understand what it was all about. All that year the war was getting more and more horrible. And the feeling that the Johnson Administration was lying to us, had been lying to us. And the enormity of the Pentagon and its power. Sucking the whole structure of the country dry, really. Not only in terms of money, but the brains of the country being pulled into this madness. It had a snowballing effect.

In the summer of 1968 my older boy went in the Peace Corps as a compromise. The other boy was still in college and had a deferment, but he was a bit more radical than his older brother. Anyway, the older boy went in the Peace Corps, had gotten married in the Peace Corps, in Peace Corps training, and then was kicked out because the girl he married had some sort of black mark against her which the Peace Corps was very obscure about. When the kids got married and they were right down to the line, she was turned down, although their belongings had been sent to Brazil. And then Petey, he was extremely radicalized by that experience. Like his mother, he had been absolutely nonpolitical, certainly not interested in killing people. Well, he then decided he'd resist, and I must say I was all for that. But then his wife, his bride, was extremely upset. She wanted him to go to Canada. Well, the way he worked it out was he finally, with some misgivings, applied for a CO [Conscientious Objector status] and got it. He really felt it was a copout.

Now, the other son, he was very much involved in the McCarthy thing. Worked as a volunteer for McCarthy that summer. He was part of the team of young people we took out from New Jersey to be of use to the New Jersey delegation. We both went to Chicago. Alan had been pretty New Left. And Chicago was a terrible experience for him. He'd never seen violence before, and it was pretty shattering. Well, anyway, this son, as a result of that, became more and more involved in new religions, self-realization and fellowship, and yoga, and so forth and so on. He was on the way to becoming a total pacifist. Then in the spring of 1969 he dropped out of college because he had mono and went to California and got involved with a religious group, a commune called The Unified Family, which to our great surprise was extremely square. Short hair, no drugs, no sex, no dancing, no nothing.

It became more and more obvious that this was a right-wing political front, and by the time the October 15 Moratorium came on, he was telling us that the Communists had infiltrated the peace movement, and on November 15, he absolutely refused to march with us in Washington. And from then on he's been completely in the hands of these people who are gathering converts day by day and have all the money in God's world to spend on their political advertising. That's a capsule of that boy.

I consider Alan in many ways a Vietnam casualty, just as much as if he had his legs blown off. There are some people who under stress are flatfoot in society, can't take it. Obviously what he was doing was rushing from one escape to another. Now, of course, this doesn't mean that if we'd had no Vietnam

War this child's life would have been serene by any means. But I think that these pressures of the last four or five years are directly responsible for the kind of escaping he chose. Perhaps that's unfair, but that's the way I feel.

Sara Sill

 They were cute; they were charming; they were clever; they were talented. . . . They had different characters. Like John, the strong, sort of satirical. And then, of course, Paul, the cutest one.

Sara Sill, a twenty-three-year-old college student, lives in New York.

I was in sixth grade when they came out with one single: "I Want To Hold Your Hand." Between the time that I first heard of them, which was about in November of 1963, and the time they came here, which was in February, things got rolling. They began to put out Beatle cards. They began to put out a lot of publicity. On the radio, about a week before their actual arrival, things had built up so that they were having countdowns. Beatle Day minus three, Beatle Day minus two, etc., etc. The day they came here I was in school. It was on a Friday. The girl in front of me had her transistor radio. It was like boys would listen to the World Series.

It was really fun to watch them. At first I couldn't tell them apart. I always laugh when I think of that, because afterwards, when you got so much information about them, to think that at one point you really couldn't tell them apart! They had captions underneath their names, a word or two about them. I remember it said, "John Lennon—Sorry, girls, he's married." The typical Beatlemania—cries, tearing your hair out, screaming—that was the form that most people saw. But the forms that I saw, in my own experience, were a more quiet type of idolization. One of my best friends was really good at drawing, so instead of going crazy she would just draw pictures of them all the time. It was sort of a fanaticism—collecting Beatle cards was like collecting baseball cards. It was just a girl's way of going through that same hero worship that a boy did for Roger Maris.

All of a sudden there were just four guys. They were cute; they were charming; they were clever; they were talented. There were so many adjectives that you could call them. And they're all entrenched in this one body. If you particularly appreciated their musicianship, which wasn't that great at the time, you could focus on that. They had different characters. Like John, the strong, sort of satirical. And then, of course, Paul, the cutest one. Each girl could sort of find her ideal mate in one of them. Guys were just sort of psychologically projecting them.

I saw them in the last concert in Shea Stadium. Two or three of my friends came over to my house from different parts of the city, since my house was closest. We got a little giddy and we made our posters. As the time came we got a little excited. One person couldn't eat dinner and one person couldn't stop eating dinner. There was a sort of nervousness. We got to Shea Stadium and there were hordes of people there. It was just very exciting. Our seats were three rows from the top. The thing I remember most about the concert is that they came on about an hour and a half after one of the groups had begun. What was so agonizing was that Ed Sullivan, or whoever it was, came out and said, "We all know who you're waiting for," and everybody would scream, because this was the moment they had been waiting for. And then they'd go, "But—before that, here is Bobby Hebb singing 'Sonny' or whatever it was."

Then the helicopters started going around. Everybody knew the traditional way of Beatle transportation. It was just a whole study that you could make. They either came in a helicopter or they came in an armored truck, and both of them happened to be around there. When the helicopters started flying around Shea Stadium, everybody got very excited. It was just a helicopter, though. They came in an armored truck. Then, to keep the audience from just going berserk, they had us singing songs, like "We Love You, Beatles." That sort of absurd thing. But that just got people more excited. It gave them something to do, but as soon as the song was over, they got more and more anxious. Finally, after what seemed like ages, they came out and it was like heaven.

I heard rumors that you couldn't hear them. I had been prepared for not being able to, especially in Shea Stadium, but it wasn't a problem. There was a basic agreement that you'd scream in between clauses unless you couldn't help yourself. What would happen is that Paul would sing the line "Yesterday" —and everybody would scream; and he'd say, "love was such an easy game to play"—and they'd scream.

Jerry Garcia

 What the Beatles did in music was really nothing innovative in the purest sense. What they did was create a lot of groovy syntheses, you know. . . . But the other stuff, the unconscious stuff, . . . has been even more far out in terms of how it's affected life.

Rated by many experts as the best pedal steel guitar player in the country, Jerry Garcia plays lead guitar for The Grateful Dead, the group that pioneered that genre of music called acid rock.

I thought the Beatles was an interesting name, and they had funny haircuts. That was like a real low point in rock 'n' roll. AM radio. And I was in a whole other kind of music. I was like in traditional music and teaching music and stuff like that. Old blues stuff. It didn't really catch on in my mind. The Beatles still didn't really mean anything. That was the first time I really had heard about them. It was the number-one group in England at that time. That was before they even were in America.

Then their records started coming out. They were catchy. A reason to listen to the AM radio while you were driving, for example. That was a good thing. That real early stuff. And then *A Hard Day's Night* came out. I think the movie had more impact on me and everybody I knew than their music did, their early music, that is. The movie was light and fun. It was satisfying on a whole lot of different levels, for people who were already Bohemian or beatniks. That was the thing that did it. The movie. In the straight world, in the other world, I guess it was the music . . . I don't really know. The impact was incredible!

What was it about the movie that made it come across so well?

The whole style of it. The delivery of it. It wasn't influential in terms of subject matter or anything. It was just light. It was the flash. Suddenly a good flash, a happy flash. Post-Kennedy assassination. Like the first good news. Maybe it was a happy flash, these guys getting away with weird shit, playing rock 'n' roll music. It was groovy. A good thing.

I was in a whole different world musically. Personally, of the English groups, I preferred the Rolling Stones because they were more into the kind of music that I've always played, which is like funky, raunchy music. Blues music. Rhythm and blues. The Beatles . . . their music seemed a little too light for me at the time. Then later on it started. I think the first record that I really liked a lot was *Rubber Soul* and the first record that really moved me heavily was *Revolver*. That was the first one that I thought "Wow!" That was the first one. All of a sudden it seemed their musical possibilities opened way up.

They've been fantastically influential in music and, in fact, a whole lot of other things. In my opinion, they sort of brought to light a whole lot of trips, put them in the above-ground, which made it much more possible for these things to exist, these things that used to be half-life trips.

When you speak of these trips, specifically?

I can't really talk in specifics. Because none of it is specific stuff. It's all gone through all kinds of interpretations. There's nothing I can point to and say, "This is a Beatles phenomenon." For example, people wearing long hair. The whole thing there is, like, I think you could key that to the Beatles.

It's just that things manifest different planes. History repeats itself and what have you. What the Beatles did in music was really nothing innovative in the purest sense. What they did was create a lot of groovy syntheses, you know. A lot of little crosses between various kinds of music that were successful, and they produced tons of fantastic melodies. I think musically that's the contribution. But the other stuff, the unconscious stuff, the stuff that wasn't music, has been even more far out in terms of how it's affected life.

But what is the "other stuff"?

Everything. The whole thing. I would say that was one of the offspring of the Beatles, or that was part of it. It's really complex.

What was Woodstock like for you and the Grateful Dead?

As a personal experience, Woodstock was a bummer for us. It was terrible to play at. The situation is extreme to say the least. Playing for four hundred thousand people is really peculiar. The situation was like we were playing at nighttime in the dark; and we were looking out, in the dark, to what we knew to be four hundred thousand people. But you couldn't see anybody. You could only see little fires and stuff out there on the hillside, and these incredible bright supertrooper spotlights shining in your eyes. The stage was all wet, so there were electric shocks from your instruments. People were freaking out here and there and crowding on the stage. People behind the amplifiers were hollering that the stage was about to collapse. All that kind of stuff. It was like a really bad psychic place to be when you're trying to play music. We didn't enjoy it, playing there, but it was definitely far out. That's all I can say about it. It was really amazing to see that many people. That was the thing really amazing about it. It was like an incredible huge people show. You just could wander around from people scene to people scene.

The thing that was far out about it was that it was all all right. You know what I mean? It was okay. There wasn't any hassle there. There wasn't anybody scoffing at it or anything like that. That's a liberating thing in itself. It's kind of like a king-size cookie jar snatch. Like the pig in the cookie jar without anybody busting you for it, you know. That sort of sensation, like in the air. Amplified a billion times. It was powerful.

It was like I knew I was at a place where history was being made. You could tell. You could be there and say, "This is history. This is a historical moment." It was obvious that it was. There was a sense . . . when you were there there was a sense of timelessness about it. You knew that nothing so big and so strong could be anything but important, and important enough to mark somewhere. I was confident that it was history. That was my feeling really. See, at the time, man, it was like all this stuff that we'd seen coming. We'd seen it coming. And it's just like scratching an itch. 'Cause it's just "Ah, here it is." And then it's on to the next one.

Ross Barnett

 That's forty-four miles of riding on a bus. Now that is just outlandishly silly. People who believe in such things haven't got any

common sense. They don't have any sympathy for little children.

A Southern Baptist, Ross Barnett was born and raised on
a Mississippi farm. He graduated from Mississippi College and the University of Mississippi School of Law and
began to practice in Jackson in 1926. From 1943 to 1944
he served as President of the Mississippi Bar Association.
Elected Governor in 1960, two years later Barnett tried
to prevent the enrollment of James Meredith, a black, at
the University of Mississippi. After his term expired in
1964, he returned to private practice.

The United States government has no right under the
shining sun to meddle with the public schools of America. The
United States Constitution simply doesn't give it that authority,
and the Supreme Court of the United States is usurping the
powers that belong to the states.

Now, back in the days when we had men on the United
States Supreme Court who were really grounded in the fundamental principles of law and constitutional government, men
who had practiced law . . . like [Benjamin] Cardozo of New York,
Oliver Wendell Holmes, like Chief Justice Taft, Chief Justice
Hughes. Men like those, they knew what the law was. As it's
constituted today and in the last few years, it's just been a group
of politicians up there in Washington.

It's just like George Washington said in his Farewell
Address. If this nation ever weakens and crumbles and falls, it's
going to be on account of internal affairs, like the Supreme
Court usurping powers that it doesn't have. He mentioned that;
ultra vires, we call it in law. That means acting beyond the scope
of the authority.

It's been going on for a long time. Whittling away each
year the rights of the states. Today, we don't have any poll taxes
in the South. At one time we had a two-dollar poll tax in about
six or eight states in the South. We don't believe in ignoramuses
and illiterates voting. They don't know how to vote. They can

be driven to the polls just like sheep. That's why we've got so many nuts in Washington.

Do you speak mostly of the Warren Court?

Yes. More than any other Court. We had a great Court during the term of Cardozo and Oliver Wendell Holmes and Chief Justice Hughes and Taft and White. We had a great Court! We had a Court of law then, a government of law; but now we have a government of men.

States' rights and local self-government are the things that truly made America the greatest nation on the face of the globe. When we get away from the rights of the states to control and direct their own activities, then we're weakening and we'll finally crumble and fall. Take for instance the public schools here in Mississippi. There's nothing in this world about busing in the Constitution, but they're controlling and directing the subject of busing. I think the people of Jackson, Mississippi, would know more about what's proper here in this state than somebody twelve hundred miles away. They have probably never seen Jackson. That is the reason why our educational system has gone down. The insanity of Governor Wallace trying to get the little Davis girl away from a school in Alabama twenty-two miles from her home. She has to ride twenty-two miles and stop many times before she gets to the school. Probably sleepy, maybe didn't get up in time to eat breakfast, and then has to ride back twenty-two miles. That's forty-four miles of riding on a bus. Now that is just outlandishly silly. People who believe in such things haven't got any common sense. They don't have any sympathy for little children.

Jack Greenberg

 You'd get some lawyer getting up to give some technical lawyerlike argument trying to uphold some deprivation of liberty ... and the Chief Justice would say, 'Yes. But is that *fair?*' And the guy would just sputter and stutter. ...

Jewish and white, forty-eight-year-old Jack Greenberg has been with the NAACP Legal Defense and Educational Fund for nearly twenty-four years. In October 1961 Mr. Greenberg succeeded Thurgood Marshall as Director-Counsel of the Fund. He has argued successfully before the Supreme Court on more than a score of occasions, dating back to the 1954 *Brown vs. Board of Education* decision, outlawing public-school segregation. More recently he argued *Alexander vs. Holmes* in 1969, a decision mandating the dissolution of dual school systems "at once."

I've been here since 1949, and I guess the important litigation that really affected the country in the Fifties were the school desegregation cases of 1954. That was followed in the Supreme Court largely by proclamations that the national government was bigger than any of the states, that Governor Faubus in Arkansas was not allowed to run his own little revolution, and neither were governors and demagogues in a lot of other places. The courts generally would not accede to these kinds of challenges, but they didn't do anything more than that. They really did not require anybody to integrate anything, except here and there—one kid, two kids, maybe ten kids. But there was no real integration. What the courts were doing was essentially waiting for the rest of the country to catch up, and that began to happen with Martin Luther King and the advent of social activism connected to the black civil rights problem.

You had Martin Luther King starting in 1955, 1956, and then that really caught on around 1960 with the sit-ins. What the Warren Court did was that, by a whole variety of techniques, it allowed the demonstrators to continue demonstrating. It reversed convictions. It granted injunctions against prosecutions. It lifted injunctions against demonstrating. It gave somewhat of an imprimatur of approval in one way or another to the demonstrators. This approval continued until the Court began splitting on it, and then ultimately began disapproving of it, as the demonstrators went beyond social activism to very serious dissidence and then violence in the later 1960s.

The Chief Justice and the rest of the Court placed very high value on free speech and free expression of various sorts, and they upheld it by a variety of techniques. Not always substantively. In fact, they tended to shy away from a substantive approval. They reversed convictions on technicalities—the statute was vague or the defendant didn't have due process of law or proper notice or things of that sort—but they did not say that you've got the right to sit at somebody's lunch counter because the Constitution gives a free speech right on somebody else's property. They never really came to a decision on those kinds of questions. Though there were some opinions of approval and disapproval, the Court as an institution avoided an ultimate decision on those questions.

Was there really a revolution in thinking within the Court, led by Chief Justice Warren?

If one were to make a guess, it might be that the Vinson Court was heading in the same direction. Warren and Vinson were both only one individual, and you wouldn't think one individual would make the difference in a unanimous decision of 9–0. Indeed, the Vinson Court had heard the school [segregation] cases in some of their earlier phases. The Vinson Court had asked certain questions of the parties for reargument and though the questions did not inextricably suggest where the

Court would come out, they basically indicated what the Court was heading towards.

One of the things people have begun to perceive about the Warren Court was that it undertook to do certain things that Congress had declined to do or hasn't wanted to do, things on which the country couldn't come to a sufficient consensus itself to move ahead. The Court simply took the lead.

Do you think the Supreme Court acted properly by assuming the role of judicial legislator?

Obviously I feel they were acting properly or I wouldn't be here. The Court is set up under the Constitution to interpret the Constitution. Unlike other aspects of government efforts to solve social problems, a court when faced with a case has to make a decision. You can go to Congress, and they can say, "Well, we don't want to go into that." You go to court—they have to decide the case. They can decide it favorably or adversely, but they *have* to decide it. The justices are supposed to have some way of sensing the moral tone of the times, and somehow infusing the written words of the Constitution with that and applying precedent and weaving it all together to come out with a decision. Courts always do that. They act out of a medley of reasons, and some of those reasons have to do with what's happening in the country. Not only were they acting properly, but they simply had to do it.

Chief Justice Warren has said his most important decision was the one on redistricting, the so-called one-man, one-vote issue. Do you agree?

I don't know. I hate to disagree with him on anything, but I would think the most important decision was the *Brown* decision, simply because it was the principal act which began the liberation of twenty per cent of the population. It is inconceivable to me . . . I mean if you tried to write the history of the country assuming the *Brown* decision had been decided the other way, it's very hard to figure out what would have happened.

How do you rate the importance of the civil liberties decisions, specifically **Miranda** *and* **Escobedo** *?*

It's hard to say. Let's look at their effects on two levels. They're frequently spoken about as having increased crime, making it more difficult for police to get convictions. I don't think that's true. I don't think it has anything to do with the crime rate. The Court was part of a process that brought the whole criminal justice system to higher visibility. They began a process undoing discrepancies in treatment between the rich and the poor, and they contributed to what is just the beginning of an awakening about crime, its causes and treatment. The way things have been approached in the past was essentially just be tough on criminals, lock 'em up and stuff 'em away under the rug. And as the result, some innocent people were convicted. Many people were treated unfairly. I think we're just beginning to see the fruits of those decisions according basic rights to criminal defendants. People are beginning to think what to do about crime and rehabilitation and treatment and social conditions.

Did Chief Justice Warren really influence the Court as its leader, or was he only first among equals?

I think the *Brown* decision would have been decided the same way with or without him. There are some who say that it was his leadership which made it possible for the decision to be unanimous and that he led the Court into certain areas of civil liberties and civil rights.

One thing, he certainly made sure that in every case involving any question at all, that considerations of basic fairness were all laid out there on the table so everyone could understand it and see it. It was very well known that he would always say "But is that fair?" He'd always say that. You'd get some lawyer getting up to give some technical lawyerlike argument trying to uphold some deprivation of liberty—they didn't raise the issue in the court below, you forfeited some right or something like that—and the Chief Justice would say, "Yes. But is that *fair?*" And the guy would just sputter and stutter because it's pretty hard to fight . . . you could say that has nothing to do with it, and he would say it has a lot to do with it. That was always there in every case and lawyers just had to be prepared to argue about it.

So he made a very substantial kind of contribution in that direction. Justice Frankfurter used to always ask different kinds of questions. He would ask, "What is the impact on the federal system?" and "What is the impact on the procedure within the federal judiciary?" and "Were the technical prerequisites met?" and "Were things done on time?" and so forth, and all that is important. But when Frankfurter was essentially dominating the bench, lawyers addressed themselves very much to that and the opinions reflected it.

Do you fear that the Burger Court might now erase much of the progress of the Warren Court?

I don't know if there is any disposition to actually erase, say, the decisions in the school desegregation cases. Certainly indications are that they're not eager and running out to do it. I don't really think there's going to be much change.

But I'm not really comfortable. I think at the moment really we are in a period of crisis because of the administration. It has found what it sees to be an attractive political issue, which it calls busing or quotas or both, and rather than try to use leadership to have the country respond to this sensibly and develop programs to deal with problems of this sort constructively, it has essentially undertaken a variation of the old Southern political trick of just getting up on the stump and yelling "Nigger." And that gets a lot of votes.

Lou Smith

 Malcolm died before he saw the beginnings of his dreams come true. Malcolm always used to ... tell us, 'Man, stop being Negro and start being black.' ... We're still moving . . . from self-hatred to self-love.

Lou Smith was first caught up in the civil rights movement in 1960. Four years later the Congress of Racial Equality (CORE) assigned him to Mississippi to replace Mickey Schwerner, one of the three civil rights workers murdered in Philadelphia, Mississippi, in June 1964. A year later Smith became Western Regional Director of CORE and remained in that position until 1968, when he resigned to found Operation Bootstrap, Inc., an ambitious attempt at black capitalism. He is now President of Bootstrap, and has an office at their Shindana Toys Division, just north of Watts.

For five years before Watts I was involved in the civil rights movement, doing crazy things. We stopped them from using blackface in the Philadelphia Mummers Parade. Then the Route Forty Freedom Ride, the very famous Route Forty, and then all kind of crazy things like that. The integrationist movement. Then I came out here and found that in the good old West conditions were just the same as they were in Mississippi, only they're more polite here. Down there they call it lynching. Up here you call it justifiable homicide.

Here were all these people, piling on planes and trains and buses and cars heading for a great march from Selma to Montgomery when their own city was getting ready to blow right up in their own goddamn faces. It was obvious! It was the thousand-mile-itis again! Here's all these people, you know. Every-thing is fine: I love everybody and God bless apple pie and motherhood. But, guess who's coming to dinner? And the shit hits the fan. This whole society is so goddamn dishonest that even the liberals who try to be honest will do anything for somebody in Mississippi and yet wouldn't touch anything in their own home town.

When we left Atlantic City in 1964 [after the Demo-cratic National Convention], sold down the fucking river, we went to Nyack, New York, to the Fellowship of Reconciliation Home, where CORE was born. It was obvious that the integra-tion and nonviolence wasn't going to work in this country. We had a revolt within CORE. We started to eliminate white people who were leading it, which everybody called "racism in reverse." I never heard one Catholic say that Protestants should run the Vatican. Yet every time it comes to one of our organizations, if we want to run it ourselves, the white people say that's racism. It's crazy; it's simple; but that's how it is!

So we told Jim Farmer [one of the founders of CORE, and from 1961–66 its National Director] that we wanted new direction for the organization. He came to the CORE Conven-tion in Durham, North Carolina, at the end of June 1965. Jim wrote a paper, "The Black Ghetto: The Awakening Giant," where he pointed out the mistakes we had made in the civil rights movement. We were so busy in the South dealing with their problems, that we had forgotten the Harlems and the Chicagos and the Philadelphias where the masses of black peo-ple were. The civil rights movement barely touched them. The movement was out for integration of the "talented tenth" of the blacks that we used to cater to. We used to say that we were fighting so that Eleanor Roosevelt and Ralph Bunche could go to the same motel. In the South we were getting down the "White Only" signs, but the millions of blacks housed in ghettos in the North we weren't touching at all.

We came back from there in July of 1965, and in August of 1965 this thing blew up, and it blew up for very simple reasons. It wasn't a "riot" as you all like to call it. It wasn't even a "revolt." It was a combination of Bar Mitzvah or Watusi killing your lions and a tremendous community tantrum. What happened was that people had sat here and watched all the concern about black people "over there." And there wasn't a damn soul paying one bit of attention to what was going on in Watts. So the black people in Watts just spontaneously rose up one day and said, "Fuck it! We're hungry. Our schools stink. We're getting the shit beat out of us. We've tried the integration route. It's obvious the integration route ain't going to work. Now we've got to go another way."

The black community became of age. You would have had to have been here. Old women . . . people tell you about the one or two per cent of people that were involved. They're up their ass! Even old people would be sitting on their porches saying, "God bless you, son. It's about time." That was the spirit. Sort of like, "America, with your lies and your hypocrisies, fuck you!" Lorraine Hansberry talked about it as a "dream deferred." What happens to a dream deferred? Does it dry up like a raisin in the sun?

The violence came from the other side. We didn't kill any whites. When you do your research, you'll find that thirty-some people are listed as killed. The only people they listed as killed in the Watts revolt were thirty-some gunshot wounds, all of them inflicted by the National Guard or the police. There were over three hundred people killed in the Watts revolt. Ask them why they didn't list the bones and the teeth they were finding when they were removing the rubble from the buildings? People who didn't get out. Ask them why they never listed even one. I was at Vernon and Central when a fireball erupted. So much was burning that a big ball of flame just jumped up over the street. Didn't it ever occur to you that wouldn't somebody have gotten burned up? Why was never one death listed by fire? Why was there never one death listed by accident? Police cars screaming up and down the street. People getting their heads clobbered. Didn't any of them ever die? Why all their gunshot wounds? Firemen will tell you different stories. People who removed rubble will tell you other stories. The last count we had —we had somebody who was working in the Police Department —there were over three hundred. Then they fired our informer, so we don't know the real count. But we don't care. There's nothing to be gained by it.

With the flames a very interesting phenomenon took place. This city was broken up into gangs. There was tremendous gang warfare going on in this city just like it's still going on in Philadelphia. Right in the middle of that revolt those kids stopped gang warring. Right in the middle of that revolt you found something else. If you'd walked into Watts this time six years ago and called somebody black, they'd have knocked you on your ass. If you walk in there now and don't, you get knocked on your ass. This community is fast moving from self-hatred to self-love. Go back and look at some of the things that Malcolm was talking about, you'll find out what it means. [Malcolm X, one of the most famous and militant black leaders of the 1950s, and early 1960s, was an eloquent Black Muslim minister who broke with Elijah Muhammad but continued to promote black power doctrines. On February 19, 1965, he was assassinated in New York.] Malcolm died before he saw the beginnings of his dreams come true. Malcolm used to always tell us, "Man, stop being Negro and start being black. The only chance we have for survival is really to go into a black acceptance." And that's all that's happened in the six years since. We're still moving fast from self-hatred to self-love, which means that there will be other types of revolt that are going to take place, outside of when we just get pissed off every now and then when the cops shoot people unnecessarily. You're going to get those kind of little eruptions, but you don't have to worry about burning down no more, the kind of sporadic shit that may blow up as a riot. We're looking at bigger things now. All that's happened is that we don't hate ourselves any more. By not hating ourselves any more we don't have to aspire to be like somebody else. We laugh now when somebody says, "Blonds have more fun." We laugh at it. We used to aspire to be like that.

What do you see this eventually leading to? Do you foresee an integrated society?

Oh, I don't know. We have no control over that. I'll tell you this. Black is beautiful and blonds have more fun. More explicitly, white racism and black pride cannot exist in the same society. And we ain't about to go to the back of the bus any more. We're not about to go through hair straightening, bleaching skin, and all that bullshit any more! It's totally up to white people what's going to happen.

How do you think they will respond?

Oh, I suspect that this country will respond in the only way she knows how. She knows no other way. *She knows no other way!* There's not one historical example I can find that will tell me that white people will change their way. Conditions are different now. We're not begging to be like you. We're fighting to be like us. And another difference is that the world has shrunk. Something like eight to nine of every ten persons on the planet have color in their skin. Every one of them has had great civilizations and has been overrun by the thing that came out of Europe five, six hundred years ago. The civilizations have been destroyed and their self-love has been eliminated. It's what Nehru used to say when he said, "One who looks at the last five hundred years of history and ignores the last five thousand is a fool."

I don't think white people can give up racism because to give up racism would mean that they would then have to answer to their kids when their kids say, "Gee, we were studying about a black pharaoh named King Tut some five thousand years ago. Where were we, Mommy?" Do you have the guts to tell your kids that you were in caves in Europe? Can you honestly tell kids that the Irish were the last major group to give up cannibalism? Do you think you could sit in the classroom right here in California without saying Columbus discovered America? It requires some tremendous soul-searching. What happened to the great civilizations that were here? If he discovered it, what did we do with the Aztecs, the Incas? If Stanley discovered Victoria Falls, how do we account for the University of Timbuktu? Where else could a racist society get up and say, "The Chinese put up a shadow light and must have gotten their technology from Russia." I thought they were firing rockets in 1200 when Marco Polo got there. What's so strange about their firing them now?

Do you think you can honestly get up one Thanksgiving Day and tell the truth of what that was about? Whites depended on the Indians to survive. The Indians had great agricultural societies. Look at the crops, from corn to tobacco to potatoes. The Indians fed them, and then they got their bellies full and killed the Indians. Can you really tell your kids this? Or are you going to keep telling your kids that there were savages here, that savages were running around the land, and we liberated it from the savages? Cortéz didn't find savages, did he? You can go to Mexico and look at the ruins of big temples and civilizations— they didn't look like savages to me. I don't know what's going to happen to whites. I really don't.

I can tell you this. The thing that burned up in Watts was our self-hatred. That's when we started talking about "Black Is Beautiful." White people are going to have to learn self-love. Racism is built out of a built-in negative self-image. It's built-in out of self-hatred. It's built-in out of an inferiority complex. So they got to run out and holler "I'm the greatest" to fortify their own self-rejection. Until white people get away from self-rejection, they're never going to get off black people's backs. Nor the rest of the world's back. Some Europeans are learning that, but Lord help this country. She's not learning it at all.

*   *   *

We're going out and build our own things. Little things like this plant. We're learning something here. You will start to see coming out of here a school. Our kids are going to be worked on from the moment they are conceived. I'll show you kids who are reading at two and a half, doing math at four, foreign languages at four and a half. We're going to build a whole school system. It's not going to change the world, but we're trying to get more black people to get involved in that kind of thing and stop trying to be like white people. Getting some of their own self-love back. Let's go exploring and building some things. Now what white America is going to do with that I have no say over. We don't have any H-bombs. We don't have two hundred-plus kill and overkill. We don't have navies and air forces. In fact, we used to kid about it. You could have stopped the Watts revolt very easily. No black people own any match factories. We certainly don't own any gasoline refineries. Everything we used to burn it you sold us. Just stop selling it to us.

No, we're not building things to destroy white people, contrary to white people's thoughts. Like, at this plant we won't even allow war toys, and we could have made a bunch of money off of that. Your revolts come when you fuck us. Your last revolt came very frankly because nobody was paying any goddamn attention. The world was going on like Watts wasn't here.

The side benefits nobody planned for. I can tell you that very honestly. No one set down and figured, "If we burned up Watts we'd start liking ourselves." There was no figuring of that at all. That was an emotional tantrum that the whole community had. After years and years, back to "Does it dry up like a raisin in the sun?" Or does it explode? We exploded, and with the explosion we heard all kinds of good intentions. Now we're going to do something. Sociologists came in and studied. All that crazy bullshit. Here we sit six years later: more unemployed, schools worse, the police killing more. We're right back worse than we were. So now what do you do? Explode again? You start building. But we're not building within the framework of what is, I'll tell you that. We have no intention of getting black people out of poverty just to put some other people in. We want the whole thing changed.

He is asked about the beginnings of Shindana toys and, more generally, Operation Bootstrap.

It came out of a realization by me and a guy named Robert Hall, who was with another little civil rights organization. It was obvious that was over. A whole new thing had come in. Where do we go from here? We were trying to find a way to deal with the poverty that we have. Incorporated into that were some very basic things that are still there. One is it's just an outright philosophy of ours—and we're not going to be changed, we're very stubborn with it—we believe that people are more important than money. Now that shit can get you on the HUAC [House Un-American Activities Committee] list. Because in this country money is more important than people. When money and people come into conflict, people lose. That's in the founding of this country. They made me property.

Another point is that "If you lay down with dogs, you come up with fleas." So we have refused, all the way down to a three-million-dollar offer from Sargent Shriver, to take any government money, any state money. We won't take it. We won't even deal . . . we sell black dolls to the Army because the black soldiers want them in their PXs so they can buy black dolls for their kids . . . that's the nearest we've come. We won't even take government contracts. Government comes in here and says, "Oh, we can find some contracts for you-all." Up your fucking ass! Take that shit back to Washington. I don't even want to see it, because you are bastards! You get in a cesspool, you come up stinking. And those same motherfuckers will go out there and pay Senator [James O.] Eastland $200,000 a year not to grow a goddamn bit of food. And Sunflower County is the biggest county for mental retardation of black people because they didn't get enough protein and their brains didn't develop. I'm going to lay down with that kind of dog? You must be kidding!

We just try to build some things. We had the best job-training center in L.A. With no money. We taught everything from keypunch, body and fender, computer programming . . . we were turning out some damn good students. We had to give it up. It reached the point where there were no jobs after you trained them. The President . . . didn't he say we had to put X number of millions of people out of work to end inflation? Then the same government turns around and says, "We don't need welfare, we need work." You fall back in your chair. What the fuck is going on here? You're telling me out of one side of your mouth that you're going to put me out of work to end inflation which is fuckin' with the rich, then you're going to turn around and tell me that if I worked hard and took some training, I'd get a job! That's what I've been hearing all my life. Columbus discovered America, "the land of the free."

Bootstrap is just a collection of us who are very honest, honest with each other. We make mistakes. We fuck up, but we have learned that mistakes are not disastrous. In fact, sometimes they do good if you learn from them. We've got a lot of dreams and a lot of ideas that we've got a lifetime to chase. It was like I told you, we had our Bar Mitzvah. We killed our lion. We gave up our dependence and we became men and women, psychologically. We grew of age. We matured. Because when I was in that civil rights movement, I was still trying to be like white people. White people were still my idols. But that's over. Over and done with.

Morris Samuel Jr. and Jlyn

 There were people down underneath this mattress trying to find a bullet slug from this person they killed, and there were people firing at us from a sawed-off shotgun.

Morris is fifteen; Jlyn is seven. Their father is a minister with a long history of involvement in the civil rights movement. Shortly after their father left for Selma in preparation for the march on the courthouse, he decided that his family should also journey to Selma to witness what he expected to be an historic occasion.

MORRIS   I was in fourth grade, and Dad was at the march. He was there for about a week or so, and then we came down. We just flew down because he wanted us to be there. We stayed in a housing area. We slept in one room, right next to the church where all of the activity was going on. I went to a Catholic school run by nuns that was all black. Somebody had to take me to school everyday because I had received threatening phone calls.

How did you react to all that was going on?

I was really amazed. I didn't think it was really happening.

Other than school, how did you occupy your time?

We played marbles a lot with the kids. I got to know the kids pretty well. I was the only white there. I got along with the kids pretty good.

Being the only white, were you treated any differently?

No, not at all. I was just kind of there. They didn't bother me at all. I became friends real easy. It was kind of funny because they were amazed, too. They didn't expect it. It had never happened.

Did they talk of the march, or the civil rights movement in general?

No. Fourth grade, you know.

Did they realize what was happening?

Oh, yes. They knew what was happening. We used to play a game called "Riot." The kids would pretend like there was a march and the police would jump out at them and everything. So they knew what was happening. They were aware of it but they didn't really talk about it.

"Riot?"

All these kids would just walk down the street and pretend they were protesting, and some other kids would pretend to be cops and they'd jump all over them and knock them down.

The first bunch would fall and they'd pretend like they were nonviolent and sit there; and the cops would hit them over the head and everything, just like a regular riot. Like they see on TV, I guess.

Were you old enough to remember Selma, Jlyn?

JLYN   I was two or one. But I remember. A lot of things. We were driving in the car. There were people down underneath this mattress trying to find a bullet slug from this person they killed, and there were people firing at us from a sawed-off shotgun.

What for?

I don't know.

Robert C. Scull

 . . . I started to buy Pop Art. I didn't understand it totally, but then again, why should I have to understand everything? I liked the idea that I didn't have to say to an artist—or to myself—'What is it?'

"I make my living from a taxicab business and a real estate business. I'm a product of the movements, of the undulations, of changes in money markets from one group of men to another. Some men make it; some don't." Such is the way Robert Scull, a fifty-five-year-old New Yorker, explains his financial success. After making his fortune in the Fifties, he spent much of it on Pop Art in the Sixties—so much so that he became the best-known patron of Pop Art.

By the end of the Fifties people had already learned how to say "Picasso" without being embarrassed about it. Most of the middle class were looking at it very shyly and possibly they were a little bit offended by it, but they were able to say the word "Picasso" and it became part of our vocabulary only fifty years after the fact. Then Abstract Expressionism with Jackson Pollock happened like a glorious thing in this country . . . finally America had found itself. Up until Jackson Pollock our paintings were European, in philosophy and thought and in the whole background of what is a painting. We always looked on a painting as a painting of something. Suddenly Pollock came along and said, "Listen, America can paint a picture, too." America has discovered something entirely new: that a painting doesn't have to be a painting *of* something. A painting *is* something. By the time the Sixties came along, Abstract Expressionism already had a rather large cult.

Then Pop Art came along. It sneaked in through the back door. I was called the "Father of Pop Art." In 1960 I started to buy Pop Art. I didn't understand it totally, but then again, why should I have to understand everything? I liked the idea that I didn't have to say to an artist—or to myself—"What is it?" This was a glass and this was a Coca-Cola bottle and these were stars and this was a nude. It suddenly rocked the world, but very few people at that time really, really dug it.

To me it was such an obvious movement that I started to buy like a madman. I thought it was the most wonderful, wonderful experience in the world. Jasper Johns taught me to take everyday objects by showing me that a bronze lightbulb . . . which is sitting there right behind you . . . if you take that bronze lightbulb and hold it in your hand you'll find out that it's not a lightbulb any more. It's now *sculpture*. Hold it, please pick it up. Now you're beginning to realize that our industry has created, every day millions of them in the factory, the most erotic shape imaginable. It's got everything rolled up into one object. Jasper Johns taught us to look at the lightbulb. It had never occurred to me to think of a lightbulb as anything but something to give us light.

So with Jasper Johns and Robert Rauschenberg opening the floodgates to possibilities of making art from objects surrounding our daily lives, Warhol was such a logical step. To take photographs in a "four-for-a-quarter" photographing booth and blow them up into art. It was just a pure step of logic because he began to use the materials, not of the traditional painter of the traditional school—but he began to use life all around him. He began to use supermarkets—everything that could show us who we are through our culture, through how we live and what we do and what we think. Everything around us tells everything about us. You pick up pottery from a dynasty three thousand years before Christ—that pottery tells us a great deal about the people and what they liked and who they were. These young fellows got the message. They started to disseminate the message and I was there to receive it. My antenna was set for that message; I understood it so well. I loved Pop Art so much. Good Pop Art.

But why is Pop Art art?

Marcel Duchamp already proved to us a long time ago the answer to that question. He took a bottlewasher and he brought it into a museum. He took a urinal and he brought it into the Armory Show, which they rejected. The object must be looked upon as an expression of what a sincere artist chooses from the forms in all the world around him as something significant that has to do with our lives. When you looked at the urinal of Marcel Duchamp, you suddenly became aware of the fact that the curves and the design of it were extraordinary. If you could forget what it was used for, it was an extraordinary experience to discover.

Andy Warhol was looked upon as a madman, but I understood Andy Warhol the day I saw his works, because he made me understand it through such powerful means: using a silk screen, making the ink heavier or lighter as he chose, using fluorescent colors, etc. To me, Andy Warhol was the most exciting thing imaginable. I conveyed this through the means that people understand the most—of putting my name on the bottom of a check and paying for it.

It spoke everything to what the American psychology

was at that time. These men spoke of their moment. That's why they were so misunderstood. Do you know any man who speaks of his moment that's understood? When Beethoven played his symphony, he knocked everybody's eardrums apart because they had just learned how to assimilate Mozart, they had just learned how to take Mozart's dissonances and chromatics. Do you think they were ready for the Sistine ceiling? My God, there was an outcry and a howl when they saw that ceiling. They said, "What the hell is this?"

Pop Art says exactly what the 1960s were all about. Plastics, color, advertising, television. Tom Wesselman had paintings with a television set in the painting. Right over here you see . . . Robert Rauschenberg in that painting used a dirty old discarded T-shirt, underwear, to create a form on that canvas. It's a fantastic painting. John Chamberlain took fenders, banged them out and whacked them into shapes, into the most baroque shapes. He took fenders, the throwaway of our automobile crashes—what can be more contemporary than a man that takes metal that was bounced off a car on the highway that went into a pole and use it for art? We'll be able to judge what America is from their paintings more than from a General Motors stock certificate.

The heroic "F-111" by James Rosenquist, the eighty-five-foot painting, must be considered a major painting of the age because of the very attempt at an eighty-five-foot painting of a subject concerning an F-111 airplane and his views of our society . . . little children under hairdryers . . . the good life of packaged cake that you buy in the stores and so forth . . . the American Dream . . . the myth of the American life . . . the good life . . . the honey-colored lights. And in the background the drone of this terrible, terrible situation that we found ourselves in in the Sixties. I remember when I heard an exceptionally loud noise when I was sleeping—the tension grew because you thought it was some kind of a bomb. You had pictures like *Dr. Strangelove*. . . . Comedies were made about a man riding a nuclear bomb down into a city by mistake. So you realize that the "F-111" was a major, major statement—even in its heroic arrogance of trying to portray it. It's heroic in the concept of being able to say, "Here is the dichotomy of American life. You guys are like a bunch of babies. You love little toys and television sets and little Japanese transistor radios. Yet at the same time you're probably the best manufacturers of planes that drone around the world that have these guys sitting with helmets and red and blue buttons all over, ready to press all kinds of things."

The high points were the concepts. The concept of people telling you, "Man, look around you and start to live. Improve on the things around you. You don't have to take a trip to the moon. You don't have to go to Paris in the spring."

Ruth Figgs

 We're used to it but we ain't happy with it. We don't feel good. . . . They've always had their ways of keeping . . . us Negroes down, and they still work it on the same old things.

Ruth Figgs lives in Marks, Mississippi, in one of the poorest counties in America. Her husband has managed the campaigns of a number of blacks running for local office. Mrs. Figgs has told him, "I'm pretty sure you're going to have to get out your sticks and guns."

Has the Poverty War helped you?

It have not. The power structure is still fighting it. When we're talking about the power structure, we're talking about the rich whites. We're talking about a white group that go together and organize their thing. They want it where they can hound us and the poor will still be submissive to them. We just have not got it yet. It's not as yet where it will benefit the poor.

You have one or two independent programs, but they cannot be beneficial because you can't get enough to help too many people, you see. We do have one or two programs that we did get by the power structure, but two or three hundred people is nothing when you've got thousands and thousands of poor folk. Then they would have handpicked Negroes. When we're talking about "handpicked," we're talking about a special Negro that he knows will go his way, let him make all the decisions. That's what we call "hand-picked." They get him and put him on the board.

This is a poor county. It was a big farming area. Eight or ten years ago folks didn't do nothin' but farm. All this country was farmland. We raised cotton and beans, all like that. When they put these mechanical machines in here, these landowners started telling the Negroes . . . they started tearing their houses down. Some of them burnt the houses down on the plantation because they didn't need them no more. They got these big machines and where they had been using twenty-five folks, probably they don't use but five out there now; and that throw a large group of people here with what? Nothing! I'm pretty sure the government thinks we should have done excellent through the food stamp office, but the poor people here still have a thing to sweat with—that lily-white over there hounding them. There's all white women working in there, and some of them is discriminating. They have a way—it don't seem like it's fair in the price—between the federal government's price and their'n over here. Some people sometime suffer because they charge them too much for those stamps.

We're used to it but we ain't happy with it. We don't feel good. You can look at the condition of our living here. If anything had been benefiting me, I could be in better shape. I'd have somewhere to live. They've always had their ways of keeping some of us Negroes down, and they still work it on the same old things. They haven't changed.

Marion Jelin

 All the way down the line, starting with the top administrator, there was a fumbling and a bumbling and a groping which to me was planless. . . . What was to be done today was changed tomorrow.

Marion Jelin worked with the Cincinnati Community Action Commission for several years. In 1971, disappointed and disillusioned, she quit the program.

Head Start is an unusual program in that it doesn't stem from the community as the other antipoverty programs are supposed to. The concept was a preschool program, early childhood development for children from the disadvantaged areas of communities. A summer program, a conventional two-month summer program would be offered to them, primarily to give them reading-readiness. Cognitive skills, the simple basic concepts of numbers and letters and sizes and colors, to prepare them to compete with their peers when they got into school, instead of coming with one arm and one leg tied behind them as was so often the case. Built into it were certain basic concepts —health, nutrition, a complete health examination.

The parent involvement was written into it then, and this is terribly important. It was required that the parents of children who were taken into the program be worked with in terms of giving them an understanding of the basic nutritional needs of children, of the emotional needs of children, the psychological dependency on the parent, of the need for stimulation. Very simply, of talking to them. So often hard-pressed parents will find that it is easier to tell a child to go away and be quiet than to answer their questions. They don't read to them as much as parents of middle-class children read to their children. The results are very obvious in the kids' behavior.

Our operation here was very modest to start with, and came on very fast. Having first heard about it in February, if we were to mount a program for the summer and hire staff and get facilities and recruit children and screen them for their eligibility, this was a monstrous job. So we decided that we would work with existing agencies. Inherent in our concept of our agency was the idea of maximum utilization of community resources, not duplicating facilities. In the interest of expense and also common sense. So the Cincinnati Board of Education and the Hamilton County Board were eager and willing and we contracted with them.

That first summer we had somewhere around one thousand youngsters with the Cincinnati Board and a couple of hundred with the Hamilton County Board. The Hamilton County Board has sixteen school districts in the outlying areas.

The summer program went off very well. I'm not sure we knew what we were doing, but we did it, and we did have a lot of children benefit from the program. Of course, as soon as the summer program was midway, we began to wonder what would happen to eligible preschoolers come the school year. We also realized that there was a limitation on what you could accomplish with youngsters in so short a period. It included a hot-lunch program also. Food was a very big item in the budget. We also heard that there might be funding available on a pilot basis for certain communities that had initiated the summer Head Start. We applied for it and we were funded. We also applied for the summer program for the following year for two counties, Campbell and Kenton in Northern Kentucky, as well as Clermont County in Ohio, and got them.

As the program evolved from year to year, different points of emphasis became worked into it. Parent involvement began to mean many different things. It began to mean parent organization and interpreting to the parents activities that would lend themselves to parent strength and understanding of how a community worked: an understanding of meetings—not just *Roberts' Rules of Order*—but how to participate in the meeting, how to speak up, how to make motions, how to become effective as a group, and then how to use your group as strength. If you will, perhaps political strength, in order to help to meet the needs of your family, your children, and your community. It became closely allied with the movement and the trend toward welfare rights organizations. The mothers and a few fathers who participated in Head Start meetings began to develop leadership qualities. The natural leadership came to the fore. It was a very interesting phenomenon to watch.

We had three day-care centers, which we had funded out of general OEO funds. After about two years we discovered that in the new regulations it was possible to fund day-cares out of Head Start monies. New Head Start monies were segregated in a separate fund nationally. They couldn't be used for anything else. Our versatile funds were being used for the day-cares and we were delighted to find we could relieve those versatile funds of the Head Start day-cares and get them funded out of the Head Start "pot." That meant that then we could do a Planned Parenthood Plan, a Foster Grandparent Plan, and put more of the versatile money into the Neighborhood Organizations Division. Then we discovered that we had cut off our nose to spite our face, because the day-care programs were not half day, they were full day for working mothers. And the Head Starts were only half day. We ran into the problem of insufficient funds for twelve months full day care, and our day care was cut to eight-month funding, along with all Head Start that year. We were able to get the four-month difference locally from the city and the Community Chest after eloquent pleas from the parents.

We ran into trouble with a Small Business Development Corporation grant, SBDC, that was short-lived. We had to work with the Labor Department and the SBA [Small Business Administration] on that. We got funded for an experimental SBDC—one of a few in the country in 1965—for giving small business loans primarily to the members of the black community who were outside the mainstream and who couldn't go to a bank and get a loan through normal channels. It was great. Except that we got the money for the administration of it, and for their guidance and processing and counseling, but the SBA didn't have the money for the loans. We got about thirty-five loans processed, I believe. We had hundreds and hundreds of applications. But it finally died nationally of its own weight because the other part of it that was an essential ingredient was the dollars for the loans, and these were not appropriated.

So businessmen and banks and operating organizations were very wary of government assistance. They were also leery of the red tape, the paperwork, the kind of record keeping. Record keeping in and of itself is a fine thing and necessary; but the changes in regulations and interpretations, rules, and forms became very burdensome. We ran into that with the MDTA [Manpower Development Training Act], which was earlier and preceded some of the later Job Corps and other Neighborhood Youth Corps assistance for youths. Employers had been burned with this kind of paperwork and were reluctant to enter into contracts even though they were paid for it. You couldn't pay for the agony, and there was very little ecstasy! It was rough.

What brought you to resign?

I felt that there were too many staff who were hired who were not competent, were not doing the job. They were just making a car payment, or using the position as a temporary steppingstone to something else. The ensuing turnover on all levels of staff created a lack of continuity, a lack of understanding, a lack of efficiency in operation, and in wastefulness that was horrendous to me.

All the way down the line, starting with the top administrator, there was a fumbling and a bumbling and a groping which to me was planless. There was no real concern. There was none of the initial dedication and concern. The initial excitement that came into the program dissipated. The rules and regulations kept changing with the top administrative turnover. As a result there was a great deal of confusion. What was to be done today was changed tomorrow. The overlay of reporting and recording that was required reached a point where pretty soon I could see that there would be nothing to record and report because everybody was recording and reporting and not doing any work. It was *ad absurdum!* There were all kinds of studies, all kinds of reports. At one time I was doing the reporting. It was done monthly. It was a one-page sheet. It made sense. When we started that, we had about eighteen agencies. It was difficult to get the information from the agencies, but we got it and we got it in on the fifteenth of the month, when it was required. After two years that was all changed. They went into a new system. We had to hire staff to do it. About a year later that was changed. Conferences were called to interpret the new Management Information System, the MIS report, and we had to get new staff to do that.

Charles 'Pete' Conrad

 After eight years I not only was ready to go, but I found it a fantastic place to be. You could look up and see the earth. It was always there.

Charles Conrad was born in Philadelphia in 1930. He earned a Bachelor of Science in Aeronautical Engineering at Princeton University in 1953, and then entered the Navy. In September 1962 NASA selected him as an astronaut. Conrad piloted the eight-day Gemini V flight and was command pilot for Gemini XI. In November 1969 he commanded the second lunar landing mission, Apollo XII. Captain Conrad has logged more than five hundred hours in space.

The first problem was to get over all the butterflies. Anybody who tells you they don't have a healthy fear for what they're doing in this business is lying, because there are certain places where your neck is out. It's minimized to the absolute greatest degree that they can, but we're not quite up to the "747 over to London" deal yet.

It took eight years to put this all together in my mind and that was the most logical trip I ever made. And it was the most logical place in the whole world for me to be. I can explain that further. On Gemini V I went for eight days in a little can. I could hardly move. I sat just the way I'm sitting here right now for eight days. We had a lot of failures. A lot of the time we were out over the ocean we couldn't talk to anybody. That was lonely! We didn't understand all the medical things that were going to happen. The doctors told us we'd die after fifteen minutes of weightlessness. Then it was one day. Then it was so many additional days. Stretching it, you know. You've got all this in your mind and you've never been there before. I worried about those retrorockets firing for eight days. If those things didn't fire. . . .

When I rode Gemini XI I was commander of the flight. My worries were strictly operational. Will I make the rendezvous? Will the radar run? Will the Agena get into orbit? I really didn't have any of those fears of sitting around thinking, "Gee, the boosters might blow up." You always have that thought right before liftoff, but you have been through it before and you're much more familiar with it. All the clanks and rattles and the sloshing of fuel of that baby underneath, if that doesn't run the old heart rate up and down!

I did project that out to the moon from Gemini V, that two hundred fifty-six thousand miles from home, I was going to be lonely, but it just didn't turn out that way at all. After eight years I not only was ready to go, but I found it a fantastic place to be. You could look up and see the earth. It was always there. The trip just wasn't lonely. One of the reasons is that you may not be talking to anybody, but you can look at the gauges always locked up on the earth and you know you can push the button and say hello and somebody is going to say hello back.

En route, you're in flight. Your machinery is machining and if you look out the window and the ground's going by or you look out the window and there's no earth and there's no moon and you're out in the middle of deep space, you're pretty damn aware of where you are. When I landed on the lunar surface, I powered the vehicle down, and we were sitting . . . we're not in flight any more, that's just the same as sitting on the end of the runway in a plane waiting to go. The fact that it was on the lunar surface didn't bother me. It was a very comforting feeling to be sitting there on the lunar surface. You kind of got the idea that nothing could go wrong as long as I'm sitting here. When you're in flight you sometimes think, "Gee, the gazimos can quit or something can happen."

The first thing I was really interested in was seeing if the Surveyor [an earlier unmanned spacecraft that had been on the surface of the moon for nearly two years] was in a shadow. I knew we were at the right crater, but I wasn't sure the scientists really knew which crater the Surveyor was in. The first thing to do was get out and make sure it was sitting on the side of the crater. It was, and that made my whole day! That's what we were really looking for, along with being able to do the geology. They wanted some parts to see what happens. We brought the TV camera back, so you've got condensers and resistors and transistors and wiring and insulation and aluminum and magnesium. They wanted to find out what the hell happens to something like that. You start talking about this grand tour . . . we want to send a spacecraft that makes a grand tour of the outer planets, the ones that we've never looked at. We're hoping to do it about 1976. That thing is going to be in deep space for nine years. For nine years that stuff has got to run. We talk about making Saturn V's five million parts all operating for twelve minutes of flight and then the rest of our five million parts for twelve days in a spacecraft!

*   *   *

When I came down here to Houston, there wasn't a building here. There was a two-lane road. NASA Bay wasn't there. There were cattle grazing in this field. There were two little towns: Webster and Seabrook, on the other end of the lake, and they'd been minding their own business for thirty years.

When we first reported in, October 1, 1962, we rented office space in downtown Houston in a bunch of different buildings—warehouses, office buildings, and everything. There was this fantastic enthusiasm. Like every other organization that starts with that kind of enthusiasm, the sky was the limit. If you wanted green gazimos with purple dots on it, that baby showed up. It didn't make any difference what it cost. Do the deal. There was an article every day in the paper about something on the space program down here. There were pictures every day. It must have gone for two years that there was at least a major article a week in the Sunday supplement on the space program. You're hard pressed to find it today. Once a month somebody says something . . . we laid off a few more employees or something.

So in July we land on the moon and it was just like falling off the end of a cliff. We hadn't done our homework because we hadn't had the money. We don't tell a very good story to Congress. We don't tell a very good story to the man in the street about what we're going to do for him now that we've gone to the moon. But we don't tell that story very well because that's where we've been cut.

I've got a deal on the budget right here as an example. The budget was supposed to go up to where it would remain approximately 5 per cent of the government budget. When we first started the program we got five billion dollars a year and the government spent one hundred billion. We now spend over two hundred billion and we're getting 3.2 per cent. I don't want to bore you with numbers, but in 1962 we got $1.8 billion; in 1963 we got $3.6 billion; in 1964, $5.1 billion; in 1965, $5.1 billion; in 1966, $5.1 billion; in 1967, we went to $4.9 billion; $4.5 in 1968; $3.9 in 1969; $3.7 in 1970; $3.3 billion in 1971; $3.3 in 1972. If you look at inflation from 1966 on we've really gotten whacked. We've had to keep the first objective, which was to go to the moon. Do the flights. We haven't spent the money on other things. So we don't tell a good story. I've got a couple of axes to gind with these social people and all their social rot. We want more cans. We've got more cars. Those guys didn't pump those cars out and then convince the people to buy them.

They built cars to the demand of the people. Now the technologist was at fault for not looking at tomorrow and the day after tomorrow when he built dirty engines. He answered the demand of people who wanted those cars, and that's the guy that's out there bitching right now. Do you know how many hair-curler sets there are in the country? I went and got the numbers because I got so tired of being licked by the kids in the schools. There are fifty-six million electric hair-curler sets in this country. There are something like sixty-one million toasters. Now that causes pollution, you know. That causes old Con Edison to belch that stuff out in New York because he's got to put out the juice to run that junk. Con Edison just can't shut that plant down tomorrow and come up with a clean plant.

If I get a guy who's a real dissenter, he forgets that when he demonstrates in New York and rides a 707 to Los Angeles to make his next demonstration, he's crapping on the thing that got him there to make him be able to demonstrate in one day in two places three thousand miles apart. He sure uses it, and man, he can sure condemn it.

I call it "social pollution." We've come along and we have the world's richest poor people and we've got the world's best-educated poor people. We educated them with the tube, as stupid as it may look. It opened up a world they never saw before. But when the social man has pushed for all the things he's pushed for, the education and everything else, he didn't look two weeks ahead either—he looked at tomorrow. Now they all want to be millionaires, and the rate we're going right now there's no way that's going to happen. Man is basically competitive. They may all start out equal but it ends right there, and I have never seen a guy in this country who worked hard who didn't make out.

The amount of bucks we spend a day is nothing. It represents 1.4 per cent of the budget. Health, education, and welfare, and all these social programs they're talking about get 43 per cent of the budget. I'll bet you my sweet bottom if they ran as efficient a program as has been run here, people wouldn't need to bitch about it. I'm not allowed to knock other government agencies because we're not theoretically in competition with them, but the public puts them in competition.

We've shut off the last three flights to the moon. I really don't understand the public's attitude. If they only realized what they are saving . . . absolutely nothing. By shutting off those three flights, they are saving less than a dollar a head in this country. A flight like Apollo XV costs $445 million to send to the moon. The operating costs out of that $445 million? About $50 million, maybe $60 million. That's what we save. The hardware's already been paid for. It was paid for in 1970, 1969, 1968. It's all just sitting there, and we've saved somewhere between $150 and $180 million dollars to sacrifice the last three flights to the moon.

It's really a shame. I don't feel badly about it. I got cut out. I would have had one of them. I think if that's what the people want`. . . but I don't think the people understand. I really don't think they understand. I don't think they realize. . . .

George Meany

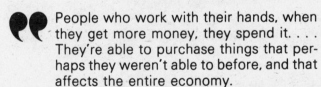

People who work with their hands, when they get more money, they spend it. . . . They're able to purchase things that perhaps they weren't able to before, and that affects the entire economy.

As President of the AFL–CIO seventy-eight-year-old George Meany represents a large share of the United States population: "In a sense more than the fourteen million membership. They have wives, they have families which make it much more than fourteen million, maybe forty million." This large following vests Meany with

enormous political leverage, which he has always been
willing to use over the past thirty years.

_____

There was tremendous progress made in the general
trade union work. General trade union work is all directed toward enhancing the welfare of workers as workers and as citizens. In other words, we're not just interested in wages and
hours. All during the long history of labor, our interests have
run far beyond wages and hours. We're interested in the worker
as a consumer; we're interested in him as a citizen in the community; we're interested in the community. We made progress in the legislative field, in the field of consumer protection,
civil rights and dozens of others. It's all in the record.

We played a major part in bringing about the enact-
ment of the education laws in the Sixties which placed the federal government in the position of responsibility for the education of all the children of America. During President Johnson's
time, federal aid to education in money terms went from a very
small amount, a billion or so, up to twenty or thirty billion
dollars. This was the first time where the federal government
accepted the theory that the education of the people of America
was a federal responsibility.

The contracts our unions made during the Sixties were
better than they had ever been before. The wages went up
considerably during the Sixties. We had inflation—not so bad
up to 1969—and of course that eats into any increases the workers get, but I would say the net increase was substantial.

How did this increase affect the people?

We don't do research work after we sign a contract that
increases wages for fifty thousand people. We assume that the
increased wages will be reflected in their standard of living and
so forth. The wage increases that came in the Sixties were reflected in a better life for the people who got the increases.
People who work with their hands, when they get more money,
they spend it. They save some of it, but a great deal of it goes

into better living. They're able to purchase things that perhaps they weren't able to purchase before, and that affects the entire economy. We don't go back to see, "Well, how did this affect you?" As far as going back and making some sort of a survey, we don't bother with that. We're always looking forward.

Saul Alinsky

 Most of the black civil rights leaders, they always come in and sit around with me late at night, going over strategy and stuff. But late at night, privately. . . .

Nearly forty years ago Saul Alinsky helped John L. Lewis organize the Congress of Industrial Organizations. Thirty years ago he united the workers, merchants, churches, and unions of Chicago's "Back of the Yards" neighborhood—the area referred to as *The Jungle* by Upton Sinclair—in a self-help program that remains powerful in Chicago today. In 1940 Alinsky founded the Industrial Areas Foundation in Chicago, a school for radical organizers where Cesar Chavez once studied. He battled city halls all across the country, as well as in other parts of the world. His goal was community control. In the summer of 1972 Saul Alinsky died at the age of sixty-three.

I remember being down at Vanderbilt or Duke and I was giving a lecture down there. This was a couple of years ago. Most of the black civil rights leaders, they always come in and sit around with me late at night, going over strategy and stuff. But late at night, privately, because the black leadership hasn't reached a point where they want to have a white seen advising them or anything of that sort. These blacks were all seated in one group off on the side of the auditorium, and I opened up by just looking at them and saying, "Well, now, I'm from the North, and up North the issues are different. I really don't know what the issues are down here in the South, but I know that they are very different because up North many of the black students are fighting for separate dormitories, they're fighting for separate eating places, separate tables. I know that you don't have those issues down here because you won that one years ago. You've had separate dormitories, separate eating places, separate everything for all these years." You could see the blacks turn around and look at each other in a state of real confusion, as if to say, "What the hell are we doing to ourselves?" Then when you sit around and you get in a conversation, they say, "Well, there's a difference between segregation and separatism. Segregation is when you, whitey, force us to do it. Separatism is when we decide on our own that we want to be separate." All I can say is what I've said to them: "You know, there's an old Portuguese cliché: 'It's the same old shit. Only the flies are different.'"

Your home base is Chicago. What was the city's reaction to the riot there in July of 1966?

Daley was laughing about it all the time. He figured it was saving the city a lot of money. The blacks burned down a lot of property in the black community, property that was marked condemned and was to be demolished. So by burning it down it saved the city the cost of demolishing this property. All they had to do was scoop it up.

They got a couple more OEO programs and they got a couple of portable swimming tanks. City hall is more conscious of it, but basically nothing has come out of it. You have to understand power. That's the argument I used to have with Dr. King. When King would have a demonstration outside of city hall, I used to say to him, "You're going to get chickenshit out of this."

Riots . . . yes, I would say they certainly exposed what was a hidden infection that a lot of whites didn't want to face, the racism of this kind of society which had always been kept under the carpet and always covered up with these cosmetic coverups, or just plain horseshit like brotherhood weeks, education and tutoring programs here, a health program here and a recreation program, Upwards Bound, Sideways Bound, and all the rest of that stuff. Job training when there weren't any jobs. When the riots broke, they had to face it, whether they wanted to or not. Now that was good. It's as good as going to a doctor finally and being diagnosed: this is your disease and you've got to take treatment. The unfortunate thing about it is that once the riot is over with, then everything cools back after a while. It's got to be a constant threat. If you had riots and riots and riots and riots, if they kept on one after another, you would have had a lot more changes. Look at Detroit after that riot. That was the worst one that we had in the country. So we got Ford and we got General Motors and we got department stores, we got everybody together in a big committee: "We've got to do something about the black situation, their living conditions, unemployment, and so forth and so on." Big programs launched. Big committees set up. There isn't a fuckin' thing on in Detroit now and there hasn't been in the last three years!

Howard Cosell

 . . . Muhammad Ali was the most important athlete of the 1960s. He was to become a figure transcendental to sports. . . .

For the past twenty years Howard Cosell has been closely tied to the sports world. He has announced most of the major heavyweight boxing matches of the decade, and has handled many other varied assignments as well. Proud of the fact that he is Phi Beta Kappa and "trained

in the law," Cosell is now the analyst on ABC television's
Monday night football games—"one of the top ten shows
in the country. I just don't understand it," he says.

You live a life in sports, and you're living a life in a
thimble. You're constantly engulfed by a worrisome lowness of
mass intelligence quotient. There still are a lot of people in this
country who want sport to be a looking-glass world, who are
shocked at somebody telling them that sport is human life and
that the same maladies that exist in the society exist in sport.

How would you characterize the development of
heavyweight boxing over the past years?

By chance, Patterson wound up in the Fourteenth
Street Gym, which was presided over by Cus D'Amato. And
Patterson, for the first time in his life, found a manner in which
to express himself. He felt secure, comfortable, part of society,
when he used his fists. Cus D'Amato understood this. Cus
D'Amato understood also that nature had somehow given this
young man enormous speed of legs and hands for his weight and
his size. The two became inseparable and Patterson's career as
a fighter was under way. He won the Golden Gloves as a middleweight in Helsinki. He came back, turned professional, and
gradually went up the ladder. He never really had the body of
a heavyweight, but Cus D'Amato was very smart, very shrewd,
very adroitly picked the right opponent. He did all the things a
manager is supposed to do for his fighter.

So the fiction grew that Floyd Patterson was a very great
fighter. He might have been a very great middleweight or light
heavyweight, but *never* a heavyweight. Nonetheless, all of the
sensitivities from his youth remained. He seemed so curiously
gentle and so curiously straight that he almost defied the public
image of a boxer, and always he had the public sympathy.
Strangely, he got the public sympathy most in the role of self-
martyrization: when he would lose, when he was knocked out by
[Ingemar] Johansson and went into seclusion. Then, extraor-

dinarily, on June 20, 1960, at the old Polo Grounds, he knocked out Johansson with as pulverizing a knockout as I've ever seen.

Then along came a man, a congenital thug, pugilism's gift to literacy and culture, named Charles "Sonny" Liston. Patterson simply could not emotionally face Liston. He couldn't have faced him physically either because, in his time, Liston was a very great fighter. And so Patterson, twice consecutively, was put to humiliating defeat by Liston; the second bout a virtual replay of the first, each first-round knockouts.

But Liston himself was nothing more nor less than a bully. He ascended to the championship at a relatively advanced age. He carried with him in his later years a birth certificate, ostensibly establishing that he was about ten years younger than most of us thought he was. And Liston, whose skills had begun to decline after the second fight against Patterson, was hardly a match for the brash young man who then came along.

Without question, the most important athlete in my lifetime and the most important athlete of the decade of the Sixties was Muhammad Ali. I amend that statement. Perhaps Muhammad Ali was not the most important athlete of my lifetime. An argument could be made, and a very good one, for Jackie Robinson. But certainly Muhammad Ali was the most important athlete of the 1960s. He was to become a figure transcendental to sports. He was to become a figure that could reveal how sport had changed through all the years, how sport was no longer a privileged sanctuary of life, a looking-glass world to be carefully protected by commissioners and operators and traditional sports writers and sport broadcasters who would feed to the public the Establishment pabulum that they had been feeding to them over all the years. Ali, as an individual, revealed how sports invaded the economics, the law, the politics, the sociology of this society. The manner in which he did this I think was self-evident, quite apart from the glory of his boxing skills.

Watching Ali fight, before his enforced idleness, was in its way as artful as listening to Heifetz play the violin, so great were Ali's skills. But the cold fact remains that Ali's boxing skills no longer matter. What will be remembered about him was not his greatness as a pugilist but rather that he symbolizes a very unpretty chapter in American history: how somehow this nation, once again, with its politics and with its sociology—with its racism, to put it squarely—could deprive a man of his constitutional rights, could utterly destroy him and yet, in the long run, actually not martyr him but glorify him. Because Ali won where it counted.

He exemplified the fact that what is popular is not always right. And what is right is not always popular. He exemplified it at a time when we were getting new leadership, governmentally, in this country. That new leadership seemed to bring out of the woodwork in its very early going all of the subterranean prejudices and hatreds that we had kept subterranean, that made us a normally civilized people despite our deficiencies of character. It was an astonishing thing in the 1960s—after two World Wars, after the Roosevelt era, after the judicial arm of the Government that had fostered such men as Marshall and Oliver Wendell Holmes and Louis Brandeis and Benjamin Cardozo and Felix Frankfurter—it was astonishing to think that on April 28, 1967, at 4800 San Jacinto Street—the Federal Customs Building in Houston, Texas—when a man rejected military induction, that within thirty minutes thereafter a politically appointed boob of a boxing commissioner in New York, by edict, could strip this man of his heavyweight championship and of his right or license to fight. But it happened, and the act was widely acclaimed, and was duplicated in all of the other states. There had been no arraignment; there had been no grand jury presentment; there had been no indictment; there had been no trial; there had been no conviction; there had been no appeal; there had been no ultimate appeal to the court of last resort, the Supreme Court of the United States.

Ultimately Ali was vindicated [by the Supreme Court], of course. But even as what happened to Ali outside the ring is the most important thing that happened in boxing in the 1960s —a matter that will be recorded in American history books, not the sport tomes put out by the men who follow the Mets and the

Jets and the Giants and the Yankees—so too we had in sports in the 1960s the growing fact that in all of sports what was happening outside of the arena was far more important than the competitions taking place within the arenas. That, to me, was the great change in sports in the American society during the 1960s.

Do you consider the events at the 1968 Olympics another example of this social importance of sports?

What [Tommie] Smith did, and what [Juan] Carlos did? That's one of the reasons I went to the Olympic Games. To cover just that kind of incident. They bowed their heads, they wore black socks, and they didn't stand at attention during the anthem. Their protest was symbolic, to indicate that they were a beleaguered people, that the beleaguerment extended even to sport. They wanted to call the attention of the entire world to the fact that they were beleaguered, that all of their people are beleaguered, and that beleaguerment did exist.

I stayed up all night and found Tommie Smith and induced him to come on the air and have him tell what he did and why he did it. Subsequently the U.S. Olympic Committee implied that the black athletes had taken payola and that they would be deprived of their medals. As the story leaked, resentment in the Olympic Village grew like a forest fire. It began in the American building with men like Harold Connally and Bill Toomey, and then to the French building, the West German building, the East German building, the British building, everywhere.

That was pure journalism. Had we not put him on the air and allowed him to tell his story, while all the newspapers around the world were carrying the protest front page, we would have been utterly deficient in our obligation, first to the public, second to the FCC, and third to ourselves. So we did what we had to do, and we did it very well. But I came back to this country and received in the mail copies of the Warren, Ohio, *Tribune,* a full-page ad taken out by a furniture dealer demanding my voluntary emigration from this country or governmental deportation for exposing the truth on the air.

*   *   *

The sports world is the toy department of human life. What kind of a society are we that people around this country can go crazy over these weekly polls? What is this terrible weakness in our society? Not ten minutes ago did I get a call from a young man in Arkansas, who was very pleasant, very cordial, then, "You said last night that Nebraska-Oklahoma would be the biggest college game since Notre Dame-Michigan State in 1966. What about the Arkansas-Texas game? I'm writing a letter of protest." How absurd that a man would spend the money to call long distance on a matter like that.

What is it about America . . . ?

I don't know, but it's a frightening and worrisome thing. I'd like to see the same fervor and the same enthusiasm that people apply to these silly events applied to an immediate cessation of hostilities in Vietnam, the leveling of the ghettos, the elimination of hunger and poverty and unemployment. I see no evidence of it in the society, except in one segment, our young people. It's our only hope. I admit that sport serves a very valid purpose in the provision of escape. People do have a hard time in just surviving, they do have problems. People are people. Prejudices and passions are inherent in all of us. So we'd probably go berserk in this society if we didn't have the escape that sport provides. But good Lord, there's got to be a mix! A balance. A sense of proportion.

PART 3

Christopher and Mary Nahas

 I don't think we want to see this war end, economically . . . the minute they hear the war is almost going to end, . . . you notice what happens in Wall Street. . . . There are so many industries depending on the war for their products.

Christopher Nahas works in the Ford Motor plant. He and his wife, Mary, have two children—a daughter just graduated from high school and a son just graduated from college. They live in northern New Jersey, a few blocks from the Lincoln Tunnel.

MRS. NAHAS We have been brought up to be patriots, defend your country and that, you know. And if my son had to go to war and defend his country, surely I would feel bad, but on the second hand I would feel that it is his duty. But this is not our war when you stop to think about it. It's obvious it's not our war. On the other hand, we cannot leave these people just be gobbled up. At least this is what they tell us.

It wasn't our war to begin with. Surely, we had compassion and went out to try and help these people, but we have had enough years to prove that what we were doing is not helping them or it would have come to an end.

So, I feel at this point, my son's losing his life for this cause will be losing it for nothing.

I don't think we want to see this war end, economically. Economically, I feel it has helped this country, because the minute they hear the war is almost going to end or we're pulling out or something, you notice what happens in Wall Street. The economy immediately takes a nosedive in Wall Street. There are so many industries depending on the war for their products.

How do you feel about the young people and their reaction to what is happening in this country?

MRS. NAHAS   As far as the hippie movement, I think there is a certain element that hurt this country, that hurt the nice boys who wanted to wear their hair a little bit longer instead of what we were accustomed to seeing. There is a certain group that I feel are just plain lazy. What do they call themselves? The love people?

MR. NAHAS   The flower people.

MRS. NAHAS   I think you can have these sort of things and still keep yourself looking well kept and holding a job or going to school, or whatever or what have you. Now, many a hippie will hear this and think I'm a terrible person to even categorize them in this respect. But I actually feel that way about some of them. I really do. They are marvelous people. I think there has been maybe more love in their heart than there has been since I was born. At least it has shown outwardly toward their fellow man. The only thing they have not been doing is their bit for society.

When they had the big thing at Woodstock, well, at first I thought what a wonderful thing that so many young people could get together and have a good time. But then we got all the information on what actually happened there. I don't think it was something that we can be especially proud of, some of the things that took place. There was smoking marijuana. And all this sort of thing was going on like it was an everyday occurrence. They went out and swam in the nude. They tell you, "We were born this way." Maybe I'm going to sound prudish, but it's not the accepted thing of society to do this sort of thing.

MR. NAHAS   Well, there are pros and cons on that Woodstock condition, if you want to call it that. Some people are for it, some are against it. There are pros and cons.

MRS. NAHAS   Culture has brought us up this way and that is why we won't change. Our generation, my husband's and mine, won't change as far as our culture and our background.

MR. NAHAS   You must figure who on earth is perfect. No one on earth is perfect.

MRS. NAHAS   This new generation thinks it is quite all right. Now that *Hair*. Did you see it? Well, Barbara went not too long ago, and I was really quite horrified when I knew what took place. I had heard it was "a little bit," you know, but then she said it was "mostly." It came dark when that [nudism] took place. She said it was beautiful. She took it as the whole generation would take it. I mean, it was a beautiful thing, you know. Letting yourself go, so to speak. But back to convention again. We were not brought up this way. I just can't sit here and tell you I think this is right.

MR. NAHAS   This is something altogether different from our childhood. This is all something new. Wow! This did not go on in our day.

Joseph A. Califano

 Most of the Great Society programs were directed toward putting people in a position where they could stand on their own

two feet and pull off their own piece of
the economic pie.

After serving as an editor of the *Harvard Law Review* and
graduating *magna cum laude* in 1955, Brooklyn-born Joseph Califano practiced law in New York for six years
before heading to Washington for a decade of public
service. In 1964 President Johnson appointed him a Special Assistant to the President. It did not take long for this
intense and energetic young lawyer to become chief architect of the social legislation of the Great Society.
Califano is now with the Washington law firm of Williams, Connolly and Califano, and numbers among his
clients the Democratic National Committee.

I came to Washington in 1961 on a leave of absence
from a New York law firm for a year to do the legal work for the
McNamara reorganization effort at the Pentagon. I went
through a series of jobs in the Pentagon—as General Counsel
of the Army and then as McNamara's assistant. Then went to
work for Lyndon Johnson in July of 1965. I didn't know the
President when I went to work for him.

I think what Johnson saw was basically this. We looked
at the country. We looked at the United States of America. We
looked at two hundred million people and essentially said,
"About one hundred fifty to one hundred sixty million people
will be taken care of if we have an economic policy with a solid
growth, a growth without inflation of about four and one-half or
five percent. The remaining forty to fifty million people will
need some extra help to get their share of the economic pie.
That help really breaks down into two kinds: first, there are
people for whom no job training programs, no education programs, can be of any assistance. Essentially these are the very
old, the totally disabled, the mentally incompetent, or what have
you. Roughly ten to fifteen million people. For those people, the
society has to provide either the services they need to live at
some level of human dignity or money so they can buy those

services. Out of that came the Medicare program and our attempts, which failed unfortunately, to extend Medicare to certain groups below sixty-five. Ultimately we would have liked to have extended it to everybody. And programs relating to increases in income maintenance for people. We looked at income-maintenance programs—they were just politically not possible in the Sixties. So what we did essentially was to pump as much money into the lowest levels of society as we could through traditional programs. That's why Social Security increases of fifty-nine percent at the lowest level were proposed. That's why we attempted to increase veterans' benefits—especially for the highly disabled veterans. That's why we tried to make changes in the welfare program and the unemployment and insurance compensation programs. Essentially using existing programs to achieve an income-maintenance structure.

The other group of people, the other twenty-five million people, are essentially people that could get their share of economic prosperity if they had essentially the kind of help that your parents or my parents or somebody in our family gave us. If they had decent health care, if they had a decent education, if they had an opportunity to go on to higher education, or if they had some job training or retraining, or if they had a decent environment to live in—a house, some reasonable police protection, what have you—if they had the material things and training necessary to have a decent family or community structure . . . it was at those people that all the manpower training programs were directed. It was at those people that the poverty programs were directed. In 1963, when John Kennedy died, the federal government was training seventy-five thousand people in manpower training programs. In January of 1969, when Lyndon Johnson left the White House, one and a half million people were being trained in federal training programs. A dramatic change in the government's role in that area.

The next element of it was, all right, if you give to a guy the training he needs or the education he needs to break into that sphere, then you've got to make sure that there are no arbitrary barriers to his either getting employed when he wants to get employed or using the money when he wants to use the money. That really was essentially the function of two kinds of programs. The civil rights program to break down the employment barrier—the Equal Employment Opportunity Commission legislation, the fair housing legislation of 1964; the 1964, 1966, 1967, 1968 civil rights bills.

The other area was a more overtly economic area and it was basically the consumer arena. Johnson's view on that was really quite simple: in the marketplace in the 1960s in America the individual was at an enormous disadvantage. The housewife in the supermarket, or the serviceman trying to buy a house, or the husband trying to buy a car had against him or her a tremendous array of talent. Advertising experts, psychologists, lawyers, accountants, marketing people, television—everything. The role of the government in that arena was to equalize the situation a little bit. In the larger context of the Great Society, the government assumed the role of trying to say, "When you earn the dollar, we'll try to get you a fair shake for the dollar. If you spend the dollar, we'll try to get you a fair shake for it."

Exactly what efforts were made along those lines?

My God! The consumer programs—there must have been at least two dozen consumer programs coming out of the Johnson Administration. The first one . . . another indication of the way things changed dramatically in the Sixties. In January of 1966, when we proposed the Automobile Safety Bill, we put it in the Transportation Department Message of the President, the message on transportation. Not in a consumer message, because we felt that consumer items were just dead as soon as they hit the Hill. Anything identified as such was dead! In January of 1967, a year later, we sent a consumer message to the Congress with almost a dozen bills in it. Even before the Traffic Safety Bill got through, thanks to General Motors and a few other mistakes that were made, we had begun calling it consumer legislation, not transportation legislation. That whole area just ballooned, and it ballooned in a funny way. When the State of the Union

Message went to the Congress in January of 1966, the next day we were reading it in the papers, and we all noticed that the Traffic Safety proposal was in the first two or three paragraphs of every newspaper story on the State of the Union Message. And it was competing with proposals like Model Cities, like four-year terms for Congressmen, clean air legislation, clean water legislation. Yet Ralph Nader's book was not even a best-seller at that point. Nobody had heard of Ralph Nader, but we had read his book in galley proof.

Lyndon Johnson is criticized for letting Vietnam destroy the Great Society. Did it?

No, I don't think it did. Most of these programs are still on the books. The programs that have suffered most have been the poverty program, which is fairly well emasculated today; and the failure of the present administration and the Congress—and they probably reflect the people—to really provide the funds and the staff to enforce the fair housing legislation. Those two areas suffered severely. The other areas are underfunded, but you've got to remember a couple of things. One: I don't think there is any reason to believe there would have been one dollar more for domestic programs had there been no Vietnam War. I think if you need any indication of that, all you have to do is look at what's happening today. There's not a penny more going into domestic programs. The Congress today is lowering taxes of the American people as fast as if not faster than the Vietnam War is winding down. That's exactly what happened after Korea; that's exactly what happened after World War One; that's exactly what happened after World War Two. So there's no equation in that sense.

There is a political equation involved, though, which was costly. We reached a point, I suppose, by mid-1967 where all the conservative elements were against the Great Society programs, and had been, but the liberals started jumping us on the war. We were faced with this constant attack from both sides, for different reasons. They both began to coincide in small ways, in ways not noticeable to the guy who's just reading *The New York Times*. Those things are noticeable today. The vote in the Senate on the Foreign Aid Bill three weeks ago [November 1971]—you never would have beaten foreign aid if the liberals and conservatives hadn't gotten together. For entirely different reasons they voted to defeat foreign aid. We were feeling that in appropriations; a few million dollars less for this, a couple hundred million dollars less for that, in our ability to move legislation through the House. If you're a liberal President, it's much more difficult to move stuff through the House than through the Senate. We were starting to feel that. We had a minor skirmish, but we lost it. We were defeated in trying to get the debt limit increased, because in addition to all the conservatives in the House in 1967, they picked up a half a dozen or a dozen liberals who voted not to increase the debt limit because they were opposed to the Vietnam War. It hurt in those ways but I don't think it hurt in the sense that we would have been able to obtain money for domestic programs. We never would have been able to get tax increases for domestic programs. They were still too controversial.

Where do you see the Great Society and Lyndon Johnson fitting into American history?

In terms of the past, I think the New Deal was essentially a "handout" and the Great Society was essentially a "hand up." Most of the New Deal programs either provided cash, welfare, public housing, service in effect or makework to a large degree. The Great Society, while keeping all of that and using that, tried to isolate those programs to the people that really needed them, the people that I told you about earlier. Most of the Great Society programs were directed toward putting people in a position where they could stand on their own two feet and pull off their own piece of the economic pie. Health, education, manpower training, vocational education, that kind of thing.

I'm not a historian so it's very hard for me to render

some Olympian judgment on the historic significance of the Great Society. I do think that most of those programs are on the books for a decade at least. The issue will be the extent to which they'll be funded. That will depend on whether, in a somewhat oversimplified way, the Republicans or Democrats win.

> *When you were sketching these programs on the drawing board, what did you think then? Did you feel that this was just a typical legislative program of the President, or was there something special?*

It was extraordinary. We *knew*. There were roughly thirty to forty federal grant-in-aid programs when Johnson took office in November of 1963. By January of 1969 there were four hundred fifty. There has never been anything like that in the history of this country. James McGregor Burns, in a lengthy book review of Johnson's book [*The Vantage Point*], pointed out that the most important and eloquent pages in the whole book are really on the back flap, where these bills are just listed. You have to remember some things. No President had ever sent the Congress a message on the cities before Lyndon Johnson was President. No President ever sent the Congress a message on air pollution. No President had ever sent the Congress a message on water pollution. President Kennedy sent a consumer message to the Congress for the first time in history which mentioned, gently, truth in packaging. Johnson sent consumer messages to the Congress that put the government in areas nobody had ever thought about before. There was a tremendous sense of action.

There was an enormous sense of the revolution in relation to the blacks. That this was it! That this was pushing them over the top. In every respect! Not only the legislative programs we were passing, but the attention that Johnson was giving to it. He put as much passion and work into that issue as he did into the Vietnam issue, and it was even more unpopular politically. The appointments: putting a black on the Supreme Court; putting a black on the Federal Reserve Board; putting a black in the

Cabinet. It had never happened before in our country. They were important acts. Symbolically important acts. They showed to young black Americans that they could get there. There it was, all the way at the top, and they could get there.

> *How do you feel about all this now? Given what's happened since . . . has your enthusiasm dwindled? What are your feelings about where this country is going?*

Among the biggest problems of this country is that people are not willing to commit to the public social problems the kinds of resources—money and talent—necessary to get those problems solved. That means more taxes. This country puts about thirty per cent of its GNP, three hundred billion dollars, into the public sector. In England, you put thirty-eight per cent in the public sector, another eighty billion dollars in comparable terms for this country. People aren't yet willing to do that. I don't know what you have to do to get them to do that. You certainly can't have much more crime in the major urban centers today. Education can't be much worse than it is in most metropolitan public school systems than it is today. Yet they're still not willing to pass bond issues. That's the gut problem, and it's aggravated enormously if you have someone in the Presidency who's not trying to get them to do that. If I look back, one of the major things we probably made a mistake on was to lower taxes as fast as we did. We probably should have cut them a little slower. Taken the economic spurt a little slower and held on to more of that public money, because it is virtually impossible to increase taxes. That, I suppose, is more frustrating to me than anything else. I think, in terms of specific programs, everything except poverty and fair housing basically will be increasingly supported with money and staff, even under a conservative administration. Largely because constituencies develop for these programs and they put more pressure on to get bigger and bigger pieces of the pie.

Will President Nixon's revenue-sharing proposal have a positive impact on these social programs?

Revenue sharing isn't going to do any good if there's no revenue to share, and there is no revenue to share. That's one of the great myths perpetrated by politicians at every level. There are mayors who say they desperately need it. There are governors who say they desperately need it. The White House saying they're going to provide it. They're going to provide it by trying to take it out of other programs. It's all coming out of the same thing and it won't make one ounce of difference in New York City if Nixon's revenue-sharing plan were in effect today. That money is funny money.

Paul Banner *

 . . . they got into fire action. . . . He got hit and he still went on and directed his team and completed the mission; then he was evacuated by helicopter. I guess that's about what happened.

Paul Banner handles the real estate for a restaurant chain in the Midwest. In his fifties, he has raised seven children —all grown or away at school. One son, John*, won the Congressional Medal of Honor in Vietnam.

My son John went through the OCS [Officer Candidate School] program and got his commission, and then he was accepted into this SEAL program to be trained. It's sea and air and land, and I don't know where the "e" part of it comes in. It's a program where first you qualify as a frogman and then after that they take you for SEAL training. I think about ninety-seven per cent of the trainees that enter the program never get through. We thought it was kind of a high risk. I'm sure that John felt that it was high risk. I'm sure that the services felt it was high risk because they give extra pay for overseas training. They drew pay as a senior parachutist and they drew extra pay as a SEAL member. So there's no question it was a high-risk area, and it was a volunteer service. I don't think you go into that without the dedication that you're doing something for your country and have something you should offer. There's a possibility of losing your life.

Had he ever contemplated using his asthma or psoriasis as an escape from the service?

As far as I'm concerned, I don't see how he possibly could have. His legs, like from his knees down to his ankles, are just completely running sores all the time. He worked hard to heal it, to cure it up. He'd take this ointment and put it on and then wrap his legs in cellophane or Saran Wrap, and keep it on his legs for several weeks so that it would cure it. You couldn't hardly say that you were trying to get out of the draft by doing it. All you'd have to do is walk in there with legs like that, and all you'd have to do is walk out in one of Kansas' wheatfields when the pollen was going, and then go down and take your physical.

Here's a boy that started off in early 1967, and you add up the years and months it's been since early 1967 to date, and this is the time that John has been involved in this thing. Even this last summer when he was operated on in Omaha and he said, "Oh, I'm just going over there to get some oral surgery at the dental clinic. Don't bother coming over." So after he gets over there and has the operation, we find out he was on the operating table seven and one half hours. So it's not a very minor-type thing. He's got five years involvement in this! That's a long time.

The actual time that he was over there was rather limited . . . the actual number of days or even hours. He got a Bronze Star for one of the activities he was on. The type activity a SEAL does . . . they'll take them in a submarine under water and let them out. They go in back of the enemy lines. The mission where he got hurt and got the Medal of Honor, he went in from the ocean side and scaled a wall of about three hundred fifty feet, descended down into the camp, and his mission was to capture these frogmen that were conducting the same kind of activity he was engaged in. Well, he captured these people.

Actually, we knew very little about what he did as far as getting the Medal of Honor until we read it on the citation. He had mentioned that he was put in for it, and then we got a notification from the Navy about it. His SEAL team went in and they scaled this high cliff from the sea side and they went down into the camp where the underwater demolition teams had been working and operating from. Their mission was to capture the personnel and bring them back for interrogation. Which they did. That was about it. John got hit with a grenade during the action and lost a leg out of it. He had quite a lot of scars all over himself where he had been hit.

Precisely why was he distinguished with the Medal of Honor?

When they got in close to the camp where the Viet Cong demolition team was operating, where their base was, well of course they got into fire action, crossfire. He got hit and he still went on and directed his team and completed the mission; then he was evacuated by helicopter. I guess that's about what happened.

What sparked his misgivings about whether or not he should accept the medal?

I don't think that he exactly ever said that he wasn't going to accept the medal.

He was just uncertain for a while?

I talked to him last night. He was back in the hospital, in the Navy Hospital in Philadelphia, where, I don't know, seven hundred amputees come in there over a period of time and then go out of there and are replaced by another seven hundred and fifty and another seven hundred fifty. A fellow like Bill Lubell* who lost both legs and his arms and half of his intestines and insides—if you look at him from his neck up, you see a person who is intelligent, a person who went back and got his degree in law; but if you look from the neck down, he's just a mess. I'm sure this is one thing that John would say, "Gee, I look at what Bill went through. It really wasn't worth it." I think you can't help but read in the papers today, you can't help but see what's going on over there and you aren't quite so sure. Now John brings up this business of going to jail. You say, "Well, John, would you go to jail today if they called you to go?" And I don't think he can answer that. Any more than I can answer it. But what he's saying is that if you knew that you yourself were going to lose both your legs and your insides and your arms, that you'd be in that kind of condition for the rest of your life; and this was the kind of thing you were going to face; and if you didn't feel that you were really serving your country, would you do this? He wants people to think about it. I tell him, "John, there must be a different way than the way you say it, rather than just saying, 'I'd go to jail.' "

*　　*　　*

Here were twelve boys receiving the Medal of Honor in Washington, D. C., and everybody was afraid that there would be demonstrations against them. They were concerned about the security. It really wasn't an atmosphere that the people of the country were behind them. They gave the ceremony but it was all a real hush-hush-type thing. They didn't parade them down the streets and say, "These are the boys who won the Medal of Honor." No, they kept you all kind of quite in the background. They got you in and they ran the thing and they got their press release and you went on home.

They even . . . and I don't know whether this was true or not . . . but they said they changed the dates on it because of security and public-relations problems. So the President's wife was not there and his daughter was.

When John came back and when he won the Medal of

Honor . . . you'd think the Mayor would write the guy a letter and say "Congratulations!" but he didn't. You'd think there would be one civic club who would say, "Would you come and talk to us," but there wasn't. You'd think the Chancellor where he's been enrolled in school would write and congratulate him, but he didn't. Most of the people . . . you kind of got the impression that you were kind of guilty because you went over and shot all these people. You did something bad. This is the reaction I get. You go along and people all look down! They won't look you in the eye. They're kind of ashamed of what went on. With this type of reaction, this type of background, and this experience that you run into—really, what is the value of the Medal of Honor? It kind of degrades him. I'll tell you an experience that John had. When he came back from the Naval Hospital, he flew into Wichita. He came in late at night and didn't have a ride out to where we live, so he announced on the speaker, "If anybody is going such and such a way, will you give me a ride?" Do you know how many people gave him a ride? Nobody! I don't think John expected everybody to stand up and play the band and everything else, but you do kind of think that somebody at least is going to say, "As the Mayor of the town, I congratulate you on winning the Medal of Honor," but they don't want to associate with you.

After all that John has gone through, do you personally feel we belong in Vietnam?

I think today that people should quit talking about the thing in Vietnam. I think . . . well, why don't we go out and do something that's constructive? You read about the river project in the Mekong Delta . . . the money we're spending in a year over there, how much good that could do! Instead of worrying whether there's a Bolshevik or a Communist or a Chinaman, how great it would be if we just spent one year's effort doing something good over there? Certainly the world . . . you have to learn to live with other people, and I feel we should start doing this. Like Tom Dooley. [The famed "jungle doctor" known for his efforts in providing medical aid to refugees fleeing North Vietnam during the Indochina War of 1954. He extended his aid to other underdeveloped countries, most notably Laos, and later was a co-founder of Medico, Inc., an international medical aid organization. He died of cancer in 1961.] See the effort that somebody like this individual put forth, see how much more good that does our country than all the bombs we send over there. And why do we assume that the North Vietnamese are going to be so horrible? It used to be that we thought the Chinese were great. We sent all the gifts we had over there. We had more hatred probably for the Japanese than the Chinese. You can run a film like *Tora, Tora, Tora* and get everybody coming out madder than heck.

James M. Roche

 It's a very simple thing to pick at the fringes of something like our system, and it is another thing to create this system and build it . . . the history of America has been one of steady progress. The automobile is a perfect example.

Sixty-four-year-old James Roche has spent forty-three of those years with General Motors, the biggest industrial concern in the world. On December 31, 1971, he resigned as Chairman of the Board, but continues as a Director. His salary reached as high as $790,000 a year when he was Chairman. In March 1966 Roche was called before a Senate subcommittee to apologize for General Motors' surveillance of Ralph Nader, following Nader's publication of *Unsafe at Any Speed,* a book highly critical of GM's Corvair.

We have reached the epitome of what any society has ever reached in the history of the world. When we look at what we have put together here in the United States over the years that we have been a nation, we have made the most remarkable progress of any other country or any other system in the history of the world. While we're far from a perfect society, it's still a better society than exists in other places: from the standpoint of our educational facilities, from the standpoint of the progress we've made in health, from the standpoint of the economic progress we've made, from the standpoint of our cultural progress, the opportunities that are available.

There will always be unfinished business. I don't think we're ever going to reach the status of our affairs where everybody is going to have everything that they aspire to. We have to look at these things on a relative basis as compared to other countries. When we compare what we've been able to achieve as a nation, as a people working within the framework of our democratic system of government, within the framework of our free enterprise system, we have made more progress than anybody else has made. That doesn't mean that the job is finished, that doesn't mean that everybody thinks that they have got what they would like to have, but collectively we *have* made this progress.

But there is a feeling in many quarters that we are pursuing the wrong goals.

I don't think that Americans have been pursuing the wrong goals. I suppose that the striving for a better objective is a natural part of the average person's makeup. The so-called dissatisfaction has been greatly exaggerated. I think that we have in the United States a great silent majority who are pretty well satisfied with their lot. If we didn't, we couldn't have the kind of a government that we have today.

Certainly we can't deny the fact that there is some poverty in our country. There's poverty throughout the world, always has been, and perhaps there always will be. Certainly we can't hide the fact that we've had discrimination in our country; we're in the process of trying to fix that. But I think in too many cases we've been accenting the negative without looking over our shoulder to see what the positives are.

Is this dissatisfaction—this constant pressing at the problems of the day—a healthy attitude for our society?

This has been the history of the United States. We're looking at the problems in a little different way today than we were before. In too many cases the alleged solutions are the result of oversimplification. We started out in this country with a lot of problems. We started out really with a wilderness, and we have had to build on that wilderness and develop and solve these problems: transportation problems, agricultural problems, the problems of making a living, creating schools, creating churches—all of the nice things that go along in life. We have done this, but we have done it with our eyes to the future without disparaging the accomplishments of the past.

The average American citizen is a pretty sound individual. I think he knows what his own situation is and I think he, in the main, enjoys his state of life. He owns a home, he owns an automobile, he has reasonable working hours, he's reasonably prosperous. The people are living a reasonably good life, and they enjoy it. Most people would like to do better than they are, but in the main I think we've got a very solid core of people in the United States who feel pretty good about the way things are going.

How do you feel about the rise of consumer interests, as led by Ralph Nader?

Consumerism is not new. Everybody who's been in business has always had a responsibility to satisfy the customer; and if they didn't discharge that responsibility, they didn't last very long. There isn't anything new about this at all. No businessman has any quarrel with the consumer, because they are the very lifeblood of his business. These things called consumerism have been blown up out of proportion to their real significance.

To take our own automobile industry, for example: an automobile is a mechanical product, mass-produced, and it's sold at a very, very low price. Any mechanical product requires service, it requires care, it requires attention. An automobile has thousands of different parts; many of them receive very little maintenance. Indeed, a large proportion of vehicles today after they leave the factory are never inside again until they go to the graveyard. We focus on the occasional problem which somebody has with an automobile instead of watching the thousands and the millions of times that a car has to start—and does—in cold and heat and rain and dry weather. We watch them streaming in and out of our cities every day, and it's very seldom that you see one that's disabled or broken down in the course of this traffic. While there may be many things that can be done, American business has done a pretty responsible job taking care of its customers. There are exceptions and there are cheats, and to this extent the so-called consumerism can play an important part, but when they attempt to impute to every business a greed and a disregard for the welfare of the customers, as some of the consumer activists do, I think they're doing our society and their country a great disservice.

Is there need for a watchdog, a person such as Ralph Nader?

We have a democratic system, a democratic political system, and our political system should take care of this without having a group of individuals, self-appointed, take it on themselves.

It's a very simple thing to pick at the fringes of something like our system, and it's another thing to create this system and build it, step by step, in a competitive market. I think we all do things that maybe we'd do differently if we had a second choice. But again, the history of America has been one of steady progress. The automobile is a perfect example. The automobile is only seventy years old as we know it in the United States today, and when you look at what we started with and at what a modern automobile does today, it's a remarkable record of progress. You can take anything . . . and we are taking everything today in the United States . . . we're taking the schools, we're taking the churches, we're taking the government, we're taking business . . . each of these areas is coming in for criticism. We've gotten these magnificent institutions in this country! It's easy to pick at the fringes and find out what the flaws are. It would be quite something else to try to start over again and say, "What kind of a system should we build?" We've got to be careful that we don't throw out what we've got. What we've got to do, whether we like it or whether we don't, is to build on the base that we have today. This is a tremendous base of accomplishment. If we just say, "Well, the hell with this, it's all wrong, we're going to throw it out and start over again," then we've really got some trouble.

Thomas P. F. Hoving

 There is a . . . middle ground between Lindsay and Daley. Both are either revered or despised, probably for the wrong reasons. . . . One has to break away from ideology.

Thomas P. F. Hoving was asked by John V. Lindsay to author a "White Paper on the Parks and Recreation" for his first Mayoralty campaign in New York City. After Lindsay's victory, Hoving took a leave from the Metropolitan Museum of Art to become Parks Commissioner of New York City. During his short term in that post, Hoving excited New York with a series of events dubbed "Hoving's Happenings." He returned to the Metropolitan Museum in 1968 as Director.

It really had come down to one word: "No." No fun, no breathing, no bicycling, no kite flying, no walking on the grass. I spent five months researching the political position paper, the "White Paper on Parks and Recreation." I had a team of three people besides myself. We visited every park in the city—two hundred seventy-six of them. We talked to community groups and hundreds of people who were using them: mothers, children, employees in the Parks Department. We took a line out of the early books on parks which said that the parks were the lungs of the city. They were the places for refreshment and were in direct contrast to the knockdown asphalt attitude and feel of the rest of the town.

The first thing that one had to do about the safety problem was to break the credibility gap. We looked into the statistics and found that the parks were far safer than the streets. We began to urge the public to use the parks on the theory that people will protect themselves. They did—well, pickpocketing went up in my regime, but major crimes and violence dropped radically.

How did the first "happenings" begin?

Rheingold Brewery and its president, Bernie Relin, started them. We went to Bernie and said, "Why not have the great singers, bands, Puerto Rican and Cuban bands, Led Zeppelin, Judy Collins, Joan Baez come and sing in the skating rink twice each evening during the summer. Make it into an exciting modern theater, charge a dollar." It happened. The place was packed every night.

We once had an enormous festival in the winter. We had the luck to have about a foot and a half of snow, and as soon as I heard the report, I told my people not to plow in Prospect Park, Van Cortlandt Park, Central Park, and in Staten Island's Silver Lake. The people had an incredible time sledding and skating. It was complete relief from the rest of the city.

Times Square had become a pressing problem at New Year's Eve. We picked the Bethesda Terrace as a new celebration place. That suddenly became the place where people came and joyfully enacted the midwinter hoopla. Eight or nine thousand people showed up the first year and fifty thousand the next.

Another project. We took Bryant Park, which is in back of the Public Library on Forty-second Street, a park which was well known for the number of bums sleeping in it at night, and the enormous amount of broken glass—more broken glass per square foot than any park in the world. We talked to the businesses in the area and asked them to contribute to afternoon musical concerts. We put in the first outdoor sculpture show—Tony Smith's works. We had fashion shows, lectures, poetry readings, minstrels, jugglers. We had a great team of acrobats come in. Suddenly, that park, which had been a real problem, stopped being a problem.

How did you go about establishing bicycling in Central Park?

Henry Barnes, the great traffic commissioner, was in charge of traffic. But I found that I was in charge of the shape, the size, the width, and the entrances of the roads. So I told Henry, "I'll just simply put up a curb three feet high at the entrances of these parks on weekends, and that's that." He screamed and beefed and yelled and said that I was killing him. The Saturday biking spree started off with a couple hundred people the first days. Now you get ten, fifteen thousand people using the parks on Saturdays, Sundays, and on Tuesday evenings. People drive in from New Jersey with bikes on top of the car.

A guy once came to me, an East Indian. He said that he was a kite flyer. He made kites and he taught kite-flying. He said that there's a local statute that prohibits the flying of kites. I said, "Well, that seems pretty silly." I had a couple of young lawyers look into why, and they found that kites were disallowed because they frightened the horses. Acting upon the belief that a General Motors car is not going to get overexcited by a kite, I waived the thing and suddenly a whole group of kite-flying clubs began to work.

My staff and I were nothing more than brokers for peoples' ideas. We'd hear of something and we'd try it. We never said "no." In some cases there were some pretty silly events, but in a large percentage of the cases it worked. The situation was ripe for it. The people wanted it. After thirty-five years of "no" suddenly there was "yes."

My efforts were a very determined attempt to go deeply into the middle class. My assessment was that New York City is primarily a middle-class city, that it is not a big ghetto area as some people think and is certainly not controlled by the effete, sophisticated small group. They're never around. They just yap sometime but they never accomplish anything. We spent most of our time finding out what people in Wabash Towers wanted, what people on Staten Island would like to see and have. I think that was the success of it, that it was based upon a very solid middle section.

How do you react to those who speak of the urban crisis?

Generally, they're probably people who have not been really walking through the streets of the city and talking to people. They've been holed up in some office or some academic institution where they are positing certain broad economic problems and trying to translate them into pieces of the quality of life. If you go into parts of the city, from the deep Jewish section, to Italian sections, even to the very solid black upper middle class in Harlem, you find there are a great many constructive ideas of what to do. You will also find a considerable amount of cash from citizens and foundations to enact some of these things.

Our festivals were enacted as fragments of overall life. You have to have some frankly kooky things sometimes, to take people's minds off the rest of the time, which is monotonous, tough. A whole city lives the way a human being does.

I don't think New York is declining, I think it's shifting. It's an organic situation. The greatest sin that a city can do is not being tough enough to update, change, and make better its buildings, its facilities, its parks.

The very important thing about any city is to realize again that it's not just one attitude, one thrust, one philosophy. This is where the Lindsay Administration went wrong: it ignored the middle class. There has been kind of a veering away from the commonsense balance. There are people who a very short period of time ago were not middle class. They have worked like hell and they have made it; they want to get their children into safe, good schools, better schools. They want their community kept up, cleaned up and so on.

That's the problem. There is a strange middle ground between Lindsay and Daley. Both are either revered or despised, probably for the wrong reasons. It was great that John went to the streets and cooled off this city because it would have been busted like Chicago, Detroit, and Washington. He did an incredible job! Incredible! But the mistake was that he thought that this was the way to handle the city all the time. The city administration is a public servant and it is for *everybody*. Hurry-up clean-up jobs and spot rehabilitation were done in certain ghetto areas, but the middle-class areas were being allowed to deteriorate. That was wrong.

So the running of cities has to be distinguished from ideology. Running a city is not to proclaim an ideology. Running a city is to make it run. One has to break away from ideology.

Carol Doda

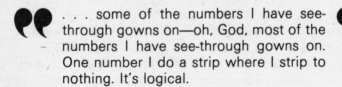 . . . some of the numbers I have see-through gowns on—oh, God, most of the numbers I have see-through gowns on. One number I do a strip where I strip to nothing. It's logical.

In early 1964 Carol Doda first danced the Swim in a
Gernreich topless (see pp. 60–64). Her act, at the Condor
in San Francisco, was a sensation and heralded the opening of hundreds of other topless nightclubs. A year later
she was arrested. Defended by Melvin Belli, she was acquitted and her act deemed "within contemporary community standards."

I was working as sort of a go-go dancer–cocktail wait-
ress combination, and one day my boss came to me and said,
"This is your new costume." Obviously, since it was topless, I
couldn't wait on the customers. I had to graduate to the stage,
which was a piano at the time, which went up and down from the
floor to the ceiling. It was like an elevator, up and down, up and
down.

Do you see yourself as a leader in the new morality?

No, I see myself as a humanitarian, whatever that
means.

I was going to say, what does that mean?

Well, it covers a lot of things. A humanitarian is somebody who does things for people. So that covers a lot of things:
entertaining people. I don't know how to go into that except to
say I'm a humanitarian. I dig entertaining people.

*And you think that the topless is far more effective
along these lines?*

Have you seen the show?

No, I haven't.

Well, maybe you'd better stick around and see it and
then add your own footnote. I don't do just topless. That was
in the early Sixties when I did just topless. I've graduated a little
bit now. We do a little production here.

You say you've graduated. Is this better?

Is what better?

Going topless, and going bottomless, and the whole bit.

I'm not "going" anywhere. It just happens that I'm known for that, right? I can't get away from it. So some of the numbers I have see-through gowns on—oh, God, most of the numbers I have see-through gowns on. One number I do a strip where I strip to nothing. It's logical.

A lot of people think it's wrong. They think it's wrong until they do it. Now, do they think it's wrong to get undressed and take a shower? Suppose they look at themselves in the mirror. Is that wrong when they see themselves nude?

Of course, they're not doing it in front of thousands of people. The more I say, it sounds like I'm defending myself; and I don't want to have to do that because we have a lot of people who come to see the show and they're not interested in just looking at topless. Okay, it *was* a fad, but now it's something.

Ruth Applewhite

 I think if people would talk about it less, there wouldn't be as much of what we call a 'generation gap.'

Ruth Applewhite lives with her husband in an apartment in Jackson, Mississippi. She is eighty years old. Her husband was a public health officer until his retirement in 1958.

How do you feel about miniskirts?

Just what do you think an old lady like me is apt to think? I don't think they've been altogether for the good. I think there's been a great deal of foolishness and maybe un-wholesomeness exhibited in dress. I don't care for the real, real short dresses that are being worn and have been worn even by the girls who are not grown. The kids that came into church this morning! A few years ago it would have stopped the services!

What is it about miniskirts that you object to?

Well, you ought to know! I really think it amounts to undue exposure. I don't think it's pretty and I don't think it's good. I've read some people who are smarter than I am that say it wasn't good. I don't think so either, even on my own. I don't think it's graceful or pretty in any way. I think most people, men and women, look better a little more covered up.

What would you say the proper length of a skirt is?

Now, not mine! Mine are longer than most people's. But I think that most any woman should have her knee covered up. Mrs. Nixon wears hers down to the knee, covers up the kneecap. I think that's a pretty length.

What brought this change about?

Oh, there are many reasons. I don't know what's bring-ing it on except it seems to be a general trend, not only in clothes but in many ways. I don't know what's the cause of it, only I think people got awfully careless. It's a lot easier to be careful and try to be particular if you're dressed right for it than if you're just going wild. If you get too careless about the way you look, you're apt to be that way about what you say and what you think. It seems to me that it's all part of the whole. I'm handicapped by realizing that I'm in a hopeless minority.

What do you think of the Beatles?

The group's broken up now, hasn't it? Well, I heard some rather derogatory things about their manner of life, and I heard some derogatory things about their music from some people who don't like that type of music. But a great many people have apparently gone crazy about them—most of the young ones, I think.

I didn't think they were going to do the country any good. I was surprised that they became as much of a fad as they did, because the kind of music they made leaves me cold.

What do you mean when you say they didn't do the country any good?

I mean by that that they were going to encourage the trends that I have not thought were good for the country. You know, people have said so much, there's been so much printed and all about young people being crazy about that kind of music and young people doing this and young people doing that, until young people think they've got to be different and think they've got to be slightly *crazy* in order to live up to their reputation. I think if people would talk about it less, there wouldn't be as much of what we call a "generation gap." I don't see how they could be so terribly much different than the young ones of a generation or two generations behind them. They're still people. I do think they've been encouraged, though, to go further than necessary.

Richard and Betty Hughes

 ... when they emerged and the translator said, 'The President and the Premier have decided they would like to meet again right here on Sunday,' I thought that was so stimulating. I thought, 'Oh, hot dog!'

In 1957 Judge Richard Hughes left the bench to return to his Newark, New Jersey, law firm. Three years later, however, he agreed to be the "willing victim" to run for

Governor of New Jersey against a heavily favored Republican candidate. He won the election and was reelected in 1965, carrying the first Democratic legislature into office since 1911. When his second term expired, he again returned to private practice. His wife, Betty, hosts a tri-state television show called *Betty Hughes and Friends*, best described as a hybrid of *The Galloping Gourmet* and the *Today Show*. The Hugheses have ten children and live in Princeton, New Jersey.

RICHARD HUGHES   It was June 1967 when we got to Glassboro [for the summit between Premier Kosygin and President Johnson]. During those earlier years of the 1960s I had sensed a difference in the feeling of strife between our country and the Soviets. I've often thought that it was probably an increase in the feeling of mutual fear; that with the terrible potential of the nuclear bomb, with which both powers were armed, we got into a philosophical frame of mind that we just couldn't let it happen.

BETTY HUGHES   We were no less afraid, but we were despairing. We had long since quit thinking that building a special little place in our cellar, with a big bucket of water and ten cans of Spaghetti-O's would really help. I don't think that any of us were any less fearful, but we had a despair. "What can we do? It's hopeless." If I turn on my radio and they say, "Alert" . . . all stations switch on, and they say, "Calling all cars, calling all cars: Here comes an atom bomb," I'd probably, if the kids were around, go kiss them; but I don't think I'd make a move. Where would I run? Feeling that way, what can you do? Preparing against it is foolish.

RICHARD HUGHES   Khrushchev's attempt to install the missiles in Cuba in 1962, and Kennedy's response to it, made the two powers grow up. The Soviets tried it; we were prepared to stop and board a Soviet ship in the blockade. Had we done that, that would have been an act of definite war, and World War Three would have started. We were told after that that we were very, very close—just an eyelash away—from an exchange of nuclear missiles. The Soviets turned back and we began to talk some more and things came along. In June 1967, when Kosygin came here to address the United Nations General Assembly, there appeared to be no chance of a visit between him and President Johnson. I read in *The New York Times* on the way to work that Kosygin was going to depart and go back to Moscow without having seen the President. I thought what a shame it was, with them about four hundred miles apart, at least not to meet each other and exchange the amenities and talk about some platitudes about world peace. I called the White House and tried to arrange that conference.

BETTY HUGHES   There was one proud man in Washington and one proud man in New York. There's no other word that I know for it—they were both sulking, worrying about face. I would suspect LBJ was saying, "Well, he knows where I am. And he can't come see me?" And Kosygin was saying, "I'm a leader of a great nation. If I've come clear across the world and he can't come four hundred miles, the heck with him." And a little nobody man, as far as history would go, named Richard J. Hughes, was reading newspapers all week and thinking, "Darn, this can't be! There has to be some way to save both their faces and give the people a chance. If that's the only thing I do while I'm Governor, I'm going to try like everything to do that."

What progress was made at Glassboro—Substantively, but also in the minds of the people of our country?

BETTY HUGHES   You feel better after every big state visit. This is why they've become a tradition. I felt that after the Pope came to New York. You figure, as long as they're talking to each other . . . I felt very, very positive. One of the most elated moments of that weekend, which was kind of wild altogether, was when they emerged. Dick and I played no part in the conference. We were kind of hanging around. The fact that he was Governor was the only way we got to stay in the backyard under the tree. We had this little kind of sawbuck table. Everybody else had to stand behind the ropes. But when they emerged and the translator said, "The President and the Premier have decided they would like to meet again right here on Sunday," I thought that was so stimulating. I thought, "Oh, hot dog!"

RICHARD HUGHES   And unexpected. Because I had really thought, even in the face of the auspicious beginnings of the meeting, that there would be an exchange of amenities and everybody would be very guarded in what they said, but it wasn't that way at all. Apparently they let their hair down and sat together privately.

The one big impression I emerged with was his feeling of reciprocal affection for people. Betty, you remember when he was saying—it was translated to us—he was telling the crowd after they applauded him that it was too bad we had to be fighting in Vietnam, that there were so many more exciting and good things that we could have done with the money and the effort and the lives. I thought to myself that he probably meant curing cancer and things like that, overcoming poverty and hunger throughout the world. Of couse, when he went back to television that night in New York, after the second day of the conference, then he had to talk tough. He had to become a tough guy again, because he was talking for the benefit of Moscow and Peking.

How did America react to Kosygin and to his meeting with Johnson?

RICHARD HUGHES   The people yearn so for a chance for peace that as you can see from the faces on this crowd . . . [*he points to a newspaper photograph from a huge scrapbook*] that crowd loved Kosygin. I don't mean that they loved him as a person, but they loved the possibility that the meeting would protect them and their children. You see most of them are holding children.

*   *   *

In August 1967 we had a terrible tragic riot in Newark in which twenty-six lives were lost. I had been alerted by the Mayor [Hugh J. Addonizio] of that city. I'd been watching the situation for a couple of days through my State Police representatives and some other people, including Dr. Paul Ylvisaker [see pp. 29–36], head of the Community Affairs Department. We had the idea, mostly because of the reassurances of the Mayor, that he had it pretty much under control. I was constantly reassured that he had many contacts and roots in the black community. I think one time he mentioned that he had one hundred fifty ministers that he was talking to all the time, but apparently that blew up.

I received a final call, the second call, about two o'clock in the morning and I went to Newark immediately. I stayed there about five days until the riot was over. During that time I was in charge of the movement of the State Police and the National Guard. The Mayor took a secondary position, turning the situation over to us. We contained it as best we could, but there were twenty-six deaths—at least twenty of which were innocent people killed in the crossfire because of the excitement and the shooting back and forth.

I almost was shot myself one morning at six o'clock. I had a State Police driver in an unidentified car. He was in civilian clothes because we didn't want to antagonize the people by too much of a show of uniforms. We were trying to get past a roadblock and another State Policeman put his rifle up. I thought he was going to take a shot at us until our man got out and put his hands up and deflected this attempt. There was a good deal of nervousness and shooting and I thought it was my duty to go out into the streets and give a feeling of composure to the people as much as I could.

What provoked the riot?

I think it was because Newark is probably foremost of all the troubled cities in the country . . . its infant mortality rate is maybe five times that of any other city. The venereal disease rate is much higher. Its tuberculosis rate is much higher. Its poverty is deeper. Its unemployment is more acute. And it's just a city that has changed to a pretty badly off city. Basically the roots of all of these problems for all of our urban communities is the fact that we have grown accustomed to putting an inordinate burden of taxation on the local property homeowner and the local small businessman. We haven't had the guts to adopt a state income tax. The same as the federal income tax. As much as we all hate it, it's the only realistic way the country can survive. New Jersey was very derelict in that for many years. In fact, the first substantial broad-based tax came into existence in my administration in 1966, when we put through a three-per-cent sales tax. I had wanted an income tax and fought very hard for it. But I lost by one vote in one house of the legislature. It passed one house. It would have been a much fairer tax. It would not have touched down on the poor and the retired teacher, the understructure of our society.

*   *   *

The Plainfield riot was very tragic. A policeman was stomped to death by the black people. That took place right after the Newark one. We were no sooner in good shape in Newark and got the National Guard out of there and the shooting had subsided, when we were called down to Plainfield. I authorized a search of the black quarter in that town because we had very good evidence that one hundred and sixty carbine rifles with ammunition had been stolen from an armory nearby and were in that community. I'm not sure that I was right in doing this, but I thought I was right. That search caused a lot of abrasive contact between the internal community and the state police, although we took great pains to have each search car occupied not only by a policeman but by a member of the Negro community.

Would you describe what a city is like when it is under siege during a riot?

Well, it's almost like a carnival. Everybody's laughing and joking and looting and kidding. You'll see a fourteen-year-old boy running out of a store with holy pictures in his hands —paintings showing different religious themes—and he'll run to his parents on the porch and they'll laugh and congratulate him for having robbed the store. Then you see poor women wheeling little tricycles out of the store for their kids, stealing them. I came up behind a Cadillac in which some black man and his wife were taking . . . he had about two hundred pairs of shoes he'd taken out of the store. I was really incensed about that because these people obviously weren't suffering the pangs of poverty. They were just thieves. I authorized a complaint against them. I don't know what ever happened to it. But it was a case of gross opportunism, and there were many such in the Newark riot.

I talked to Martin Luther King on the phone that first night. He told me that he had read about our problem and that he was deeply affected by it. He told me that I was right in trying to stamp out the killing and the shootings by very strong measures, and that if he could help, he would be glad to come up. We had offers from various black sports people—Elston Howard offered to come in. But it was the feeling of the people that I was working with, the moderate and very fine black people, that we ought not to get too many strangers in. We ought to try to settle it ourselves.

I did very hard work. I talked to Ramsey Clark. I must have talked to him five times during one of those nights. He shook up the presidents of the A & Ps and the Food Fairs. There was actual starvation in Newark then. You see, some of these black people lived in apartments and were only able to buy a day or two in advance. On the fourth day, when they were afraid to go into the streets, their kids were hungry. We opened federal food depots. We had the cooperation from the chain stores that opened their stores, although they had sworn up and down they wouldn't dare to open them up because of the fear of looting and attack. But they opened them. When we withdrew the National Guard and the State Police, we left National Guard trucks merely to dispense food for the black population.

Carolina Vasquez

 I fasted in front of the Food Fair in Philadelphia for nine days to try to convince the company that what we said was true and we were nonviolent . . . on the ninth day they . . . decided they would give us a break . . .

Carolina Vasquez says of herself: "I am Cherokee and from New Mexico, but my mother brought us to California when we were very little when my father died. I was about six years old then. I have lived picking cotton and working in the Coast picking prunes and plums.

"I was twenty-two when I worked with the union [United Farmworkers Organizing Committee] in the Delano area. I walked a lot in the picket lines. I made a march to Sacramento; I am one of the original marchers to talk to Governor Brown. I sing a lot. I used to sing with the Farm Workers Theatre—we travel all over the state of California to bring the issue to the people of our movement. Later I met my brother-in-law; he was one of our picket sign captains. Through him I met his brother, Miguel, which now he is my husband. I married him in Connecticut because of the boycott. Now we are living here in California."

When he got out as President of the CSO [Community Service Oganization], Cesar [Chavez] came to Delano and studied and wrote a lot about the industry of the growers in California.

The strike started in Coachella in 1965. The Filipinos started the strike there, asking for a ten-cent raise, but the growers automatically started making trouble. These Filipinos are workers that got out after the Second World War and came to

America and they started working for these growers from real young ages. Some traveled from Coachella to Delano to work at the time of the real busy season. So they asked the growers for a ten-cent raise, and the growers refused. They refused after so many years to give them a raise, so the Filipinos struck. The contractors started bringing in loads and loads of trucks and buses to break the strike, workers from Mexico, what you call wetbacks. This happened every day in the strike areas covering a forty-mile area.

During this time Cesar was organizing in Delano. He started with friends of the family and had his meetings at homes because he had no other place. Many of us began to go to these meetings and hear what he had to say about organizing ourselves, trying to make a better life and a better future for the kids and for ourselves in farm labor, because many of us, like myself, got out of school to work from very young ages. Finally, when Cesar struck Delano, we joined together with the Filipinos one week later. These farm workers don't know nothing about unions. We don't know what it means. All we do is work and eat and work and eat.

Cesar would talk to reporters; he would talk to church and labor men; he would talk in general to people who wanted to know about the union and about the farm workers. People would ask me questions about what local number it was. I would just shrug my shoulders and just wonder what they meant by that. It turned out that my mother came to Delano one time and she found this little pamphlet. We began to learn from this little book. It said that we were going to fight for better wages. It said that we were going to have to suffer. At the very bottom of the sheet it had the address where people could go and hear more about this, and to learn more about what we could do to help ourselves. That's where I met Cesar. He had a little office in Delano, at 102 Albany Street, which was constantly burned down. They constantly stole the papers. It was a real problem.

We would try to talk to the workers in the fields that were brought from Mexico, talk to them in Spanish; but not knowing the language, it's very hard. I tried anyway and at least

I stopped them from working. We had many camps that were empty because the workers would strike, but by the next Saturday they were back full again. We'd tell them to pretend they were sick or whatever. It was up to them to decide. At first it was hard because they didn't understand. Many of them who were accustomed to working year after year, to them it was so hard to miss two days or a week of work. Then they began to realize that we could spend the rest of our lives and die there and never have nothing. They never owned a car. They never owned a home or never had gotten married. They just worked and worked all their lives. They never had nothing. The growers didn't mind it because they had them camped and they had them a cook in the camp and they would make a party that would bring in women so that they could have fun with these women.

What was Chavez like in the early days of the organizing?

During that time, of course, he was just like one of us. He worked in the fields all his life himself. His family came from Arizona, and his mother and father live in San Jose; and he traveled from one end of the place to another, living under bridges as many of us do. He just said, "We don't want violence. We want to get at the heart of it, but we want to make people understand with words instead of beating their brains out and hurting them." But when the growers started losing money, they started using violence on us and on many of the strikers in Delano. They used their dogs from the ranches. They would bring in workers to beat these farm workers on the picket line. The workers that they recruited . . . they would tell them that we are troublemakers or that we were Communists or that we were lazy people and did not want to work. They would beat us up. Unfortunately, it happened to me one time too.

How large did the boycott finally become?

Oh, my goodness! It's international. We have offices all over the United States and we have one in France. In many places, like in England, they would stop the ships before they unloaded the product. There were loads and loads of grapes that were going down that way. We have already won with the grape growers, with the pressure we made of the boycott internationally and all over the East. Myself, I worked for three years in Connecticut, Boston, Philadelphia, and New York.

When we first went to New York, we went on a school bus—which was a Christmas gift to all of us and to the children in Delano, which included canned food and clothes—to fight the growers in the boycott. We would go to the terminal market and talk to the men, these guys that were carrying the product that we were fighting against—the grapes. We would talk to them and tell them that was a scab product. We asked them not to patronize it. We would picket the stalls there in New York. The labor union found out that we were picketing, so they began to give us their support with contributions to be sent to the families that were behind: to pay the bills, and to buy food or whatever.

Were you immediately successful at the markets in New York? What did the store managers say?

They'd say, "Oh, no, no, no! I can't do that. Grapes is my biggest sale in this store." All of them would say that. That grapes were just something that people enjoyed eating. Some people would say, "Oh, I'll die without grapes. I can't do without grapes." But they began to realize later that they could do without them. We would send literature—a picture of a little girl in a labor camp—and show it to the people in the East what the conditions are, what children have to go through waiting for the parents all afternoon; how when the parents come to make supper, by that time the children are asleep and it's late. People began to understand, but it took a lot of organizing and a lot of work.

I was sent alone to Philadelphia to work with two other ladies, to go and try to stop the grapes that were being shipped there. I was to talk to the managers of the large chain stores to try to convince them why we were striking in California. We didn't want to hurt them; we only wanted their cooperation. But it took time and it took millions and millions of literature to inform them that farm workers all over the United States, all over the continent, are suffering because we have no protection of the law. I fasted in front of the Food Fair in Philadelphia for nine days to try to convince the company that what we said was true and we were nonviolent. We were trying to concentrate on the bigger chain stores that were carrying more products of grapes during that time. The guy says, "Look, you're fasting and I don't want to be responsible for your health, so okay, we'll have a meeting with you and see what you're going to tell us. We want to know what's going on in California because we've never been there. We only sell the products." They had a meeting with us and the main guys were there—their attorney was there, the guy from the cold storage where they put their products was there. They began to realize that we had a lot of support from the unions and churches and mostly housewives, and so they finally decided that they were going to think about it. I fasted for nine days and finally on the ninth day they had decided that they would give us a break, that they wouldn't order any grapes if the other food stores would not order grapes. That meant a lot of work and a lot of coordination to stop the other stores from ordering grapes so that Food Fair wouldn't take it back.

Where were you when the growers finally gave in during the summer of 1969?

Oh, God! How can you say it in words? It was something that you just can't say in words. I was in Philadelphia and I was in the ladies' room and Hope [Lopez] received a call from Delano. She screamed, "I got a call from Delano from my Cesar." I said, "What's going on, Hope? Is there something new?" She said, "It seems like we're breaking through to them." During that time I had been working with her to talk to the bishops and the church organizations, because you know they really never wanted to do very much about our kind of organization. She started jumping up and down and her eyes were crying and I was wondering what was going on.

I said, "Is it possible that after all these three long years the growers are finally giving in; they finally realize that we don't want to hurt them, that we just want benefits and insurance and toilet facilities and water in the fields?" It was like up in the air. It was something . . . I don't know how to really express it to you. I just felt the hot tears running down my cheek. And thanking God . . . all the suffering we had done in the past years. I was wondering if it was really, really true, if the growers had finally signed.

After all the growers began to sign the contracts and we're all peparing to come home and make a conference to see what we're going to do next, we finally realized that we were working now for the lettuce growers. We started working, getting all our supporters to now start changing their product to lettuce.

Paul Davis

 . . . there was and still is a lot of danger for a man like Chavez, but I think that it's a model of how that sort of thing ought to be operated.

A thirty-four-year-old free-lance artist, Paul Davis works mostly in magazines and advertising. One of his best-known posters was for a Carnegie Hall benefit in support of "La Causa," Cesar Chavez's grape boycott. The poster was selected for the Mead Library Show and won many other prizes.

I come from Oklahoma. I knew a few people who were migrant workers when I was a kid. They used to go out to California and work six months out of the year picking, a whole

Grapes of Wrath kind of a story. Out here on Long Island we have a lot of migrant workers too, but they just go unnoticed. They're just forgotten about.

A guy from the poster company called me. He told me that they were going to have a benefit for Chavez's group and asked me to do the poster for the Carnegie Hall concert. I looked all over to find someone to model for it, and the guy whose face is on the poster is not a migrant farm worker or even Mexican: he's a kid from New York. I don't know why it worked out as well as it did. It's a funny thing. I was really worried about it because I didn't have any grapes in it, or any grape fields or anything to relate to migrant workers at all . . . just a face.

Af first I thought I was going to do a picture of Chavez, and I got a lot of photographs of him. But I realized that Chavez really isn't, and probably doesn't want to be, a kind of star in that way. I really shouldn't use him to represent the movement, because a typical worker is more important than the leader in a situation like that. I really wanted to show someone young. People would be more sympathetic to someone young who they figure is going to spend his life out there picking grapes. It ought to be better for him than it is. At least it ought to be fair. It's really a crappy life: the people are exploited more than anybody. They make less money for harder, more backbreaking work than almost anyone does. And they get cheated because they really are not residents anywhere. They don't stay anywhere long enough to vote, so they aren't important to anybody except these guys who are making a lot of money off of them. It's sort of like slavery.

I didn't want it to be sentimental. I didn't want you to feel sorry for him. In fact, I wanted him to be a kind of optimistic figure, that maybe there's a new day coming kind of thing. That hopefully there will be more in it for him in his life than there was in his father's life or his grandfather's life. I keep coming back to the actual people. The cycle is so deadly because most of these kids don't get educated. Not only do they not get educated, but they're undernourished half the time. It's such a vicious circle, that whole poverty thing they're stuck in. Yet they're people with an extraordinary amount of dignity considering the way they get kicked around. I think that's an important thing too—the dignity. I was trying to show a sympathetic, dignified, hopeful figure.

Why was "La Causa" so successful?

The credit really goes to the political organization that Chavez had. He's responsible for having the energy and the tenacity to keep things organized and keep it going. It was one of the longest strikes there ever was in this country, certainly one of the longest boycotts. They began to represent poor people everywhere.

I didn't eat any grapes, but then nobody was. That wasn't any big deal. It was no sacrifice. Nobody was buying them, and that's really what finally broke the growers.

People want to express themselves. They may not want to get personally involved with a migrant worker, but they want to express their feelings about him. It's unfortunate that the government and the people who really ought to be doing something, making laws and doing things about this, are so slow to respond to that kind of obvious groundswell of feeling. One of the things that was going on during the grape strike is that they were buying grapes and sending them over to Vietnam to the soldiers. The Department of the Army was actually subsidizing the growers. It's really strange that the government is the one that you have to fight. The bureaucracy seems to always be in the way.

They did have a lot of success, and I think they'll have more. It's like Gandhi or someone. They developed the techniques for dealing with it and they've really become a model for other groups that want to accomplish something. There was no violence. There was a lot of hostility, I'm sure, and there was and still is a lot of danger for a man like Chavez, but I think that it's a model of how that sort of thing ought to be operated.

Francis S. Johnson

 In spite of the skepticism that I offer about man's useful role in space, . . . I still think we had no choice in this. . . . It's been a worthwhile activity to maintain our place in the world.

In the infancy of the space program—long before the days of NASA—Dr. Francis Johnson served the program in an advisory capacity. His work was concentrated on ionospheric physics and planetary atmospheres. Having recently stepped down as Acting President of the University of Texas at Dallas, he now directs the Center for Advanced Studies there.

What was your reaction when President Kennedy first set a moon landing as our national goal?

It seemed Buck Rogerish, impractical, unlikely to me. I felt then, as I feel now, that it was a program undertaken for reasons that were largely political. There had been statements from time to time trying to justify Apollo in terms of its science, but these are really pretty weak. It's not unsympathetic toward science, but certainly it wasn't undertaken for the science return. It was very much undertaken for other reasons, and I think it has been very effective in those. I sort of hate to think how we would feel if we didn't have the Apollo program and if the Russians were as active as they have been.

During the International Geophysical Year, or close to it, this first Russian satellite was flown. The scientists were virtually incredulous to find that this had been done. I was living in California at the time, but I remember going out and seeing that thing pass over. It gave you something of a funny sensation to see that Russian vehicle pass overhead. The whole country began to wonder, "Are we seriously behind?" The whole school system tended to undergo some change. A great emphasis came in on science.

The space project has been sympathetic to science, in the sense that they are willing to take science along and do what they can. Some of the criticism of the Apollo Program has been, particularly with regard to its continuation, "Well, we landed a man on the moon. We did that once. Why go again?" That's right in terms of a milestone accomplishment. By undertaking this national commitment, Kennedy greatly narrowed the horizon for American space activities. He had one clear focus, and it assured that not only would we accomplish that objective magnificently, but that we wouldn't be able to do much of anything else for another decade or two to come. Right now the organization that's put man on the moon is a factor in this. What do they want to do? Well, first of all, they would probably like to continue putting men on the moon. If they can't do that, well, most anything else where they can use the same sort of organization.

Skylab [a new program of long-duration manned missions], I think, is the perfect example, that part of Skylab that's associated with earth resources. While the instruments that will be in Skylab in several respects are much more powerful than those in the Earth Technology Satellite [an unmanned project], the disparity in cost and the disparity in coverage are just overwhelming. That is, the dollar spent in Earth is worth many, many times the dollar spent in Skylab. It just costs a lot to insert man in the operation. I don't think they'd ever have Skylab if it weren't that they've got astronauts and an organization that needs support.

It's darn hard to find an example where if you set out to get certain data, that you can do it more effectively by putting a man into the operation, because it escalates the cost just tremendously. I don't know exactly what it will cost to fly one Skylab, but you'd be hard-pressed to put a pricetag of less than a billion dollars on it. The Earth Satellites—the two of them that are going—will cost less than one-tenth as much, and will give ten times as much data.

In spite of the skepticism that I offer about *man*'s useful role in space, I'd like to emphasize that I still think we had no choice in this. We might not have gone to the moon, but if we hadn't at least done something to roughly compete with what the Russians were doing, we'd look much less prestigious on the world scene. It's been a worthwhile activity to maintain our place in the world.

Paul Morrissey

 Somebody piles glass on the floor and that's art. Somebody digs a hole and that's art. . . . And to think of the mindless ninnies who devote attention to this gibberish.

Paul Morrissey is one of pop artist Andy Warhol's closest associates and has directed some of the Warhol films.

Well, I'll tell you what happened in the Sixties. In the Fifties and into the Forties, you had this development of this pathetic craft called abstract art. This is like a contradiction of terms. It came out of Picasso. You know, the museums paid four hundred thousand dollars for that crap. And Andy [Warhol] came from the Fifties. He was an illustrator for commercial newspapers and magazines of the product that was sold. By that time the art world was no more than an in joke, a joke upon itself. All Pop Art was was a return to the figure and a ridicule, a further ridicule, of what's called "art," or what you might call "wall hangings." You know, stuff sold in galleries to hang on walls.

Historically, Pop Art was certainly a wonderful thing, because it immediately stopped the sale of the garbage Abstract Expressionism or whatever you want to call it. Of course, because it happened in the Fifties museums still have to buy abstract art, because they think it's part of the culture, the history of the period. I suppose that's true—to show how mindless people were in those days.

The Pop Art was simply a gesture against all that, and a ridicule of it, and people responded to it, not critically but emotionally. They said, "Oh, what a relief to have a joke on the wall, instead of that other joke." An obvious joke instead of a pretentious joke. So historically, Pop Art really makes sense.

But the other thing, I think really that it was an honest thing. It was completely literal and it was extraordinarily direct. It was a reflex of art, like a person dying. They wiggle their toes or something. It was that kind of an emotion. But if you really understand what it is, you realize that it is a gesture at the end of a cycle, then you don't take Pop Art and then develop something from it. You leave it. But all the other people keep doing it or trying to extend it, and they've become the same kind of joke the Abstract Expressionists have become. Because they take it seriously. In the end you never could take that kind of art seriously, so why don't you leave it? It only took Andy three years to realize it. He began in 1961 and by 1964 he had stopped. His last exhibition, I think, was early 1966, which was helium pillows and wallpaper, and it was just like "What more can you do?" You put the objects on wallpaper now. To go on kicking a dead horse and making a living off the dead horse carcass of the art world is a pretty boring thing. Andy didn't want to do that. You spit on the carcass and then you walk away from it. You don't keep spitting on it for ten years like some other pop artists are still doing.

Of course, when you think of the movements that followed Pop Art. . . . Somebody who takes his clothes off and burns the hair on his chest and photographs it and puts it in an art book. That's art. Somebody piles glass on the floor and that's art. Somebody digs a hole and that's art. Yes, that's art. Anything you want to say is art, that's art. Oh, yes. And you vacuum-clean the room and that's art. Blah, blah, blah. That's art. And to think of the mindless ninnies who devote attention to this gibberish.

Was Andy poking fun just at art, or was he poking fun at society?

No, not society, because society is people. He did very nice silk-screen portraits of people. And then when he did his films, he did films of people. He wasn't ever criticizing society, I don't think, at all. His notion was not to criticize. If he was critical of anything, it was forms: art forms and film forms. He was always out to simplify, to make form a very simple thing.

I think that any artist who works in a period, if he's a genuine artist and has an artistic validity, reflects the period, no matter what he does. I guess Andy was interested in reflecting the period. But the way he did it was that he reflected the period by finding people who somehow reflected the period. He took on this notion of modern popular art form being not a question of form but a question of content. Which means you're dealing with content and your content is people and in effect your form is people too. Form and content is merged into people. So it's like a painter who paints portraits, like Rembrandt or anybody. They're interested in people. The face of the person is what's interesting. Now you can put people on sort of a canvas where they speak and you can hear the way they talk, and the impulse. What I was going to say about it, why I think Andy was so interesting in the Sixties, I think he's sort of returning to the notion of the Renaissance, if you want. The Greeks. The study of man is man. The study of man is not art. It's not abstract slop on a canvas. The study of art is not the mind of the artist, it's the study of people.

Among Warhol's most popular works are his Campbell's Soup cans. What do they sell for?

Well, when they came out they didn't sell for anything. Now, oh, I don't know, maybe twenty to thirty thousand dollars. A little can of soup which up to two years ago, three years ago, you could have bought for four to five thousand dollars. When they came out, nobody bought them. And they were on sale for five hundred dollars, one thousand dollars. I think they're quite interesting things if you want to hang something on a wall and you want to hang a period of historical interest on a wall, and with modern furnishings. Things that Andy did adapt very well with modern furnishings. They have a great look to them. They are very much a part of the modernistic styling, which you cannot say Abstract Expressionism or abstract art ever was. Abstract art was connected with nothing, except probably mental disorder.

Craig Kreutz

 I think that laws are there to protect the criminals more than they are the innocent people. . . . I take my hat off to the police force. I think they're doing a great job and they're out to protect you.

Forty-eight-year-old Craig Kreutz owns a small furniture-frame business in Portland, Oregon. The Kreutzes have two college-age daughters and a son just returned from Vietnam.

I'd like to move to Australia, yeah! Or New Zealand. I think the pace of life is slower. I think a guy would live longer.

If he could live at all, he'd live longer, because you wouldn't have the pressures that you have here.

No, I haven't always felt this way. Hell! I'm not still patriotic. I used to think that the government couldn't do anything wrong. But I've had some experiences in bankruptcy courts and so forth, and they never seemed to work out the way it seemed to me it should. . . .

*   *   *

I don't believe in votes. I actually don't believe that your vote amounts to anything. You can vote any way you want to; the majority can go that way. Whatever happens, somebody decides they want it, and baby, you got it. It's like the eighteen-year-old vote. Here in Oregon it was "thumbs down." It was a majority landslide. We got it though. The government said it was legal to vote on federal situations, which is fine. Well, then all of a sudden a certain percentage of the states went that way and then everybody had to go that way. It didn't matter how the state voted.

Do you follow national politics at all?

Oh, I don't follow them that closely. I used to when I was first old enough to vote, when I came back from service and everything. I used to think it was interesting. I used to sit up and listen to it on the radio until three, four, five o'clock in the morning. I thought that was the greatest thing in the world. But it's gotten so that when they have these things any more, that's all you hear. I've gotten so I shut them off. They overdo everything.

*   *   *

I think that laws are there to protect the criminals more than they are the innocent people. I believe the innocent person is at everybody's mercy, other than the police force. I take my hat off to the police force. I think they're doing a great job and they're out to protect you. But they're sticking their necks out every time they do. The innocent person has nowhere to go. I think the laws are to protect the crooks. It's just like this new law that they have—it's something about a criminal code law: if a person breaks into your house, unless you know for sure that he's going to do you bodily injury, if you happen to shoot that guy, you're in the wrong. If a guy comes into your house and he's stealing or something—maybe the lights are out and you can't see him—if you happen to shoot him and he's a fourteen-year-old kid or a seventeen-year-old kid and he doesn't have a gun, you're in bad shape. I believe that anybody that comes in my door after I'm in bed, if I shoot him, I believe I should be in the right. But I'm not.

The police are doing the best job that they can possibly do. Do you realize that when they arrest somebody that commits a crime, usually that guy is out of jail before that cop gets finished filling out the papers? What protection has the cop got in a case like that? What's the reason for him risking his life to have something like that happen? We had a case here when the same three people, a girl and two boys, firebombed two separate places. They caught them, and they took them down to jail, and they turned one kid loose on his own recognizance before the cop even got out of the jailhouse. Now, is that right? If these guys are brazen enough to go around firebombing . . . I don't know, I suppose they were probably colored. I'm not positive but it was in that area and that was about the time they were having that problem. But why in the devil would they turn that kid loose?

Like I told my daughter a while back, there's something wrong and I don't know what it is—but I don't like it. It's as simple as that. And I don't know how to go about straightening it out. I don't even know what's wrong. But something's got to be wrong because there are so many different things that are going haywire. I'm going to get the hell out of here.

I believe that inflation has something to do with it. I think it's just plain greed. And, like I told you, the pace that you have to live in this country. The fact that a person says, "I've got to make mine now and the heck with everybody else." It didn't used to be that way around here a few years ago. Nobody had anything and they just figured they never would have anything. And they weren't tearing everybody up so bad. Everybody's trying to get ahead of the other guy. And I believe that's ninety per cent of our problem, and that's one of the reasons why I've talked about living in a country like New Zealand or Australia where the pace is slower. Canada would be all right, certain areas of Canada.

Charles Schulz

 I like to think that I'm talking about things that are more important. The whole Lucy psychiatric thing is more important than making cracks about the President.

A fifty-year-old father of five, Charles Schulz is the renowned creator of "Peanuts."

It's difficult to talk about what I do, because I do it so I don't have to talk about it. If I talked about the things that I draw, I'd probably be a lecturer or a novelist, but I draw comic strips because somehow I have feelings way in the back of my mind that come out in little pictures and in funny little sayings.

I've been trying in the last couple of years to show how these little kids are searching for something. The thing that has delighted me the most recently is the discussions between Peppermint Patty and Chuck. Peppermint Patty seems to be searching for something. She doesn't know quite what it is. She's always asking Chuck what he thinks love is. He never gives her a satisfactory answer.

Did "Peanuts" reflect the American attitude?

I think they probably did. But in a deeper and more profound way than. . . . Just because people talk about politics and draw Senators in their comics and make cracks about who-

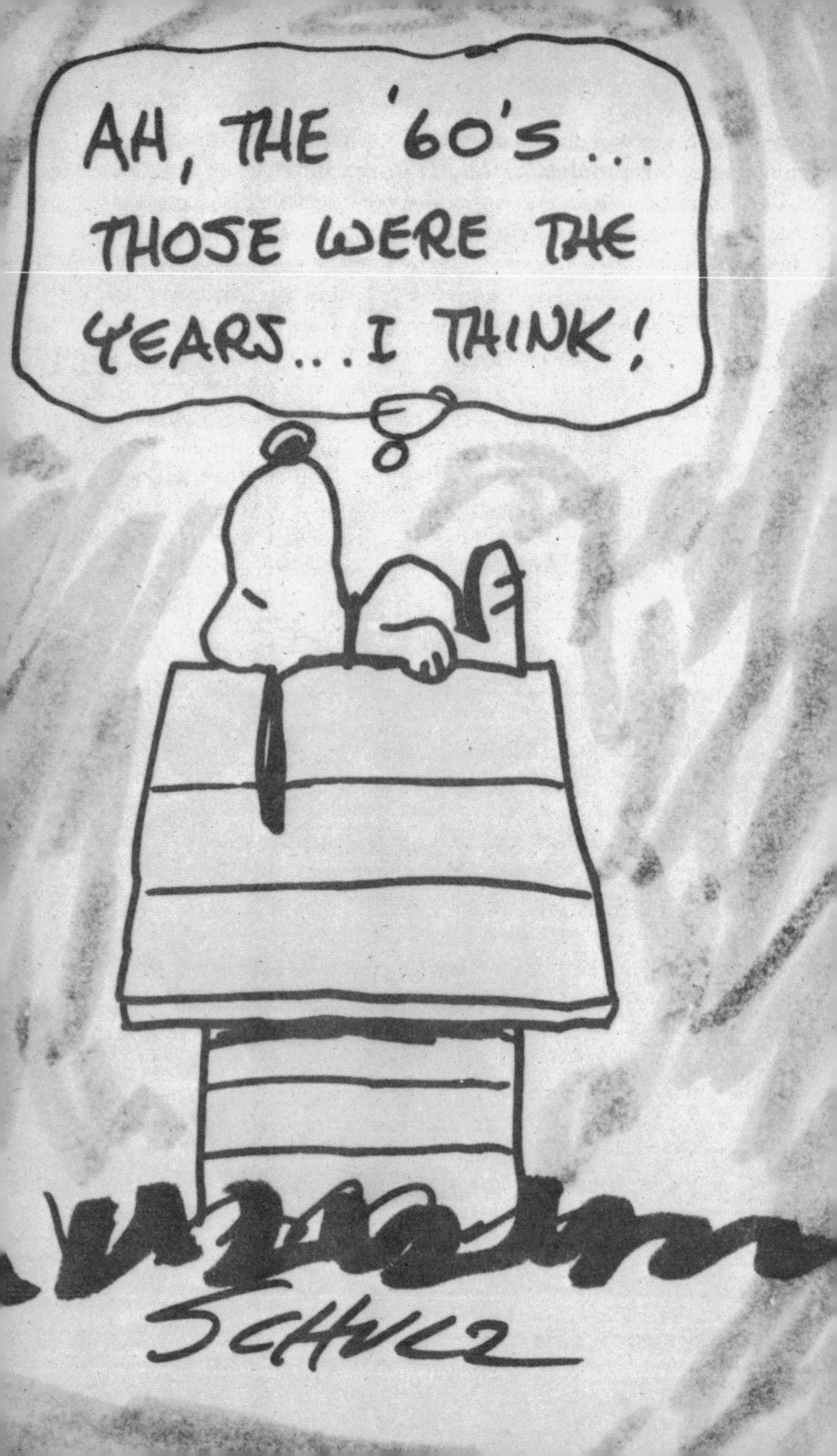
AH, THE '60'S ... THOSE WERE THE YEARS... I THINK!
SCHULZ

ever is President, I don't necessarily think that's making social comments. I like to think that I'm talking about things that are more important than making cracks about the President. It's getting down to the problems that people have. Fears and anxieties. . . . Charlie Brown says, "I've developed a new philosophy . . . I only dread one day at a time." This was a generation that really did fear the next day, sometimes wasn't sure if the next day was going to come. I suppose Charlie Brown's baseball team and his constant losing—so many people were able to identify with him. Then the age-old problem of trying to find someone to love who would love you equally in return. It seems almost never to happen in real life. Unrequited love . . . it seems to happen all the time. The strip is filled with little unrequited love affairs. Sally likes Linus and he can't stand her. Charlie Brown likes the little redhaired girl, but he can't even get to meet her.

Is your overall appraisal of the times negative?

Oh, God, no! I don't think we're in any worse shape than we've ever been. Do you know how nice it is to have little children and not to have to worry about whether they're going to get polio? Have you ever seen a parent that saw summer come when you lived in the Midwest, where there are lots of lakes and the kids started to go swimming, and all of a sudden the newspapers started to run lists of fifteen polio attacks a day? You could just feel the fear among all your friends who were parents. It's gone now! If that doesn't make life easier, I don't know what does.

There are still a lot of terrible things around, but I don't think we're on the brink of disaster. We are now at a point in history where war is a complete bore and it's utterly stupid. We see no glory in it. Little by little, we've been chipping away at the glory image. Cartooning views have changed, songs about war have changed. World War One had some great war songs. World War Two started off with *See Here, Private Hargrove* and cartoons about KP. Then Bill Mauldin suddenly saw that war was not funny; and since then, we haven't had any war songs and there aren't any more war jokes about KP because it isn't funny any more.

It's a lot easier to be upset, and a lot easier to preach discontent than it is to preach positive solutions. This is why the evangelists and the doom theologians are so successful. It's simply a lot easier to preach this kind of doctrine than to preach love and hope. You can run a very successful radio-preaching ministry by preaching that we're right on the brink of disaster and the world is going to end very soon. You won't get very many listeners if you preach love and kindness. It isn't that interesting. It's a lot harder too.

Eugene Carson Blake

 If you take the decade of the Sixties, when historians write it, it will be a tremendous, almost miraculous development of the idea of the unity of the one church of Jesus Christ.

The Rev. Dr. Eugene Carson Blake, sixty-five years old and a Presbyterian from New Canaan, Connecticut, headed the World Council of Churches from 1966 to 1972. Based in Geneva, the council comprises more than 250 Protestant, Anglican, and Orthodox churches.

The Fifties were considered a boom time for religion, but there were some of us who weren't convinced. The statistics were all good organizationally, but when you really looked at how people were deciding things, it seemed to me that the churches were failing.

If you take the decade of the Sixties, when historians

write it, it will be a tremendous, almost miraculous development of the idea of the unity of the one church of Jesus Christ. It has happened all over. I went over to Geneva in June before the first session of Vatican Council II and I asked all my friends, "What's going to happen?" Nobody was hopeful that anything was going to happen. Then, the first vote the next fall of that Vatican Council showed a sixty-per-cent majority on a progressive new wave, and the thing changed from that moment on. It was a miracle. Maybe not technically a miracle but, it was an act of God, not of men, for which nobody really could see the cause.

So now you have ecumenical activity going on all over. It's spotty. It is not everywhere. I go to Dubuque, Iowa, for example—ten years between visits—1955 to 1965. Dubuque was full of distrust in 1955. It was a German community which had imported old-time European prejudices. By 1965 the Lutherans and the Presbyterians and the Roman Catholics were thick as thieves, working together on a common theological program.

What happened in this country was that a great many Christians who were disciplined members of their church suddenly found a great release. It was possible to have not simply tolerant relationships, as in a Rotary Club, but Christian relationships with people in the other ecclesiastic communities.

What spurred this new openness, this receptivity to others?

Let me dig a little bit deeper. The Sixties are the climax. I remember very vividly what we felt like at the end of World War Two. There were lots of positive things. We had a real hope in the best tradition of America—since we had come out so strong, ideologically, militarily, and economically at that time—that these next years, twenty-five years, were going to be an American age: we would be leading the world. By 1970, everybody who has thought about it at all knows that we flopped completely.

I'm not sure what spurred ecumenism. You do have the

breakups of the old patterns. Two World Wars in this century, with a third one threatening from the time of Hiroshima. I think that people had to begin to think, "Where are we going?" It's been very slow, actually. You talk to a great many people and they are dodging really asking the deepest questions yet. I think the younger generation, before they get into jobs and their own life pattern, see it clearer. Most of the older of us at some point begin to dodge the ultimate issues: What is human life? You look at our cities and they're getting worse. We're the wealthiest in the world and we can't put together the things to make decent human life for most of the people.

John McCarthy

 . . . I seen him bring the whole team back out and teach them the fundamentals of baseball. Base running, throwing, setting up a cutoff man. He just went through it like it was spring training. Only this was October!

John McCarthy worked for the Allied Maintenance Corporation at Yankee Stadium, then "When the Mets came into being, I just moved over with the same company as groundskeeper for the Mets."

The first year or two we went for name ballplayers. Fellows that were beyond their peak—let's put it that way—but names. Like Frank Thomas, Richie Ashburn. These fellows were not really over the hill, but it was their final days in the game. Gil Hodges, even. They were an attraction. People remembered them from when the Giants and the Dodgers were in town.

And when they got on the field?

They lost pretty bad. They lost pretty bad! You didn't expect them to beat anybody. When they did, it was a real novelty. They hurt a lot of people, though, in pennant drives. I remember they took four in a row from Cincinnati and nearly crushed their season for them. They could hurt you, in their own little way. Then they started a youth movement and it eventually paid off.

What about Casey Stengel?

He called me "Doctor." I worked under him for fifteen years and he never called me by my right name. He called me "Doctor" all the time, and that wasn't because I doctored the field up. He's a funny guy. He'd have you splitting your sides laughing.

Why did the Mets become such a hit in New York?

It's the coming from the underdog. And I'm talking a *real* underdog. Each and every time they lost they found a new way to do it. That's the way it appeared. Ron Swoboda, when he first came up, would run after a ball and run right into a wall. And people would laugh. That kind of thing. You could go back to Jimmy Piersall in the Polo Grounds. When we got him, it was just about the end of his career and he hit his hundredth home run and ran the bases backwards. Jimmy Piersall was capable of doing just about anything. But he was also one of our Mets. Marv Throneberry hit a home run and when he got into the dugout and they were clapping him on the back, the umpire called him out. He forgot to touch first base.

How did Stengel react to all this?

He could cope with just about anything, being a winner or a loser. He knew how to handle the situation. I remember the second year in the Polo Grounds and it was the final game of the season. Everyone was going home for the winter. Supposedly.

Casey waited until everybody left the stands—all the employees and what not. I was on my way out the door and I seen him bring the whole team back out and teach them the fundamentals of baseball. Base running, throwing, setting up a cutoff man. He just went through it like it was spring training. Only this was October! I've never heard of this before.

Were you surprised with what happened in 1969?

I didn't think they'd go all the way. The pennant first and then the playoffs and then the Series—that was quite an achievement. Especially for the Mets! I believe they won seventy-some games the year before. I believe they were setting their goal for eighty wins for 1969, in that they had improved that much over the previous year. Around the middle of August they took over from the Cubs. The Cubs had it really sewed up all year and everybody thought they were going to win it. Then they went into a real nosedive. And we picked it up from there. We had it clinched maybe a week before the end of the season.

What was Shea Stadium like the day they clinched it?

It was a madhouse. Actually everybody just seems to recall the day they won the Series here, whereby the fans came out on the field and picked up the grass. They tore out all the team emblems that we had out on the field and what have you. Part of the fence. They ripped out seats and what have you. But they'd done this two times previously! They'd done it when the Mets won the pennant during the course of the regular season, and they done it when the Mets won the playoff here in Shea Stadium. Three different times they ripped up this field! They took big circles and squares of grass out of the field. We actually replaced fifty-five hundred square feet of sod after the World Series was over—as we had the two times previous to that. Little patches of grass all around the place. People wanted souvenirs. They worshiped the ground the Mets walked on.

I couldn't see them beating Baltimore, Baltimore being the big powerful team that it is. All the hitters, and some very good pitching too. I just couldn't see them in the same race with them. But they did it. They beat them. In five games yet! They lost the first one and then took the next four in a row.

How did you feel after that final game of the World Series?

I felt like crying and laughing at the same time because of what the fans had done on the field. This is my job and they're wrecking it on me! But at the same time you have to be so happy and elated over the fact that they won. It's an odd feeling, a very odd feeling. A very rare feeling.

What was the victory party like?

I didn't go into the clubhouse. I came out and I was measuring to resod it. I was actually measuring the divots and the spaces where they had removed the grass so that I could order the grass that night and replace it the first thing in the morning. That's what I was doing until it got dark out.

They were very nice to us. They voted the ground crew a full share of World Series money, which was like eighteen thousand dollars and some change. Which was very nice of them.

Sam Shemtob

 That was astronomical. That was like a hundred-to-one shot at the races. It was something that wasn't figured in the books. It was against everything that was humanly possible.

Sam Shemtob is a friendly, rotund hot-dog vendor at the Willets Point subway station, just outside Shea Stadium in Queens, where the Mets play.

They were considered such underdogs, and they really tried their darndest in a game to really get ahead. But they had nine dogs on the team, that's all. Everybody was bad. They just couldn't do anything right. Yet they captured the New York crowd somehow. They've got a certain flair about them. The younger generation just seems to go haywire over it, even though they're losing and they're not doing the things right.

Were you a fan in their "losing days," stretching back to 1962?

Oh, sure. I went to the Polo Grounds to see them. I was also a Yankee fan at that time. And a Brooklyn Dodger fan. And a New York Giant fan. But thank God we got the Mets! They really keep New York going.

Sometimes they play good ball and sometimes they're just a bunch of idiots. When they had that big upset in 1969, then that's when I became a Mets fan. That was astronomical. That was like a hundred-to-one shot at the races. It was something that wasn't figured in the books. It was against everything that was humanly possible.

New York loved the Mets as losers. How is it now that they're winners?

Oh, they still love them! They still love them a hell of a lot! You can tell by the attendance we get over here for some of the games that are very unimportant. We still get forty, fifty thousand.

Lula Belle Weathersby

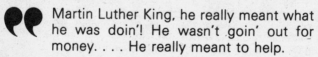

Martin Luther King, he really meant what he was doin'! He wasn't goin' out for money. . . . He really meant to help.

In her upper fifties, Lula Belle Weathersby has lived all
her life in Mississippi. She and her husband were among
those who journeyed to Washington, D.C., in April 1968
to set up Resurrection City.

What was it like to be in Washington during Resurrection City?

We went up on the bus from Marks [Mississippi]. Five
hundred! We had twelve busloads. When we got there, they had
not started to build the city. We got there on Sunday, and on
Monday we all gathered out on the spot where they were going
to build Resurrection City. I was there when [The Rev. Ralph]
Abernathy drove that first nail. It was in that big beautiful park,
right off from the Lincoln Memorial.

They built low board houses with this canvas, big
striped stuff. This canvas, the duckin'-lookin' stuff, that was the
top. Marks was the first town got there because Martin Luther
King asked Marks to be the first ones to get to the city.

I was there a month, but the rest of them stayed about
two months. We had a death in the family and we had to come
home. They teargassed them away. I believe there are some of
them would be right there now if . . . *I* didn't want to come
home!

You see, when we were up there, we didn't have to
worry about our food and clothing. Truckloads of clothes were
coming in there all through the day. We didn't have to worry
about nothin'! And we were livin' comfortable! We didn't want
to come back here and get under what we had been under all
the time. It was too rough on us here. It was better there than
it was here.

Where were the food and clothes coming from?

The world! The whole world! They were sending us
food and clothes from all over the world. They really treated us

nice up there. We had a good time. I lived better than I ever
lived in my life.

Better than you ever lived in your life?

Better than I ever lived in my life! On that trip. That
seems funny, but it's true. People in Washington and all along
the way there. When we were going up there, at different places
we would stop. They would flag us down. Sometimes they would
have roadside parks full of food, and then they'd even load the
buses upstairs full of food. All the way there at different
churches we stopped. We stopped and had services along the
way, and the people would accept us with gladness. The officers
and all. They were real nice to us on that trip. We didn't have
any trouble whatsoever. Even when they teargassed them out.
Martin Luther King had taught them that if they would be bothered, never to fight back. We didn't fight back.

*What made Martin Luther King stand out so as a
leader?*

I had a feeling that he meant . . . he wasn't fraudin' or
nothin'. He really wanted to see it better for poor people. He
didn't only work for black people, he worked for poor people as
a whole. That's really what made him stand out in my mind.
Martin Luther King, he really meant what he was doin'! He
wasn't goin' out for money. He really meant what he was doin'.
He really meant to help.

We liked the nonviolent part he carried on with. He
believed in God. And God didn't believe in wrath and fightin'
and goin' on. He was a Christian man. That's the reason he
believed in nonviolence. Then when he received the Nobel
Peace Prize, I thought it was just wonderful. I felt like he deserved it. Of course, I heard some different on the television,
like he didn't deserve it. But we felt like he deserved it! Wish we
had another man like him!

How did you react to the assassination?

I'll be straight honest. My first reaction, when I *first* heard it, it looked like to me violence kind of blurried up in my mind. I got angry, but it wasn't no time before I could think what he had taught us and it soon passed away. I tell you, after that anger flew up and I settled down from there, it was just sobbing and tears and sorry then. We had three silent marches here coming up to his funeral. Quiet marches. We went to the courthouse and we had a service on the courthouse steps. It was very sad that day.

What place do you think Martin Luther King holds in history?

A man of justice and a man of peace. That's the way I feel he should go down. A man of justice. For all! Not just for black folks. He wanted justice but he wanted to bring it about by peace. He wanted to outtalk people and show them why they were unjust.

Howard Baugh

 Nobody ever figured that M.L. would become a messiah. Nobody ever figured that he would become anything more than a good preacher.

Superintendent Howard Baugh heads the Crime Prevention Center of the Atlanta Police Department. His office is in a storefront in a black section of Atlanta.

M.L. [Martin Luther King] and I became friends in childhood. We lived in the same neighborhood and later lived next door to each other. Our childhood was not really one of those type relationships where you could say we were the closest of friends. We were friends because we lived next door to each other. We never had an opportunity to really play because he never had a lot of opportunity to play. He was always most astute in his ways of life. He was involved in his father's church affairs. He was involved in his studies. I remember on one occasion he had committed some misdeed and his father gave him a whipping. His father told him—and I remember very, very distinctly —that he was going to make something out of him if he had to beat him to death. He really wanted him to become a real man.

He was an ordinary person. He was the type person as a kid that you could respect as a kid. Nobody ever figured that M.L. would become a messiah. Nobody ever figured that he would become anything more than a good preacher. He practiced hard at that profession even as a child.

In the later years M.L. went off to school, and I didn't see very much of him after that until he had become a minister in Montgomery, Alabama. The trolley boycott later led him to this area. I was already a policeman with the City of Atlanta Police Department, working on the detective force, and Chief Herbert T. Jenkins assigned me as his aide and protector while he was in this area. The first night, I remember, was at Wheat Street Baptist Church. He came to dramatize the methods that had been used to start desegregation methods in Montgomery. We met, renewed our old friendship and acquaintanceship, and from that point on we saw quite a bit of each other.

We talked at length many, many times. I won't forget my feelings about his feelings on the Vietnam War. I could not bring myself to understand why a man that had acclaimed himself in this country and the world had taken on this tremendous responsibility of speaking out against the United States government and the President's actions in this manner. One Saturday afternoon I decided to go by the church when I knew that he was preparing his Sunday sermon and had an opportunity to really sit down and talk with him. He took the time and really went into the matter with me. That was my first time of beginning to realize what he meant by the Vietnam War. I think maybe that was my first realization to myself that maybe he was right.

Originally, he had not said anything about Vietnam. Then he had these ideas and feelings about war, that all wars were bad. Being a veteran—I had participated in the invasion of Iwo Jima as a Marine, and had felt that I had performed my services and duties as an American citizen should—it was difficult for me to feel that other people did not have that same right to do the same thing. He mentioned to me that day that this was an undeclared war, that it was a war that had very little meaning for people. From that point on, I began to really admire M.L. because of his stand, and because of the courage with which he made his stand. He was lashing out at all of America.

*   *   *

I was on duty, and I was preparing within the next day or so to take a trip to Washington to the demonstrations there, so as to get an idea of what it would be like if that same situation became real here. I was patrolling through the streets that night when the news came over my police radio to go to Dr. King's home, and on the way there I learned that he had been wounded in Memphis. I was met by his oldest daughter, Yolanda; his oldest son, Martin; and his next boy, Dexter. His youngest daughter, Bunny, was asleep. Mrs. King had already left the house to go to the airport and take the trip over to Memphis.

Word came that he had passed, and I was given the task of telling his older son that his father had been assassinated. This was a very difficult job for me, and it was even more difficult to see the expressions on the children's faces about their father. They accepted it quite calmly. His oldest, Yolanda, was not able to absorb the shock as much as the other youngsters were. Being older, it struck her with more of a shock. She just talked of the loss of her father. She spoke of his teachings and the things that he had said. The other children accepted it very calmly, although they wept for some time. They were quite strong. There was no bitterness. Not from that moment. And this is the unique part of the whole situation. There was bitterness in the minds of the people, there was bitterness in the minds of those who walked the streets, there was bitterness in the minds of blacks all over this country. But not one time did I ever hear one bitter remark by one member of his family. Not one.

The reaction of this community was hostile, to the point of hatred, bitterness, revenge. After he was funeralized I had a call to come to an area where the rest of my men had been assigned. There was a group of black militants from all over the country who were assembled here for the funeral. They had decided they wanted to get revenge in some way against the society that had taken M.L. away from us. They intended to destroy our city. But his family's action, through M.L.'s past teachings, saved this city.

*   *   *

I think that the point of violence that we have reached in this country today was generated by the killing of such people as John F. Kennedy, Bob Kennedy, and Martin Luther King. It's a universal feeling in the minds of people that we've *got* to do something to bring people around to the nonviolent feeling. But how do we do it? You don't have a leader to teach it any more. Martin Luther King was a guy that really had the authority and knowhow to show me how to do it. There are other people that are knowledgeable but without the expertise or time or effort. This man went to India and talked with the greatest philosophers in the world. Meditated to the extent that he could accept abuse, hurt, and pain without holding it against mankind. Only God has been able to do this.

I'm not claiming that M.L. was God. But we know that there are people who live in the image of God, and they live in that image so strictly that they are like God. It's only logical to feel that M.L. King was this kind of man. Because if he were not, how could the whole complexity of the world have changed so much in his short years?

E. Moore

They just worked among the niggers down here. They wanted the niggers to do this, that, and the other. Get out and mix with the white people. That just didn't go down here.

"My name's Euel, but everybody calls me E. I've been here only since 1929. Raised in the Free State of Jones County. Jones County didn't sign up with the Union until afterwards." Thus E. Moore introduces himself. In 1934 he opened E. Moore's Hardware and Implement in Philadelphia, Mississippi, the quiet Southern town where in June 1964 three civil rights workers—Andrew Goodman, James Chaney, and Michael Schwerner—were murdered. On August 4, 1964, their decomposed bodies were found in an earthen dam on the outskirts of town. Six months later the FBI arrested twenty-one persons for the slayings, including Sheriff Lawrence Rainey. All were later released or acquitted on the murder charges, although a number of them are serving time for conspiracy.

I think the Sixties were pretty good times considering the times that we had. I've seen the times here back before the Sixties, you couldn't have got enough cash business in this town to run one store, let alone several like we have now. We have a motor place, U.S. Motors, which is a division of the Emerson Company. The Wills-Lamont people here who make gloves; it's a division of the Hammond Organ Company. Then we have the Weyerhaeuser Lumber industry. That used to be Dewey's, but they've increased the capacity of it a whole lot—I imagine it's nearly doubled what Dewey used to have.

We operated here at one time mostly on credit, on

account of the farmers: they didn't have a monthly payroll. Of course, now the farmers here they have electric lights, they have telephones—it's almost like living in the city. We just live so much better.

*   *   *

We had lots of civil rights trouble here. I say lots—the killing of the white boys, we had that trouble here. That kind of paralyzed business down a little bit. I believe it was 1965 we had three civil rights workers killed here. They had men arrested down around Meridian. They never could convict them on the killings, but the United States government got them on conspiracy. There are six or eight or nine in the federal penitentiary serving time.

They were having trouble down there in Meridian; so, in the meantime, we had a little old church to burn here. That's what the civil rights workers were doing up here. They came up to investigate the church-burning. The bunch from Meridian telephones up here that they were coming and wanted this bunch up here to take care of them. They had done something in Meridian. Therefore, when it happened, Neshoba County got the blame for it. It's been hard on Neshoba County ever since.

What type of work were the civil rights workers doing?

They didn't do anything.

Then why did they come South?

They just worked among the niggers down here. They wanted the niggers to do this, that, and the other. Get out and mix with the white people. That just didn't go down here.

How did the people here in Philadelphia react to the killings?

You couldn't hardly tell it. Except there, for about three or four months, there were hardly any people here on the streets.

Has the South really changed its stand on the Negroes?
We've changed some. The schools are integrated.

Have your attitudes changed?
Not too much. Not too much.

Could you tell me what your attitudes are?
No, I couldn't.

Why is that?
I wouldn't say. I wouldn't say.

This attempt to mix the Negroes and the whites—is this a good thing?
Right now, the schools are integrated and the niggers would go back to their schools if they could. They would go back to their schools and be happy. The niggers are dissatisfied as well as the whites.

Charlotte Curtis

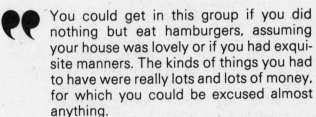 You could get in this group if you did nothing but eat hamburgers, assuming your house was lovely or if you had exquisite manners. The kinds of things you had to have were really lots and lots of money, for which you could be excused almost anything.

Charlotte Curtis joined *The New York Times* as a reporter in 1961, and became the Family/Style Editor in 1965.

Throughout the Sixties she chronicled the exploits of the Jet Set for *Times* readers.

The moment you had jet airplanes and people who flew on them, you began to have a Jet Set. It really didn't get its name until the early Sixties, when people began to forsake travel by ocean liner and go almost exclusively by jet. Flit about the world: this season in London and this season in Paris, this season in Rome, New York, California.

I can't look at those people as a moment's Camelot, as though they came out of the sky and then went away. They are a continuing long line of people who landed here in 1600. The very upper echelon of any part of American society has always been watched, stared at, enjoyed vicariously by other people within the society. During the depths of the Depression people were just fascinated by Doris Duke's coming-out party, which cost thousands and thousands of dollars. People were fascinated by J. P. Morgan's yachts, and this was all in the worst economic times we've ever had. In the 1890s, when there was recession and then there was boom time, you had fascination throughout.

The difference is in the Thirties. They were "Café Society," because that's where they gathered and that's kind of what they did. People who thought they were a waste of time used to call them "Nescafé Society." In those years society, so-called, was overshadowed by the movie stars. You could trot out all these incredible numbers of celebrated people whose names were household words, so that that was the Thirties and the Forties, the Forties through the war. And then you came to the Fifties and everybody's really recovering from the war and you still had movie stars. By the time you got to the Sixties, movie stars weren't important. Of course, Elizabeth Taylor, but there weren't twenty-five or thirty women's names that were just automatic. After the war they became known as the Jet Set. Today the "Jet Set" really is a passé term; it's really more the International Set in the sense that how they get there isn't important: it's where they go that's important. *Everybody* goes by jet plane.

It's a very distinct group of people—people whose standards of taste have to do with food, and how their houses are put together, and how they dress, and the kinds of parties they give. This kind of thing is important to them. These were the showy rich. When I used to write about them then, I used to say that "essentially they were everything that's not nailed down." It was as though they were flying out to something all the time.

They were known for their clothes; they were known for their houses; they were known for their parties; they were known for their jewels; they were known for their horses; they were known for their yachts; they were known for the number of houses they had; they were known for the people they knew; they were known by the events they attended, which were always elegant. *Their* charity balls and *their* dinner parties and lunches in *their* clubs.

There were a lot of nouveaux riches, but there were also a lot of aristocrats. There weren't many outsiders forever pushing to get into this group. It was too easy. You simply had to have lots of money and a flair for entertaining in exquisite and interesting ways. You could get in this group if you did nothing but eat hamburgers, assuming your house was lovely or if you had exquisite manners. The kinds of things you had to have were really lots and lots of money, for which you could be excused almost anything. Or you had to have some kind of charm or fascination or wit or intelligence. It was all kind of amorphous except that it had to do with taste and exquisiteness and elegance.

What's an example of a "Jet Set function"?

For example, the one that was the most talked about was the April in Paris Ball. They would bring from France maybe twenty thousand, forty thousand roses, which would have to clear Customs and they'd have to be fumigated especially to get into this country, and then arranged. There would be five wines. There would be a seven-course dinner. All this collection of names from all over the world would be there. The decorations routinely cost between fifteen and twenty-five thousand dollars, just for the flowers or the horses' heads. One year they made it look like a little discothèque in the south of France, and another year they made it look like Deauville; other years it was papier-mâché vegetables or animals. Then you'd see three or four million dollars' worth of diamonds on the women. The ball gowns universally were a thousand dollars and up.

They're slightly quieter now. They're in hiding, waiting in part for the next renaissance. And one reason they came out in the Sixties was because there was money everywhere. Everybody had money. It was a boom time. Everybody had more money, despite the figures about poverty. It was all right to be something of a hedonist. It was a time, after all, when *Time* magazine had a cover wondering whether God was dead. The Puritan ethic was certainly getting a drumming, not just from the younger generation, but from the older generation. It was all right to spend thirty-five dollars for lunch, and it was all right to go out and buy a diamond the size of an ice cube.

The Vietnam war was the first thing to catch up with this. These people . . . I can remember going to Palm Beach and never hearing the war discussed through many seasons. And all of a sudden Palm Beach became quite aware that there was a war. They were very much against the war. As it turns out, they're pacifists. They then began to do things more quietly. With the recession they toned down only because it wasn't right for people to be doing this sort of thing when there were so many problems in the country. In a way it had something to do with the Democratic administration. You could raise a kind of elegant hell under the Democrats, but by golly you'd better not under the Republicans.

Mario Procaccino

 I thought I owed the city something. . . . And when I saw the darn thing was going down the drain, well, I tried to persuade my wife, but she was against it. She said, 'People don't appreciate it. You're too honest.'

Beginning his public career in 1944 as an assistant counsel for Mayor Fiorello La Guardia, Mario Procaccino was later appointed to the bench by Mayor Robert F. Wagner. In 1965 he was elected Controller of New York City. Four years later he won the Democratic Mayoral nomination against a field of liberal rivals. Despite the defection of many prominent liberal Democrats to John Lindsay, who ran as an independent candidate, Procaccino nearly unseated the Mayor, coming in a close second in a three-way race.

I took a five-thousand-dollar cut in salary to become a judge. They wondered why I was doing that, and I said, now, where I was born, a judge was a great person in my home town. When a judge came to town, he was a big man, an important man. I've held many positions. I've always felt that, especially to me, the country was good to me, you know. After all, I was a shoemaker. And my father was a shoemaker. I fixed shoes when I went to school. It was through scholarships that I was able to go to school, to get an education. And in those days scholarships meant that you had to be bright to get them, not just that you needed money. Today if you need money, they call it a scholarship. In those days, it was competitive.

I thought I owed the city something. I really did. And

when I saw the darn thing was going down the drain, well, I tried to persuade my wife, but she was against it. She said, "People don't appreciate it. You're too honest. You can't do it, you can't do it." I never really considered it until I saw what the heck was happening to the City of New York. The city is shot. This is a beautiful place. This is a wonderful place. This is the greatest city in the world. To think what the hell it's become! It's becoming a haven now for what I call the "limousine liberals." I coined that phrase. It's being used all over the county. I think the Vice President [Agnew] used it. You've got to be either very rich or very poor now to live in New York. A fellow that's working for a living can't do it any more. This is a city of crisis, and this fellow Lindsay is responsible. My wife has a good name for him —Mortimer Snerd. He came in and he said he was going to cut down, economize. He added over one hundred thousand people —they say ninety thousand—but it's over one hundred thousand people he added on the payroll. Over one hundred thousand! The budget went from 3.8 billion dollars to almost ten billion dollars, and you're not getting better service! The filthiest streets, the filthiest place in the world. I've been all over the world. I walked on the streets of Israel, Jerusalem, Athens, Rome, Tel Aviv. Three o'clock in the morning. Nobody bothers you. You don't dare walk here. After dark in New York, you're in trouble. So they called me a bigot because I wanted a safe city.

Dustin Hoffman

 It showed people not knowing where they were going. It did not have a really Hollywood happy ending; it had a down, Sixties ending. . . . It was the beginning of the whole movement. . . .

Dustin Hoffman has starred in *The Graduate, Midnight Cowboy, Little Big Man, Straw Dogs,* and other movies.

The Fifties? You go to church every Sunday and you live your Norman Rockwell fantasy of life. And your kids are clean and scrubbed. You can still hate the niggers and still hate the Jews and be out to win the war. And if your wife is a good housewife, the reward is right there.

The Sixties have been terrific times. It was a great explosion! It hurt. It was a great opening, and when you open something, all the ugly odors come out. A reexamining . . . those ten years did it. The whole reexamination of what we are, what the marriage institution is. What is a man? What is a woman? It was a great ten years in terms . . . not to live in, maybe, but certainly in terms of what it's going to do for us in the Seventies.

The Sixties were the beginning of an operation, the beginning of a surgical procedure. For years and years and years the body of America was there, and people were wondering, "Should we operate?" Biopsies had been made here and here. They were all standing around wondering whether they should operate and looking about.

While they were talking, suddenly something exploded right in front of them, and they got blood all over their faces. They *had* to operate. It just exploded by itself and all the stink came out. This country—a country that had always said what a great country and what a great people they were—was suddenly forced to look at itself turning over buses.

*   *   *

The Graduate is an excellently made film, but as a reflection of real life it's terribly naïve. It's film life, and by being film life, it becomes romanticized in its vision. *The Graduate* is a romanticized vision of a young person, of a juvenile, of a college kid. It's not a true portrait of American life; it's a caricature of parents, the Establishment. It's a romanticized view of the rebel, this time 1967 style. It's someone who we identify with his mind rather than his physical prowess. But nevertheless just as romanticized, just as written, drawn, and shown, just as one-sided.

It left the audience thinking, but I'm not sure they weren't tricked by it. If they were tricked, it was because it had a freshness to it. A great deal of it had to do with the music. It kept one thinking in an emotional way, but it was not a deep movie in the sense that a great novel is deep. They laughed and they were moved by it. At the end some of them cried. It was not without truths. It showed people not knowing where they were going. It did not have a really Hollywood happy ending; it had a down, Sixties ending, I guess. It was the beginning of the whole movement or the whole revolution. Benjamin Braddock still had rather short hair. Two years later Benjamin Braddock would have very long hair and be much more radicalized. I was one of the first actors playing the so-called lead romantic role of my type. I was not the average good-looking Hollywood type of a guy. I was more average-looking. Through the Sixties the so-called matinée idols changed and the so-called uglies have now had their day. But not so in regard to women: women still have to be very pretty. Even Jane Fonda, who's somewhat of a rebel, nevertheless is very attractive. Only Streisand, who is able to sing, or Liza Minelli, whose main thing is that she's a singer, are allowed into this category. But if you're going to be a starlet or a matinée idol and you're a female, you still have to look like Fonda or Candice Bergen or Faye Dunaway or Raquel Welch. That has not changed. Yet if we're sincere in our so-called new attitudes, it certainly should. I would hope that a new female star who did not fulfill these standard chauvinistic measurements might come on the scene.

What do you think of the films of the later part of the decade: **Midnight Cowboy, Joe, Easy Rider, Five Easy Pieces?**

With the exception of *Five Easy Pieces* all those fit in the same category in the sense that none of them are really accurate. None of them is really true. They're all romanticized. *The Gradu-*

ate is not really the story of that boy. Things are left out. It's not really dealing with why he's having so much fun screwing the mother and then the daughter. What's the power struggle behind it? What's the other side of the character that we are never allowed to see? Even when he goes to the toilet, you hear the "Sounds of Silence."

Midnight Cowboy is a loaded picture also: that's not a real hustler, the Cowboy, that's a romanticized idea—the real hustler doesn't look like that. *Trash* [an Andy Warhol film directed by Paul Morrissey—see pp. 279–282] was more accurate. To me, the guy they used in *Trash* was the real Midnight Cowboy. In the first frame you saw a closeup of his ass. He was being blown by a girl, and as the camera pulled back you saw that he was being blown. But I remember the ass was full of pimples. In *Midnight Cowboy* you saw a part where Jon Voight was showering and his body was very light, tan and smoothed and unpimpled and made-up. He was an innocent, whereas in *Trash* the character was not an innocent. In the *Cowboy* he didn't seem to know what was going on—he was just lost in this world. He had come to New York to hustle because he thought he was good-looking and he was gong to get rich women to live with him. The psychological side, his latent homosexual thing, was not gone into. What makes a guy want to be a hustler?

Easy Rider is not a real film. It's not about real people. *Easy Rider* is about two guys who are dealing in drug traffic and we see a very romanticized side of them. It's the good guys and the bad guys. To me the film offered little except a very, very wonderful performance by Jack Nicholson. *Joe* had an excellent performance by Peter Boyle, but without him, the film had nothing to stand on. It's cheap; it's vulgar, it's exploitive, it panders to the most unthinking parts of the audience—the real comic-strip kind of intelligence. *Five Easy Pieces* does not stand in the category of any of these films. Not only is there a fine performance there, but there is an honesty of intention in the film: there was nothing exploitive about it; there's nothing really romanticized about it.

*   *   *

The movies are not a real art form. I think of it as a minor-league art form. It can't break out because you're not doing it for the truth of it. You're doing it to sell it. I like movies. They're fun, but I think they should be thought of as entertainment. I think it's sad that there's so much fuckin' talk and time spent on movies. We've been brought up on movies and television and that means that we've been brought up to sit on our ass in a very passive kind of atmosphere. Movies demand nothing of you. All you do is sit there and dull your mind.

The film critics today are more powerful than they've ever been in the history of the world. You can go by a marquee and you see no actors' names, no director's name; it will say, "Rex Reed Says 'It's a Knockout.'" They throw their shit back and forth and analyze this and analyze that and you think they're talking about great works of art. They talk about Peter Bogdanovich like he's Dostoevsky. It's crap in the sense that if you take all art and put it together, film art—except for a very few —is going to be at the bottom.

Thomas S. Buechner

 You go through fifty years of Boy Scout calendars and that kind of thing and then you hit this. . . . This thing really looks like the cry of hurt animals.

Thomas Buechner began his career as a painter of portraits, landscapes, and illustrations. As a Director and Trustee, he has been associated with the Corning Museum of Glass for over twenty years and is now Director of the Brooklyn Museum. In 1969 he authored a coffee-table collection of Norman Rockwell's works.

How do you explain the enduring phenomenon of Norman Rockwell?

He was working in a way which was out of fashion. Cubism had come in in a big way and Abstract Expressionism was all around, and here was a guy who just wasn't paying any attention to it at all. But Norman would be the first to say this himself, he would not be considered an artist in the sense that Rembrandt is an artist. It's a different kind of thing. In the first place, Rembrandt deals usually with very ennobling themes. When Rembrandt does a family, or a mother and a baby and a father in a seventeenth-century peasant shack, it's the Holy Family. You know. It's not just a family. When Norman does it, it's a typical American family, right down to the most precise kind of details. So that Rembrandt's taken big generalities of big subjects that are very moving, with the intensity that he devotes to them; whereas Norman has picked out a little vignette aspect of life common to all.

This is the delicate area. An artist likes everyone to feel that he's making a statement. A commercial artist and an illustrator has certain talents which are for hire. So Norman Rockwell is a pro in the sense that if somebody comes to him and offers him a job and he feels he can do it, he does it. I would say that that was the *Look* situation. I don't think that he elected to make statements about racial issues. I think that that's what his market asked for.

The work that he did for *Look* in the Sixties certainly reflected the interest in the whole racial phenomenon. I think his earliest, most popular one of the Sixties was the Little Rock one, of the little Negro girl being walked between four sheriffs against which a motto was splashed and the word "nigger" had been written. A very moving picture. A very compassionate picture. Then he did more recently, much more recently, about five years later, a picture of a black New York family moving into a white suburb: the white kids looking at the black kids, showing the evenness, the similarities with them. These would be scenes that he wouldn't have touched twenty years earlier because they weren't things that interested the country.

There's one he did for *Look* that is like no other picture he had ever done. It's a sketch all in brown, no color. It's a black boy that's been shot and a white boy is trying to hold him up. But it's just a sketch. It's very simply done. It's not finished at all. It's so brutal that . . . and yet it's terribly moving. Particularly in the context of all of Norman Rockwell's work. You go through fifty years of Boy Scout calendars and that kind of thing and then you hit this. . . . This thing really looks like the cry of hurt animals. That's the one thing that stands out. It's not a finished professional piece of work. It's just a crude little sketch. But he just said it so perfectly and so movingly that there's nowhere else to go with it.

Peter Kircheimer

 People read about it and . . . started . . . acting on their own. . . . [The] student reaction in the late Sixties was a fantastic thing. I'm not sure it got us anywhere.

Now attending Columbia Law School, Peter Kircheimer was involved, as an undergraduate, in the April 1968 campus revolt at Columbia University. His father was a Columbia professor.

The specific issue was that the university decided to build this new gym which they had been trying to build for some forty years, the present facility being a temporary gym, which was temporary in like 1920 and it had been temporary ever since. They pushed through a deal in Albany and were given the land in return for the promise that they'd reserve a small part of the facilities for community use. There was opposition to this in the community and among the students who were working with the community. Opposition was on the basis of, first, how Columbia went about it. Deciding on building its gym in the park, pushing the legislation and authorization for it through Albany and the City Council, and now saying it's a *fait accompli.* "The gym will be built in the community and we're going to let you have the ground floor." Secondly, there was just large distrust over whether the community was ever going to get to see any of the parts of that gym. Thirdly, the gym was a symbol of Columbia's housing policies in general. Ten thousand housing units had been removed from the area in the past ten years and then ten thousand more housing units would probably be removed in the next ten years following. The gym itself was not going to remove any housing units: it was just symbolic of the way the university operated. There's a conscious policy on the part of the university of sanitizing the area—getting rid of low-income people and making it safer for the people who lived there, for the professors and students.

The sun dial rally started at noon. All sun dial rallies started at noon. You had speeches, you went down to the gym site, came back from the gym site for more speeches, and then someone from the sun dial suggested that if we can't go to Low Library to make our complaints better heard, let's go take Hamilton Hall. Hamilton Hall was the main classroom building for the college and there were also other deans' offices there. The Dean of the College's office was there. The speakers on the sun dial could feel the force of the crowd, that this was not just a normal sun dial rally. It had more people and more of a willingness to do something. So we went and took it. Three hundred people sitting around the lobby. There was no prevention of people passing in or out to their classes.

The real cause was this common feeling of the students, which was more than just the gym. It was anger against the university, anger against society in general for the war in Vietnam and for the social injustices that were going on, and against the university for its complicity in these things. The thing that people were most concerned with was the war and what the university was and wasn't doing about it. Specifically, ROTC [Reserve Officers Training Corps] and defense research and the Institute for Defense Analysis [IDA].

A central committee went off to talk about a list of demands. The original committee was composed mostly of SDS [Students for a Democratic Society] leadership and Afro-American Society leadership. I was left in charge of moderating the speakers in the lobby while the committee went off to talk. The committee talked until three or four or five o'clock; they talked on into the night. People decided to stay there, just spread out over the building and sleep.

The demonstration kept getting bigger and bigger all the time. People just kept pouring in. Around three o'clock in the morning everybody was awakened and told that all the whites had to get out of the building, that the blacks were taking over. There was no ability to come to terms between the white leadership, namely SDS, and the black leadership, on how the building was going to be organized—specifically, whether barricades were going to be built, whether entry was going to be permitted or not, and what kind of defense was going to be taken if the police were called to kick people out. Since there was no agreement on tactics, they decided to split it up. All the whites split, at three o'clock in the morning. A group of people said, "We're going to take our own building," and went to Low Library. I went home. I was tired at three in the morning! The next morning Low Library had been occupied. I climbed in a window.

The university cops and the regular [New York Police Department] cops came into the office. They removed a Rembrandt that was hanging in the office. It was all the administration appeared to be concerned about. They ripped out the wires of the centrex telephone communication center and they split. At the time the cops came in to take out the Rembrandt, people thought that they were coming in for a bust, and most of the people left. They voted to decide whether to leave or stay when the cops came to arrest them and a small group of twenty or thirty decided to stay. The majority split, jumped out the window. The twenty or thirty who stayed were sitting on a rug when the cops came in.

Then people started taking other buildings. In the middle of the night a bunch of people took the Math Building. And later on Fayerweather and Avery. Hamilton remained all black. Avery was taken by members of the Architecture School, with the consent of the Dean of that school. Fayerweather was the biggest . . . it had a couple of hundred people in it.

Then there was a week of continual meetings with the central committee on the issues. You had a very disparate group, and it was loosely agreed that nobody would leave their building until everybody else left. Most of the time the blacks from Hamilton didn't come to the meetings.

There was an ad hoc faculty committee formed to try to negotiate a settlement. Alan Westin was president pro tem of the ad hoc faculty committee. There were lengthy negotiations with the faculty committee which ended finally when Mark Rudd stood up and said "Bullshit" in the middle of the meeting. Whereupon Westin decided that a student standing up and saying "Bullshit" in front of faculty members was more than could be stood for and he dissolved the committee and quit.

Somehow it became obvious that there was going to be a bust, that the administration wasn't changing and we weren't changing. They did not seem to be willing to grant amnesty to the students. That was the big hangup. There were almost perpetual, continual meetings going on during the whole time, both between the faculty people and the administration people and between the faculty people and the negotiating committee. There were meetings inside the buildings all the time to discuss that specific building's policy toward defense, toward maintaining life. You were in there for a week—you had to get food in, you had to have sanitary stuff, you had to have sleeping areas, and all that kind of stuff. Everything was always fluctuating. It was like a perpetual meeting. Three years later it's really hard to remember anything that happened at any of the meetings. Some people decided they were going to passively resist, they were going to be carried out. They grouped themselves all together in the bottom floor. Everybody else was just spread out over the building in rooms. I was in a room with five or six other people. We barricaded the door. We put a desk against the door and put a filing cabinet against the desk and just sat there. I might add that there was absolutely no destruction of the property that was in the building except for . . . well, you know, people were living in the building for a week, so there were coffee stains all over the rug. But there was no destruction at all of the physical property of the building or the furniture. Just plain absolutely none! Until the cops came in.

And they tore the place apart. We had barricaded ourselves in an office. What they did was they took a crowbar and they crowbarred the door open the wrong way through the frame, thus tearing the frame out of the wall.

There were thousands of cops on the campus. They threw a cordon around the building. They made a *pro forma* statement through the bullhorn: "You are obviously trespassing. You are asked to leave. If you do not leave, you will be arrested." They came on in and carried people out. Carried people who were passively resisting. In our specific building the only people who got roughed up were the people who were passively resisting. I was on the top floor and we were looking out the window. The ones who were on higher floors were just dragged, face down, all the way down the metal steps from whatever floor they were on. The ones I saw in the police station were in very, very bad shape. Also, once they got them outside, they just tossed them on the lawn in front of the building. The people who did not passively resist simply walked out.

The first to be busted was the Afro-American Society building, Hamilton Hall, with the blacks in it. There was absolutely zero violence there. Half of the Mayor's office and a couple of captains and inspectors were standing around watching. They were scared shitless. There were riots going on in cities around the country at the time and they were scared shitless at the reaction of the black community if there was massive violence used against the blacks on campus. There was intense, close supervision of that operation. People from the Mayor's office and higher-up cops; they all split as soon as that was done. Then the cops went in and did the violence in the other buildings—in Avery and in Fayerweather . . . they were just beating the hell out of people all over the place.

I didn't see the violence. It didn't happen to me. It happened to some of the people in my building. The larger part of the violence happened to the people standing outside and watching who were not involved. They probably were beaten worse than most of the people inside the building. The cops cleared the campus several times, beating everybody indiscriminately. A bunch of the people who had come to watch, who were on the side of the university, who thought that the cops should have been called in, ended up having their heads busted by cops. They had their ideas changed rather radically by being on the end of the nightstick.

It didn't stop with the bust. After the bust there was a strike. The university closed down for the rest of the year, like a month or so, from the point of the strike. The strike came about as an immense reaction on the part of all the students to the violence the cops had used in the bust. It started out with the students not going to class for about a week. It was very, very successful, like ninety to ninety-five per cent successful among the college; among the professional schools it varied. Eventually the university reacted to the strike by just ending that scholastic year a month early, and giving the professors the option of giving incompletes or giving pass-fail gradings or final exams as they wished.

*　　*　　*

The tactics that were used there and demonstrated widely there were used in other universities. It was like an igniting thing, a spark. It was on the front page of *The New York Times* for two, three weeks. People read about it and it started people thinking and acting on their own. That was terribly, terribly important. I feel that student reaction in the late Sixties was a fantastic thing. I'm not sure it got us anywhere. We're still in Vietnam, people are still dying. To be a moral man, you had to try and change what was going on because it was bad. That I'd still do again. We changed Columbia some; we didn't change Columbia much. It rearranged its relations with IDA so that the same thing was happening but less obviously. It finally did get rid of ROTC. The gym was stopped. . . .

James Dougherty

 That's when all the clubbing took place, and people resisting arrest. . . . Things like that will happen when you form yourselves into mobs. . . . That's something I guess young people haven't learned.

Fifty-one-year-old James Dougherty is an industrial relations expert in Houston, Texas. A graduate of Columbia University, he has four children.

This is one of those things that, when you first heard about it, you thought it was something that would be over in a day or two and forgotten about. There had been others. But this thing just rolled on and on and on. There was obviously a lot of mishandling going on. I've heard about some fantastic mishandling of events. Of course, I resent most of all those kids up there. I'm sure they were doing what they thought was right, but in satisfying their relatively minor grievances, they were doing, as I say, grave damage to the university, which they had no right to do.

How did you understand their grievances? What were the issues?

I couldn't see them at all. The issues were ridiculous. Even now none of them claim that the issues were important. The gym business, for instance. The university gratuitously built this gym so that half of it could be used by the Harlem troops and half of it by the university. There's no need for a university to build a public gym. Instead of that being something that they welcomed . . . incidentally it was being built on a rocky hillside that I remember very well—it's not quite a ninety-degree angle but something like a seventy-degree slope . . . they said it was taking away all the playground, and they were giving them the back door! It just so happens that they were at the foot of this precipice and one had to be the front and one had to be the back. I don't think it's asking too much to let the front be at the university side. They were doing the building. This was the main issue. And I'm delighted that they agreed not to put that gymnasium there and put it on the campus instead.

How did you feel when President Grayson Kirk called in the police?

I reacted with sheer joy. They should have called them in the first evening, and they almost did, according to private word we got down here. A small group was at one building and Grayson Kirk was calling the police in the middle of the night. He was supposed to have gotten an emergency urgent call from Mayor Lindsay that Harlem was going to be burned down if they put those rioters out of that building. He held off that night, and then some of our noble faculty decided they could negotiate with these people, and so that negotiation carried on a week or two and then it was too late to save the situation. It was a shambles after that.

When the police finally came, as I understand it, they did clear them out. That's when all the clubbing took place, and people resisting arrest. And whatever happened happened. Things like that will happen when you form yourselves into mobs and gangs. That's something I guess young people haven't learned.

You said it's done grave damage. In what way?

Applications for admission have fallen off. I am told that a lot of faculty left on account of this. They're just now getting back on their feet. They've run a pretty stable ship for a few years here. They're back on the road now, but really there was some doubt as to whether the thing could survive in its form. There was talk of moving it out of New York City and into the suburbs; in effect, giving up the whole thing.

Stuart Magee

 . . .if they're short, I like them. I mean, depending on what they look like. . . .

Stu Magee is thirteen years old and lives in Lincoln, Nebraska.

Do you remember long skirts in the days before the miniskirt?

I never looked at them, so I really wouldn't remember. I wasn't interested in them. I guess I first started noticing them probably about four years ago.

Do you know any people today who don't wear miniskirts?

Just older people. I don't know anybody that's in their early twenties or something like that. I even notice people forty that wear them!

What do you think of them?

Well, if they're short, I like them. I mean, depending on what they look like. If there's an old lady, you know, and she's got bruised-up ugly old legs, I'm not going to really like it or look at them. But if there's some chick, sixteen, seventeen, about my size, with goods legs, a nice pair of legs, I'll look twice, maybe three times.

Cyrus Vance

 This was the first time that an American had sat down with any North Vietnamese official in a long while. It was therefore with anticipation and eagerness that I went into that first meeting . . . at the Majestic Hotel in Paris.

Cyrus Vance held a wide range of public positions during the Sixties. Starting as general counsel to the Department of Defense, he was next sent by President Johnson to oversee the crises in Cyprus and the Dominican Republic. The President also dispatched him to Detroit and Washington, D.C., as liaison between the local and federal officials during racial disturbances. He was a deputy to Averell Harriman at the Paris Peace Talks, and remained there one month into President Nixon's term before resigning. Having returned to his Wall Street law firm, Vance continued his public service as a member of the Knapp Commission on police corruption in New York City.

The President, as you may recall, announced in his speech of late March [1968] that the bombing was being partially halted over North Vietnam and that we were prepared to sit down with the North Vietnamese and enter into negotiations looking towards a solution of the Vietnam problem. Within forty-eight hours after the statement of the President, word came back from Vietnam that they were prepared to enter into discussions with the United States. They said they would send an emissary to meet with one of our emissaries in an attempt to reach agreement upon the place for the talks.

About three weeks transpired before I left for Paris.

During that period I spent a good deal of time in Washington putting together the staff and assembling the necessary background materials for my own education. Also in working out, along with [former New York] Governor [W. Averell] Harriman, the Secretary of State, and the White House, the guidelines which would be our bible during the opening phases of the talks. We finally left for Paris on May ninth or twelfth.

We left with some optimism. We expected that the talks would be difficult and protracted. We believed, however, that there was a possibility that we could reach a negotiated solution. We were encouraged by the prompt response of the North Vietnamese to the President's initiative, and we thought that this augured well for the talks.

How did the very first meeting with the North Vietnamese go?

It went very well. I was terribly pleased with it. This was the first time that an American had sat down with any North Vietnamese official in a long while. It was therefore with anticipation and eagerness that I went into that first meeting, which was held at the Majestic Hotel in Paris. There were only three of us, as I recall it, on our side: Phil Habib [Deputy Assistant Secretary of State for East Asian and Pacific Affairs], Bill Jorden [spokesman for the American delegation to the talks], an interpreter, and I. On the other side was Ambassador Lau, Mr. Vy, a notetaker, and an interpreter. We exchanged draft proposals with respect to the procedures to be followed and then discussed each other's suggestions. We reached agreement on many of the items and decided, after about two hours of discussion, to meet again a couple of days later, hopefully to conclude our discussions. The meeting was courteous, not an unfriendly one. We shook hands again when we left the Majestic Hotel and went back to our respective missions. The next meeting we cleaned up all the remaining items and in a period of forty-eight hours had agreed on all the procedures for the start of our talks with the North Vietnamese. We were excited and pleased that the procedural details had been agreed upon so quickly because we had some fears that the problems that appeared in the Korean talks might face us there. The fact that we got through the procedures so quickly gave us hope that perhaps we could do the same thing on the substantive side.

One of the preliminaries which received the most publicity in this country was the shape of the bargaining table.

That didn't come up until after we had agreed on the total bombing halt and on expanding the talks to include both the National Liberation Front and the Republic of South Vietnam representatives. The issue of the shape of the table, I think, actually came up on November sixth. We had reached agreement that the four parties would sit down on the sixth of November. On the sixth of November we could not sit down because the South Vietnamese had refused to come to Paris—I'm talking about the Republic of South Vietnam people—and because of that the talks could not go forward. It was after that that the issue of the shape of the table and the order of speaking and the other procedural questions were raised. In my own judgment, had we been able to sit down as agreed upon on the sixth of November, the procedural questions which plagued us for the next seven weeks never would have arisen. That whole silly argument about the shape of the table simply would have not existed.

Why weren't the South Vietnamese there on November sixth?

I wish I really knew. They had committed to our government that they would come. They subsequently changed their minds and said that they were not coming. There are a couple of reasons that are given for this and I can't, of firsthand knowledge, say which, or whether both are in fact true or not. One is that it was domestic political activities in South Vietnam that dictated their refusal to come. There are others who charge that pressure was put on the South Vietnam government not to come at the time of the U.S. domestic election, and to wait until after the new administration came in when allegedly they would get a better deal.

We discussed the subject with the North Vietnamese, and at that time the subject of the order of speaking also was thrown into the pot. From there on we went through I hate to think how many different meetings with how many different shapes of tables proposed and how many different variations on speaking order. It really was a silly, tragic process.

What shape was finally decided upon?

A round table, with two smaller oblong tables a few inches from the outer rim of the round table. It was a circle with two projections on each side.

What kind of substantive progress do you feel was made at Paris?

Several things were accomplished. First of all, there was a total cessation of the bombing of North Vietnam. Without that, in my judgment, no talks could have ever started. It was necessary that this be done to get the talks under way. Secondly, it was understood that in return for the bombing halt certain actions would be taken on the part of the North Vietnamese with respect to actions in and around the demilitarized zone and in South Vietnam. Further, it was agreed that the four parties would sit down together to start talking about a political solution, without which there could be no solution to the Vietnam problem. That was absolutely essential to resolve the problem. Actually, the cessation of the bombing, and the concomitant action taken by the North Vietnamese and the NLF, resulted in a lowering of the casualties of the North Vietnamese, the South Vietnamese, the NLF and the U.S. thereafter. Never again were the casualties, military and civilian, as high as they were prior to the reaching of that agreement.

The parties were brought together where they could

start to talk about a political settlement. The opportunity then existed to make progress. It did not make progress, and for a variety of reasons. Lost opportunities on the part of both sides. Unfortunately, I'm afraid, the time has come, or the time has passed, so that the likelihood of a settlement coming out of the Paris Peace Talks is virtually nonexistent. I think there was an opportunity for a political settlement. I think if we had been able to sit down the first week in November as agreed, we really might have made some progress. The North Vietnamese had agreed to waive all procedural questions if we could sit down on November sixth. To me that indicated that they were serious about wanting to talk about the substantive issues. It was just a tragedy that the talks never were able to start.

> *Would it be misinterpreting those comments to infer that you don't think the South Vietnamese were as serious as the North Vietnamese in wanting to sit down and discuss the substantive issues?*

No, you don't misinterpret me at all. I think it's an absolute tragedy that the South Vietnamese didn't show up at that time. I think that hindered, if not destroyed, any chances of progress in the talks.

Glenn T. Seaborg

 The fear of the bomb is understandable. . . . It hasn't disappeared, but . . . just the passage of . . . time tends to diminish the fear.

A Nobel laureate in chemistry, Dr. Glenn Seaborg chaired the Atomic Energy Commission from 1961 to

1971. He is now at the University of California at Berkeley as Visiting Professor of Chemistry and Associate Director of the Lawrence Radiation Laboratory.

Radiation has always been mysterious. It is invisible, and people are afraid of what they don't understand. That fact explains the fear of "fallout." The fear of the bomb is understandable. It's just the apprehension that with several of the world powers having this awesome weapon, that it might someday be used. I think that was more in people's minds in 1960 than it is now. It hasn't disappeared, but ten or eleven years without that ultimate disaster happening, just the passage of that time tends to diminish the fear.

A decade ago there were only a few experimental nuclear power reactors and the total electricity-producing capacity was negligible. Progress was made during the decade by the reactor manufacturers and there began to develop . . . not a shortage of fossil fuels, but fossil fuels began to go up in price. By fossil fuels, I mean coal and oil and gas. There also was a recognition of the health dangers of air pollution—which nuclear energy is free of—so that there was a gradual turning to nuclear energy. About the middle of the decade utilities began to order nuclear power plants, which by this time were bigger than they had been. Nuclear power has a characteristic that it's more economic relative to fossil fuel in the large sizes, and the reactor vendors were learning how to build larger nuclear power plants—five hundred and six hundred thousand kilowatts by the middle 1960s. Utilities then began to order nuclear power plants at a rate that was just about equal to that at which they were ordering fossil fuel plants. By the end of the decade one-million-kilowatt nuclear power plants were commonplace. If you add up all of the nuclear power plants in the United States that are operating, or under construction, or planned by utilities, this totals about a hundred thirty, with a gross total electric generating capacity of one hundred ten million kilowatts, compared to about three hundred fifty million kilowatts for the total in the United States.

Without nuclear power we wouldn't be able to meet our electric requirements, and eventually, by the twenty-first century, civilization would slowly grind to a halt.

John J. Gilligan

 The unchallengeable belief in America's virtue and righteousness and incomparable military strength, and our unchallengeable right to use that military power as we saw fit to maintain peace and order in the world—as we define peace and order. Now that *is* under challenge. . . . we are on the threshold of making some brand-new evaluations . . . about what our society is all about.

An outspoken liberal from southern Ohio, John Gilligan served in Congress in 1965 and 1966 before being unseated by Robert Taft, Jr. He was also defeated in a bid for the Senate prior to winning the governorship of Ohio in 1970. During his stay in Congress, Gilligan strongly supported the social legislation of President Johnson's Great Society.

There was an enormous explosion of scientific endeavor in the educational field following the launching of Sputnik in 1958. As usual, like most things in this country, they can't be undertaken unless they're somehow related to defense or war. When they want to build an interstate highway system, they have to call it the National *Defense* Highway System in order to get it going. If we want to do something in the field of education, we have to call it the National *Defense* Education Act.

So Sputnik generated a great deal of concern in the

country. The Russians were getting out ahead of us in technological advance, education, and so forth and so on. So the government began pouring very substantial amounts of money into those areas. Within a very short time eighty per cent of all medical research in this country was handled directly or indirectly by federal grants. Hospital expansion. Educational advancement. At one time in the middle Sixties, I think, three out of every five graduate students in this country, especially in the fields of the physical sciences, were on some form of federal scholarship or assistance program of some kind. There were research grants of all kinds. Not all of the expenditure of this money was productive, but it did find an enormous, simply fantastic expansion in national effort to promote scientific investigations, technological development, and so forth. The same thing, of course, applied in spades when you threw in the NASA space effort. It has been estimated that NASA absorbed sixty per cent of all the scientific brainpower we had in this country, directly or indirectly. All of it strictly federally sponsored. Now, was that altogether good? Perhaps not, but again the spinoff in terms of electronic research and everything else is really hard to calculate.

The curious thing is that while we were expanding scientific knowledge, scientific training, technological breakthroughs of all kinds, the delivery systems of putting this new knowledge at the service of the people of the country—whether in the fields of health, education, or welfare—didn't develop at all. When I was in Congress in the middle Sixties—1965, 1966 —the so-called DeBakey Report came through. That was commissioned preparing for the 1964 campaign of Lyndon Johnson. Dr. Michael DeBakey, the heart surgeon [see pp. 369–371], came through with a report that described the great gulf between advancing technology and the inability of the practitioner in the field to keep up with it. He said that while we are light-years ahead of where we were in medical and scientific knowledge thirty years ago, the average general practitioner and the specialist in the field today are practicing the medicine of thirty years ago. Beyond that, the hospital systems, the clinical systems that are giving care to people are relatively unchanged in fifty years. In some respects these can even be said to have deteriorated. The curious thing is not this enormous explosion of knowledge, backed up by billions and billions of dollars, but the unwillingness of the nation to spend anything at all to provide services to people who need them. There were other nations that weren't advancing nearly as rapidly as we were in scientific knowhow, but who were spending significantly greater portions of their national wealth, national resources on people.

It's this lack of desire. It's this built-in doctrinaire fear in this country of "socialism"—whatever that means. We don't mind bailing out Penn Central, lending a quarter of a billion dollars to Lockheed. We don't mind government contracts of all kinds in the defense industry. That's fine. But the programs designed in the fields of health, education, and welfare to meet the needs of the people get labeled "socialism." We hate welfare in this country, for instance. We hate the concept of paying people for not working. At the same time we spend billions of dollars to support farmers for not plowing their fields and for not planting crops. This is a game in which logic will get you nowhere. Welfare is a heinous operation to get people the necessities of life—that's bad. But to pay a farmer for not planting his field—that's good. How it makes any sense at all . . . !

*   *   *

I think what happened in the closing period of this decade will quite probably signal the dawning of a new day. One reason is the Vietnam War and the public reaction to it. It's caused a search of the nation's conscience that we probably haven't undertaken since the days of the Civil War. This is a national convulsion. The My Lai incident and all these things have just caused people to ask themselves and others questions about this country and what we're up to. These questions really haven't been asked in a very long time.

The second reason is the whole question of the environment, the ecology. Up to now it's been a given that any kind of scientific and/or industrial development, production, and so forth and so on was an unchallengeable good. Now all of a sudden lots of people are beginning to ask, "Do we really want more production if the production costs are such and so?" Poisoned streams and lakes, black air, and so forth. To raise these two questions challenges the whole folklore of the American operation: The unchallengeable belief in America's virtue and righteousness and incomparable military strength, and our unchallengeable right to use that military power as we saw fit to maintain peace and order in the world—as we define peace and order. Now that *is* under challenge. The second one is the idea that anything done in terms of industrial or commercial progress is an unchallengeable good. Now we're beginning to question that. At the conclusion of the Sixties, it seems to me, we are on the threshold of making some brand-new evaluations and decisions about what our society is all about.

As a member of the platform committee at the 1968 Democratic Convention, you were one of the backers of the so-called Peace Plank. What was its purpose and its effect?

Humphrey was obviously so explicitly concerned with offending the Johnson Administration. He was really afraid that Johnson, by some device or another, would take the nomination away from him, even by running again himself. So it was decided that if Hubert couldn't do it for himself, we'd do it for him. We'd do for him what he had done for Truman in 1948. Humphrey came up with a Civil Rights Plank which forced Truman way out into a position which I don't think he would have willingly taken if the Convention hadn't forced him to.

We knew we would be defeated in the committee, because after a week we had pretty good soundings as to how people felt. We had the hearings with Rusk and the other people up there—you could tell from the questioning who we were going to get and who we weren't. But we thought we might do better on the floor. In the meantime we were trying to get Humphrey. We didn't expect him to come out and embrace the plank, but we wanted him to pass the word gently that he could live with it. And then, after we got our platform passed, to stand up and accept the nomination and say, "I accept your nomination and I accept your platform." Then the break would be clear and he'd be off in the blue.

I was told one night in negotiations with a couple of Humphrey's people that "There isn't a dime's worth of difference between the Vice President's position and this plank." A nickel apiece. We kept trying to get at least a tacit okay out of Humphrey. Both of the other candidates endorsed it openly— [Eugene] McCarthy and [George] McGovern. Then they tried to put the debate off until after midnight on Tuesday night, knowing that most of the people would be in bed. So we got the Convention adjourned until the next afternoon, Wednesday afternoon. In so doing, we got ourselves a bigger television audience. We got the full debate on television, but we probably lost the Peace Plank, because the night before they were still talking about Teddy Kennedy running. The word was out that McCarthy had quit but Kennedy was still a possibility. The word was all over the hall and everything else that maybe Kennedy was going to go. It was known that Kennedy was a dove, and if the Convention were going to go for a dove, it gave strength to the adherents of the Peace Plank. Over Tuesday night we found that Kennedy had had it out with [Mayor Richard] Daley and some of the other people and had declared flat out he would not go. When the word came out that McCarthy had offered to throw his votes to Kennedy if he'd come in, that meant that any lingering doubts about who the nominee was going to be were gone. The question hinged even more on what does the candidate want. When Humphrey declined to give any slightest suggestion of acceptance to the Peace Plan, that pretty well finished it. We still got forty-three per cent of the vote on the floor. In the President's own party. And when you take out of that Texas and Illinois that voted unit rule—so there was nobody in Texas that wanted peace and only about two per cent of the Illinois population did—you got a situation where it was an absolutely extraordinary thing.

Having lost, what was achieved by the Peace Plank, if anything?

Getting the debate! The question had never been debated as such in any deliberative body. Never on the floor of the House, never on the floor of the Senate. Unless you want to talk about the Bay of Tonkin Resolution, and that really wasn't a debate on the issues of the war at all. It was not debated—it was hardly mentioned—at Miami. So getting the debate, getting it thrashed out and getting the Peace Plank written, going through the procedural battle of getting it to the floor, and then getting something like forty-two to forty-three per cent of the delegates to stand up to say, "You're wrong, you're really wrong." It was a very considerable accomplishment.

What effect did Eugene McCarthy have on events that year?

McCarthy's achievement is not what it seemed to be. Eugene McCarthy is a very talented and very complex personality. When we were in Washington for the hearings on the Peace Plank, I went over to him and I said, "Senator, there are two kinds of credibility gaps at work in this Convention, or what is about to be a Convention: one of them is killing Hubert and one of them is killing you. The delegates don't believe that Hubert can be his own man. They don't believe he can ever shake loose of Lyndon Johnson. And the thing that's killing you is that the delegates don't believe you really want to be President of the United States. They think you want to win the debate, but do you really want to be President? Do you really want to sit in that awful oval office and pull all those grimy knobs and levers of power and make all those grimy decisions with all those grimy people. If you're really interested, go out and start now. Start with Dick Daley—he's the kind of guy you're going to have to deal with when you're President of the United States. If you can't or won't deal with him now, what makes you think you're going to be ready to do it after you're inaugurated President?"

What turned the delegates off is what the kids later saw.

First he [McCarthy] was a holdout during the course of the campaign. He knew Richard Nixon and he knew Hubert Humphrey. It's conceivable he could have elected Hubert Humphrey. Then giving up his place on the Foreign Relations Committee. His vote against Teddy for the Whip. The total kiss-off. I think he really did disillusion an awful lot of the young people. They had built an image of him that really wasn't quite fair. A total Galahad! He's a very human guy. And they didn't want a human, they wanted a hero.

PART 4

Robert McDonald

 Our plan has grown more sophisticated each year. The first plan was about fifty pages; now we have about a four-hundred-dred-page plan.

Robert McDonald, at forty-eight, is the administrator of the Appalachian Program in Alabama. His wife works for the Office of Economic Opportunity.

The Appalachian Development Act of 1965 is set up within the Office of the President. The structure is such that each of the thirteen Appalachian governors vote on commission policy. It was a result of President Kennedy's touring West Virginia. You remember he made some inroads in his campaign in West Virginia and he promised the people that he would try to do something about their area. The Appalachian region is one that's been bypassed through the years. The mines are gone in many cases. The people are living up in the hollows in pretty destitute circumstances. This area we are in right now is the southernmost reach of the Appalachian Mountains.

339

How has this specific poverty program developed from its first days back in 1965?

We didn't think of ourselves in terms of the word "poverty." That's sort of a taboo word with the Appalachian Program. It was a program to give the states a block grant of money. Within certain broad categories, the states were allowed to design their own program. Each year we've had an Appalachian Development Plan for Alabama, designed for the state. The University of Alabama in Tuscaloosa does the major input into it. Part of the plan are growth centers. These are areas that have shown a potential for future growth based on their past; industry is there; it's a moving place. We can't afford to invest our few public dollars out in the boonies where it won't show any return. Our plan has grown more sophisticated each year. The first plan was about fifty pages; now we have about a four-hundred-page plan.

How do the Appalachian people react to the attention and interest surrounding them?

I'm not sure that they're even aware of it, if you want an honest answer. The community leaders are quite aware of our program and the features of it, but the Appalachian people I have no contacts with.

Allen Funt

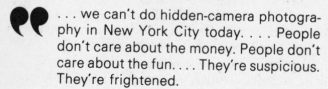

. . . we can't do hidden-camera photography in New York City today. . . . People don't care about the money. People don't care about the fun. . . . They're suspicious. They're frightened.

Best known as the producer and host of *Candid Camera*—the show ran until 1968 and was the nation's number-one television show from 1962 to 1963—Allen Funt has been described by David Riesman as the "second most ingenious sociologist in America." Over the past quarter century, on radio and TV, he and his crew have recorded and photographed countless people caught unaware in frustrating situations by his hidden microphones and hidden cameras.

People have changed enormously, and for the worse. At least in the early part of the Sixties the people were relaxed. In our particular context they could smile at themselves. To jump to the most severe comparison, we can't do hidden-camera photography in New York City today. All of the reasons why we could approach them before fail to exist now. People don't care about the money. People don't care about the fun. People don't care about the entertainment. They're suspicious. They're frightened. They're antagonistic in general. They haven't the sense of humor. The sense of humor is one of the first senses to dry up in this type of atmosphere. We wouldn't even try to work in New York.

When we went to the Midwest, the South, believe it or not, it's a less frantic, less fearful atmosphere. Now I have no clear measure about the rest of the country in the Sixties, but I suspect that the people were better in 1960 than they were in 1970 wherever they were.

When we finish filming somebody, we have to get a release. That's the moment of truth for us. There was a time in the Sixties when our average of failures to get a release was three in a thousand, and those three normally were people who were in the wrong place at the wrong time. Not people who had any principles, who had any fear. They would have loved to do it, but if the guy's with the wrong woman, that's the end of it. Nowadays, they're so suspicious. They're scared. "What the hell's this going to do to my life?" "Who are you?" "Where are you using this?" All this overall concern.

What provoked this change?

The things that provoked it, the things that brought it on are . . . perhaps the war is most important. The economic difficulties is a second subject. The racial thing is a third subject. I'll give you an example in any one of those spheres. We did films in Harlem during the Sixties. We took a crew in Harlem. It's absolutely inconceivable that you could take a white crew in Harlem now—that would be on the race basis. On the basis of the war, what a weird thing it is that in the early Sixties, soldiers, any uniformed personnel, could be a part of any show. We used wonderful sequences involving soldiers and sailors. Now you wouldn't dream of putting a uniformed person on television. They would never allow you to. The motion pictures would never allow it. So there's a sense of the military. In the sense of economics: our one source of popular expression that is missed by so many people is organized labor. We did enormously successful films of the teamsters and the dockworkers—very funny sequences. Now you couldn't even ask them to allow you to do it. They are all preoccupied. They're all scared. I wish I could find some new key to why we are behaving the way we are, but I don't really think it is a question of a new discovery. The obvious things make a pretty good explanation for it.

I have a feeling that the Seventies may very well prove to be a better time for living than the Sixties, and I say that because I don't think things can continue this way without a sort of cleansing explosion of some sort. The Sixties were successful in hiding the malaise of our society, or postponing the eventual showdown. I think the Seventies are going to find those things are mounting to the point where they're less hideable.

Didn't the showdown come during the Sixties?

Not really. I think the explosions took place, but it didn't really bring a showdown. It brought a confrontation without really any decision. Name one basic thing that's been changed. The students' uprising—nothing really happened. The race situation today, it seems to me, is worse than it was at the time of most of the riots—simply because one has a sense of something being done about it, but I don't think anything has.

I think we had a very strange false issue in the early Sixties—at least it turned out to be a false issue—and that is, we were all afraid of atomic warfare. That was the abiding fear. It diverted us from many real issues of our time. I have a feeling that the returning soldiers will crystallize the racial situation. I think that the economic thing is going to make a showdown in the struggle between capital and labor. The stalemate in the major power struggle of the world is the ideal—no, not the ideal —but the best possible balance of trouble. There's an equilibrium among the major powers that looks quite secure, so I don't think there'll be any huge holocaust, which leaves us relatively free to face the real issues.

My major regret is that I don't really have a place to enlist. I can't identify with the quarrels of the young. I don't have a real stake in the racial or economic struggles. People of my age are terribly left out, really. We can sort of pretend to be involved, and we can sort of ruminate a little bit for one side, but we really don't have any stake.

As I would judge it, it was a period of really a pleasant lull before the storm. It was only a prelude to harder times. It had to be, because it wasn't solving anything. It wasn't facing anything.

Susan Lottman[*]

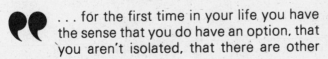

... for the first time in your life you have the sense that you do have an option, that you aren't isolated, that there are other women to help you, that these aren't just your own travails.

At twenty-three Susan Lottman has decided to pursue her studies by working toward a doctorate in American Studies. After her graduation from college, she worked in child welfare for a year and spent one evening a week counseling at an abortion clinic.

Every woman has a gut awareness that something is wrong in the world. For women things were going along pretty much as they were in the Fifties, with women just really trapped in the suburban households, and women being sent to college and then coming out and being cheated, being told, "Here we are in the marvelous twentieth century and you have the vote and everything is all right."

At the same time this thing called the sexual revolution was happening. That brought even more pressure to bear on us because you were made to feel that if you weren't in the avant-garde of your sex—what that meant was that you slept with anybody who asked you to—then there was something wrong with you and you were still hung up on the mores of your mother.

I went to college and my freshman year I was at a place that had a five-to-one ratio and had incredibly bright women there. It was much harder to get in as a woman than as a man. So supposedly you have all these bright women, very challenging women, and they supposedly have some life of their own; but instead the identity of a woman was just totally dependent on the prestige of the man she dated. There were just incredible pressures for dating. It didn't matter if you were really involved in your major or if you were really involved in something in the community. The only thing that mattered was if you could get a date with a football player.

There was also this kind of mental bargaining going on all the time with yourself and with the people around you of just how much of your sexual favors could you give away to get a date or to get an engagement ring. So in my sophomore year my friends and I got involved in this sexual liberation bit. When I think back on it, the atrocities that we committed on each other and on the women around us were really horrifying. The community of women which I was involved with was divided into the women who slept with men and the women who didn't sleep with men, and they were at each other's throats constantly.

What happened after you transferred to Princeton?

I would come home at night and I would just get all frightened because I was afraid somebody would call me on the phone and I didn't want to talk to them. Then when I hung up somebody else would start calling me on the phone. What I lacked completely was just a room of my own. I was just besieged on all sides by people making demands on me. People turning me into somebody that I wasn't. People turned me into a woman that loved them and I didn't really. That was when I picked up an article in *Mademoiselle* magazine that just told me that there was a thing called the oppression of women. It went into great detail comparing the role of women to the role of blacks in our society. There was the realization that came to hundreds of women that their resentments were legitimate, and that their resentments were not only legitimate, but they were political—that the anger and the hatred you were feeling was no longer your own personal hangup, but that it was shared by your sisters too. It was liberation.

Consciousness-raising groups sprang up. Consciousness-raising just meant that a couple of women got together and would choose a topic like work, and they would start talking about that topic, and about how they related to this topic as women. What came out of it was this incredibly exciting realization, for example, that you got sick and tired, *too*, of hearing your boss call you a girl all the time when you were thirty-two years old, or you got tired, *too*, of dialing your boss's hotels to make reservations when he could have dialed just as easily himself.

The first movement of women's liberation that went

into consciousness-raising groups is now expanding into tremendously positive action. Women are doing theater together and they're teaching each other how to do gynecological exams on each other and they're doing abortion counseling and they're setting up health clinics and they're setting up radical care groups for each other.

There are a lot of women who just missed the first wave of feminism, who got out of college, say, in 1963, got married —because there was pretty much nothing else to do—and they were like five years into a marriage with maybe one child when this desolate feeling came over them that they were just ruined, that they no longer had any use for whatever education or whatever talents they had. Here came these other women saying, "You can. You can do it if you want to. You can say to your husband, 'You're going to have to start sharing the dishes with me.' You can say to your husband even something as radical as wanting to split a work week." Those things are coming, very, very slowly, but they're coming to be more and more accepted.

I don't think that feminism is instant happiness, but there's a quote from a Frenchman of the eighteenth century that pretty much says it all. I'm obviously going to misquote it, but he is comparing the feminists in eighteenth-century France to the women who today say, "I love to be a slave. I love to be a wife and mother and work ten hours a day." [*She laughs.*] He says, "There are women who would rather exchange the larger responsibilities and joys of freedom for the easier luxuries of being a slave." That's what women's liberation is about. Being a feminist does not mean that suddenly you're going to be able to go in to your boss and say, "I want that promotion that you didn't give me two years ago and gave to a man," and you aren't going to be able to say to your husband, "I'm walking out unless you start sharing the housekeeping duties with me"; but it does mean that finally, for the first time in your life you have the sense that you do have an option, that you aren't isolated, that there are other women to help you, that these aren't just your own travails. Most of all, that you can gain some kind of control over your life.

As for myself, it has made a difference because I've become very close to a number of women for the first time in my life. I always have the knowledge that the man in my life is not the only thing that there is. That in itself is a tremendous freedom, because I can remember times when there was just this kind of gut terror that would strike me, this archetypal fear of the high school dance, of standing in the corner when no one asks you to dance. That happens all the way through to women —it just doesn't end in the seventh grade.

Richard Fleming

 How do you feel about Women's Lib?

Well, I feel in-between.

Richard Fleming is eight years old. He has a younger sister, Katy.

What is women's liberation?

It's like . . . Women's Lib is like . . . women are always doing housework, like washing the dishes, and they want the husbands to do that sometimes, and go out and do some of the work in their garden and stuff.

Bill Graham

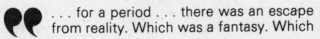 . . . for a period . . . there was an escape from reality. Which was a fantasy. Which

was flower power. 'Oh, aren't the streets
beautiful?' No, they have shit in them!
'Well, I'll just dance on the shit then.' No!
Try to clean it. 'Oh, no, no. That's work.
That's reality.'

After a stint in the business world, Bill Graham joined the
San Francisco Mime Troupe in 1965. He organized a
benefit to help the troupe out of financial difficulties. One
benefit led to another, and he soon opened the Fillmore
in San Francisco, to be followed by Fillmore East in New
York. The two Fillmores soon became the central show-
cases of the rock world. In 1971 Graham closed both of
them.

The Beatles? When you talk about rock, I'm like everybody else—there's nobody to compare them to. You talk about
who is the greatest group ever. It's hard to say. What is your
favorite food? Who's your favorite being? First you talk about
God and you put him away and then you talk about everybody
else. The Beatles are up there.

If they wrote one or two good songs, you could say they
were good writers who wrote a couple of nice things, but they
wrote twenty, twenty-five great things! Melodic! They weren't
putting on anything. They weren't just rock 'n' roll. They wrote
intricate patterns that were hummable and rememberable. And
memorable. Debussy or Mozart is good music. The common
man can't remember a whole symphony. The Beatles' songs—
the words were interesting, some of them made you think, con-
template, but more than anything else about their songs is—this
sounds crazy but this is the key to popularity—they were hummable. You could hum their songs. There's a joy in them. Take
Harrison's "Something"—it's an incredible song! "Norwegian
Wood"—I love that, just the flow of it. If you listen, it's a symphony. It's music! It's not fucking rock, it's music!

The words have a nice flow about them. Nothing com-
pares with them. The songs that they wrote were good and

they were many. So there's the quality there and the quantity there.

The Beatles, earlier than anybody realized, went through the whole drug syndrome looking for that fantasy world. They stopped in 1968, I think. They signaled to us that that fantasy world isn't real. They were the first ones. One by one they dropped out. They went into the meditation thing after the drug thing. A lot of their songs were written during their drug era—1966, 1967—some of their good songs. Every interviewer usually asks one question: "Mr. Graham, do you think drugs played any major part of any sort in the rock revolution?" What a stupid fucking question! Of course it did. But I think having gone through that, it must have brought the Beatles around to the realization that while drugs may have helped their songwriting to some extent as far as their heads were concerned, the true test comes when your head is clean.

You have to go back to the barest level. A man, John Lennon, lives in a neighborhood, has a family. Who is he? The real man? Take away the drugs, take away . . . I think they have, all along, since 1967, 1968, been making the attempt to find out who they really are. George Harrison going to India and back. Ringo Starr leaving and raising a family. The relation between Lennon and McCartney. As writers I have the greatest admiration for them. As people I have great respect for their attempt to find out who they really are. And boy, they really tried!

*   *   *

There's so much discussion about freedom of expression and letting it all hang out and flower power and love and togetherness. At that particular gathering [the first benefit he organized, in 1965] I saw it in its purest form. Because there it was real. It was as if we turned over the rock of Bohemia and all the worms were there and they were fresh and they mingled with each other. What I liked about it is that everything was experimental. Guys came with their cameras and guys came with their liquid projection. People came with their musical instruments. Or with their poetry. There wasn't any phony fanfare. People danced freely with each other and smiled and exchanged dialogue. A bunch of people would sit in the corner and rap. Some other people would be having some refreshments in another corner, and they were feeling no pain. It was an open, honest feeling of expression. Honest! Later on . . . of course we all know what happened in the scene. Everybody tried to hide from reality through flowers or through Goodwill retreads or tie-dyed shirts and what not. The thing I liked about that evening was that everybody just really had a good time.

I did promise that I would do another benefit to raise some money. It was not just a financial success—I think we made four, five thousand dollars—but it was the way we made it. It was fun. It wasn't just hard work. We had fruit hung from the girders and we had two garbage cans lined with aluminum wrap and we put ninety per cent vodka and ten per cent grapefuit juice in them. The spirit was what I liked. After that we got hundreds of calls and letters: "Let's do some more, whether it's benefits or not." So I had to find a bigger place. About a month later I found a place in the middle of the ghetto area here. It happened to be a film auditorium. It was sitting there vacant and I rented it for sixty dollars, and we did another benefit. And then we did another one. I just gravitated into that field.

What happened with the music and with the young generation is that it went into a period of wanting to forget the world around them and using music as the gasoline to get there. Having failed after six or seven years, they're now back down to earth.

The young people used rock 'n' roll to say to the world, "We can be independents. This is our way of life. We're revolutionaries. This is the background. This is the scene for our play. We shall overcome our parents' misunderstanding us. We shall overcome poverty and sickness and the fact that there's a war. Whether we know where Vietnam is is really not material." A desire to escape. Rock and its derivatives—the drugs, the commune, the wanting to dress differently from our predecessors— all of that was backed up by the sounds. There was nothing wrong with it except that there was very little doing. There was a lot of thinking and a lot of escaping.

What's happening now is that we're in the period of going down the other side of the mountain, having peaked in 1969. There was an attempt to get to a utopia that never was. A fantasy that could never become real. The kids who put flowers in their hair and dreamt about the wonderful world of Bali Bali didn't stop along the way to find out what it takes to make the world that way. There was never an active part. A writer some years ago described the Beatniks as "a group of people that had neither the guts nor the ability to change the world they hate." They're forever putting down: "Down with the pigs!" "Down with Washington!" "Down with Nixon!" "Get out of Vietnam." But other than yelling and screaming, what are they doing?

The music did the same thing, you see. When the fantasy was over, people reasoned that the world isn't going to get any better just by yelling about it. We're now back to how the mass of young people relate to reality. They now go to concerts differently. During that period they went to dances . . . you know, lovely. They didn't have to know anybody. They walked in and joined a circle of people and started dancing. They walked up to them and felt like they were sisters and brothers. Today they go to rumble or to make out or to pick up, and maybe to listen to the music.

But it all relates to the times also. They realized that the world around them isn't very pretty. They also don't do anything about it. There's an acceptance of negativism where, for a period of time, there was an escape from reality. Which was a fantasy. Which was flower power. "Oh, aren't the streets beautiful?" No, they have shit in them! "Well, I'll just dance on the shit then." No! Try to clean it. "Oh, no, no. That's work. That's reality." You have to relate to music in the same terms.

There was an honest capitalization by a lot of groups and a lot of writers about utopia. "And there we were, two of us, as one, walking on the beach of tomorrow"—I'm making this up—"the beach of tomorrow. And the colors. Call it the rainbow of life." What is he saying? It's this wonderful dream world, *out there,* that you grasp. You get high one night and the world is beautiful and you wake up the next day and you say, "My God,

the world isn't beautiful. I've got to get away from this reality."
And you get high again. Four years later you're still high and you
get up every morning and you say, "How come the tree of life
isn't ripe? How come things aren't happening?" It's because you
think the same as your brother who lives in the next hut and he
is saying, "How come our neighbor isn't doing things? Why isn't
the tree ripe? Maybe I should ask George, or Charlotte, or Peter,
or Susie." Everybody's waiting for somebody else to do something, and nobody's doing anything.

Well, here we are. It's 1971, and what happened about
all the marches about Vietnam, and all the nine thousand communes, and all your hi-fis, and all the musicians who were small
at one time who are now superstars, who, when they were small,
said, "Community, relate, exchange, dialogue. No Cadillacs. No
real estate ownership. We should all live together, one world."
What they are now is what they really were then but they just
couldn't say it. It's very easy to put down something and make
people think he really doesn't want that—he couldn't afford it!
So you have the musicians today who are writing what will sell.
Not all of them, the majority of them. [You have some artists
who are still men and ladies who are women.] But the majority
of the artists today? The majority are in it to make money.
Nothing wrong with that—except one thing: say it. I respect
Sinatra because he says, "I'm an entertainer. I make a hundred
thousand dollars a week and I go out and try to put on a good
show. When I'm finished, I get into my Learjet and go to my
Palm Springs hideaway." He doesn't say, "Let's all get together
and relate and exchange and make the world a better place to
live in. Let's buy clay for the kids. And hospitals for the sick."
He goes and does a benefit for a St. Luke's Hospital somewhere
and raises eighty thousand dollars. He just does it.

Jesse Unruh

  What's happening in California is an understanding of what massive numbers of people do to an area. . . . We have to reorient our thinking.

A member of the California State Assembly since 1954 and Speaker since 1961, Jesse Unruh has become a powerful political force in California as well as on the national political scene. He was the unsuccessful Democratic candidate to unseat Governor Ronald Reagan in 1970.

The in-migration into California has slowed down. At one point we were getting about a thousand people a day into California. Last year [1970] it was twenty-six thousand for the entire year. There was unbounded optimism about the future of California in the late Fifties and the early Sixties. We saw no end to the number of new freeways we were going to build. We used to be proud of quoting the statistics that we had to build a new grammar school every week in order to meet the educational needs of our children. I remember one of the phrases was that all of the people in the United States would eventually be living in California. The health and welfare of the State of California was built on that philosophy of expansion.

Why was California so attractive to all of these people?

There were two things that attracted them: our climate certainly is an inducement; the other thing that attracted people was jobs. In those days, when we were building more houses, more schools, more office buildings, more freeways—and all the concomitant service demands that go along with those construction industries: the truck drivers to drive those trucks, the automobiles to occupy those freeways, the mechanics to overhaul the automobiles, the production workers to build them—those jobs were all available in California. And unfilled. As a consequence, people came to California. They got there, they found out the climate was magnificent, the cost of living quite low. The educational system was good. Admission to colleges was inexpensive.

For twenty years we've been working now on filling the backlog of demand: housing, recreational facilities, and all the other things that go along with the population expansion and stepped-up demand. What's happening in California is an understanding of what massive numbers of people do to an area. We've filled that demand and now we're at a level of static economy. We have to reorient our thinking.

The backlash to expansion is setting in with a lot of people understanding the demands that our millions of automobiles and our millions of people put on the environment.

What is your reaction to the poll indicating that over one-third of the California residents wanted to leave California in the near future?

An awful lot of people would like to say right offhand that Reagan has contributed to that, but Reagan may very well be more of a symptom than a cause of California's problems. He's voicing a lot of the disenchantment with the philosophy of growth and expansion and giving something to everybody, because all of a sudden there is a scarcity of the good things in California.

*   *   *

1965, 1966, 1967 were years of gradual, in some cases shocking, disillusionment for me. I could begin to feel some of the social unrest and the unsatisfactoriness of many of our governmental solutions as early as 1963, when I began to raise some questions about whether fair-housing legislation was really going to do anything other than destroy the Democratic Party in

California. It did. Destroy may be too violent a word, but certainly damage it for a long time. In 1965 we had the Watts riot [see pp. 166–171] which was a clear indication to many of us that much of the Kennedy-Johnson domestic programs were not working, either rapidly enough or visibly enough. 1966—the people went backward in the election drastically. That's when we got the Ronald Reagans of this world. And 1967, the disillusionment with the war was really beginning to hit many of us who hadn't questioned it significantly up to that point.

I started out in the fall of 1967 understanding that Lyndon Johnson had had it in this country; that if he got re-elected, he probably couldn't govern the country. Looking around for both a political alternative, and an alternative in life in general, that's when I really became a strong pusher for Bob Kennedy. I thought we really hadn't made any progress since the Watts and Detroit riots. As a consequence, we had to have a political leader who understood that the programs of the past were not going to significantly change that. At the same time have enough ongoing following to survive the violent wrenchings that he was going to have to go through to change relationships between the races and between the poor and the affluent. That's what I saw in Bob Kennedy. The shock of his assassination was seeing what I thought was really the only symbol of hope on the horizon—hope in terms of the short run—wrenched out from under us! That assassination had a wild effect on politics and also life in general. An awful lot of people who had just gotten geared up to come back . . . a lot of people, I think, were looking in that election to the governmental system for a solution. That was yanked out from under by the assassination.

We lost the Democratic majority in California in the Legislature that year because of the assassination. I just sat around and drank and cried for two months, which was a crucial time for registration. Democrats in California don't win unless we have a massive registration drive in our marginal areas.

It's interesting what happened during the course of the Kennedy campaign. He came in when Johnson was still there for the people to hate. He came in and I thought he was absolutely unstoppable. Then all of a sudden when Johnson was out of it, when it wasn't possible to vent the spleen on Johnson, it turned on him. All the petty little hates and jealousies of our society suddenly turned on Bobby Kennedy.

On Election Day I was cautiously optimistic, but scared as hell! In the morning I visited a number of my headquarters in my district—I was running for reelection that year myself—and I had gone out in the early afternoon and walked the precinct. Then I went to the racetrack to meet five or six of the guys in the dead period of the afternoon, which is like from two to five o'clock. When I drove into the racetrack, the parking attendants and the gatekeeper were all white, of various ethnic backgrounds. Almost all of them recognized me. They knew my connection with Bob Kennedy, and to a man they told me they had voted for him. So I guess for the first time in the last month of that campaign I felt absolutely sure we were going to win.

During the course of the evening, we went to the Ambassador Hotel. I had a suite there and Kennedy had a suite on the next floor. That was the first time we had gone to machine voting in California, so they couldn't get the precinct snap tallies that they'd always gotten before. CBS was wildly off. They were predicting fifty-two per cent for Kennedy and thirty-eight per cent for McCarthy. We just sat there, not quite knowing whether to claim victory, until very late.

Finally, about eleven-fifteen, I said, "Well, the crowd is getting terribly impatient down there in the ballroom. I think we can claim victory now." At that point the figures showed we were running about forty-seven to forty-one—something like that. He said, "You go on down and talk to the crowd for a while." I went down and just sort of made a general ass of myself, cracking jokes and so on and so forth. Finally I introduced Steve Smith, [Kennedy's brother-in-law] and he talked for a couple of minutes and then Bobby came down. He kidded around for a little bit, about two minutes, and then in a reasonably serious little pitch said, "On to Chicago," and walked off the platform.

I recall the Convention as sort of a big emotional blur.

I had absolutely no political motivation at the Convention, no plan of action. I say myself as having really only one task there, and that was to lead the California delegation as close to what I thought Bob Kennedy would want as I could. They didn't much care who won the Convention. They were just there as a sort of memoriam.

Mercy Anne Wright

 . . . the feeling of hopelessness came the moment I realized they had shot him. I knew it was all over, that there was no more reason for hope, because there wasn't anybody else on the scene.

Twenty-six-year-old Mercy Anne Wright graduated from St. Philip Neri, a private girls' school in Portland, Oregon —the only black girl in her class. "By the time the sit-ins were occurring, I was more than a little angry, more than ready to do something." She joined the Portland chapter of the Student Non-Violent Coordinating Committee in 1963, and a year later—at the age of eighteen—addressed the 1964 Democratic Convention in behalf of the Mississippi Freedom Democratic Party. She worked long hard hours for Robert Kennedy in 1968, opening a campaign office in Albina, the black section of Portland. A nurse, she now does volunteer work at a Black Panther clinic.

My attitudes changed so much and so rapidly, from going to peaceful things, like marching and praying, to really being able to relate to what was going on in Watts. You know, "Burn, Baby, Burn." Really having a spirit of *feeling* even though I had never lived in a ghetto per se. Of knowing where it was at and knowing which part I stood on. I stood with my black brothers and sisters no matter what they did. If they had to burn it down to make the people listen, then damn it, if the time came, I'd help them burn it down. But Bobby Kennedy seemed to offer an alternative to that.

We found a building and painted a sign. Oh, God! It was fantastic! My senior year in college . . . going to school and then straight to the office and working until two or three in the morning! It was delightful, the kind of people that came out. Not a lot of people from the college, but high-school kids and grade-school kids who related to Bobby Kennedy. They were all turned on by this man. Older people. Doing things like getting the black community active in registering voters. You went house to house and you got people out. You said, "I'm for Kennedy," and people could relate. You really didn't have to sit down and talk about it. People who'd never registered to vote and were in their forties and fifties and had lived in Portland I don't know how many years. . . . A really grassroots kind of thing.

Then it began to get involved. I began to see politics for what it really was—a very dirty game. Somehow my idealism going into it . . . I wasn't really expecting it; what went on at the local level . . . pushing and shoving and everybody fighting for their little bit of power.

Kennedy came to open that particular little office. It was funny because all these people came out, these white people who had nothing to do with the office. They had, of course, supported it, but it had been the little people who cleaned the office and organized the thing, and they were all there. I can remember meeting the Senator and shaking his hand and talking. It was really funny because when you saw the thing later on television you couldn't see me because I'm barely five foot three. You could see all these other people who somehow made it look like this whole thing was them, but then you did get a chance to see him relating to the kids who were there. There were some even in preschool who were shouting "Bobby, Bobby!" It was amazing, the feeling and the hope that everybody had in him. As we talked about this and that and all this uproar was going on around him, you didn't have to tell him "I did this or I did that or the little people did this or that." He knew it. This was the amazing thing about him because anyone else would have been carried away with the bigger people, the people who have the names.

We knew he would win in California. So things really quieted down and there wasn't a lot done because the big push was in California. When he won there and went to Chicago that was when things were to open up again.

That never took place.

Somehow, that morning . . . I remember going to bed that night, knowing he was winning in California. I had to go to work that next day. My parents sent my younger sister to waken me because they were afraid of how I was going to react. She woke me up and said, "They shot Bobby Kennedy." I was just sitting there for what seemed like an eternity, trying to relate to what she was saying. Then finally I started down the stairs. I almost tripped down the stairs and the television was on. I remember taking a shoe and banging it on our dining-room table, totally hysterical. And then I sat and I watched it and it was kind of a numbing thing. With the other Kennedy supporters who watched and waited. . . . Will he live? He's just got to! But then he's only going to be a vegetable . . . all these kinds of feelings that went on. The biggest anger and the feeling of hopelessness came the moment I realized that they had shot him. I knew it was all over, that there was no more reason for hope, because there wasn't anybody else on the scene. A real hopelessness set in—for me and for a whole lot of other people. I remember it dramatically affected my life to the point where I got up and I went to work and it was, "What the hell? The system isn't going to change now." What's happened in the last few years for me more than validated that.

It's like you don't care. Schools *are* all black. It's just "Give us good teachers and good books. I don't really care to have my kids go to integrated schools." That's the philosophy of not only the young blacks but a lot of middle-aged blacks. Integration . . . there's no such thing now. It's kind of like they were giving us "pie in the sky" and then we realized it. All that was supposed to occur during the time of the Reconstruction when bills and laws were passed, but they didn't do much about them then and they don't do much now. And then you've got Nixon, which is just incredible.

George Plimpton

 The interesting thing about Bobby is that the people who would normally have been against him—the Wallaceites, the rednecks, the hardhats—really had a sort of grudging admiration for him, for his pugnacity.

Author and editor George Plimpton is best known to the masses of America for his exploits as an amateur sportsman, and the books he has written chronicling those exploits, including *Paper Lion*. Since 1953 he has been Editor-in-Chief of the *Paris Review*. His office-apartment on Manhattan's Upper East Side has been a literary and social gathering place for a wide circle of celebrated writers and personalities. In 1968 he campaigned for Senator Robert F. Kennedy.

Robert Kennedy was a very pugnacious fellow, I remember thinking when I first knew him, very little sense of humor that I could find; shy, very, very, shy; very difficult to get along with compared to the gregariousness of his two brothers, Teddy and the President. If I had to list those in the family that I really had the pleasure of being with, he would be at the bottom of the list. He was more difficult to understand, and I remember thinking there really was a certain amount of woe when he was around.

He was a man whose attitude was rather different from most political figures'. His apparatus was different. Somehow his orientation was visceral, whereas most politicians rely on the mail that comes in from their constituents. They rely on packages of political data which have been set up for them, or they are told what to do by the party whip or special interest groups within their state. They get locked in. It becomes sort of insular. I'm not saying this is true of all of them, but I think that Bobby was terribly different in his reactions to what he saw around him. It produced a visceral response which made it possible for him to change his mind, and to change his commitments, and that's very rare in a politician. He reacted to a person getting slugged during the early Freedom Rides as if he'd been slugged himself. His response to it was different from what most people's might be. For him it somehow dramatized the position, the difficulties they had to struggle with.

He had extraordinary ability with children, great love of competition, great love of the people around him, but somehow there was something about his character which made it very difficult for people to see all this. He was shy, withdrawn, yet all of a sudden these other qualities of greatness began to emerge and you began to realize that perhaps he was the greatest one all along, and perhaps we hadn't known it.

*   *   *

He always referred to his brother as the President. He never referred to him as John or Jack or anything like that. I think that he was probably more stricken by the assassination than any of the other Kennedys, which is saying a tremendous amount because they're all very emotional people with a tremendous sense of family. He went into a shell, and for a couple of months was just a completely haunted man, because I think that with a mind like his—which was one of a plan, a type of dream, which only his brother could run—it was as if everything had been swept away. There was no future. Then, as everyone does in a tragedy, you realize that life goes on and the country continues to run and you can set yourself into the machinery of it again.

He was one of the people that was very upset that Johnson was ever the Vice Presidential candidate at all. Why he disliked Johnson as much as he did I really don't know. Again, maybe that was one of those visceral things. He was always perfectly polite with Johnson in every way. I remember seeing Johnson at many parties they had. He was always there as a matter of courtesy. His life style was entirely different from the Kennedys'. He always came in strange powder-blue dinner jackets and there was always a lot of chuckling behind the hand about how one felt about this sort of thing. I think Johnson was aware of that. I don't suppose it was very comfortable for him either. Thus Johnson's considerable suspicion of the Eastern Establishment grew. The real reason for Bobby's dismay was that right after the assassination, here was this man sitting, through absolutely no choice of his own, of course, but still sitting in the position that his brother had been in. I don't think Kennedy could ever look at him without thinking, "My brother should be there." Then I think he saw that the programs that his brother had initiated began to be taken over by Johnson, and that such commitments as Vietnam, which he thought his brother was going to get out of, were reversed by Johnson. It was a double-barreled thing.

*   *   *

I arrived in California—I guess he was in the second month of his campaign, the last week—and helped him campaign there.

To go through Watts with him, to see such an unbelievable response—not so much adulation as . . . hope, "soul brother," they called him. It wasn't that they jumped like they did when President Kennedy was campaigning—the squeals and all that.

It's very weird to watch this happen to someone who's a friend of yours. . . . He played these games with these audiences which always used to make me squirm a little bit, because he's playing on this visceral response and he'd kid with them. He'd kid with them about Governor Reagan in a singsong voice as if he were scolding children. Then he'd shift gears. I suppose the kidding was because he'd decided he wasn't going to use up any strong political juice giving a strong talk because he had them anyway. But it always used to upset me slightly because I always assumed political figures had to win your minds, not your funny bones.

It's very strange, watching a friend of yours being a political figure, because it moves him up on some elevated scale. No longer a friend, he becomes a metaphor, a symbol. One's awe here increases tremendously because you realize the stakes he's playing for.

Eugene McCarthy simply did not have this ability to bring people together. The interesting thing about Bobby is that the people who would normally have been against him—the Wallaceites, the rednecks, the hardhats—really had a sort of grudging admiration for him, for his pugnacity. They understood that, and I think they accepted it since it came from him. They wouldn't accept any such thing from McCarthy because he was a living symbol of what they were suspicious of, quoting Plato and all that. Bobby, even though he does do a lot of quoting Aeschylus, still there was something about his character, his forcefulness and pugnacity that they could understand. He was the only person around who had this ability to grow, to change—not with the wind, mind you, but to change so that some rectification was being done through a process of proper moral exercise and consideration.

What, finally, do you remember of that last night in Los Angeles?

Disbelief. Stunned. I thought the guy who did it was a Mexican. I think I went out of control for a while. I never looked where the Senator was. Just sickness! Even then, right at the beginning, this awful sense of loss, this existential sense of the powerlessness of things. A lot of doors had slammed shut. Then just the horror that we were all going to have to face. The shift in temperature. We were on our way to celebrate at The Factory or some place like that. We had won California. Everybody's walking a little bit taller. . . . Then this little sound of the popping of balloons. Even without knowing, there was this deep, obvious sharp drop in temperature.

*   *   *

He was really just getting in position to have an effect on the Seventies. His brother's effect on the decade has always puzzled me a bit, because all the seeds of the tragedies of the Sixties were in some way planted by him. It was almost as if a close relation had come along to set them right, or to root up the ground and start again. I think his brother [the President] was really out of a political mode of the past. When you read something like his Inauguration speech, you realize that his speech wouldn't have made it today. Then suddenly here was a man who was going to turn everything around and make the Seventies a more brightly lighted room.

Arnold Palmer

 . . . this man died with a golf club in his hand. He was a hammer boss in a steel mill, and he found out how great the game was and what a . . . challenge it was.

Few people would question that Arnold Palmer was the golfer of the decade; indeed, many considered him sportsman of the decade. Most famous for his charges late in the match, Palmer commanded such a loyal following that his fans came to be known as Arnie's Army. While the forty-three-year-old golfer won large purses on the links, he was equally successful in the business world. Now head of a web of enterprises that have made him a millionaire several times over, he is still ranked among the world's top golfers.

In the early Sixties I felt that things started to go reasonably well for me. I won the Masters starting off in 1960. The crowds and everything . . . I noticed the differences in the crowds. They were much larger, and they were larger because people were more conscious of golf and they were participating more. This happened because of Eisenhower playing golf and being President; it happened because of television; and it happened because . . . whatever credit I can take for it was the fact that I was really starting to move when television and these other things were coming on at the same time. They pyramided in the early Sixties. The participating in golf became tremendous—the building of golf courses, all the things that made golf as big as it is now, the bigger purses.

What was the impetus for this surge?

It came with the economic surge. The fact that people that worked in steel mills, people that worked in coal mines, people that worked on the railroads—labor became interested in golf and became participants. When I was much younger, I would talk to a father of a friend of mine and he would say, "What are you doing playing that game of golf? Why not football or some baseball?" I, of course, would always say that I thought that this was a greater game than either football or baseball, and he would kind of laugh. But this man died with a golf club in his hand. He was a hammer boss in a steel mill, and he found out how great the game was and what a terrific challenge it was. He became a participant himself to the extent that he was a fanatic about it.

People simply had more time to participate than in the late Forties and the Fifties. In the early Sixties it picked up tremendously. People's lives were influenced greatly by sport. It became as much a part of their life as their work, because they spent as much time doing it. The Sixties might well be noted for the fact that we had a sports revolution: from a participation standpoint, from a viewing standpoint, from every standpoint. Sports conversation now is as common as business conversation in most groups. You find that the two now intermingle a great deal more than they ever have in history. Sports can have a great part to play in business deals. I myself entertain thousands of people a year, where we're doing business on the golf course.

*   *   *

There is one blemish that we all are going to look at for a long time and try to decide whether it was right or wrong. I have an opinion that people much more brilliant than myself decided that it was something that we should do, and for me to say that it wasn't the right thing to do is not right. I'm speaking, of course, of the Vietnam War. Aside from that, I can't think of anything but the great things that we've had in the Sixties in America. The country has progressed tremendously from all standpoints, and I think we all should be very proud of it. That's the only thing that bothers me—that some people aren't proud. We have ills. We have a lot of things that are wrong, but if any one of us, if ninety per cent of the total population of America took a good look at himself, how could he say that he was ever any better off? How could he be any better off? Our economy has never sagged that much. Our living has increased . . . we're probably at the highest standard of living we've ever been. We eat, we drink—it just couldn't be any better.

Jane Abell

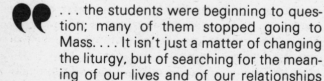

. . . the students were beginning to question; many of them stopped going to Mass. . . . It isn't just a matter of changing the liturgy, but of searching for the meaning of our lives and of our relationships with each other.

Sister Jane Abell has spent twenty-four of her forty-four years as a Dominican nun. She now works with younger sisters in a mansion-turned-convent ten miles south of the Astrodome in Houston, Texas.

Vatican II *has* made a difference, although it wasn't the Council really. The theologians were already doing the preparations. It's just that Pope John and the Council gave them a chance to go ahead with it. There is a real effort to rethink theology, to rethink the meaning of revelation and faith.

How has this theological rethinking affected you? What does it mean concretely?

It's affected my life personally as far as my own understanding of faith, well, life itself. And what it means to them [*she gestures toward some young people playing noisily in the background*]. The fact that we don't have all the answers to everything. It's not all cut and dried. It's not already answered. It's there to be sought after and discovered.

It's made me kind of "awaken"—awaken to the fact of how life's an ongoing process. In our life we are *becoming* always. The way I was raised, in both the tradition and the theology, everything was already answered. We just learned the answers. That's the way we educated the children in the school in every respect. The answers were there. We learned the catechism questions and answers. Every question had been answered. Now I think I've learned to just continue to ask questions, and realize that we don't have all of the answers. We may spend a whole lifetime searching after God: who He is; what the meaning of human existence is; how does Jesus Christ give us the answer to the meaning of human life today? So many things happened at once that it's hard to apply it just to theology.

Things happen to you by way of people. All this began to happen to me simultaneously because I went back to work with the young sisters, some of whom are those that I had in the novitiate. They asked me questions. Why do we do this? Why do we do that? And then I began to ask questions. I began to wonder why we do this and why we are doing that. They were people who were alive. The best experience that ever happened to me was to be with these people and to have to change. To have to try to be open to their questions and responsive to them. I had to change from a very settled routine of long years of religious life to rediscover again *my* life. At that time the theology had not changed that much, but we were beginning to get the documents of Vatican II, beginning to hear the fact that we had to renew.

It's just like everything kind of opening up. That's the way I feel about the theology now. The really good theology that's given to us is beginning to open up life to us. Ourselves: who we are, the meaning of life, the meaning of our relationships to other people—and through this, coming to see our relationships with God. I feel like I'm just beginning! I feel like I'm beginning life all over again. We're becoming more aware of our relativeness to others. The whole question of social justice, the poor. I think we have to be careful that we don't do this in a superficial way, that we don't just kind of get on the bandwagon.

Did Pope Paul's encyclical prohibiting birth control have any significant impact?

No. Most of the young married people I have talked to had already made up their minds. They've come to read and think for themselves in many instances. We've changed the idea that "you ask Father." I think we've hardly begun to see the changes. We're beginning to see it where in high school . . . like when I was teaching in St. Pius, the students were beginning to question; many of them stopped going to Mass, this kind of thing. It isn't just a matter of changing the liturgy, but of searching for the meaning of our lives and of our relationships with each other.

Michael E. DeBakey

Finding out what causes arteriosclerosis and then preventing it. . . . That's far more important to society than a transplantation . . . a much more economical way of dealing with it.

Dr. Michael DeBakey is one of the world's leading heart surgeons. Since the increase in their numbers in the latter 1960s, however, he has become increasingly critical of heart transplants and has directed most of his work toward development of an artificial heart. Based at the Methodist Hospital in Houston, Texas, Dr. DeBakey regularly works sixteen- to eighteen-hour days, seven-day weeks.

We had been working in our experimental laboratories. In fact, we began doing heart transplants in animals about five or six years prior to that time. The problems were recognized as being rejection and the control of it. It was known that it could be done technically, very simply; but the survival rate in animals was not very good. However, it was felt that this was as far as we could go experimentally. No one could predict exactly what the rejection problem would be in human beings just from extrapolating the animal work. We knew from other experiences, such as kidney, that the response in human beings is much better, and the control of rejection in kidney transplants is actually easier in human beings. In patients who are certain to die of their heart disease because there's nothing to do for them—certain to die in a relatively short period of time—it was worthwhile taking that chance.

So there was no surprise when Doc Barnard [Dr. Christiaan Barnard] first did it. The only surprising thing about Barnard doing it was the fact that no one, I don't believe, really expected *him* to do it because he wasn't known in this field. His experience in this field wasn't recognized because he had published virtually nothing on this subject and nobody knew that he was even working on it. Then it was a surprise to the rest of the world that it was done *there* [Capetown, South Africa], especially since that was not a place known as a cardiovascular center. But someone was going to do it—that was imminent.

*   *   *

The public's image of heart transplantation is misleading. To some extent, the public was misled by the way it was presented to them in the news media: a great dramatic breakthrough, which it was not. It was unfortunate that both the news media and some of the doctors did not point out the limitations of the procedures in terms of its usefulness in treating heart disease.

These limitations still exist today. One is rejection, which causes high mortality. The other one is the limitation of available donors. What isn't understood about this is that, at least at the present time, a donor has to be a relatively young healthy individual—and he has to die. Now there are very few young healthy individuals who die a natural death. They have to be killed. Therefore they're killed, usually in an accident, but they just can't be killed outright. They have to be killed in a rather special way, by causing brain damage, primarily, and then survive long enough to get to the hospital to be kept alive until they can be matched and studies done to determine whether or not the procedure can go on. This so limits the procedure that only a very few heart transplants could be done.

"Heart disease," as it is generally used, involves many forms of diseases. The great majority of patients who have severe heart disease, for which transplantation is most used, are due to what we call coronary artery disease. Very common—it's due to arteriosclerosis. It causes more deaths in our country than all other diseases combined. Now the solution to these problems is not going to ultimately be replacement of the organ;

it's going to be a resolution of the cause of the disease. Finding out what causes arteriosclerosis and then preventing it, specifically. That's far more important to society than a transplantation. Prevention is a much more efficient way of dealing with it, a much more economical way of dealing with it.

Erika Taylor

 I had said, 'Oh, marijuana, what's that all about? I'll never smoke grass. And then my younger sister turned me on . . . the next week we took acid. A month later I moved away from home and lived up on this mountain. . . .

At nineteen Erika Taylor left home to travel with the Hog Farm commune. Now twenty-three, she lives on a seventy-acre farm in Oregon with her husband, Bobby Flash. A dozen more people round out the semi-commune. Erika spends much of her time in the garden—hoeing the soil and harvesting vegetables.

I went to California in 1966 after I graduated from high school. My parents moved out there, and I went too. It was just when all that good stuff was happening. There was just the most incredible energy. I'd come from the Main Line in Philadelphia, really posh, egotistical, money-oriented scene, where our social stuff was based around drinking. I started trying to get in with the kids who looked like and acted like my friends back East, but for some reason nothing was happening. I just didn't like those people. I started noticing all the people with long hair, and these guys were the nice people. I had said, "Oh, marijuana, what's that all about? I'll never smoke grass." And then my younger sister turned me on. I went out with her and her friends and we started getting stoned, and then the next week we took acid. A month later I moved away from home and lived up on this mountain, which was just about a half hour away from where my parents lived. It was up in the redwoods. There was a little log cabin up there. It was the first commune that I ever lived in. A bunch of really nice people. We used to just take walks in the woods. It was a really natural, friendly scene. I went through a lot of changes in California just through the stuff that happened there. The beginning of that whole scene was really good. You'd go into a park and people would turn you on and smile, and you could just hold a stranger's hand and walk along and talk, and just feel really at ease. Then a lot of hard drugs started showing up, a lot of speed, and that naturally changed a lot.

We were working for Earth People's Park, turning people onto an idea of buying some land. Putting money together, putting your money where your heart is, buying some free land where everybody could come and live. It involved a lot of other stuff. We had a real beautiful scene there before we went to Woodstock. We just acquired this land and we were working on buildings. We didn't have hardly any money but it didn't seem to matter because we were working together. There were a lot of Chicano neighbors and we were having Spanish class every day, where we'd get together in our barn and pass whatever dope there was and this one girl who spoke Spanish real well was teaching us, just so that we could communicate with our neighbors the way we should be able to. That was real good.

But then, after Woodstock, the address got published and folks started coming out with everything they owned tied to their cars. And this was like fifteen acres of land, most of it with a road running right through it. This was in New Mexico. We traveled from back East, Pennsylvania, to New Mexico. It was just such a scene! So many new faces. There became very little past history with people. People came and went so often. So much confused energy without any center at all that I just got to a point where I didn't want to say hello to anyone. I almost couldn't acknowledge any new faces because I wasn't getting any feedback. There were a lot of young kids, and that had a lot to do with it. Most of the older guys left.

We were doing shows, that's what we were doing. A light show. Talking to people and collecting money. It wasn't a self-supporting scene at all, the people donated stuff. I got to feel like a scavenger after a while, and I didn't like that at all. You have to put as much into it as you're getting out of it and a lot of times that wasn't so. The balance wasn't there.

After I made the decision to leave, a lot of things became really clear to me about my own ideas. There was supposedly this group consciousness; we were as one as a group, to a point where I lost my individuality. I got to the point where I didn't know what my own beliefs were. I knew what we were supposed to be doing, but somehow I wasn't getting high doing it at all. I wasn't feeling it, and therefore I shouldn't be there. I was awakened at this point, because I could see that there were a lot of folks who were tagging along and hanging around and not doing anything. They were just a weight, a burden, for the people who were putting out energy.

Were your parents very upset when you first left home?

Yes, but I didn't realize it then. I had completely turned myself off to them. That's something I realized later: "How could I do that to my parents? How could I have not written them for a month at a time?" This was all during that Charlie Manson thing, too, which was really freaking them out. But after Woodstock they saw all the good stuff written about it and that pulled them out a little bit.

Many people are often turned off by the supposed free sex on the communes. Was it really all that free?

It was an individual thing. There were some people . . . some guys who slept with a lot of girls because that was their thing to do, but actually there was very little of it. There were very few couples. Most of the couples who were there in the very beginning of the Hog Farm got to where they were not finan-

cially able to take care of their families the way they wanted to.
So they left and got jobs and a lot of them are living in San
Francisco and having babies now, having a family. They all do
different stuff: some of them are mechanics, one guy works for
the railroad, one guy works for the telephone company, Hal
Foster works for IBM.

They're living their lives the way they want to. Otherwise they wouldn't be doing it. They just want to live a certain
way, and it becomes obvious after you reach a certain age that
if you don't have money, you've got to work for it.

Robert Greenblatt

 There was a tremendous reluctance to all
ideology; somehow that was alien to
America. SDS really never pulled itself together. It just became more cumbersome.

Robert Greenblatt came to the United States when he was
eleven, a survivor of the German concentration camps.
After studying for seven years for the Orthodox rabbin-
ate, a year from ordination he switched to Cornell and a
doctorate in mathematics. Now a professor at Columbia
University, Greenblatt coordinated the March on the
Pentagon in October 1967.

---

*You said you **used** to be a member of SDS.*

There isn't much to be a member of. After the split in
1968, SDS ceased being a mass organization. On the campus of
Cornell there was one community of people that did most of the
work. Sometimes it was under the SDS banner, sometimes under another name. I was not very active within SDS as such,
although I worked with SDS a lot in the coalition.

The biggest single influence that helped the formation of SDS was John F. Kennedy: "The youth of America can get America moving." There was a tremendous gap between our potential and our promise and what we actually do. There's hypocrisy in America which we have the resources to turn around if we only had the will to turn it around. That was very much the spirit of early SDS. It was very much the spirit of the Port Huron Statement. The candidacy of John F. Kennedy in 1960 was in fact very much of an impetus to that whole development. The first break in that stride happened with the assassination in 1963. Even in 1964—people might not want to remember this right now—but in 1964 a major slogan of SDS was "Part of the Way with LBJ." The official slogan of the Johnson campaign was "All the Way with LBJ," and SDS's response was "Part of the Way with LBJ." Hardly a revolutionary slogan.

What was the general direction of the Port Huron Statement, the founding document of SDS?

It was a radical departure from the preceding decade, but it was not a radical statement, historically. SDS was the youth arm of something called the League for Industrial Democracy, and the League for Industrial Democracy contains such people as Hubert Humphrey. It was pretty much the left-of-center wing of the Democratic Party.

The Port Huron Statement is a manifesto of very intent, very sincere children of the middle class. It's an idealistic post-scarcity statement. There is no reason why America, given its resources, given its political development, should be so crass about the needs of the poor people. It was an antibureaucratic statement. The welfare state, instead of living out its promises, had really become a bureaucracy alienated from the people it served. Some of the slogans of SDS, aside from "Part of the Way with LBJ," emphasized the whole notion of participatory democracy, which meant an antiadministrative, antibureaucratic, anti-institutional kind of setup. An early battle cry of SDS was that people have a right to control their own lives, as opposed to saying people have a right to control the institutions that govern the country. That became, "Not with my life, you don't." It was a populism in a way, but it never really developed a political feeling.

There were some experimentations later in the Sixties. Some people who had been in SDS for a while began to realize, "Well, our slogans are based simply on vague aspirations. We've got to develop some kind of understanding of what the real forces are." They began to hear that there's something called Marxism, but that's old hat, that's Old Left. You don't dare dabble in that because somehow you're out of mode. Yet there was a need. There was a plethora of something called new working-class theories: that Marx was right in his day but what we have is not simply a new relationship between the working class and the ruling class, but it is a whole new kind of working class —the so-called semiprofessional and the technocrats and so on. But it never really took off. There was tremendous reluctance to all ideology; somehow that was alien to America. SDS really never pulled itself together. It just became more cumbersome.

The clash that developed has one line which says, "The only answer is to simply go back to the traditional industrial working class; that unless you do that, you're isolated from the base; you can't talk about revolutionary change. Students shouldn't be in the forefront of the leadership anyway." That's basically the line that the Progressive Labor Party took. The other pole that developed, which is the Weathermen pole, is in fact an overly simplistic internationalism—that there is no hope for any revolutionary change in America because the United States has to be seen as part of a worldwide system. You don't make a revolution in the capital. Everybody, even the workers in America, share the fruits of imperialism by virtue of being Americans, and therefore revolution in this country by and large is not possible. The only thing you can do in this country is to disrupt its normal functions so that the forces around the world that are fighting against the American empire have a better chance. White America is irrevocably racist—and whatever the source of that racism, it's now beyond repair. The only thing to do is to take up the gun to get that portion of America.

SDS split, with each side claiming they had control. One group set up the Weather Underground, the Weather Machine. It was to be a clandestine operation which was to be an underground army within the United States; acts of destruction, terrorism, revolutionary violence against certain types of targets. The bombings in New York a couple of years ago, Chicago, San Francisco, and a number of other places—in a number of these cases there were communiqués issued afterwards by the Weather Underground taking credit for these actions.

At that time they took very much a line that that's the only political action that made any sense. That line has changed. Last year they came out with a major manifesto called "New Morning, Changing Weather." A new Weather station. It was printed onto a large sheet and there was a rainbow on it.

What did it was the bomb explosion thing on Eleventh Street. There was a townhouse on Eleventh Street near Fifth Avenue [in Greenwich Village] which blew up. It was totally demolished. A townhouse right next door to Dustin Hoffman's. It is generally accepted that there were Weathermen in the house. The police found three charred bodies. Two girls escaped, and they're still underground. Subsequent to that, one didn't hear from the Weather Underground for some months. That simply, in a very tragic way, just said "Stop!"

Janice Branch*

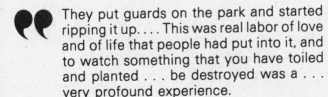

They put guards on the park and started ripping it up. . . . This was real labor of love and of life that people had put into it, and to watch something that you have toiled and planted . . . be destroyed was a . . . very profound experience.

Janice Branch is twenty-five years old, mother of a four-year-old son, and divorced. She attributes her marital breakup to her involvement with the women's liberation movement. She lives in Berkeley and has been close to most of the political ferment there throughout the decade.

Some people decided to build a park out of a terrible parking lot. The land was lying totally unused. It was dangerous—gutted, rutted, mud puddles, broken glass. The land was not being used at all. It was property that did belong to the university, no doubt about that. People just started building a park. The first weekend there were maybe twenty-five, fifty people gathered around.

We started clearing the land and filling up the holes and collecting money to buy grass. We got tools and people were just doing their own thing. It was just this incredibly beautiful, spontaneous thing that grew up. People came and built sculptures. People donated things. Somebody saw that the kids needed a swing and they went and built a beautiful wooden swing out of logs. It was a very open kind of thing. There was a bulldozer rented and people brought things from their own gardens—flowers. Free dinners were cooked while people were working. It was mostly done in four or five weeks.

There were meetings in the park about whether we should build a pond or not, whether that would be dangerous for the kids. How big and where and why. It was a beautiful thing that people wanted. People's Park was something that the entire community was in favor of—from little old ladies to liberals in the hills to street people to university students to the College of Environmental Design to the City Council.

Why was the university so intransigent?

It was private property and they couldn't allow that. They couldn't allow that kind of thing to happen. People hadn't asked permission and it was private property. The City Council even offered to lease it from the university. But they had a ten-year plan. . . .

People were expecting something to happen after having dealt with the university for many, many years. They were expecting that something was going to come of it. They weren't going to let us continue to do that, even though it was obviously a very pro-life beautiful thing. At five o'clock in the morning one day they went out and they put up a chain-link fence all the way around the park. They put guards on the park and started ripping it up. Ripping up trees and stripping it up. This was real labor of love and of life that people had put into it, and to watch something that you have toiled and planted and loved be destroyed was a very, very profound experience. The morning that the fence went up, I think it was a Friday, you could just feel in the air almost a calling, a getting ready for battle. There was a kind of seriousness and warning and silence over the town. People were so dumbstruck they didn't know what to do. They felt so incredibly powerless. We had a rally on campus and went down to the park. Then it all started.

People went down to look and to see, and the police were there in force. It was a street battle, a very bloody street battle where they were using live ammunition and shooting at people. It's the first time I've ever been shot at and I've been in a hell of a lot of demonstrations. It was the first time in these many, many years of trying to deal with the law enforcement things and billy clubs and so forth, it was the first time that they had used live ammunition and shot at white middle-class students.

One person was killed—James Rector. An artist was blinded: he was shot in the eyes, buckshot. I don't even know how many people were shot. Seven, eight, ten, twenty-five. People were running down the streets. There were Alameda County sheriff's deputies using birdshot, buckshot, twenty-twos. They were shooting at *people!*

Then the National Guard was called in, and a curfew imposed. It felt very much like a state of war: Army trucks going down the street; lines of jeeps filled with soldiers, setting up bivouac centers down at the marina and at People's Park.

We came down here to build this park as an alternative. We just said we're going to build another park. You can't stop us. And a thousand parks shall bloom! Marches all over the street. There must have been twenty thousand people by the last day of the march.

What took place at that last march?

The troops were being withdrawn finally, and there was a big march by the park. There was a big dispute about whether to have it be a celebration or whether we were going to do it again and risk having some more people killed. The community was divided over how we should handle the situation. Whether we should try to rip down the fence or just say, "Okay, you won this one," and have a festival and make our resolve to continue to fight. Twenty-three thousand people, and it was incredible! The sense of it was "cool it."

They couldn't get anybody to do anything with the land for years.

It's a parking lot now, isn't it?

It's a parking lot and a grass field, but nobody ever uses it. It's an incredible piece of real estate, just looking at it in the monetary sense. They tried incredible tricks. They tried to get black kids in the ghetto to lease it out as a kind of "Project Self-Help" or something. But they wouldn't do it, they wouldn't touch it. Nobody would touch the land. The stigma of it was so bad that nobody wanted anything to do with it. They had guards and floodlights all around that thing all the time. They built their parking lot for the dormitories. Nobody in the dormitories would sign up for the parking lot. They have a grass field now for basketball. Nobody will play on it. Nobody will use that land.

Ken Kesey

 We had built up this armor that would not let us look left or right to the gardens on both sides. The road that was straight in front of us led straight down to the Bank of America, and nothing could have changed it nearly so much as acid. Acid was a gift from the gods. . . .

As king of the Merry Pranksters—a group that traveled the West Coast staging acid tests, happenings, and anything else sufficiently far out—Ken Kesey organized the fabled and epic psychedelic cross-country bus trip that was chronicled in Tom Wolfe's *The Electric Kool-Aid Acid Test* (see pp. 36–40). Highly regarded as a novelist, Kesey wrote *One Flew Over the Cuckoo's Nest* and *Sometimes a Great Notion.* He now lives in a barn on a farm in Eugene, Oregon, with his wife, Fay, their three children, and a motley of other pranksters, friends, and acquaintances.

I was given LSD—I guess psilocybin was the first thing they gave me—by the United States government. Twenty bucks they paid me. Every Tuesday I went in there. They gave me this pill or shot me up with this something that they didn't tell me what it was. Then for eight hours they watched me: recorded my blood, my breathing. When I was finished with that, I got a job at the same place so I could take these drugs from the ward. I ended up finding out that the key I was given opened the doctor's office. I found out I could get into the stuff that he had in his office—which I didn't feel it was right for the doctor to have because he wasn't taking it. If he was really interested in what the drugs were doing, he would have taken it, but he didn't. He was just more of the rap-runner, and I didn't feel that those drugs' value was to see how it changed your heart or your electroencephalographic graph. I was high on psychedelics before I was drunk, except for one time when I got drunk in my fraternity house and crawled all the way under the rug.

What was their value?

I had written two books before then, neither of which are worth mentioning. With the taking of that acid, suddenly I was shifted over to where I was able to see where I had been looking full front at a world; and by shifting over, I was seeing it from another position. It became dimensional. I saw that everything that you see from this position, if you're also able to see it from over here, you've got two views of it. Everything that's going on has an allegorical level. If you're into psychology, it's called "ideas of reference." If you're into religion, it's called "revelation." If you're into politics, it's called "paranoia." Enough stuff happened out of it that it was undeniable. I have never had anything reiterated quite the same way.

You can take, say, three books ... open them at random and start reading from one to the other [he does so] .... "I cut the switch to a tiny fingernail and together with the force of ourself and the crack of a whip we find the gatepost and mix inside with shrieks of dismay until the second thought that we find is the pearl of a new wisdom, and there in a household panorama of earth delicately balanced between a few chords, we lead ourselves to sunup."

That change, that little thing that I did with those three books is a thing that [Bob] Dylan discovered and it's the thing that our whole generation of minds discovered: There is lateral thinking as well as linear thinking, and in lateral thinking is where discovery lies. Linear thinking will only lead you on paths you've already traveled.

When we headed out on the bus, the theme song came to be Ray Charles's "Hit the Road, Jack." I knew it was a theme song the way it would always come up at a pertinent time. The thing that bothered me was that "Hit the road, Jack, Don't you come back no more, no more, no more . . ." means that once you've viewed this kind of thinking you really can't come back any more. You've changed. All you can do is tidy up the corners so that the change doesn't bother the people that you come across too much.

*   *   *

Me and Kramer and a couple of other guys, when we were doing the supplement [*Whole Earth Catalogue Supplement*], we drove down past La Honda and then turned and went right down the coast highway. And we passed this guy, he was about fifty, pushing a bicycle. First you saw him come down the hill up there. It was like something from the apocalypse. The bicycle was completely loaded with all his possessions. There were two other bicycles on the bicycle. He was pushing it down the hill. This grim brown man in castoff clothes, castoff shoes, coming down this road. We went on down and we went to this place which had been gouged in the mountain during 1945 by the Coast Guard when they would go out there, crawl through this tunnel, crawl one hundred yards through this tunnel cut through living rock. It looked out over a cliff where they could sit with binoculars and watch over the top of this gun all day long for this Japanese submarine that never did come. We'd sit out there and we'd smoke some dope and watch the sun go down and listen to the ocean. We got back in the car, headed back toward where we were working on the magazine, and on down about another two, three miles from where we'd seen him there was this guy. Only by this time he was on the other side of the road. He was pushing the bicycle up the hill. We were all coming on, talking, and we were really affected to see this guy for the second time. I pulled up behind him with the convertible, and I hollered to him. "Can we give you a hand?" And he turns and he looks back and with this grim, outraged voice yells, "NO!" He turns back and pushes his bike on.

To me, it was a sight into the future. This guy had kicked the petroleum habit. He wasn't going to be tempted into joy popping. I could see that fifty, a hundred years from now there'll still be cars shrieking back and forth on the highway, but there will be more and more of this old guy, who just refused to participate in a form of life that we know is eventually poisonous. It means a sacrifice of all the things that we consider the juices. But this guy, you looked at him, man, he was fierce inside of himself. He was total. He was not going to be distracted. He made you feel humble to be around him. He made you feel ashamed. We drove on and all three of us in the car, we sat there very affected by it.

*   *   *

Every time an airplane flies over there's one guy up there who is signifying that what he is doing is so important that he can take the sweat of thousands and convert it into pollution for ten thousands. The government man, the businessman, he's a fascist. Everytime I ride in an airplane . . . I flew to New York and back and by the time I got back here I thought if I heard that guy say, "This is your captain, Captain Jamieson here. The weather in San Francisco is a little overcast, but you're going to have a fine time. Sit back and enjoy the friendly skies of United." And pretty soon I just wanted to go up there and say, "Just knock it off. It's awful enough anyway. There's no way you can cover it up with all these smiles and all this food and all these pretty girls." It finally becomes so obvious that any more of this casual "everything is all right" attitude is finally driving us mad.

Have you ever been high on acid and had a drink of Tab and felt what seemed to you like a good thing? When you've just kind of gone along and you want to fit into the Pepsi Generation, but you feel that stuff going in there so alien and awful, your body just revolts at the whole thing. I did it one time and I've never since taken any of it. Those cyclamates! Your body can tell. It's saying "NO!" Sugar itself is bad enough, but this stuff, which isn't even . . . it's created junk. Ersatz junk. It's not even real junk.

Have you ever been concerned by the purported medical dangers of drugs?

I feel it's untrue, but I feel it's also worth the risk, because we were in a terminal state as a consciousness, as a people. We had lost connection with our soul. We had built up this armor that would not let us look left or right to the gardens on both sides. The road that was straight in front of us led straight down to the Bank of America, and nothing could have changed it nearly so much as acid. Acid was a gift from the gods at that time. Dope of all sizes.

The thing that's important to a human is the shape that his books are in; and when you start fooling with dope, what you're doing is asking to see your books. The first few highs are gratis. There's a grace given you, but then it's like they say, "You want to see the books, huh?" This hand grabs you by the back of the neck and turns you and for eight hours you're forced to look at your own history of transgression against your fellow creatures. Not only that, but you're forced to look at the fact that you will, one day, be worms. That your physical body will turn into this. Your soul will continue on. It's how your soul is doing in its path to eternity, not how your body is doing in its path through this life, that's important. The guys that come back from Vietnam, the junkies that are coming back from Vietnam, are in far better shape karmically than the guys who are coming back from Vietnam who have no excuse.

We have forged the beginning of an ethic in the last decade that is now like a new karate trick or a muscle that nobody can avoid. You can go into a room and wield this ethic . . . you don't even have to say anything. It's like the blacks with "Here Come the Judge." There's no stopping it once it's started. There's avoiding it and procrastinating from it, but it's already making itself felt everywhere. Ecology and our treatment of the races . . . we're still fighting the Japs. When the Marines are trained they're trained to fight an inferior being. We were raised over here to believe in a certain hierarchy that was up here. That all collapses when you do dope. You can't maintain it.

When a person takes acid, a lot of acid, it's not going to hurt his chromosomes. It's going to hurt something that's a whole lot more dear to him—which is his image of himself. There's a ghost that's being held at bay from America with every possible resource. With television, with one fashion after the other, with one movement after another. The war. It's like in *1984*—if you can keep the people interested in this, it doesn't make any difference whether it's the peace movement or the war. It's to keep them from going mad and rushing the frontiers and demanding the right to their own destinies instead of having it legislated.

David Brinkley

 People are fond of saying the problem with poor people is they don't have any money. Well, that's nice. That's cute. But there's more to it than that. If we gave them money, some people would wind up with a lot of it and some people would soon wind up, again, with none of it.

On October 29, 1956, two obscure NBC reporters sat down before the television cameras—one in Washington and one in New York—and thus was *The Huntley-Brinkley Report* born. Over the next thirteen years the team won every major news award and had a nightly audience of more than twenty million people. Chet Huntley has since retired to Montana, while David Brinkley now presents *David Brinkley's Journal* each evening. Brinkley has distinguished himself most with his biting wit.

We evolved a little cliché in the Sixties which led people to say, in relation to almost every social problem we had, "If we can land man on the moon, why can't we . . . ?" and you fill in the blank. It's been applied to almost everything: curing cancer, clearing slums. Hundreds of problems had that little recipe applied. It has a kind of superficial charm, but I don't believe it really holds up because the problems are not really comparable. When we decided to land a man on the moon, we knew precisely what it was we wanted to do, we knew pretty well how to do it, the objective was clear, the methods were reasonably clear and, because it was government, the financing was freely available. There was no question of profit or loss. So the space objective was achieved.

Whereas a great many, or most, if not all, of our social objectives were not. But again, I don't think the two are at all comparable. In the case of poverty, the goal is obviously to eliminate poverty, but we don't know how to do it. We really don't know how to do it. People are fond of saying the problem with poor people is they don't have any money. Well, that's nice. That's cute. But there's more to it than that. If we gave them money, some people would wind up with a lot of it and some people would soon wind up, again, with none of it.

Compared to the problems we have to solve on earth, flying to the moon is child's play. If all it required is the assembling of a group of scientists and engineers, giving them the money and the facilities, and telling them precisely what we wanted done, we could get it done. In the case of curing cancer, just to choose another example, we don't know. We know we want to cure it but we don't know how to do it. We could assemble all the scientists and engineers and medical technicians on earth, but we don't know how to tell them to do it. That was one of the many little thought patterns that grew up in the Sixties that I thought perhaps charming, but not very useful.

*   *   *

The news from downtown Chicago traveled very fast, and within a half an hour or so the delegates in the Cow Palace were aware of what was happening. Their reactions depended on their points of view, as reactions often do. The more perceptive of them realized that the Democratic Party was, as of that hour, in the process of losing the next election, as I think it did.

They seemed to be advertising the fact that the party could not manage its own affairs very well, that it couldn't have a Convention with free and open discussions of the issues.

The Convention had all been rigged by Lyndon Johnson to achieve two purposes: one was to coerce the Convention into endorsing his war policy, and the other was to nominate Hubert Humphrey. It succeeded in one, but not in the other. It succeeded in nominating Humphrey under such chaotic circumstances that it almost guaranteed his defeat.

By the time the Convention was over, any except the most devoted ideologist had become very lonely men. Any except the most devoted ideologists realized that the Convention had been a horrible mess, both in the hall and out. It was all rigged so their only real choice was to endorse Lyndon Johnson's war and, again, to nominate Humphrey. They were frustrated and angry. They thought—those who thought about it— that the protesters in Chciago could have been allowed to come to town and express their views and have their rallies and demonstrations peacefully. If the Daley organization in Chicago had not chosen to resist, to fight, if instead of sending the police out they had let them have Soldier Field and allowed them to have their rallies and their speeches, then they could have done it and could have left town without having all the violence. I think everyone in Chicago who knew anything knew that there had been a terrible mess created. It was mainly a self-inflicted wound. They all could predict the results, and I think most of them did.

In the face of Johnson's rigging, did Eugene McCarthy ever really stand a chance?

McCarthy was the first well-known national politician to announce himself as a candidate for President openly opposed to the war, and so therefore he attracted a great deal of attention and a substantial following on that basis alone. On that basis he did fairly well in the primaries in New Hampshire and the others that came along, until Bobby Kennedy joined in. I think maybe his campaign was not more successful because of his personality difficulties. He never was able really to effectively head the army of younger and older people who fell in behind him. He was even accused of being somewhat lazy. In any case, he attracted an army, but he was never able to lead it, to inspire it, to encourage it. Then Bobby Kennedy joined in, which drained away some of his support. And then, of course, Lyndon Johnson rigged the Convention so he couldn't have been nominated anyway. I suspect the failure of the McCarthy campaign was a combination of those three things: the fact that Bobby Kennedy, who stood for many of the same policies, divided the antiwar movement and took away a lot of McCarthy's support; plus McCarthy's personality; plus Lyndon Johnson's absolute determination to nominate Humphrey to be the President.

You refer to Johnson's rigging of the Convention. How did he do this?

He did it in a number of different ways: by seeing to it that the delegates chosen in the various states were supporters of the war. There are many many different ways of choosing delegates. Some states have primaries. Some states have conventions. In some states they are simply appointed by the governor, simply arbitrarily appointed by the governor; he is accountable to nobody. That's being changed now, but that's the way it was in 1968. Johnson used all the influence he had to see to it that delegates friendly to his war were chosen, and to a great extent he succeeded. Not entirely. You may recall that they had before the Convention a so-called Peace Plank which didn't disown the war—I don't remember exactly what it said—but it was at least a partial repudiation of Johnson's war. The Convention defeated it, but only by about a ratio of sixty to forty. In effect, it was a defeat for Johnson, because this was not a vote of the general public, it was a vote of hand-picked Democratic delegates, hand-picked Democratic Party officials, leaders; and out of that crowd he was only able to get sixty per cent.

What did you actually see at the Convention?

I saw pretty much what anyone else saw who tuned it in. A minority of the delegates, such as those from California and New York and Wisconsin and a few others, were angry and frustrated because they thought they represented the current public point of view, and I believe they did. Angry and frustrated because they knew they were vastly outnumbered by the hand-picked party leaders who didn't represent the public, but who represented Lyndon Johnson. The leader of the delegation from Wisconsin, Jesse Unruh from California [see pp. 353–357], the New York delegation—they knew they'd been had. And they *had* been had. So they were angry. There was a deep division of opinion on the floor. Johnson had seen to it that these dissident delegations from these states had been spaced widely, scattered over the Convention floor, so they could not come together as a group in one part of the hall. He put California at one end, New York at the other end, to keep them widely separated. That was another part of the rigging that went on. What we saw on the floor was a huge exercise in anger and frustration by people who felt they represented the public point of view being outvoted and to some extent trampled by a lot of professional party leaders, hangers-on, and hacks who represented nobody's views but their own—and Lyndon Johnson's. A democratic exercise turned into a very undemocratic one.

Quentin Young

 We attempted to do such revolutionary things as get toilet facilities in Lincoln Park for the thousands of people who were going to camp there. We got an enormous runaround.

A leading member of the Chicago Chapter of the Medical Committee for Human Rights, Dr. Quentin Young teaches at the Chicago campus of Illinois University. The Medical Committee for Human Rights was actively involved during the turmoil of the 1968 Democratic Convention. Dr. Young was later called before the House Un-American Activities Committee, along with most of the "Chicago Eight" defendants.

The Medical Committee for Human Rights was started as an arm of the civil rights movement in 1964 during the so-called Freedom Summer. In Freedom Summer, you recall, they sent a whole bunch of white middle-class kids into the South. The official story isn't true, that we were invited to come down and offer medical services: the mothers and fathers of those kids just decided their nutty kids could go down there, but not without a doctor. Very quickly we entered into what came to be known as Medical Presence, an organization deeply committed to localism by supporting free clinics, drug rescue stuff, fighting discrimination in the local institutions. . . .

You have to remember in the pre-Convention setting that they were talking not of five or ten or twenty thousand people, but hundreds of thousands who would come down for McCarthy's thing. Idiots were talking about half a million! But maybe many times the number who actually came were frightened off by the overt threats of violence.

Overt threats?

The city did a whole bunch of things to indicate that there was going to be no friendliness toward outside visitors.

Could you give a couple of examples?

We attempted to do such revolutionary things as get toilet facilities in Lincoln Park for the thousands of people who were going to camp there. We got an enormous runaround. We wanted to have some kind of an emergency service in case of insurrection. We wanted to be able to offer clothing and housing and medication. We were negotiating for all this and it became clear that every city agency was in a negative mood, to put it generously. They were under orders not to cooperate in any way.

What we did in preparation for this was to go through our usual base, which is several score of doctors, several times that in nurses and other health workers, and urge them to sign up for what was going to be a week-long event with all kinds of demonstrations and so on. We got commitments, like "I'll be there on Wednesday night" and "I can come down Friday; it's my day off." We started with about seventy-five part-time volunteers. After that first night in the park we were inundated with volunteers. We ended up with four hundred people participating in our Medical Presence effort. We had headquarters in the Church Federation downtown.

Daley almost had to cancel the Convention because of a telephone strike. But for some reasons that were never clear to us, *we* were able to get a whole bunch of lines. Plus a big donation from the telephone workers for our efforts. We got our cadre needs immediately filled by the tremendous reaction by the people, many of whom were unknown to us, and we unknown to them; some few very conservative in their viewpoint. The whole house staff at Presbyterian St. Luke's, a major hospital, volunteered to serve on all their off time.

*   *   *

Daley, after this remarkably unprecedented attack on citizens, alleged that there was a preliminary count that showed that sixty-six people had been injured and went to hospitals. He issued this under an attack on the demonstrators entitled "The Strategy of Confusion." We issued a counter-paper entitled "The Strategy of Contusion" and we said they were right, it was sixty-six people hurt, give or take a thousand, because we had records on about a thousand people.

The first night there was a good deal of violence in the effort to clear the park. All of a sudden the park, where citizens had been sleeping on hot summer days since antiquity—and it was a hot summer day—all of a sudden the law calling for an eleven-o'clock curfew was enforced.

We had our little teams, teams of people who have various skills; hopefully, at least one physician with every group, and medical students and nurses. The main equipment for Medical Presence is first-aid stock. Lots of water to wash teargas out of eyes and noses, dressings for any kind of contusions, things to rouse people who might have fainted from heatstroke, and litters if you have occasion to get people out. I remember just standing around quite late at night. There was a series of minor confrontations with the students and the police, and pretty soon it got more active. It got darker, and finally the order was to go, and then there were some pitched battles here and there.

Then the scene outside Lincoln Park. The police were remarkably aggressive. I mean, they beat people who came out on their front porches to see what the hell was going on. They chased people into houses. They must have been really hoked up. This was just the first of six or eight really major mass brutalities, not to mention the uncountable individual ones. The stuff that took place at the railing when somebody put the flag upside down. At least one massive charge where the police came out of these huge vans—there was no question of the police being individually taunted or assessing the scene, they just came out of the vans swinging their clubs. They couldn't have known what was going on. Endless mass brutality!

I guess they reasoned that eventually they would cow people—nobody wants to risk their head being split. I don't think it ever worked in that particular demonstration. The crowd never really ran away from being hit. To me, the really amazing thing—and others share the view—is that some police were not killed. I'm certain there were some hard-line people present who felt that the police were their enemy and who, after two or three days of getting their heads caved in, had pretty good evidence. I'm just making the point that it would have been . . . at a distance . . . with a weapon, or up close with a gun

. . . the police were there. I don't know what kind of mass discipline kept that from happening.

One of the biggest things to emphasize is that half the time the control of the crowd was in the hands of the National Guard, and the Illinois National Guard is a bunch of draft-dodgers. Nice guys who didn't want to go to Vietnam, and virtually no casualties occurred, with one exception. There was one day when the National Guard did something, peanuts compared to what the police did every time they were on duty.

Another thing is the abuse of emergency rooms. Police would go to emergency rooms and they would intervene and arrest people. To their discredit. That's an area of contention of medical responsibility: the need to defend the neutrality, and more, the inviolability, of the emergency room as a treatment place. The only way to do that is to guarantee that the police have no access. It should be at least like a person's home. There's more than just violation of rights: there's a possibility of contamination, not knowing whether they're free from germs.

What types of injuries were most common?

The biggest number were teargas and some Mace. That's a mass thing and hundreds got that, some really bad. Hundreds of contusions, and from the location of these wounds we were able to determine that people were struck on the head from behind. Not a few groin injuries—obviously to people who were down.

Max Schmidt*

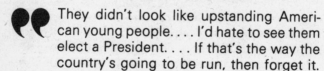

They didn't look like upstanding American young people. . . . I'd hate to see them elect a President. . . . If that's the way the country's going to be run, then forget it.

Max Schmidt was on duty as a doorman at a leading Michigan Avenue hotel during the 1968 Democratic Convention in Chicago.

We were sort of in-between here. If the Convention hadn't been held here, then there would have been no business. We're out to see business come in. Without the business, we don't make any money. So, I think we were looking forward to that one being here. Of course, when you came to work every day, you didn't know what was going to happen that night, and some of it was pretty rough. The roughest was on the Wednesday night and the Thursday night following.

I started work at three-thirty. Things were pretty calm. By that time most of the delegates were still out in the amphitheater and they wouldn't come back until around five. That's when things started. They started massing over in the park. It was for those delegates' benefit, as they came back on the buses. That's who they tried to impress. The Wednesday of the Convention—that's when they had competition over there with the bandshell area, over at the stone wall, and the Army dropped the teargas. It drifted over this way—this was when it really hit us. We found out how serious it was.

I saw a lot of provocation on the part of the demonstrators, and I thought the police were really restrained. Not charging. They were standing there with their hands . . . well, the parade dress status.

What type of provocations?

They were throwing everything at them that they could get. If there had been that many civilians, instead of the police, where each one was on his own instead of under orders like the police were, they would probably have charged those demonstrators. The citizens wouldn't have taken it. But the police were under orders. That's the reason they couldn't move.

They were trying to prompt the police into charging.

That's the impression you got out there. They were just hurling insults where I was standing duty. If it had been civilians up there and everybody was on their own, not under orders, they would have thrown it back. You got the guys over there with the bullhorns, urging the people on, urging the demonstrators on. And they predicted they were going to do this before they ever came. Now how do you stop this? You've got to do something. You've got to try to stop them somehow. It would have been a riot, too. It was not really a riot.

It wasn't a riot?

They quelled everything. The National Guard had everything under control. Like the next night, when they stopped them at Eleventh Street and Michigan. Well, they drew the line and that's as far as they got. That was it. I think they were going to march to Mayor Daley's neighborhood or something like that.

I have a cousin who lives in California and he called me at home and wanted to know if my family was in any danger. I live twelve miles away from here, but that's the impression he got from television. Everything was overexpressed. I wasn't in any danger. There was no danger other than right here at Grant Park or at the amphitheater. That's the only place that anybody was subjected to anything, but he got the impression from the television that the whole of Chicago was in danger.

Could you describe the demonstrators? What type of people were they?

They didn't look like upstanding American young people. They just weren't the type that you would think . . . I can't see a President trying to get them as his backers. I'd hate to see them elect a President and that President get in the White House and try to represent everyone. You see what I mean? If that's the way the country's going to be run, then forget it.

Like living out in the park. That thing was filthy. Right across Michigan Avenue. When they left, they dug up everything and resodded the whole thing. That was their own private bathroom. Everything! It was ridiculous. But that's the way they want to live. But I don't want to live like that. See. Now if you can get a President in that condones this thing, well. . . . They weren't able to vote anyway, but they will in the future. Then if they can sway a President, then the country's in trouble.

You'd have to see it to believe it. You tell people who don't live in this city or never seen anything like that, they don't believe you. They think you're exaggerating. I have a neighbor, a young fellow, school age. I told him—he came over to see me the next day—I'd tell him what was going on and he didn't believe it. So he came down here one night when they raised the Viet Cong flag up here. Then he believed it. Things like that. They were just trying to disrupt everything that was going on. The Convention itself went right along in the amphitheater. They elected the Presidential nominee and that's what they wanted to prevent.

Duane Hall

 We really didn't believe it was happening. It was just like a regular movie set. The lights were coming from both sides . . . continual policemen charging down. They came charging right into the crowd.

A twenty-six-year-old North Carolinian, Duane Hall went to work for the Chicago *Sun-Times* as a photographer in 1966. His photographs of the street scenes outside the Democratic Convention in 1968 were later published in *Life* as well as in the *Sun-Times*. Many of the photographs were also used in the court cases arising from the disturbances.

The first incident happened in Lincoln Park on Sunday evening. There were a lot of people there in the park. I'd say about fifty per cent of the people in the park were onlookers. From all around they had come to see what was happening. They had read the papers and the reports of all the strange stuff that was going on. So they came down to look, which made the mob look a lot bigger. There was a group of maybe twenty or thirty people on a flatbed truck who tried to start yelling. They weren't really doing anything except running around yelling. The police were on edge, and some kid started deliberately getting himself arrested. He ran into the police lines and started yelling and the police grabbed him and started working on him. So there was a little emotion and the police arrested a couple and beat them, kind of. One of those Chicago-type arrests.

A Chicago-type arrest? What do you mean?

That's an old Chicago arrest. It's not like any other city. In some cities I've seen them beat, but in Chicago when they arrest they have to beat them into the ground. Long before the Convention I saw it. One night I was on Madison Street, a slum area, trying to get some pictures of slums, so I was dressed ruggedly and sitting on the curb. I had my camera in a paper bag. One of the bums was drunk or something and I saw him yell something and the policeman yell something at him and then the policeman chased him down with his wagon and went around the building. I knew the police station wasn't that way, so I went down to the corner and looked through the alley and they were beating the hell out of him, really beating him bad. The man came out of the alley and he was crying. He was a grown man. All of a sudden he sobered up and he was begging me to get out of there or the same thing would happen to me. The police didn't arrest him; they just left him. The same way at the Convention. The majority of the people at the Democratic Convention weren't arrested; they were just beaten and left.

After the first arrest the kids started yelling and charging. They didn't know what was happening and people were trying to get out of the park. They kept pretty calm, though. The marshals were pretty good. They tried to get everybody to calm down. This was in the early evening, three or four in the evening, still daylight. The police had them completely circled in the park, so they wound up there singing and humming. The police had kept telling the people that there was an eleven o'clock curfew, and that they demanded the people get out of the park. It was kind of an ultimatum or facedown. Some of the people were saying they weren't going to leave the park, some said they would leave the park, and some didn't know what they'd do. Night came and they were still there, building little fires and still not knowing what they were going to do. Eleven o'clock came and the police said it was time to move. Some of the people started to move and some said they wouldn't move, but everybody else stayed back to see what the others would do. Instead of leaving, they were waiting to see, and they waited until the last minute. They were still there and it was eleven o'clock so the police started charging through. They came charging through the east end of the park and pushed them out the west end. There was nowhere to go—all these thousands of people all getting on this street at the same time. All they needed was one guy to get in front and start marching and they'd follow him down the street.

Thousands were in the street heading down South Street and no place to go. The police were chasing them from behind with teargas. They started beating the people. There was very little rock throwing or anything like that. They were just marching down the street and yelling. There were a couple of them turning over trash cans and they would throw a rock, but the other people would tell them to stop, don't do that. They must have been all up La Salle and down to Beechum somewhere near to Michigan Avenue. By Michigan Avenue, when they got there they were pretty well dispersed. The police threw a line across Michigan Avenue. They had told us before . . . they had had a talk with some of the newsmen and they told us if something like this happens, the riots and all, to go to the police lines. So some of the press men started crossing the bridge to go to the police lines because they saw there might be a confrontation, and some of the policemen ran out of the lines and started beating the press men. I turned to photograph the people being beat on the side of the bridge and some policeman came up and started hitting me with his club. He hit my head and my hand and knocked my camera out and stuff. I didn't even see him. I was shooting a picture to my right of the other man getting beat, and this other guy came up and he started hitting me as I was trying to get across the bridge. Another one of the photographers, a guy from *Newsweek* or *Business Week*, got his name. A guy from one of the other magazines got his picture. There was a federal indictment against him but he won the indictment. They had his picture, a couple of witnesses, his name. He was found not guilty.

I stayed on the street. I'd get up at four in the evening and go straight to the street. I'd stay there until about three in the morning and then go straight home. Three days, four days, whatever it was. Each day it seemed like it kept getting . . . more contempt, more fear . . . it just kept building up and building up. The Balbo-Michigan thing was, I guess, the biggest publicized confrontation. It probably wasn't the very biggest, but it just so happened at that point all the television cameras were there at the Hilton with their lights and their trucks. It was like a television movie setting. Everything was right in front of them happening. The police . . . I saw one guy run up behind a bunch of kids with the butt of his rifle and knock a couple of them down, hollering "Kill the motherfuckers!" I saw another guy pulling his gun and shooting over their heads. There was a building here they just tore down last week. There were still bullet holes in it just five feet over the heads of these people. The guy was shooting five feet over their heads from one hundred feet off! The police were panicking, because for days they were telling them that the guys were out there with everything from black widows to shit to throw at them. They were really scared, I guess. They threatened me about the second day or so. They knew I was a news photographer and they threatened me. They said, "Tonight we're going to get you. We're just waiting for the sun to go down." After the newspapers came out with some of the pictures of what was happening, they knew that they were in trouble if they got their pictures in the paper unmercifully beating some guy that was sitting in the grass, not wearing their badges, smoking cigarettes. They stopped that by getting the cameras that shot the pictures.

At Balbo and Michigan, the night they had the big one, they came charging. . . . I was by the stoplight right in the center of the intersection and one policeman tried to get me but he couldn't climb the stoplight. They were beating them all around under me. The atmosphere. . . . We really didn't believe it was happening. It was just like a regular movie set. The lights were coming from both sides. People were yelling. Some guys had makeup on just like a regular setting. It was really hard to believe it was actually happening. You see it but you can't believe it.

The night of the Balbo-Michigan thing, they had a big rally at Grant Park at the Band Shell, and from the Band Shell they were going to march to the amphitheater. When they started to march out the police stopped them and told them they couldn't march and blocked their way. Allen Ginsberg was in the march then, but of course once they started marching, he'd always vanish. Like in Lincoln Park before the confrontation, he'd vanish. He's a real elusive guy. I guess that was good. Keep out of trouble. To go over the IC tracks to get to Michigan and the Hilton there were bridges and they had all those blocked. The kids kept going up further and further north until they found one that was open, and they charged across to Michigan Avenue and came down to the Hilton. I didn't see Ginsberg after that.

They came down—the group had crossed at about Jackson—they crossed the IC tracks onto Michigan Avenue. It was a strange fact that the Bread Basket had a mule train coming down Michigan Avenue. Some kind of a protest march with Jesse Jackson. Anyway, they both met at the intersection up there, and they were yelling, "Hello, hello. Hi, hi." And they started running down Michigan Avenue. By the end there was a hell of a lot of people. They filled the whole street. I don't know how the police ever let them across there, but they did. They kept coming down to the intersection of Balbo and Michigan where the police had thrown a line across. The National Guard was down the street backing them up. Everybody was standing up so nobody could see what was happening. I was in the center and everybody was asking, "What's happening? What's happening?" The police around the edges were yelling with megaphones, "Clear the street," and the policeman on the other side was yelling, "Clear the street" that way. They didn't know where to go. The thousands in the middle didn't know what was happening, and the guys on the edges didn't have any place to go. I got up on the edge of the stoplight—by then it had started to become dark—and I saw that down Eastern Avenue and down Balbo, coming toward the Hilton, there were TV lights on top of the Hilton on this wing thing . . . continual policemen charging down. They came charging right into the crowd. The people at the beginning of the crowd started screaming. They were getting beat, and the people about the middle of the street were still completely fenced in. They couldn't run and they didn't know what was happening. By the time they started beating pretty hard, the people were falling and running every which way. There were people all around, girls and everything. They didn't know which way to run because they couldn't be sure which way the police were coming from. You could hear them but you didn't know where. I climbed up atop the stoplight and the police came charging through, beating everybody. Most of them ran into the park and some of the police ran into the park after them, and some of them even chased them all the way up Balbo. After they finally got the intersection cleared, there were shoes and purses and everything laying in the intersection. Everybody just dropped everything and ran.

Were any charges brought against the police for brutality?

There were eight against the police and eight against the conspirators. Of the police, none were convicted. I think one of the policeman now is still in court, suing one of the press men. He was found not guilty, so now he's suing them for something. Then, of course, they had the eight conspirators. . . .

When the names came out, some of the people you never even heard of. I was here when [Bobby] Seale made his speech in Lincoln Park that they arrested him for. It was more rhetoric that the blacks have been yelling about for I don't know how long. It was in the evening and most of the people there who were listening to it, they had heard it I don't know how many times before. It didn't stir up anybody. It's the same stupid rhetoric and garbage that's normal—big deal. I guess he flew in and made that speech and then left. That was why he was a conspirator. The others? Very few people around here had ever even heard of them. When they came up with these names, they were wondering who the hell those people were.

Anyway, they had the trial for them, and of course it was played up real big. The papers covered the trial pretty good, I think. There was a lot of contempt there. I kind of felt sorry for [Judge Julius] Hoffman in a way—and then in a way I don't. He was hit with this stuff and it was a different world, a different trial. He had never seen anything like this. I think even if he hadn't said a word in the court, just their appearance would have shut him up.

William R. Zwecker

 But nobody got killed in Chicago. Nobody got killed. He didn't have one killing in all those tens of thousands of rioters who were in Chicago.

When World War II broke out, William Zwecker was an executive with the Altesse-Olleschair Paper Mills, with

offices in Vienna and Prague. At the age of thirty he came
to the United States "to fight Hitler," planning to return
to Vienna, but he decided to stay because "America sold
itself to me."

Why I give Mayor Daley credit is that he was the first
mayor who was not a thief, the first mayor who has really improved, you can say physically, the city. Also, in certain sociological ways, to improve it. When I came here, there was a Mayor
Kelly who was a big thief, tremendous. After him came a guy
named Kennelly, who was a do-nothing—a wealthy man but
never did anything at all. So in my thirty years in Chicago, Daley
is the first mayor who has really produced. He's a producer. And
when people speak against him . . . at the Democratic Convention they said he was strict, that he had the police out, and they
called the storm troopers out. But nobody got killed in Chicago.
Nobody got killed. He didn't have one killing in all those tens
of thousands of rioters who were in Chicago. You have to realize
that to control masses as he did. . . . After all, those people came
here to cause trouble. They didn't come here just to walk on
Michigan Avenue and to throw out some candies to the people.
They were looking for some action. I think Daley has done, in
my opinion, my very humble opinion, a very nice job. He's the
first mayor I respect in the city here.

Paul Brown

 We had an advantage in that we played
on Sunday afternoon primarily, and our
big competition . . . was the Philharmonic.
The common guy didn't know much
about that caliber of music. He had far
more interest in football. . . .

Paul Brown founded the Cleveland Browns in 1946; then twenty-two years later—after a brief absence from the gridiron—he founded the Cincinnati Bengals. He served as general manager and coach of the Browns, as he now does with the Bengals, and with thirty-seven years and over three hundred victories behind him, Brown has become a legend in the annals of professional football.

Television has been a big factor. It just really didn't get under way until the Fifties and was just getting into full bloom for Sunday-afternoon looking, say, in the start of the Sixties. This gave us a tremendous decade of growth and strength in professional football. We had an advantage in that we played on Sunday afternoon primarily, and our big competition on the so-called television exposure was the Philharmonic. The common guy didn't know much about that caliber of music. He had far more interest in football than in that! The television was a tremendous factor in the rapid growth of professional football for another reason: professional football lends itself especially well to televising; it's action; you can follow the ball. For me to look on TV and see something that's live—something that I don't know how it's going to end up until I see it develop—is much more interesting than just seeing something that's not that way.

The networks vie with one another. In fact, we're on all three networks now. Even going to Monday night turned out to be a tremendous thing for ABC. What's happening is the female interest in this thing has increased by leaps and bounds. You just can't have it in your house every Sunday afternoon and Monday night without almost being overwhelmed. You *have* to look at some of it, at least to be around your husband, shall we say? I know that gets a lot of jesting and smarty answers, but the American male likes this kind of thing apparently. The knowledge of the game is becoming more widespread because of television. More and more husbands have to explain to their wives "why." There are some wives that are just finding out that it takes four downs to make a first and ten.

Do you think the violence of football is related to that of society?

You've been listening to too many of those college guys make words! Nobody is battering themselves into submission. They wear shoulder pads, hip pads, they're all padded up. I wish you could see my Cleveland Browns team of, say, 1950. You couldn't see today more handsome, fine physical specimens, with lovely wives and families, than this group of people. These are the same people that you just now were talking about massacring each other.

People like the miniature wars as compared to the pastime aspects of things. They aren't satisfied maybe to just drink beer and pop and eat peanuts and hot dogs.

Michael Tigar

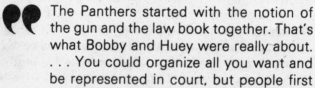 The Panthers started with the notion of the gun and the law book together. That's what Bobby and Huey were really about. . . . You could organize all you want and be represented in court, but people first had to know you were serious.

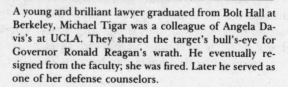
A young and brilliant lawyer graduated from Bolt Hall at Berkeley, Michael Tigar was a colleague of Angela Davis's at UCLA. They shared the target's bull's-eye for Governor Ronald Reagan's wrath. He eventually resigned from the faculty; she was fired. Later he served as one of her defense counselors.

In 1961, 1962, the Far Left spoke of Cuba, of the Third World. Later there seemed to be a greater concentration on the United States and its domestic problems. What brought about this shift?

I think what happened . . . this is a phenomenon really of later in the Sixties. There was concern with the sit-in movement of the South. Sit-ins and Freedom Rides, the whole pacifist nonviolent movement of Martin Luther King dominated a certain segment of college politics for a while. The big peace marches were an imitation of the tactics of the nonviolent movement in the South. The major change came, though, as a result of two kinds of fads. First of all, in the summer of 1964. . . . To go back a moment, within the South, the style of the big demonstration—"let's get everybody arrested and go to court,"—the sit-in tactics—had already begun to be shown bankrupt in the South. SNCC had moved into Mississippi and had begun the concept of the community-based political organization. In 1964 white students went south and black students went south during the summer, culminating in the Democratic Convention. That showed a lot of things. First of all, it showed a hostility in the Southern movement toward any kind of change. Burnings, bombings, beatings. Goodman, Schwerner, Chaney. The news came over the radio day by day as it turned out that the sheriff and his henchmen had killed them. Then the Democratic Party's inability in 1964 in Atlantic City to do anything about the South. It was the beginning of the new kind of politics in the South. Then the students went back home after the summer, and it turned out there was racism up there in the North that they hadn't known about before. It turned out that racism wasn't calling people "nigger." Racism was an economic system that rested on the superexploitation of blacks. At the same time, the black movement was undergoing its own kind of internal dynamics. Somewhere along the line the black community went through a black nationalist stage which pretty well left the whites out. It's hard to see all the things that happened, to put it all in perspective. . . .

What is clear is this: in this process the movement for change began to understand something about power. They began to understand that most of the talk about the power of love was bullshit. That power meant people, people in motion, people willing to take risks. One can talk about the beginning of that consciousness only. . . . Take the Free Speech Movement in Berkeley in 1964. The Free Speech Movement began because the Republican Convention was in San Francisco and some students wanted to pass out "Scranton for President" bumper stickers. They weren't permitted to.

It started with a coalition that included many elements, and in its many political elements, you can see a kind of image of the Sixties. You've got the liberal Republicans and the sort of straight-out political liberals who believed that soon the administration would capitulate to our just demands. If they don't, we can work through the liberal faculty members; and if that doesn't work, we'll have a lawsuit and the courts will tell the university to behave itself. That faith was held in varying degrees and with varying intensities for varying reasons by almost all segments in the Free Speech Movement. It shades over to the kind of activists of the FSM who believed, "No, we have to play it confrontation style, mobilize masses of students in support of our positions and then we might have a sit-in or something else. But then we'll get arrested and we'll be like the Southerners; we'll go to court and the judge will acquit us, and in acquitting us will say, 'Boy, it's a good thing you had all this courage and stood up for the Constitution and I'm letting you go now.'" It didn't work.

The Panthers started with the notion of the gun and the law book together. That's what Bobby [Seale] and Huey [Newton] were really about. The idea that here were these rights that had been denied to a whole group of black people, and they *needed* their rights. But you also need to have a gun, which is one of your rights—to have it; because one of the main reasons that the pigs didn't recognize your rights was because they thought you were indefensible. You could organize all you want and be represented in the court, but people first had to know you were serious.

The liberals come at it—those who move into and out of Columbia, the Columbia University shutdown—they come through an entirely different position. They come at it as people who are used to those rights. They've had everything. They've been raised to believe that the system really does answer when you call.

I must say that it's a process that I find really difficult to understand. There's this tremendous frustration and feeling of betrayal when a man realizes that to believe in and advocate radical solutions is to really become an outlaw. An actual outlaw. If you believed that the black man was largely stalled, if you believe that the hope for America lies principally in the weakening of the American empire through revolutions of the Third World and then the liberation of this country by a combination of Third World people who attack this country as the place where workers are exploited and subjugated, then the role of the white middle-class person is to get ready.

You have a theory of history that says this is going to happen and you should get ready for it. How do you get ready for it? The most important step in kindling a revolutionary consciousness is that a person have a consciousness that he or she is an outlaw and has no regard for the law except a sort of technical regard for it. In jurisprudential terms you can see it as rules for behavior; rules of laws become not rules for a section of the populace but merely the basis for maxims of prudence. There's a rule that says you can't have a gun unless it's registered. The corresponding maxim of prudence for the outlaw is, "You can't have an unregistered gun unless you hide it from the pigs."

Now, in building the consciousness, in moving people to the position of outlawism, you also have to have a program. Things for people to do which will begin to show that it's possible to strike, that it's possible for people who are now swimming in a stream of radical sympathy toward a hostile society to take action against the political and economic mainstays of the country, to show that it's possible. That's the style of revolutionary works in the US for a specific class of people who have no base in an exploited community. That style of politics almost necessarily is Weathermen politics. You blow up buildings. You take other kinds of action to demonstrate you are powerful, strong, committed. . . .

I think the Weathermen have made a great many errors. The decision to go underground worked against them. It's hard to have a political organization from underground. The Weathermen—people who were some of the most recipient and articulate and committed theorists of the American revolutionary Left—are now gone from the midst of the movement for change. And that's a great loss. Because Weathermen politics was an important part of that. It moved a number of people to reconsider their own position. They are people who would not have been *arriviste*. They had *struggled*.

Where does that leave the movement now?

The movement has never been more fragmented, ingrown, petty, nasty, brutish, and short-tempered.

It's a great loss to American society. The fact is that unparalleled resources are being devoted to crushing and silencing this country. The beefing up of the Internal Security Division, the revival in the parlance of the highest government officials of the old McCarthy clichés of the Fifties, the turning to the cause of suppression this enormous bureaucratic apparatus —Justice Department, strike forces, and special prosecution and so on. All this together indicates that the Nixon Administration is about to kill off the Left.

Barbara Walters

 I remember saying, 'Mrs. Cleaver, I have a child and you have a child about to be born. . . . What about our children? What about their life together? What do you want for your son?' And she said, 'May he light the first match.'

As hostess of the *Today Show* since 1961, Barbara Walters has interviewed an extraordinary list of world luminaries. *Ladies' Home Journal* has named her "One of America's 75 Most Important Women." Married to a theatrical producer, she has a four-year-old daughter.

I received a telephone call one day from someone on *Ramparts* magazine asking if I would be interested in doing an interview with Kathleen Cleaver, the wife of Eldridge Cleaver. At that time she had not been interviewed on television, and we decided that it might be a very good thing for us to do. I did as much research as was possible on her, and I was surprised to find that her father was a member of the government; he was working in some capacity for the State Department. She had been brought up in India, where there had not been that much of a difference between the sexes or between the races. I was interested in at what point in her life she had become a militant.

The interview was arranged in the penthouse apartment of some friend of hers here in New York. I went to do it feeling that I understood and that we were from a mutual area of concern. I remember the interview because I never had one quite like it. It was an eye-opener for me. No matter what I asked, no matter what approach I made, she would have none of it. The interview was one, on her part, of controlled anger, not at me, but at the whole system, at the fact that I was white. It was the first time that I had heard very distinctly what the goals of the Black Panther Party were, what their constitution was.

She was pregnant with their son, and my little girl had just been born. I remember saying, "Mrs. Cleaver, I have a child and you have a child about to be born. You have said that you hoped that in the future this country would burn. What about our children? What about their life together? What do you want for your son?" And she said, "May he light the first match." I felt then that I understood a great deal of the animosity of the militant black towards the white liberal. I thought, "I can't possibly understand her experience or the experience of blacks in this country. No white person can. And furthermore, they don't want us to."

What was the Panther constitution?

It was a total revolution of the social system of this country including the hope that all blacks should be released from prisons regardless of their crimes because the feeling was they had not been tried by their peers: no blacks should serve in the armed forces . . . these were not the most important points, but it was a total change of the social and economic system of the country which would give the blacks the power that they needed.

What happened at the party that Mr. and Mrs. Leonard Bernstein held for the Panthers? [The Bernsteins hosted a fund-raising party for the Panthers in their midtown Manhattan apartment.]

I had been asked to come, interestingly enough, by the Black Panthers. There was a trial going on in New York for ten of the Panthers and the reason for the meeting at Bernstein's house was to raise money for attorneys' fees and to protect their civil liberties. There had been a great deal of question at that time whether they were going to have a fair trial, whether their civil liberties were being protected, whether they have a right to bail, and so on. I knew when the evening was over with that it was not just an interesting evening, but a staggering evening. I remember coming home and talking about it with my husband. By the way, I asked my husband to go and he said, "No, I won't. They have an extremely anti-Semitic stance and I won't go and be a part of it."

Leaving aside the party and whether hors d'oeuvres were served and whether they weren't, what struck me about it —and I sat there very quietly—was the naïveté of the people who were there. I give Mr. and Mrs. Bernstein an enormous amount of credit for their compassion and their sensitivity and their feeling that the civil rights of this country must be celebrated and backed and so on, but the naïveté of the people there appalled me. The Black Panther who spoke talked about free lunch for children and all the good works that they were doing, and there was never any mention at all of this ten-point program which I had heard maybe six months earlier from Mrs. Cleaver. None whatsoever. No mention of violence. It was all kind of Boy Scout do-goodism. I remember a friend of ours coming in late in black tie and raising his hand and his question was, "When can I give a party for you?" And young lovely blond ladies saying, "Can we come and work for your free lunch program?" Finally, when I raised my hand, I said, "Look, is it possible for you to exist and have what you want, and for *us* to exist? For me, a white liberal, married to a white capitalist?"

One of the Panther wives turned around and said, "You sound as if you're afraid of us." I said, "I am. I'm not afraid of *you*, but I'm afraid that what *you* want will not make it possible for what *I* want for this country." The same thing I said to Mrs. Cleaver, that if "your child lives in the world that you want, my child will not." ‘

J. Edgar Hoover maintained that the Panthers were a serious threat to the national security. Do you agree?

I don't think they were a serious danger to society because they were really a relatively small movement. I didn't have the feeling that they were going to take over the country. I thought they would have an enormous influence over the young blacks, that there could be an eventual change. Many of the things that they wanted, certainly many of the changes that they were advocating, were important changes. How do you move the center unless you have the extremists? And the Black Panthers certainly were extremists. What they were fighting for was a kind of justice, a justice which excluded white participation. When I say white participation, I really mean white existence! I felt that they had to be listened to and reckoned with, and the way to reckon was not to shoot them.

Do you sympathize with the Panthers' advocacy of separatism?

They want control over their neighborhood schools. We're back really to a large degree to the separate . . . separate but what? I don't think you can have a society of separate pockets. Somehow we're going to have to evolve—not to the integrated society that we thought of ten years ago, of everyone living merrily, black and white together, the liberal intermarriage, etc.—we're going to find that blacks want very much to have their own culture, to have their own marriages, to have their own life, and that whites do as well. And that we can have this still living side by side, or block by block. This sort of feeling that we had that we're all going to mesh and become light brown . . . and I'm not just speaking in terms of marriage, but that they're going to have our culture, that we're going to have their culture. . . . I think there's a great desire these days for people to maintain their own identity.

Leonard B. Boudin

 . . . I'm not sure it makes much difference whether you use physical torture or mental torture, whether you send a man to jail or . . . deprive his family of his chance to earn a living. It's about the same. The East and the West were exactly the same.

Sixty-two-year-old Leonard Boudin is an exacting constitutional lawyer, and his roster of cases is long and of great social significance. He overturned the ban on Henry Miller's *Tropic of Cancer;* he regained Julian Bond's seat in the Georgia legislature. He defended more people before the

McCarthy committee than any other lawyer. He defended Dr. Benjamin Spock (see pp. 153–156) against the government's conspiracy charges, and he represented Eqbal Ahmad in the trial of the Harrisburg Eight and Daniel Ellsberg in the Pentagon Papers case. His daughter Kathy is wanted by the FBI. The "wanted" poster claims she "has been associated with persons who advocate the use of explosives, and may have acquired firearms. Consider dangerous." Kathy is supposed to have crawled from a Weathermen bomb factory in Greenwich Village after the explosion in the spring of 1970; the bodies of three Weathermen were found in the debris.

I've never been active in politics, so we'll begin with that limitation. Secondly, I'm afraid of big government and I'm afraid of people with unlimited power. Here my views are those frequently expressed by Justices Douglas and Brandeis and by Clarence Darrow and Alexander Meiklejohn. I've yet to see the exercise of power handled with the limitations that I think should be imposed upon it.

Are you afraid of government?

I think most governments behave badly normally.

On what basis?

Berrigan. Spock. Angela Davis. The attitude of the United States government toward Cuba. The attitude of the United States government toward Chile. I represent both Chile and Cuba in their litigation in the United States. The power that corporations exercise; the failure of government ever to control that power. The failure of government not to be controlled by great corporate power.

Have you given any thought to how this problem might be remedied?

It never could be remedied. I think man's inhumanity to man is the key. I don't see much hope. I haven't seen any evidence of it yet. I took a young man out to dinner the night before last who was sleeping out there outside the courthouse.

I sat down with him at dinner and I asked him why he was here. Well, he was just wandering through the country and Harrisburg was a place to wander to because something was happening. He never even tried to get into that courthouse. He just sat in line. He was there at eight at night till the next morning and he never bothered to go into the courthouse. He seemed lost on drugs . . . or life or whatever it was. His sense of helplessness seemed to me to be symptomatic of so many people in the country.

I've always had this feeling about government and about political parties. I've always been skeptical of every political party, whether the left or the right, but particularly the latter. I've always found that they're centers of power and that human beings behave badly with power, whether they're in the government or whether they're in small governments called trade unions or political parties or otherwise.

If you're asking whether I can see great changes and improvements in the country, the answer is "no."

The government became worse in the late Forties and the Fifties and the Sixties. We had some reason for optimism as a result of the work of the Supreme Court, the Warren Court. The thing came to a pitch right after the war when the problem of the atomic bomb and nuclear warfare arose and terrorized the East and terrorized the West. Then in Europe those Lansky-type trials occurred and in the United States we had the McCarthy-type investigations and political trials such as Alger Hiss, Carl Marzani, the Communist Party leaders, and the denial of passports and loss of government employment. While I have boasted of and compared the United States favorably to other countries, I'm not sure it makes much difference whether you use physical torture or mental torture, whether you send a man to jail or whether you deprive his family of his chance to earn a living. It's about the same. The East and the West were exactly the same. I think our pretensions are a little greater. We are exactly as bad as what is so often called "the other side." I'm not at all talking about what happens in Vietnam; there I'm not even equating the United States with the people of Vietnam. There I consider there is only one side that's decent, and that is the people of Vietnam. The United States government's behavior is completely indecent.

Is there any better system of government?

No. I think that our system remains the better. As a political system our system is about the top that I've seen so far. In practice it often works dreadfully.

You attribute these problems to "man's inhumanity to man." Is it possible that man's human nature might better itself?

[*Long pause*] When a jury places the future of two human beings, like Phil Berrigan and Elizabeth McAlister, in the hands of a federal judge with the power to impose substantial punishments, my view of the way in which human beings operate in our society is confirmed.

[*Long pause*] I don't know. I look at these wonderful little kids—seven years old, eight years old, and I wish for a world in which they could remain as good when they grow up. I suppose that if we go back to the civil rights movement in the Sixties and we saw all these young people doing what they did . . . maybe I'm unduly harsh and perhaps I can say that if they did it then, if they tried to do what they did then, maybe there is some hope.

Does your daughter Kathy share your pessimism with regard to man's basic inhumanity?

Kathy has more hope for the country than I have in the long run. I believe that she was always prepared to make greater sacrifices than I am for the future. I can't say any more since I don't know enough of what she's thinking or what she's thought to be able to discuss it. The only thing I can give you is my conclusion.

Are her actions really aimed at the betterment of the United States or at its destruction?

I can't discuss the actions to which you refer which are the basis of criminal charges, since I don't know what they were. But I can say unequivocally that throughout her life she has devoted herself to the betterment of her fellowman: in civil rights in the North and South, in poverty areas, among college students, in her legal and other writings, as a camp counselor with blind and crippled children, and best of all in relation with her family and friends.

I know, of course, of the charges made by the government, state and federal, in its conspiracy indictments against her. I consider the conspiracy indictments under the 1968 and 1970 crime acts to be stupid and unconstitutional since they are based upon an attempt to have the federal government enforce minor local laws. As far as the Chicago indictments are concerned they were absurd. The sentences given to the people involved were quite insubstantial, and if she had been there she would have been given the same insubstantial sentence.

Do you harbor a bitterness toward the government?

No . . . contempt for the present administration. Tremendous contempt for its indifference to the welfare of human beings here and elsewhere.

Hillaire Valiquette

 Every time we have a program the first thing we do is go out there and put a red *X* on the foreheads of the people we're supposed to be helping.

A Franciscan priest, Father Hillaire Valiquette was ordained in 1964. He taught theology in college for a time, then studied in Germany. "I came back and taught for a year at Fort Wayne High School. Then down to Cincinnati with nothing to do and tied in with the Basin Ministry."

It's hard to say what we did at the Basin Ministry. I got up here in 1967 which was right after the rebellion [referring to the 1967 riots in Cincinnati] or whatever—a summer of fun. I thought everything was hot to trot. We were heavy in welfare rights organizing at the time, getting welfare recipients together. Getting community councils, neighborhood groups, to work together in a thing called the Coordinating Committee of Community Councils. Both of them were relatively successful in the sense that there were a lot of people involved, things were happening. We had all kinds of confrontations and great fun. About 1968 the OEO kind of things were finally going full blast. They were going before 1967 but they kind of got their strings out by 1968. Whether anything really got affected, it's hard to say. I guess I don't think so. Some poor people, some low-income people, were able to get themselves together by these programs. Some of them in the sense that they made money. Some of them in the sense that by the fact that they fought over the issues they gained some self-respect and some dignity. This summer [1971] it's the worst since 1967 as far as employment, as far as recreation, as far as despair and discouragement. So all the people who worked hard, or thought they worked hard, during the poverty programs are back to zero.

The great War on Poverty . . . it's kind of like the welfare program. People can be very concerned, but they still fuck up because they don't know what to do. They don't recognize the way they treat people. Every time we have a program the first thing we do is go out there and put a red X on the foreheads of the people we're supposed to be helping. "You are a welfare recipient and we're going to take care of you" . . . or mess you up—however they want to put it. Just go down to the welfare department and sit in the waiting room where people are sitting there holding their little number waiting to be called.

People are treated and helped at the convenience of the system, of the caseworker. Not only the convenience of the persons in the system, but the convenience of the categories in the system, the conveniences of a very arbitrary figure on how much people should get—about thirty-two dollars a month, which nobody can live on! That's for food and clothing plus all the ballgames and the two cars that everybody thinks welfare people have. The way people have to beg the system! Even if their caseworker is a nice person, it doesn't make a bit of difference. The caseworkers, the social workers, the community organizers or whatever they want to call themselves are all nice persons—sincere, dedicated, and all that crap—but it doesn't make any difference. No matter what they want to do, they are still representing a system that is screwing people up.

We were getting welfare people together to get the things out of the system that they already had a right to by law. It's a pretty fair way to organize people because you can get some small successes. The fact that the law says you've got a right to a refrigerator or you've got a right to so much clothing. If you don't have it, then they have to give you a voucher or a special grant. So you go down and you shake the hell out of them a little bit. Here come ten welfare recipients saying, "We're behind Mrs. Jones and according to the handbook, page so-and-so, Mrs. Jones deserves a refrigerator and you'd better damn well give it to her." This is just a total new way for a welfare recipient to act. We went up to Columbus a number of times and raised some hell. We raised hell with the welfare people, went down and sat at their desks and a few other things. We went to Washington a couple of times. The basic issue was that the recipient no longer became a recipient and became an active person. Many of the people that were in the welfare rights organization at that time, that was in 1967, are still on welfare, but I think a good number of them got themselves together. Like it doesn't matter if you're on welfare.

Was much antagonism stirred up?

That was the purpose of it. The purpose of it was to stir up antagonism. Because the welfare recipient hated the caseworker and the caseworker hated the recipient, but they both had to be polite. Or the middle-class society hates the welfare recipient, but you've got to show people that's the way it is. All of a sudden welfare recipients walked down the street claiming they were welfare recipients. Sort of like gay liberation, you know. The whole straight society hates the homosexual. What they really hate is when they get uppity.

Do your successes give you reason for optimism?

I don't see that we're heading toward any kind of new world. It's the same old shit. It's a matter of keeping your sanity while it happens.

Michael Butler

 Hair suddenly came out and really said something in a very strong way.... A new format was used. . . . It just looked like incredible chaos, but it was *organized* chaos.

The Butler Company is the oldest privately held company in Illinois. Descendants of the renegade Irish gentry that settled in Massachusetts in 1653, the Butlers are among the founding fathers of the state. Although he is the scion of a family of industrialists, it was as the producer of *Hair* that Michael Butler achieved international fame. His interests, however, do not stop with *Hair.* His public-relations firm bills him as "Polo player, yachtsman, land developer, political candidate, night-club entrepreneur, sales executive, Commissioner of the Port of Chicago, President of the Illinois Sports Council, Chan-

cellor of the Lincoln Academy of Illinois, Chairman of
the Organization for Economic Development of Illinois. . . ."

It blew my mind. I thought *Hair* was a piece of theater
that, from a satiric point of view, needed some work to make it
interesting and acceptable to the general public, but I thought
it had something very important to say that should be said. I felt
that I wanted to be involved with it, whether it was a business
proposition or in any sense. There are a lot of funny things
about *Hair,* the people who are involved in it. There are many
of us who feel that we're in it because of reasons other than just
being producers.

We feel that we have a responsibility, that we had a
responsibility and still do to get across our basic message of
freedoms in several areas. This was more important than producing the show, and for this reason we've done many things
within *Hair* that one might question. We're much more deeply
involved with all the actors; we're more into the social implica-
tions. It's like if you treat *Hair* right, it will treat you right.
There's a mysticism, in a rather pragmatic way, about what many
of us are into; a much more deep involvement than just the
involvement with the theater. We've had ten or twenty busts for
grass in the show. We arranged for bail to be put up, arranged
for legal help, everything like that. This freaks out the business
people in our organization. From a business viewpoint, that is
very imprudent. That's an extreme example. We arrange that
they can get vitamins wholesale. We have very close personal
relations. A lot of friendships are involved.

You said **Hair** *was saying many things that had to be
said?*

Hair is against war. It's against hypocrisy. It's for freedom of speech, the right to smoke grass if you feel like it, the
right to do what you want to do with your own body. It tries to
and succeeds pretty well in breaking down a lot of the sexual

taboos that are around. It has some very strong points on pollution, ecology.

It's had a very strong effect on people. It's been a very definite bridge between generations, a bridge between a lot of viewpoints. It has converted an awful lot of people who are at least saying, "Hmmm, there's something worthwhile on the other side of these questions."

What *Hair* did was, at a time when musicals, when the theater was pretty well controlled and handled by formula musicals, very dull, very boring, *Hair* suddenly came out and really said something in a very strong way and got through. A new format was used; a new approach. It just looked like incredible chaos, but it was *organized* chaos. It was really an expanding, mind-blowing experience for people who saw it because they had never seen anything like that before. *Hair* is essentially taking the rock idiom, that whole popular approach, and putting that on the stage for the first time. A lot of things you had heard over the radio you were finally hearing on stage.

People who compare *Calcutta* with *Hair* don't even know what they're talking about. I think that *Calcutta* has some interesting points. Last night I saw my first X-rated movie. I left in about fifteen minutes because it was so boring. *Hair* is not a sex piece. Anybody who considers it that obviously doesn't know what he's talking about.

Hair *and* Oh! Calcutta! *did have one thing in common —they were both highly successful.*

It's because they jumped on the so-called bandwagon. People were so stunned by the nudity in *Hair* that instantly we get into a so-called extrapermissive attitude. Things should be open, they should be permitted. Why? Because in my opinion it takes the pressure off. A lot of the sexual things that you have in Denmark, that's incredibly boring as far as I'm concerned, but I suspect that they do a great good in letting other people participate or watch in an area where otherwise they'd feel restricted or inhibited. Sexually speaking, if they've got some hangups, isn't it better to let them out?

Zodiac

 It was a phenomenon! It was something that happened and I was there. It was like being one molecule in a big organism. There was a whole bunch of stuff you had no control over. . . . You were just there.

Zodiac's real name is Michael Alan Carl. He is twenty-two years old and lives on Ken Kesey's farm in Oregon (see pp. 381–386).

Woodstock? We had a hard time finding where the place actually was. I'd hitchhiked there from Chicago. There was a highway turnoff where you got off the turnpike and was headed . . . I'm not sure of the direction . . . but it was up. You had to go up off the turnpike to Woodstock. I figured it was the Woodstock festival, so I went up to Woodstock. I remember going into the town there, and there were a lot of other people looking for the place too. Nobody was really sure. So we got a map and found out where it was and it was sixty miles away. I got in with these people in about a 1948 De Soto. We were driving up there and there was no back seat and a couple of girls and a guy and me. We stopped at the store, I remember. We got there and I thought, "Should I hang around with these folks, or just go off on my own?" Not knowing anything about the scene or anything, I took off and started walking, this way and that way; and I saw this guy and he was pointing this way and that way to other people. I asked him what was going on; "Are there any people here from Oregon?" He said there were four busloads on the other side of these trees. I walked over there and I was walking through the clearing and I saw Ramrod, sitting there on a log.

I knew Ramrod from Chicago. I stopped to say hello and he pointed on to where the buses were. I just went over there. I had a little pack, one new shirt and a couple of old shirts. I sat my pack down and I met Maria and some other people. There were about five hundred people scattered around, with some tents going up. It was nice. It was a sunny day.

Were you surprised by the numbers of people involved?

It was more than surprise. It was far out! It happened so subtly and gradually. I remember when the buses were first parked in a semicircle at the top of this one hill, and then we moved them down into this valley because they were going to put up a gate or something.

We moved down there and this was like two miles or so away from where the main stage was. We were over there, the Hog Farm was near us, and it started getting crowded. You looked around and could see thousands of people around; and you'd say, "God damn, we're camped here and there are three or four thousand people here!" And that night, we played all night. We had a little stage set up, made out of two-by-fours and plywood. We just laid it out. A big floor. A whole bunch of people . . . the old hammer-and-nail concerto. [*Rat-a-tat-tat . . . rat-a-tat-tat . . . he demonstrates, rhythmically hitting a stick against the log he is resting against.*] Then we had to carry it about a hundred yards down this hill.

We were kind of secluded, a little bit. It was late and everybody was high on acid. The lights were flickering on and off. We'd strung Christmas tree lights around, and the buses were parked in a semicircle. I was sleeping . . . under the bus, I think. And then the next day the main festival was going on, starting that day. Me and this guy John, who is Liz's brother, I said, "Well, let's walk over and check out the area." We started walking, walking. You had to go up out of our valley and across a big open field, past a fence they'd put up, a cyclone fence. Then you took a left and walked up this road. As you walked up this road, the hill along your right side was getting higher and higher. Then you finally got up . . . you went about halfway up because it sloped over. Then you took a right and there was another big clearing where a guy had built a huge tepee out of logs. He'd hung from the center three long, long leather ropes, and there was a big rock hanging there. A rock four or five feet across, and it just hung there. It was amazing. It was amazing! You walked by that and there were people hanging around, and you walked over this big field. Pretty soon, God, it was just colors—light blues and pinks. You could see the stage w-a—a—y down there. I turned to John and I said, "Look at all those colors. That's amazing." He said, "Those are all people." I couldn't believe it, because we were looking out over what turned out to be two or three hundred thousand people. It was just wild.

I remember hanging around down at the big stage for a little while and seeing John Sebastian play. I went up there when The Grateful Dead played. I made several trips back and forth. I remember being out walking around in the audience. You see, when you're walking around . . . and I mean I was stoned all the time I was there, most people were . . . there was a movement. It was like whirlpools and tides and river streams. There was a flow in there and you were caught, you were in it. You were there! You had to go with the flow. You could have a direction but you couldn't walk from here to there straight. The route that you took to get there was completely in another hand.

The whole thing stands out in my mind as a single thing. It was a phenomenal thing. It was a phenomenon! It was something that happened and I was there. It was like being one molecule in a big organism. There was a whole bunch of stuff that you had no control over or nothin'. You were just there.

I remember the rain. It was just another amazing thing. It was raining like shit and there was nothing you could do. You could find a warm spot inside a tent or something. For me, I had no tent of my own. I would stand with these people I'd met on these buses, and the buses were pretty full, so I had no right to anything. Yet when there was room and I was there, I filled the space that was there.

*   *   *

There's something I want to add. It has to do with a certain respect that you have to give other people. You have to give everyone a certain respect that they're doing each thing that they do for the best possible reasons. They're working their thing out. Everyone makes mistakes and so forth. You give them that respect that they're doing what they're doing for the good of everyone else.

Clark Clifford

 I couldn't get the right answers out of the Joint Chiefs of Staff. . . . We had never fought a jungle war before, where you have no lines, where the enemy is acquainted with the terrain [and] can live off the country. . . .

Clark Clifford has had a telling influence on the course of public affairs since the Truman years. As one of President Truman's closest advisors, he co-authored the Truman Doctrine and masterminded the upset victory over Thomas E. Dewey in 1948. Later he helped formulate the legislation that created the Department of Defense in 1949. He retired to his Washington law firm in 1952 to become one of the wealthiest and most prominent corporation lawyers in the country. His special talent was advising his firm's clients (among them AT&T, RCA, and DuPont) on strategies in their affairs with the government. After the 1960 elections President-elect Kennedy appointed Clifford as liaison with the Eisenhower Administration to smooth the customary problems involved in the transfer of power. Later, he served on Kennedy's Foreign Intelligence Advisory Board, becoming chairman of that body in 1963. In 1962 he was the President's personal negotiator with the steel industry. After the assassination, Lyndon Johnson sought out Clifford again to help direct the transition. As one of the President's foremost advisors on foreign policy, Clifford tried to dissuade Johnson from calling the temporary halt on the bombing of North Vietnam. Two and a half years later, Clifford reversed himself and encouraged the President to halt the bombing of the North and to initiate negotiations with Hanoi. Johnson followed this advice in his famous speech of March 31, 1968. This reversal of judgment came not quite three months after Clifford accepted appointment as Secretary of Defense. He is now back with his law firm, and an outspoken advocate of withdrawal from Vietnam.

When President Kennedy came into office in January of 1961, I had for the preceding months been his liaison with the Eisenhower Administration, and I sat in the meetings that he had with President Eisenhower. One of them took place on January 19, 1961, at which time President Eisenhower discussed the major problems that would confront President-elect Kennedy. What he emphasized more than any other was Southeast Asia. President Eisenhower stated at that time—I can almost remember his words—that he considered it one of the most pressing problems that this country had, and that he felt that this nation should come to the assistance of the countries of Southeast Asia, who, in his words, were being confronted with Communist aggression. He said we should try to persuade our friends to help us in preventing a Communist takeover, but if they will not join with us, then we must go it alone. And the purport of his comments was such that it left no doubt upon those present that he meant that this country should come to the military assistance of the nations of Southeast Asia. At that time, South Vietnam was not quite so clearly in focus as was Laos.

So, when President Kennedy came in, he had behind him the experience and the attitude of President Eisenhower.

During the Kennedy Administration, from time to time I would be called in. I would say that I generally approved of the policy. I believe I had the feeling at the time, as most of us did, that limited assistance to South Vietnam and Laos would very likely perform the function that was needed and gain the desired result. During the period of the Kennedy Administration, during that some three years, the situation gradually worsened in Southeast Asia. When President Kennedy came in there were maybe four, five thousand advisers and instructors there, and that number must have reached twelve to fourteen thousand by the time President Kennedy was assassinated in November of 1963. So when President Johnson came in, he inherited this situation. It was really very similar to the one that President Kennedy had inherited, with one exceedingly important addition: he also inherited the advisers that President Kennedy had. When he came into office, Johnson retained his main advisers, all able, dedicated, patriotic Americans: Secretary of State [Dean] Rusk [see pp. 54–59], Secretary of Defense [Robert] McNamara, McGeorge Bundy [see pp. 11–15] as his staff member for National Security, others of that kind. So the pattern was quite well formed when President Johnson came in. The decisions had already been made to assist the nations of Southeast Asia. That was being done. The number of our advisers or instructors had increased threefold during the Kennedy Administration. There were public statements by President Kennedy, pointing out the importance of our presence there and that we were going to see the situation through. Again I accepted the wisdom of that course of action. I hoped that with a minor investment of men and our treasury that we could obtain the result that we were seeking at the time, and that was a non-Communist Southeast Asia.

By the time 1965 came, the situation had worsened to the extent that definite decisions had to be made. No longer could the posture of affairs in Southeast Asia be maintained by just advisers or instructors or consultants. I do not know a single Southeast Asian expert who disagrees with the position that had the United States not sent in troops, South Vietnam would have fallen. So this was a situation that confronted President Johnson that did not confront his predecessors. He faced up to that in the spring, and he sent in some seventy-five thousand Marines.

I was not involved in that decision. I was not in the government at the time, but I think I would have to say in all honesty that I very likely approved of the policy. It had been one that we had been conducting consistently for years, through the Fifties and on into the Sixties. I generally accepted it. It was found out during 1965 that the first contingent wasn't adequate to do the task. So more troops were sent in. And more were sent in the following year. So from 1965 through 1968 we continued to send troops in.

When I came into the Defense Department in the beginning of 1968, one of the first problems I had was the request from the military that another two hundred six thousand troops be sent to South Vietnam. President Johnson made me head of a task force to investigate the need for the men and how they would be selected and how we could meet the demand of our military leaders. Then it was, as the result of this investigation into the whole war, that I began to get serious questions in my mind. I went through days and evenings of these meetings, asking questions which I thought were appropriate questions, and not getting satisfactory answers. I couldn't get the right answers out of the Joint Chiefs of Staff. When I asked whether two hundred six thousand men would be enough, they said they didn't know. Then I said, "Can you tell me how many more men you're likely to be needing?" They didn't know. When I asked what the plan was for military victory, I finally concluded they had none. The only plan was one of sending more men to fight and die in Vietnam in the hope that ultimately attrition would so adversely affect the North Vietnamese effort that they would sue for some kind of negotiated disposition of the war. So even in the early days of my tenure in the Pentagon, I began to have the deepest kind of reservations about our presence there. As time went on, those reservations became basic doubts. The doubts in turn began to develop into an attitude on my part—and the attitude later became a conviction—that we had done all that we should do in that part of the world. That we should get out.

So in that regard I wrote about it, published an article

in the spring of 1969 in *Foreign Affairs,* making that recommendation. I wrote about it again in 1970 in an article in *Life* magazine. During those years it became a conviction which today I might say has become an obsession with me. I believe that our presence in Vietnam is tearing the country apart. I believe that the only solution to many of our problems today will be our departure from Vietnam. The impact upon our young people today is poisonous. There are racial overtones that are very serious. The economic result of this continuous waste of our treasure is having an exceedingly denigrating effect upon our economy. So that I am convinced that we ought to get out.

I believe now, as we look back at it with twenty-twenty vision, which President Truman used to say people with hindsight always had, I have the feeling that had President Kennedy or President Johnson known that our ultimate investment would have been in the neighborhood of forty-five to fifty thousand young Americans killed in action, and that the cost in our treasury would have amounted to one hundred and thirty billions of dollars, I think we would have decided at that time, as a nation, that the stakes involved did not warrant that kind of investment. I have a sneaking notion—and it's not based on any record, but based more upon a visceral reaction that I had during the time that I was in the Pentagon—it is my belief that the military felt in the early days, in the early Sixties, that the situation could be cleaned up at relatively little cost. That with the enormous firepower that the American troops had, with complete control of the air, with the Navy in complete control of the sea and the coastline, that with those great assets our forces could bring that situation to an early and successful conclusion. It proved to be a gross misevaluation. One of the reasons is that we have never fought a previous war like the one we are fighting in Vietnam. We had never fought a jungle war before, where the enemy can live off the country—those enormous advantages which enemy forces have which we do not possess. Plus the fact that there is a sense of dedication and commitment on the part of the North Vietnamese troops that I think has been underestimated by our experts. And I think we do not yet know whether there is a sufficient sense of dedication on the part of the South Vietnamese troops for them to carry on successfully if and when the time comes that we will move out.

President Nixon had a glorious opportunity in the first three months of his administration in early 1969 to inform the American people that he felt that one of the reasons he had been elected was to disengage the United States from the war in Indochina. He chose not to do that. I thought it was one of the greatest opportunities I've ever known a President to have. As time went on and I explored why he did not avail himself of the opportunity, I reached a very clear conclusion in my own mind that President Nixon believes in the rightness of the war. I believe that President Nixon feels we are engaged in a basic struggle between the forces of evil and the forces of freedom and that we must stay with that engagement. He has mentioned it in many different ways. I have made it my business to go back and read every word he has either spoken or written with reference to Indochina or Southeast Asia, and the trend of his thinking is inescapable and most dramatic. He actually believes that President Kennedy and President Johnson did not do enough during their tenure in the White House. You get the distinct impression that had he been President during that period, there would have been more men and broader attacks and an ultimate successful military conclusion to it. Which I believe now, as I believed during my tenure in the Pentagon, is impossible of achievement.

Right now, President Nixon has informed the American people that we are engaged in an irreversible process of withdrawal from Indochina. Yet, when you turn the policy over and read the small print on the other side, you find that he has so hedged that with conditions that I have reached the inescapable conclusion that he does not intend to get our forces out of Vietnam. Also, both he and Secretary of Defense [Melvin] Laird have pretty well told the American people that even after the so-called withdrawal takes place, we are going to leave substantial air forces, naval forces, and logistic support forces. I consider this to be inordinately dangerous. I believe that as American troops are withdrawn down to a certain point, it makes them vulnerable. I do not believe from what I've learned that the South Vietnamese are likely to have the sense of dedication that would be necessary. The deepest concern I have today is that in the event hostilities should substantially increase this year and next year, and with our forces being cut all the while, that a point could be reached where our forces would be in great danger. What concerns me most is the manner in which President Nixon would react to a situation of that kind. I believe that it is possible that we would have to reinstitute sending new troops. We would have to expand our bombing. I do not know what he would do, but he has said time and time again that we are not going to be driven out of Vietnam.

I believe that the present policy in Indochina is wrong. That our involvement in the war has done inestimable damage to the United States. It has torn our country apart. It has cost us in manpower and material amounts that far exceed anything contemplated by our leaders when we got into it. I believe as we look back on it now we can see why we got into it, but at the same time those nations which do not learn from the past are doomed to perish. I feel no sense of embarrassment whatsoever in saying that I once had one opinion with reference to it, but I now have changed. If we don't change as a result of this experience, then I think we're doomed.

During your tenure as Secretary of Defense, what actions did you take to impress President Johnson with your conviction, and what type of reception did you receive?

I can't go into detail. Others have written a great deal about it. I shall not write about it. I think it is inappropriate for a Cabinet officer to write about those personal relationships that exist between a Cabinet officer and a President. I can say to you generally what is already known.

After those early days of conducting the task force in early 1968, I reached the conclusion that we should not send any more men to Vietnam. That debate went on during the entire month of March. Sometimes I thought we were making progress. Sometimes I felt that we who believed in that manner were not making progress. Ultimately, on March 31, 1968, President Johnson made his decision and announced that we were not going to send any more men to Vietnam, except another small contingent of ten or twelve thousand troops that had already been promised as support troops. Also, I reached the conclusion that if we were ever going to get any negotiations started, we should cut back on the bombing. President Johnson was not willing to stop all the bombing at that time. I took the position that if we cut back part of the bombing, that would be a step toward finding some basis for negotiation. I recall saying that if we took even a small timid step, then Hanoi might take a step. Then we might take a little bolder step and they might take one. I remember saying that before a baby can walk, a baby has to crawl, and that the stopping of the bombing was sort of the starting of the baby crawling. To our surprise, including me, Hanoi responded at once in early April, saying, yes, they were willing to sit down and talk.

During the time those talks went on, during the rest of 1968, the dispute continued with reference to the bombing. When we were not successful in reaching agreement as expeditiously as we hoped to do in Paris, there were a number of those in the administration who thought we should resume the bombing of all of North Vietnam. So we had quite a problem in that time, persuading the President not to resume the bombing. Then the question came up of stopping all the bombing, that we might be able to reach an additional understanding with Hanoi. If we stopped all the bombing, then the Saigon government could come into the talks, and after they did come in, we had hopes at that time that we might reach some agreement. Those hopes were pretty well dashed by the attitude of the government of Saigon, which in my opinion was utterly and completely intransigent. During that entire year of 1968, some of us constantly made an effort to reduce the level of the war. We went on to persuade the President to issue different orders to our field commanders: not to seek and destroy the enemy, to try to avoid contact, combat, stop the bombing, reduce the level of the war, cut down the number of our casualties, produce a climate in which negotiations could be successful. We made some progress during 1968 in that regard.

Sam Brown

 . . . there's tremendous sort of sexual insecurities which lead people to be afraid to say that they're for values which have traditionally been associated with being cowardly. They want to love the flag and don't understand it's possible to care about America and at the same time oppose what it's doing.

After serving as a youth coordinator for Eugene McCarthy's campaign in 1968, Sam Brown went to the Harvard Divinity School as a Fellow in Ethics. In April 1969 a Boston businessman approached him with the idea for the Vietnam Moratorium. What followed was a fury of intensive organizing that culminated in the October and November Moratoria in 1969. Now just under thirty, Brown opted out of national politics in 1972 and worked with a group in Denver concerned with the Winter Olympics to be held there in 1976. "Every real estate developer and hotel owner and tourism promoter in the State of Colorado is on the Olympic Committee. Sort of a super version of 'Let's sell the West.' I've been working with a group of people trying to get that stopped."

We knew there was going to be a lot going on. By the first of October it was pretty clear that the timing seemed to be working; that people were, in fact, disgusted with Nixon for not having done anything. The administration was beginning to respond nervously: they threw out General [Lewis B.] Hershey [Director of the Selective Service] and replaced him, made announcements that there would be major speeches on the war. We knew that there was going to be a lot going on in the country, that in a variety of places it was going to happen. The major thing we worried about was to make it something different than and hopefully broader and more appealing than simply another march.

In immediate terms, October fifteenth was something of a success in that people in all sorts of little towns, in the middle of nowhere, there was something going on. On the other hand, a lot of us were disappointed that as the momentum built toward October fifteenth, there became an increasing emphasis on doing marches and vigils. For instance, in New York City, there was initially a tremendous effort on the part of law students to get appointments to talk to lawyers in downtown law firms and to set up seminars and to try to discuss the legality of the war with the legal community. As October fifteenth got closer, it became much more exciting to go to the candlelight vigil at St. Patrick's, and go to the march here, and go to the rally in Bryant Park. And much less effort was spent on doing the kind of one-to-one work that we had hoped for. The final fear we had, and one that overcame us all day long, was hoping that there wouldn't be untoward incidents that would permit the press to say, "It's a bunch of crazy people at it again." We really were very worried that there would be violence some place or another. In a lot of little towns where there had never been any peace activity before, we were terrified that the police would respond to even the notion of a candlelight vigil by beating up a bunch of people.

There was one little town in Kansas where they rang a bell which hadn't been rung since the end of World War Two. It had been the "peace" bell in the community, the bell that had rung on V-E Day and V-J Day. They started ringing it twenty-four hours earlier, one ring for each dead in Vietnam, so they had to ring it forty thousand times. They had shifts of people to ring the bell. There were a lot of candlelight vigils. That whole notion of the silent vigil really caught on, and in little towns there would be vigils with people representing the number of dead from that town or county or state, wearing mourning clothes and marching through the streets of the city. There were a hell of a lot of rallies. We had put together a speakers' bureau and we were very proud of it. There were some events that I remember very clearly: the rally in Wall Street, for instance, where a number of Establishment figures who hadn't previously spoken about the war—Roswell Gilpatric, Townsend Hoopes, people like that—for the first time publicly spoke against the war. There was a meeting at Trinity Church over lunch hour on that day at Wall Street, with Establishmentarian Wall Street lawyers speaking to each other. Arthur Goldberg and Averell Harriman spoke that day in Washington, D.C., at a church down near Lafayette Park. It was those kinds of things. The Bryant Park rally where Senator [Eugene] McCarthy spoke.

How many people participated in the Moratorium nationwide?

The press that day said something over a million. I have no idea.

After October the plan was to continue it every month, escalating it a day at a time. What happened?

A tremendous amount of energy got diverted in the March on Washington the following month. The Mobilization Committee had been planning that. You know, it's exciting and it's psychologically rewarding and it's all sort of warm and brotherly, let's all get together and love one another. You get on a bus and go to Washington and then you've done your thing for peace. That became, in my mind, a very diversionary activity from what people should have been doing.

The march was the fifteenth. We had said that we would try to do something the thirteenth and fourteenth. There were a variety of vigils, departure celebrations for people coming to

Washington, departure rallies. The March against Death in Washington, where there was one person carrying the name of each of the forty thousand war dead, filing from Arlington to Washington in what I thought was the most moving and really dramatic kind of symbolic opposition to the war that there had ever been. The March against Death was really a beautiful ceremony, really almost a religious event. It was from Arlington Cemetery to the Capitol. People left Arlington, carrying the name of one person who had been killed in Vietnam, marching from there past the White House to the Capitol. A march which, single file, lasted for two days. When they arrived at the Capitol, they took the name of the person and put it into a coffin at the Capitol. The coffins were later laid at the steps of the White House on Saturday during the big march.

How did President Nixon react to having these coffins deposited at his doorstep?

He said he was watching a football game that day; he didn't know what was going on. They ringed the White House with buses, bumper to bumper, to protect the President from the people. I've always suspected, like Senator McCarthy, that maybe it was the other way around: it was to protect the people from the President.

Do you think the Moratoria had an effect? Do you think you actually did pull Nixon away from the football game?

Yes. He began to do a whole series of things. He had been in office eight months and hadn't even made a statement about the war. He hadn't done anything about the draft. I like to think that in some way we began to make politically respectable the opposition to the war—that it isn't just a bunch of kids who were out there, that it was a cross-section of the American population who were seriously concerned and wanted to do something; that you didn't have to be crazy or a pinko or some sort of long-haired freak in the eyes of the great middle American public to be against the war. To some extent, I think we were successful. We began to find people in little towns in which there had never been anything going. The greatest feeling of accomplishment that I have about any of that was not that there were forty thousand people in Bryant Park, but that there were two thousand people in Des Moines, Iowa. This is a much more significant kind of reflection of the tone of the country.

*   *   *

I really have great faith that if you can find a way to talk to people, to give them the factual basis, that they respond in very rational and thoughtful ways and that there's really a great opportunity to make a difference. Then sometimes I feel, like after Kent State, "What the hell's the whole thing worth if sixty-some per cent of the country support the National Guard? What difference does it all really make?"

I guess on balance I come out thinking that given a chance, the American people are, underneath it all . . . no, I have to hedge all of that. Every time you say anything it sort of sounds silly unless you hedge it with the obvious thing that Americans have a tendency to be violence-prone, that there's the whole thing about guns, that there's tremendous sort of sexual insecurities which lead people to be afraid to say that they're for values which have traditionally been associated with being cowardly. They want to love the flag and don't understand that it's possible to care about America and at the same time oppose what it's doing. There's all those qualifications, but in the final analysis, I come out thinking that there's really some sort of chance. You can't get up in the morning unless you believe that it's possible to some extent. I really believe it *is* possible.

Gabrielle Oppenheim-Errera

 When you haven't got all that history behind you—America has only two hundred
years of history—then of course you can
go quickly to everywhere you want to go.
There's nothing that holds you back.

A cosmopolitan gentlewoman from Brussels, Gabrielle
Oppenheim-Errera and her husband came to Princeton,
New Jersey, about thirty years ago to be with their close
friend, Albert Einstein. Mrs. Oppenheim-Errera still re-
turns to Brussels every summer.

When I came to America the students weren't interested in politics at all. They went to the war, but they were not
interested at all. Nobody spoke about that and I was astonished
because it was so vital for the Europeans. It was against the Nazis
and everything. I didn't understand.

The difference between then and now is so big because
now they are interested in everything—about the inner politics,
about the outer politics, about the politics in Europe, about the
politics in Asia. They're much more *vivant,* more lively.

I was very interested in one thing. When I came here,
I thought that all Americans were alike. They had all to me the
same faces. Little by little, when I knew them more, then of
course I saw there were big differences. But now, they haven't
got the same faces, and if I came now from Europe, I wouldn't
have that idea at all. The individualities come out more. The
"keep smiling" is not so much, that education that made everybody one like the other.

America has not a very deep tradition. When you are in

France or Belgium, the tradition is much more than here. The people here are much more individualistic. When you haven't got all that history behind you—America has only two hundred years of history—then of course you can go quickly to everywhere you want to go. There's nothing that holds you back.

The blacks, they have come a very long way, but never enough, not enough. That's very important. In the olden days when I went to Paris from Brussels, I saw beautiful blond Americans with quite black Negroes, but never in the State of New York. But now it's absolutely—you don't even look at it. It's quite natural that they go—black, white, yellow. It doesn't matter at all. That's a big, big difference. But never enough. A little more, we must try to have much more.

*   *   *

What I don't understand now is the lull that there is, much more than before. It might be disillusionment because everything that they did last year didn't even finish the war. It didn't have enormous repercussions. Perhaps a feeling of helplessness because they can't influence the government. The donnybrook continues all the same. The result is very good, but not enough to change really the government. The people, however, became more individualistic, more outspoken. It's individually much better, but for the nation it's not a lot of difference.

Are the students today happier than they were before?

That I don't know. Why do people in this country much more than in other countries take drugs? I think to have a kick. It's because they don't have enough kick with other things. Everything is so easy. There was a time when sex wasn't so easy because it wasn't done that way. Now it's . . . phssst! You see, it's like you take a glass of beer. Everything is so much more easy. The affluence they had in America was enormous too. So that altogether was such that nothing made an impression. They must have something more. A revolution or violence, because that's still a little bit more.

I don't know if they're happier. I don't think so. When

everything is in a pattern, it is easier. That is why people who are so religious are much happier than the people that are not religious. The people that are religious, they know what they always have to do. The students now are just looking. When we look, we are not so happy as when we know exactly what to do.

Kenneth A. Gibson

 They're talking about dealing with some of these critical problems. Not enough, but they're talking about it.

The soft-spoken and philosophical black Mayor of Newark, New Jersey, Kenneth Gibson half-jokingly announces that he speaks from where "I sit—and stand and run." He took office on July 1, 1970.

What I found when I took office was many years of a steady degeneration of atmosphere, of intangible things, like the image of the city, civic pride. Those degenerative effects had taken place over at least ten years. The feeling that people had about life in the city suffered. What I call the quality of life—health, education, housing—had declined, and the civic pride had declined because of the changing populations in the various neighborhoods. Not just the change from white to black in neighborhoods, but the change in those people who had lived there for say twenty, thirty years, to new residents, whether they be blacks or Puerto Ricans or other whites.

How serious is the urban crisis in Newark?

It is serious . . . but everything is relative. The biggest immediate problem I had was budget. We could not anticipate enough revenue to take care of our expenditures. The city itself can only raise revenue today by property tax. The property tax is designed historically only to provide certain basics: to collect the garbage, to pay policemen, to pay firemen. The property tax was never designed to provide for the educational load that's required in a city like Newark. It was never really designed to provide health services, and it certainly wasn't designed to build any houses. So I immediately had to go before the State Legislature to get what I considered regressive taxation for the city, to impose taxes in Newark that had never been imposed before— payroll tax, parking receipts tax, liquor sales tax.

Following taxes, in priority of crises, was the whole question of narcotics and crime in the city. We have an epidemic of not just the use of narcotics, but all those things that are attendant to their use. The crime problem in the city is multiplied many times just because of the fact that you have a narcotic addiction problem. The safety in the streets issue is sometimes used as a bogeyman, but the real problem is that you have so many addicts who are desperate people, who will attack their own family if necessary to get a fix. My father was mugged in the streets of Newark. You have a decrease in the social life in the city because the people are not willing to go out at night to social functions and attend meetings. I get more complaints about breaking and entering, muggings, fear of just movement, than I get about anything else.

Next comes the whole problem of keeping the city clean, the appearance of the city. Sweep-up, clean-up, fix-up kinds of things.

We have to think about what supportive services are needed for the quality of life of those people who live here. We ought to help to provide those people jobs. I don't mean that the city government ought to do it, but we ought to be able to attract industry and business, because that *does* provide jobs. At the same time, a man or a woman working has a family, children. So we ought to talk about those other items—housing, education, health services—because therein lies the real determination as to whether or not a family has a decent life. That's the government's problem. The city doesn't provide education; the

Board of Education provides it, but we can influence it. The city doesn't provide housing because the city doesn't build housing. But we try to make it profitable for private developers to provide housing in the city, whether it be an apartment house, garden apartments, or other housing construction. We try to work out a relationship with the private health providers. Again, the city really doesn't provide health services. It tries to coordinate health services for the people who live in the city. The key is providing supportive services to the family, and helping to make it profitable for business to move in.

The decline still exists, but I think the slope of the decline has leveled off. Attention has been brought and focused on the problem. The fact that we have traveled around the country, the fact that we've had appearances before the various Congressional and Senatorial committees . . . many people now talk about the urban crisis, many people now talk about crime, they talk about drug problems. The federal government is coming up with special-emphasis programs on drugs and crime impact. They're coming out with special health programs. They're talking about dealing with some of these critical problems. Not enough, but they're talking about it. In the early Sixties and in the Fifties they weren't even talking about it. We're not bringing to bear the resources that are necessary to solve the problem, but at least we're beginning, and that's a sign of hope to me.

I don't go home at night and say, "What's the use?" I know that sooner or later, and hopefully sooner for Newark, the resources of the state, that revision in tax policy, several steps will be taken in order for the survival of the city to occur. I think that New Jersey will revise its tax policy within two years. I don't think they have any choice. That will give a city like Newark a kind of breather, which will allow for some planning rather than the survival techniques that we use every day now. I live from day to day now, certainly from budget preparation time to budget preparation time . . . just surviving. The next step then would be the allocation of the state's resources, an allocation of the state's income tax money, based on need. If you use any other formula, it doesn't make sense. You can devote any kind of need formula you want, if you use any yardstick of need, Newark has to get a higher proportionate share of that state resource. We're beginning to make some moves.

Evie Joseph, Kris Lennon, and Mary Sue Edwards

 I mean I'm just afraid that the world is going to get worse and worse, and maybe it will end while they are alive. . . . That's the only reason I don't want to have kids.

Three fairly typical Midwestern thirteen-year-olds, Evie, Kris, and Mary Sue are talking among themselves at a slumber party at Kris's house.

Do you think America of today or America of 1800 would have been a better time to live?

EVIE: Way back when they just came to America, it was different because the people were spread out and the people really didn't need the government that much, because they could manage pretty well themselves. It seems that the more civilized you become, the more problems you get.

KRIS: Just think, though, if we didn't have all the things like dishwashers. I couldn't live without a dishwasher. And what about radios and things like that? See, there's some good things and some bad things about it. Would you like to wash your clothes in a creek?

How about you, Mary Sue? Would you prefer to live now or back around 1800, when life was simpler?

MARY SUE: In between. I like it just when we're starting developing everything and we're not looking at the end of the world, but now you have to because we're getting closer.

KRIS: I disagree with that, because I've heard it said that in the year 2000 peace will be in the world.

MARY SUE: I don't know. Look at pollution. Maybe we could solve pollution, maybe somebody could invent something. But population is just like, I don't know about this, but poverty . . . it looks like some people just want the poor people to die so we can have less population.

KRIS: Yes, I know what you mean, but with the pill nowadays, I'm sure that there are a lot less children coming into the world than when the pill wasn't here.

MARY SUE: I'm never going to take the pill!

Why do you feel so pessimistic?

MARY SUE: Well, back to population. I mean our country, it's getting more businesslike. We're losing good fertile land, and it's going to happen much quicker in the next few years, and population is growing too much. I don't know. I've been trying to think of a way, but it's just pretty hard. We need some miracles to happen. There's not so many people that are acting trying to solve it.

KRIS: There aren't enough people who care in this world. I know that there are a lot of kids that care. Kids! But we're too young to do anything about it. The hippies, they want to get a point across, they want peace and love in this world. There's nothing wrong with the hippies, but the people that started the riots, they want some kind of attention or something. They're not getting—well, maybe they are getting a point across —but they're not getting anything accomplished. Nothing is getting accomplished by the way they're acting.

EVIE: There's a lot of kids that say they're going to do something, but they never do.

MARY SUE: That just might happen with me, too, but I'm going to try.

EVIE: I mean, they say the kids are all so idealistic when they're younger, but when they grow up, they just forget all about it. They just give up because it's so hard.

About ten years from now you will all probably be married and raising your own children. Does it ever frighten you to think about that, about what the world will be like then?

MARY SUE: It sure does!

KRIS: It doesn't scare me. I've seen how far the world has come so far, and I just wonder how much farther advanced from here the world can go. Things aren't that bad at all.

MARY SUE: Well, one thing is about the end of the world. A lot of people understand, but some don't, and they say us kids are going through a lot more pressures than they used to, 'cause of all these problems wrapped up in our minds, and a lot more other things. The things people are doing, like marijuana, and we get tempted, and that just makes things worse. And I'm afraid that my kids will get too wrapped up. I mean I'm just afraid that the world is going to get worse and worse, and maybe it will end while they are alive. I don't know. I just don't want them to go through all that. That's the only reason I don't want to have kids.

Jimmy Breslin

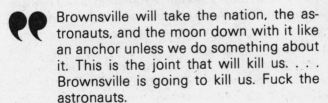

Brownsville will take the nation, the astronauts, and the moon down with it like an anchor unless we do something about it. This is the joint that will kill us. . . . Brownsville is going to kill us. Fuck the astronauts.

A throwback to Ring Lardner but very much his own man-in-the-street, Jimmy Breslin is an outspoken forty-two-year-old New Yorker whose feature columns and articles have cut to the core of the gut issues he writes about with telling humor and, when the occasion demands, real pathos. He is perhaps best known for his novel, *The Gang That Couldn't Shoot Straight,* and a rogues' gallery of barstool zanies of his own creation, including one Marvin the Torch. In 1969 he ran for President of the New York City Council on a ticket headed by Norman Mailer (with the slogan "Vote the Rascals In") and polled forty thousand votes.

I think America to me represents a night in 1964 when I got into a cab. . . .

In the summer of 1964 there were disturbances in Harlem. We call them disturbances now; at that time we called them riots. Being naïve and not understanding, we thought it was a great, huge riot. The Harlem riot of 1964. It wasn't a riot. It was a disturbance compared to what was coming, and could come.

But it was a very disturbing thing to be in the middle of it. On the third night of this, to see the hatred of people who truly hated you—you're white and they told you with their eyes. Underneath all the noise and all the running through the streets was this terrible, strange, straight glare you were getting from the people from Harlem. That was terrible. I'd rather have them yell and threaten to kill you than give you that flat look of hatred.

I was coming down in a cab from 125th Street at Seventh Avenue. The police had to get you out to 110th, and then I was able to get a cab at 110th at Fifth Avenue. I was coming down to go to the New York *Herald Tribune,* which was a newspaper on West Forty-first Street, to write a column for the later edition of the newspaper. You had the afternoon riot, as we called it, and then you changed the column to take in the start of the evening activities. I was coming down Seventh Avenue and I was sitting back in the back of the cab, dirty from rolling in gutters, and I was very depressed, awfully depressed. We passed the Americana Hotel on Seventh Avenue. All of a sudden you burst out of the blight and noise and theater district and here on the steps of the Americana Hotel was a Shriners' band. There was a Shriners' Convention at the Americana. And there must have been four hundred people in the band, standing on the steps of the hotel and out onto the sidewalk on Seventh Avenue, blaring away, playing the music, with their fezes on and these ridiculous silk shirts. Everyone clapping, a great show. And you know, you open the window and say to one of the guys with these fezes, "Hey, you're a fuckin' adult, aren't you?" I mean dressed like this in this ridiculous regalia. And I thought, what the hell have we got, is everybody nuts?

You know, the indifference was so . . . to move fifty blocks north, where there is the first faint suggestions of the violence coming, which may take ten or fifteen years to come, but the way we're going now it most certainly is going to come. At that time, 1964, it was just the first faint suggestion that something is going to happen someday. And you come down fifty blocks to all this glitter . . . people who paid more for these silly ridiculous uniforms they're wearing than the people in Harlem earned in a month. A fellow had it on his back, you know. I thought it was nuts. That's always hit me as the way it is . . . you know, the contrast in the country.

The movie *Midnight Cowboy* shocked America. You couldn't show that in Harlem. What the hell, they see that every five minutes. What would be new to them? They know more about life. It's a very brittle time, though. Very brittle, hard, dull, uncaring time.

Let's put a tax on prejudice. If you want to live in an all-white neighborhood, in an all-white school district, you don't want anybody there, you don't want any blacks near you, fine! That's your prerogative, you're allowed to hate. Give me fifteen hundred dollars a year tax extra because you're living in an all-white neighborhood and we'll put that money on Harlem and Bedford-Stuyvesant. The blacks would tell you gladly: "Live in Garden City and go fuck yourself in Garden City, just give us something to fix our schools in Bedford-Stuyvesant." So let's put a tax on prejudice. A physical tax!

There is a school district in Levittown, Long Island. They're very proud of it. It has four schools in the district without one black kid in them. Four schools in the district! Do you know how many kids that is—without one black kid in it? So that's not an education. That's a put-on. But if they want to live that way, if they want to live in what they think is the world—and it's just an illusion—fine, let them live that way. But I want a state tax on that system, a very heavy school tax on anybody in the school district. And the money to go to Buffalo, the black section of Buffalo, the black section of Brooklyn, to Harlem.

The people have this vague hatred, what is known as the vague hatred that stirs when they get afraid—the Great American Thing, my fifty yards. Don't touch my fifty yards. You draw a circle around a house and that's what you'll come up with, fifty yards of territory. That's what they all protect—with locks and fences and police dogs. And a mental attitude. Even if they see a face on television, a black face, they think that's threatening their fifty yards. Let them have their fucking fifty yards. But at least make them aware of this terrible hatred they have. Put it in concrete terms for them. And there's only one concrete term this country understands—cash money. Tax the sonofabitch for livin' in an all-white place. Special tax. Pay your taxes proportionally to the breakdown in your school system. It's good. Then you can be a bigot. Go ahead. Wonderful! Enjoy it. Give me seventeen hundred and fifty dollars a year to go to Ocean Hill-Brownsville in Brooklyn. That's all I want. That's all I want out of you.

It's so easy to appeal to the meaner parts of man, and so very, very difficult to strike the proper chord that will lead them to something better. It's so much easier to appeal to their nasty side. And most politicians can't resist doing it, you know, for their own gain. It's so hard and delicate to tell people that you're better than this, that we should live better than this. Why should we have to live like this? We can do better. It's so hard to tell them that and to get them to understand. That's the tough problem. Because you're bucking my fifty yards. That comes down to the good life of the Sixties: my fifty yards, my car, my color television set, my money. It's hard. It's hard to tell them.

You've been outspoken on the Vietnam War. Why do you think the country has tolerated it?

I'll tell you why the war went on so long. My friend Owen Duffy, his brother is the President of Local 138, Operating Engineers Local in Long Island. Big tough union. The New York police went out to them and said, "How come there's been no Italian gangsters cutting in on your union?"; and the President of the union at that time, Billy Duffy, he said, "Maybe they don't want to come here." Meaning tough Irish gangsters, the last of the Irish gangsters, were in that union.

When Billy Duffy took over that union, Owen said to me, "Why don't you come out some night? We'll have a few drinks and talk to the guys. It would be fun. One thing, though, don't talk about the war." I said, "Why? That's the only thing I can talk about. That's the only thing I'm interested in. I'm berserk on that war." I said, "It's costing them money. The work isn't as good." He said, "Look, they don't understand that. You could tell them and prove it. That the money's going into bombs. They can't see the bombs. All they can see is the nigger on the corner collecting welfare. That's where they think their money's going. They can't see the F-111. They can only see the black fellow on the corner.

"Secondly, most of these fellows have had only one things in their lives. They went into the military service, and they went away and got into a war like Korea or World War Two and they saw things they never thought they'd see. They experienced every range of human emotion, from exhilaration to absolute terror to complete sadism to manly togetherness to camaraderie to anything you want. They went from A to Z on the scale of life, and it is the greatest thing and only thing ever to happen to them in their lives. Everything that happened before and everything that happened after is nothing. It's just one day going into another, and the days becoming weeks, and the weeks becoming months and the months becoming years. The only thing that changes in their lives is the date on the calendar. That's all that changes. The war is the greatest experience. The military and the war is the only experience they've ever had in their lives. When you stand up there and tell them it's bad, you are taking away from them the only thing they've had. And they resent you for it."

That's it. The Local 138 Operating Engineers like the war, and that's it. They like the military service 'cause that's all they ever had out of life. That's one thing Senator Eugene McCarthy, God bless him, didn't understand; and the Reverend [Joseph] Duffy in Connecticut, when he ran, didn't understand. An awful lot of people don't understand. That's why they could vote so easily for Robert Kennedy, or George Wallace if Kennedy isn't there. Because they represent the guy to them that would understand where they are in life.

That's what gets me nuts about why they would like a Nixon. That kills me. The reverse side of that makes me throw up. Because Richard Nixon wouldn't last twenty minutes in the Operating Engineers 138 Hall. Drinking beer. Some guy would say, "Get this motherfucker out of here. I've had enough of his shit." He's a fraud, but he appeals to all their meaner parts, and therefore they like him. He ingratiates himself. He worms his way. He's probably America's greatest social climber. He really made it all the way—from a third-string end in a little Quaker college to the big man riding standing up in a jeep in front of the Marines while the band plays. He made it all the way. He's very hung up on what a man is. That's a whole lot of bullshit.

The war has been a great divisive fact of life in America, while the space program has kept our pride going. How do you view our putting men on the moon?

The night they went on the moon in 1969 I stood on Sutter Avenue in Brownsville, Brooklyn. There's a lot on the corner of Sutter Avenue and Hinsdale Street with a wire fence around it. I threw rocks in there and watched. Every time a rock went in—it's just a mound of garbage—every time you threw a rock in there, you could see five and six rats scurry away from the commotion the rock caused. All the tenements there, and there are only one or two families living in them. Most people have moved out, fled the area. Women have to sit up all night with their children. There's only one or two fit people in these houses, these crumbling houses. The women have to sit up all night watching television—it was good the moon shot was on all night. It gave them something a little bit different to watch. Otherwise kids from the neighborhood, the mental kids, come into these houses and set fires in empty apartments. If the woman falls asleep . . . they're all women on welfare, no husbands . . . she could fall asleep and the fire would start in the empty apartment next door and come through the wall and burn her children alive while she's asleep. So they stay up all night watching television. Then in the daytime they go out and sit on chairs in front of the doors to these seamy apartment buildings and doze. Doze in the afternoons when the kids are in the streets. Somebody would pass by in the car and say, "Look at those niggers; they're lazy, they don't work; they're asleep all day."

I went there that night. I watched it in an apartment with some Puerto Rican people crowded in this tiny little room with the linoleum floor. Kids from previous marriages—busted out and loused up—the way the poor always are loused up. You know, a rich man stumbles and nothing happens, a poor man stumbles and breaks his toe. That's the way life goes. I watched that moon shot in these circumstances and I had to conclude that we're nuts. We're just nuts. Brownsville will take the nation, the astronauts, and the moon down with it like an anchor unless we do something about it. This is the joint that will kill us. The moon's never going to hurt us. That fuckin' thing was there for centuries and never meant anything. Brownsville is going to kill us. Fuck the astronauts.

Tom Wicker

 Things which we had come to accept almost as articles of faith have been shown to be hollow. . . . I'm one that believes disillusionment is enlightenment. . . .

A native of North Carolina who received his early training in journalism there, Tom Wicker joined the Washington bureau of *The New York Times* in 1960 and was later promoted to bureau chief. Now forty-five years old, he is an associate editor of the *Times* and, as a regular columnist, one of the nation's most eloquent liberal spokesmen.

I don't think it's been a discouraging decade. Rather, a very wounding decade because a lot of things that one felt, believed in, hoped for, have just been simply blown out of the water. Many of us have suffered grievous disillusionment with the actions of the United States as a nation. Things which we had come to accept almost as articles of faith have been shown to be hollow. Men have been shown to be hollow. I'm one that believes that disillusionment is enlightenment, and I think that despite all the turmoil and struggle, in the long run we came out in 1970 better off then we went into 1960. Not because of the situation in 1970 or the President or the program or anything of that sort, but just simply because we were more mature people. We had a clearer perspective on ourselves, even though there were a hell of a lot of people who still wouldn't accept it. I think we more nearly knew that we too had feet of clay, that the way is long and hard.

In the long run it means that we will much more clearly understand ourselves in the future as being human beings with human problems rather than as some kind of specially gifted race whose businesses, institutions, and ideas were supposed to have been handed down from Mount Sinai. I think that's been shaken in everybody's mind.

INDEX

ACKNOWLEDGMENTS

Since I first started work on *Good Times* two years ago, hundreds of people have helped me with the project. Most important are the 250 people I interviewed, for they are the substance of *Good Times*. Their receptivity to the project and their willingness to invest their time made this work possible. To those who do and those who do not appear in the published book I am equally indebted: their words and their thoughts helped mold it into its present form.

Originally, *Good Times* was undertaken as a Senior Thesis at Princeton University. Professor Eric F. Goldman was my advisor, and it was his initial enthusiasm that eventually convinced me to undertake the project. His follow-up of criticism and encouragement proved to be invaluable. John and Joan Fleming helped in several ways, the two most important being their close criticism of my writing and their gracious encouragement. Sheldon Hackney and Robert Scott also generously advised my work. Irving Dilliard criticized my writing style.

Carla Danziger and Donna Nitchun cheerfully handled my mail and telephone messages at the Woodrow Wilson School. My roommates—Norman Axler, Jim Lawson, Robert Nahas, John O'Donnell, and John Prechtel—answered the forever-ringing telephone, and generally put up with me during the ups and downs of the work. Other students also assisted me: Michael Rodemeyer, Carole Grayson, Robert Ramsay, Bob Noto, Pam Karr, Julia O'Brien, and Jan Miller Zellner. My travels depended heavily on the kindnesses of those whose paths I crossed. To them and their families I say thank you—especially to Marty Franks, Tim Johnson, Bill Zwecker, Mark Wine, Bruce Magee, John Prechtel, Tim Ramis, David Grais, Dick Mahoney,

Jon Buchan, Luther Munford, Norman Mott, Jim Dougherty, Laurie Watson, P. A. O'Donnell, Cheryl Smith, Mr. and Mrs. James Seff, Mr. and Mrs. Rinaldo Brutoco, Mr. and Mrs. William Franklin, and Mr. and Mrs. Clifford Durr.

Ellen Kahn's criticism helped improve the quality of writing. She and Norman Axler did one interview apiece when I was unavailable myself.

The thesis was done jointly for the Woodrow Wilson School of Public and International Affairs and the History Department, and both these departments generously awarded me grants and prizes that helped make *Good Times* financially possible. Most of the cost, however, came from the profits of the Student Weenie Agency, so to all the managers, the peddlers, and the purchasers, thank you very much.

The contribution of one person, however, outweighed that of everyone else to *Good Times*. Not only did Helen Keeler struggle through miles of tapes that took months to transcribe on thousands of pages, but she also continually advised and criticized the work as it progressed. It was not long before we became friends, and it is a friendship that I value highly. Above all others Helen Keeler made this book possible. To her husband and children I must offer an apology: they patiently and cheerfully endured dozens of nights when Mrs. Keeler typed later than perhaps she should have. To Bob and Bill and Tricia, too, my thanks.

After the thesis was completed, George Hirsch and Sterling Lord introduced me to the publishing world, specifically to Dick Kluger and Carol Rinzler at Charterhouse Books. They have been extraordinarily helpful in converting the thesis into the book.

There are yet many others—to all of you, thank you very much.

472

ABOUT THE AUTHOR

Peter Joseph is a twenty-two-year-old native of Cincinnati. He earned his bachelor's degree at Princeton University in 1972 and was the recipient of the Harold Willis Dodds Achievement Award at graduation. *Good Times* is a version of his Senior Thesis, written at Princeton and awarded the Dewitt Clinton Poole Prize and the Woodrow Wilson Prize for a Senior Thesis "of unusual merit." Mr. Joseph is continuing his studies at Princeton in the areas of history and public affairs.